Passages
to
Freedom

a story of capture and escape

Passages
to
Freedom

*a story of capture
and escape*

*by
Joseph S. Frelinghuysen*

Sunflower University Press ®

1531 Yuma (Box 1009), Manhattan, Kansas 66502-4228 USA

ISBN 0-89745-131-7

Layout by Lori L. Daniel

Cover artist George R. Chayko served five years in the U.S. Navy, including Korea, as an aerial combat photographer, and 15 years in Naval Reserve in graphics and audiovisual.

He studied electronics at DeVry Institute of Technology and audio-visual for two years at Eastman Kodak School. He has done engineering design and illustrating for the U.S. Army, and presently does graphic artwork in a wide range of fields.

To Richard M. Rossbach

IN MEMORIAM

and

Berardino

INTER VIVOS

ESCAPE FROM FONTE d'AMORE TO CASTIGLIONE
23 SEPTEMBER - 15 NOVEMBER 1943

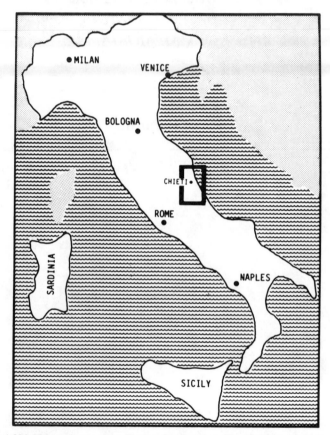

Adapted from the 1:200,000 road map of the Touring Club Italiano. (Reprinted under license from the T.C.I., Milan, Italy.)

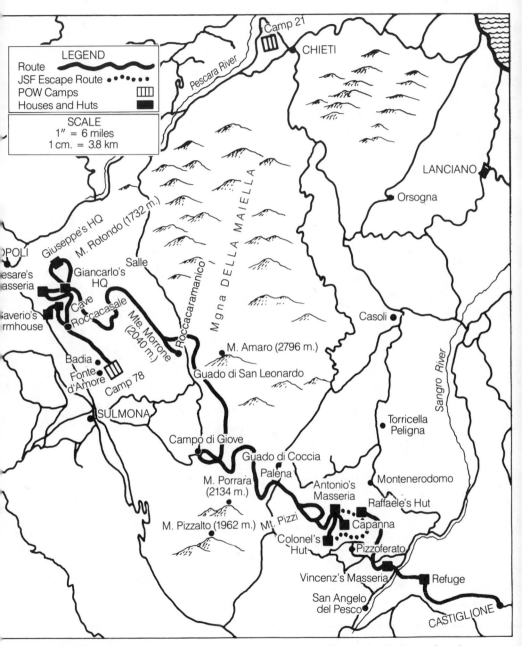

LEGEND
Route
JSF Escape Route
POW Camps
Houses and Huts

SCALE
1" = 6 miles
1 cm. = 3.8 km

Camp 21
CHIETI
Pescara River

LANCIANO
Orsogna

Giuseppe's HQ
M. Rotondo (1732 m.)
Salle
OPOLI
esare's
asseria
Giancarlo's
HQ
Cave
averio's
rmhouse
Roccacasale
Mte. Morrone
(2040 m.)
Roccaramanico
Mgⁿa DELLA MAIELLA
Casoli
M. Amaro (2796 m.)
Badia
Fonte
d'Amore
Camp 78
Guado di San Leonardo
SULMONA

Sangro River

Torricella
Peligna

Campo di Giove
Guado di Coccia
Palena
Montenerodomo
M. Porrara
(2134 m.)
Antonio's
Masseria
Raffaele's Hut
M. Pizzalto (1962 m.)
Mt. Pizzi
Capanna
Colonel's
Hut
Pizzoferato
Vincenz's Masseria
Refuge
San Angelo
del Pesco
CASTIGLIONE

Adapted from the 1:200,000 road map of the Touring Club Italiano. (Reprinted under license from the
T.C.I., Milan, Italy.)

Author's Note

This story begins in 1941, when Germany had driven France to a surrender and England was fighting for survival. In the Atlantic sea lanes and around Europe, German U-boats were already shadowing U.S. ships. In the Pacific, Japan was menacing America.

In all this, we Americans faced potential consequences more grave than at any time since the Declaration of Independence. From early 1940 it had seemed clear to me that we would have to go to war — and win — or our people and their descendants for generations would live in virtual slavery. And from the first moment I heard Hitler on the radio, I knew we would have to go: the maniacal voice, the screaming invective, and, underneath it all, the English translator intoning those apocalyptic words.

In the years from 1940 to 1945 the U.S. Army was expanded by enlistments and Selective Service from some 200,000 regular troops to 8 million men and women, most of them noncareer, wartime soldiers like myself. The size of this immense army bore witness to the depth of our commitment to the cause of freedom. What we did to defend that cause has been the theme of thousands of books, many of which are military accounts presented from strategic and tactical points of view. This is not a military book in that sense, even though the action takes place mainly in the battle zones of North Africa and Italy. Rather it is a personal story that emphasizes the human side of soldiers and civilians who were engulfed in bitter disasters not of their own making, or in combat errors they had not yet learned how to avoid. This personal account must, *de natura*, deal with the protagonists' most private feelings, matters that are seldom touched upon in military literature.

The human side always seems to be involved in questions from young people who never knew World War II, and who ask, "What was it like to be caught up in those disasters? How did you feel?" I have tried very hard here to answer such questions, though at times being frank and honest with myself proved painful indeed.

During the war years, my personal odyssey took me from a training "war" to a real war, to capture, and ultimately to freedom. Yet freedom, when it came, was surprisingly neither simple to understand nor easy to embrace. Before the war I had, as had so many others, taken freedom for granted. Therefore, I now tell this story not just to record a difficult and frightening time in my life, but to remind us all, as Thomas Paine did, that "what we obtain too cheap, we esteem too lightly; 'tis dearness only that gives everything its value. . . ." Freedom, once lost, was not regained cheaply for me, and never again would I esteem it lightly or take it for granted.

JSF

Acknowledgments

When I came home in December 1943, my wife, Emily, produced an old Dictaphone machine with a case of wax cylinders. Then she ordered me to sit down and dictate until I could think of nothing more to say about the months I had spent in North Africa and Italy.

After weeks on the run, I was quite happy to sit for a while. But I was tied up in knots between Top Secret security regulations and my own turbulent state, although in another sense I needed badly to get the story off my chest. Consequently, it was a great relief to be able to tell it to an inanimate black box.

For weeks, Emily typed away on an ancient Corona, until she had eventually transcribed some 85 pages. I hereby acknowledge, with eternal gratitude, her determination in forcing me to do the dictation and her perseverance in producing the document at that most difficult time. It became the basis of this book and has been my principal memory bank for an incredible amount of information. The details were put down when fresh in my mind — not merely fresh, but seared into my brain by the still white-hot emotions of the time.

In addition to those dictated notes, I leaned very heavily on Dick Rossbach, while he was still with us, and at one time even asked if he wanted to be a co-author. Although he declined, insisting that this was my story to write, he never hesitated to give me his time and efforts most generously, as well as his clear recollections.

At my right hand, too, I have had another vital source of facts, my dear friend Berardino, who, I have discovered, has a random access memory that would shame the latest "state-of-the-art" computer.

I am also deeply grateful to Bob Tyson, now Brigadier General, U.S. Army-Ret., for his excellent advice and for his introduction to Brig. Gen. James L. Collins, Jr., Chief of Military History, Department of the Army. General Collins made available to me all his command's records of the North African campaigns, through Department Historian Moreau B.C. Chambers. To them go my sincere thanks.

I also want to thank Rex Rawie, Len Warren, and Verne Rottstedt for their assistance in verifying dates and names and places that were vital in presenting an accurate picture of events preceding and during the ambush at Djedeida. In the years since the war I have been back to Abruzzo twice. On the second trip, which was in 1972, I was able to locate several old friends who had helped me 29 years before. They gave me much important information, and in the process proved that Abruzzese hospitality had not depreciated one iota. One unexpected reaction arose, however: No one who had been associated with the Communist Party wanted his name mentioned. Naturally I have respected the wishes of those individuals and have used pseudonyms or *noms de guerre* where appropriate. Names of a few other people as well have been changed, in cases where my account might have caused embarrassment.

For their literary and editorial guidance, I acknowledge with deep appreciation the skilled and painstaking assistance of Jane Bernstein, author, playwright, and former instructor of English and journalism, Rutgers University; and more recently of Frank J. Korn, author, lecturer, and professor of English, County College of Morris. Their many months of hard labor and patience with my stylistic vagaries deserve special recognition.

To John Cox, many thanks for his invaluable and highly professional editorial consultation. And last, and assuredly the most important, my humble and heartfelt gratitude goes to Elizabeth Mihaly for her enduring patience and splendid typing and retyping of the manuscript.

Contents

Chapter 1

German Hospitality

9:00 a.m., 29 November 1942

The waiting began to get to me. I imagined every kind of beating and torture I'd ever heard of: red-hot wires under your fingernails, electrodes on your genitals. Suddenly I heard the prison guard call, in the old German accent, *"Hauptmann Frelinghäusen."* The pronunciation was too authentic.

Struggling to maintain my composure, I strode into the office and halted before a sallow-faced officer sitting behind a small wooden table. I saluted smartly, as demanded by military courtesy, even between enemies.

Here was a man in his forties with short gray hair, wearing a blue-gray uniform bedecked with medals, colonel's insignia, and a high-peaked garrison cap. Hating him, I also loathed myself for being afraid of him.

He returned my salute with a corner of his mouth curling. "You may be seated, *Frelinghäusen*; I want to ask you a few questions. Now, if you will be helpful, you will be back with your comrades in a few minutes and can look forward to a splendid trip to Germany." He spoke English with an Oxford accent. All this time the guard stood behind me with his machine-pistol at my back.

I stared back at him in silence, a lump tightening my chest. His legs stuck out from under the table, and I could see the red trouser stripe of the German General Staff. This was to be a top-level interrogation. I forced myself to keep my face impassive.

"Frelinghäusen" — he pronounced it with an exaggerated German accent — "you should be with us, not the Americans. That is a German name."

"It is not," I said, irritated. "It's Holland Dutch."

"You're wrong. The family came from Schwerte in Westphalia, not far from the *Holländische* border." He paused a moment and leaned forward.

"Now, *Frelinghäusen*, you were with the artillery of the First Infantry Division, were you not?"

"My name is Joseph S. Frelinghuysen, Captain, serial number 0-313280."

Suddenly he smiled. "Here, have a Camel." He held out a package of cigarettes.

I declined the offer. "Where did you get those?"

"Oh, we get them through Tangier; in fact, we get any of your products that we want." Then he added curtly, "You were sent over here from Oran, in general support of what the British call their First Army. We know you landed at Arzew with 105-mm howitzers. What was your armament here?"

I sat still without answering, feeling my stomach churn. The voice across the desk grew flinty. "If you wish to be stubborn, *Frelinghäusen*, we have ways of making you talk, and I never hesitate to use them."

If I hadn't been so panic-stricken, the bastard might have been comical — right out of a grade B movie. But his threat had sounded too damn believable. I recalled an old World War I story I had heard: a sadistic Hun who liked to experiment with interrogations made an offer to each American prisoner who refused to answer questions. The interrogator would point to two doors. The first, he said, led either to freedom or to their Chinese cooks, who would kill the prisoner with slow torture. The second door led to a firing squad. After only brief consideration, each prisoner had chosen the firing squad. I wondered what I would do if I were ever given such a choice.

But the German colonel was waiting. "I see my little suggestion gave you pause for thought," he said with a malicious smile. His voice rose, "Now, for the last time, what was your armament here?"

I sat there without speaking, the knot in my chest growing more unbearable with each question. Every time I either refused to answer or repeated my name, rank, and serial number, the German became angrier. The tension increased until I was unable to speak at all.

Then, surprisingly, he said rapidly, "Well, *Frelinghäusen*, it's lucky for you one of your men broke down and gave me this information. I was merely looking for verification. If I don't get more from one of the others, I'll see you again. Then, if you persist in being stupid, you may not live to enjoy your vacation in Germany. Now get out!"

I stood up — knees shaking — saluted, and was waved out the door by the guard's machine-pistol. For the next hour or more, I sweated in a strange cell, wondering if I'd be called back, and if I would ever see the other prisoners again.

Chapter 2

Tradition

Learning to shoot at an early age was a matter of course for the men in my family. America had just entered World War I when, at age five, I fired my first gun, an old muzzleloader owned by my Uncle South, who had fought with the Union Army in the Civil War. Uncle was ancient. His striped shirt and unpressed trousers hung on a scarecrow frame; his long, sweeping mustache was stained yellow from 60 years of smoking bright Virginia, which he rolled himself.

Collecting guns had been Uncle South's lifetime hobby. And besides a fascination for the dueling pistols, derringers, six-shooters, and single-shot rifles that adorned the walls of his study, he implanted in me the idea that in almost every generation some family member had fought for his country.

How vividly I recall watching him, wide-eyed, while he poured in the powder and rammed the wads, and finally added the shot. He held his arms around me as I aimed out a window at a square of paper on the lawn and pulled the trigger. It made an ear-splitting *boom*!, jolted my shoulder black and blue, and poured out clouds of smoke. Within seconds, my Aunt Charlotte had come waddling at maximum speed to give us both a fearful scolding.

Knowing how to shoot was only part of our tradition of military service, which was dramatized by paintings that hung on the walls of the old family house. The earliest of these was one in uniform of my great-great-grandfather, who had commanded a company of artillery at the Battle of Princeton in the Revolutionary War. In the dining room there was a portrait of my great-grandfather, looking very determined. I was frequently reminded that he had commanded a detachment of troops in the War of 1812 and had been promoted to brigadier general. In the front hall hung a full-length oil of my father when he had served with Squadron A, 101st Cavalry. His uniform consisted of the broad-brimmed campaign hat, olive-drab tunic, trousers, puttees, and a wide canvas belt with a huge brass buckle. A heavy cavalry saber hung at his side, and he sported a long, curling, gray mustache. From early childhood I remembered his account of landing with the 101st in Cuba in '99, when the Spanish fleet was threatening both that island and the Florida coast.

Thus it was foreordained that when I entered Princeton in 1930 I would join the ROTC, along with some 200 other freshmen. In the summer of 1934, just after graduating with a commission as a second lieutenant, I spent two months in field artillery camps. In the succeeding years I occasionally went off again to camp while trying to cope with a frustrating insurance job in New York.

By the late thirties, as the threat of war in Europe intensified, the training in these camps grew more serious. Day after day, papers and newsreels blazoned grim-faced hordes of goose-stepping Nazi Storm Troopers called *Schutzstaffeln*, or SS. We were told that each SS member must be of "pure" Aryan stock, and that "openly and mercilessly he fights the Reich's most dangerous enemies: Jews, Freemasons, Jesuits, and Political Clergy." I was frightened and deeply disturbed.

In May of 1940 my wife, Emily, and I drove to Charlottesville, Virginia, to visit friends. One evening we were among the guests at a dinner given by Ethel and Franklin Roosevelt, Jr. I had known Franklin since boarding-school days. Later that evening, while we were playing bridge, he was called to the phone to speak to his father. He came back, looking pale and stern, and reported that the Germans had invaded Holland and Belgium in force. The bridge game broke up, and we sat in a group while Franklin detailed what had happened. Afterwards we talked in quiet but tense voices, and, when we got up and exchanged goodnights, no one smiled. Each wife clung to her husband in silence as we walked to our cars in the cool spring evening.

June of 1940 was hot, steaming, tense. Germany was storming through the low countries and into France, while the British were embattled around Dunkirk. Those of us who had doubts before now left them far behind. I signed up for temporary active duty and spent most of June on maneuvers in upstate New York with the 5th Field Artillery, 1st Division. When I was leaving to return to the city, Col. Jesse B. Hunt, the battalion CO, asked me to come back for extended duty.

For the rest of that summer New York City glared and hummed under a mid-nineties sun, oblivious to the war 3,500 miles away. Each morning as I came out of the subway on Fulton Street, the smell of roasting coffee blew over from the ovens on the east side. I had liked its fresh aroma, but now I could not stand it. My insurance job seemed pointless; with the army hanging over me, I hated the work and had to force myself to go through the motions.

The realities of the war could not be ignored. Finally, in March 1941 I sent my request for extended active duty to Colonel Hunt and plunged into my reserve officers' courses with renewed vigor. My orders came through in a couple of months.

But although my decision to go on active duty had now become unequivocal, it had not been an easy one. Leaving my family tore me apart — one side of my nature driving me to go, the other telling me I was making a cruel mistake. I detested going, and the need for it stirred a deep resentment. In those last days before my departure I growled at everyone, drank excessively, snapped at my wife and daughter, both of whom I adored.

29 July 1941

When the inevitable day arrived, I went out and threw my army footlocker into the '37 Dodge and came back into the house, feeling empty and strange. For perhaps the tenth time, I checked my uniform in the hall mirror: garrison cap, blouse, or jacket, OD (olive drab), shiny brass "U.S." on the corners of the collar, field artillery crossed cannons underneath. I was secretly proud of the rig.

Emily had crept up quietly and was standing behind me. She had a huge green maternity dress wrapped around her. Her light brown hair fell to her shoulders, her eyes were full. The baby was due in a week, and she would deliver it without me there. Mardie, our daughter, peeked around, clinging to her mother's hand. Her blond hair was rumpled and her face flushed. "Daddy, when are you coming back?" she inquired earnestly.

I started to speak, but the words stuck in my throat. Finally, I managed, "I don't know, Sweetie. It could be a very long time." Mardie turned and ran to her room. I followed her and kissed her goodbye, but she wouldn't even look at me. I was deserting her.

I returned and said quietly to Emily, "I have to go now."

She nodded. "Mardie will be upset for a while, but she'll be OK. It's always better when you tell her the truth."

We hugged awkwardly. Then she whispered, "Go!"

The old car skidded on the gravel driveway. I had to blink hard when I came to the highway and turned north on Route 202.

4:00 p.m.

At the main gate at Fort Devens, Massachusetts, I pompously returned the guard's salute, showed him my orders, and parked by a sign reading, "Visitors." My legs were somewhat unsteady, and I felt hollow as I walked along a dusty path leading to a white frame building. Over the door hung an emblem: a big red "1" on an OD shield. Underneath were the words, "Headquarters, 1st Division, U.S.A."

At the end of a long hall I found the right desk, saluted, and said, "First Lieutenant Frelinghuysen reporting for duty."

The Division personnel officer nodded and shuffled some papers. "Hello, Frelinghuysen," he said, "you're early. At least that's a good start. Now, report to Headquarters, 5th Field."

At the 5th, a coldly polite adjutant instructed me: "Report to Commanding Officer, Battery C." How much longer could this go on? I'd already sweated through my blouse. The other troops all wore cotton khaki summer uniforms.

I walked past precise rows of trucks adorned in U.S. Army camouflage paint. One row had four 155-mm howitzers coupled behind them, six-inch weapons from World War I. At least I knew what they did.

Capt. Robert N. Tyson, class of 1934, U.S. Military Academy, was CO of Battery C, 5th Field. He had reddish-brown hair, uncompromising gray eyes, and a way of thrusting out his head toward you as he spoke that left no doubt he was the battery commander. This was the man who would order my life during the coming months.

Being assigned to a regular army battalion as a reserve 1st lieutenant was for me anything but easy. At 29, I was six to seven years older than my fellow officers. Though it helped to be six-feet-two and to be able to make a certain amount of noise, I relied on my ingrained reticence, as well as my age, to build a wall between myself and the grating struggle of army life. It was a constant fight against loneliness among thousands of men, while longing for a wife and daughter, and worrying about the arrival of a new baby.

Living in a six-by-eight cubicle in bachelor officers' quarters, known as BOQ, I got to know the junior battery officers, who were also mostly reserves. But nothing I had ever done in seven years as a reserve lieutenant had taught me what I needed badly to know about handling regular army troops. I had to get up in front of them and give exactly the right commands, for they would follow an incorrect one with gleeful precision, especially when a senior officer was present. A certain amount of that stuff got by, because green lieutenants were fair game. I was sure Captain Tyson was aware that this went on, but I suspected that if matters got out of hand it would be my neck, not theirs.

Ten days after my arrival at Devens I got a telegram from Emily saying that we had a son and that, as we'd agreed, he would be named "Joe."

When I phoned that night from a booth, she answered, "Oh, thank God you called. I wondered if you'd heard."

"Yes, I got the telegram. Are you OK? Do you feel all right? And is he OK?"

"He's wonderful, couldn't be healthier."

"But you, how are you?"

"Oh, I'm just fine, fine, absolutely marvelous —"

The phone went silent, then I heard her sobbing. "Please don't, please," I said. "You make things so hard."

"Hard for *you*? Hard for *you*? That's all you think of. What the hell do you think I feel? You go running off to that goddamned old army —" The receiver fell silent again.

"Please don't take it out on me," I pleaded. "I had to do this. It'll be better than if I had waited to be drafted."

She spoke again, but so low I could hardly hear her: "Never mind, never mind. I'll talk to you some other time, but please write me. It'll be better that way." I said goodbye and hung up, wishing I had never called.

October 1941

Succeeding days and nights offered anxiety, frustration, or sleep. Each morning I would awaken to the fears of another day. This new existence did not start to make sense until all of the First Army, of which the 1st Division was a part, was ordered south for maneuvers. Five hundred thousand men were going into the field.

We drove our trucks, pulling our howitzers, in military convoy from Fort Devens to Candor, North Carolina. There we camped, in red dust that blew on broiling hot days and got in our eyes till brown rivulets ran down our cheeks. Just when I had begun to get used to army life in the field, Captain Tyson, my battery CO, was moved up to Battalion Executive, the second in command. War was in the air. The army was expanding and needed some of its professional officers for new outfits. With only three months of active duty, I was suddenly put in command of Battery C with 156 men, right in the middle of maneuvers.

Colonel Hunt had command of the 5th. A World War I veteran, he was the quintessential cool, experienced, regular army officer, both loved and feared by his subordinates. Since I was still short on field training, he had Tyson hover over me. But Hunt was there himself, right on the spot, the night one of my five-ton howitzers turned over.

The column had been going too fast. It was dusk, and the heavy cannon had skidded and flipped over on its side. When I got to the scene, the armorplate shield was cracked right across and the upper wheel was turning lazily. The gun looked like a wounded dinosaur pawing the air. I hadn't the foggiest idea what to do.

Then I saw Colonel Hunt standing on a bank above the debacle. "Well, Frelinghuysen, have you learned something?" His voice was low and quiet — too quiet. It chilled me.

"Yes, sir. I was in the wrong place."

"Why?"

"I dropped back to check our column, sir."

"Well, now you know. Send one of your officers back there. That way you can control the speed from the head of your battery. Too damn fast." As he walked away, I found myself saluting his back in the darkness.

The motor sergeant, the gun mechanic, and several men uncoupled the gun, turned around the heavy ten-wheel truck that pulled it, and hitched the winch cable to the howitzer. Within minutes, they had it righted. For these men I simply did not exist. They had known their jobs for years, and I was merely a figurehead. A few days later the gun mechanic got an oxyacetylene torch and welded the armorplate shield.

After eight weeks of dusty, exhausting, snafued maneuvers, from Rocky Mount, Durham, and Greensboro down to the Georgia border, the 5th rolled north from the Carolinas.

At midnight on 6 December the battalion reached Fort Devens. It was 5° below zero, but this time at least there were heated barracks and hot showers waiting for us when the trucks and gun sections had been parked. Orders said 7 December would be a day off. Four of us got a quart of bourbon and sat around talking and half-listening to a radio playing "God Bless America" and "Don't Sit under the Apple Tree."

All next morning I wondered what the hell had been in the bourbon to cause that hammer pounding in my head. The icy wind eased the ache a little as I walked around the battery, checking equipment. With three-fourths of the men on pass, the place seemed deserted except for a few working details, looking miserable in the cold. The first sergeant, whom I found in the battery orderly room, was checking the morning report and shaking his head. "Five AWOL, sir," he said. "Two since last night. Army isn't what it used to be with them Selective Service men."

They were the first pick of the draft, and I thought they were terrific guys, but I wasn't about to argue with a 20-year regular army veteran. Together we checked the list. I signed the reports, knowing I'd catch hell for the AWOLs, and went back to BOQ to get some sleep. Collapsing on the bunk fully dressed, I was gone in seconds.

In my stupor, I became aware that someone was banging on my door. I wondered, "Are some of those guys still drinking that ghastly bourbon?" I looked at my watch: 4:00 p.m., 1600 hours in army parlance.

Now someone was shouting. Len Warren, B Battery commander and a reserve officer, stuck his head in the door. "Hey, for God's sake, Joe, wake up and get your ass out of that sack!"

"Hi, Len, what the hell's all the excitement about?"

"Just that the entire 1st Division has been put on combat alert."

"Oh, come off it, Len." I heard footsteps running in the hall.

"You better get up fast. It's no joke. This one's straight from the War Department in Washington. Something's coming over the radio now."

With that, I got to my feet in a hurry and scrambled down the hall toward a blaring radio. Outside the room with the radio a dozen officers in all stages of dress were standing, looking worried and grim. I heard: "Half an hour ago, President Roosevelt announced in a special news bulletin that the Japanese have launched a major attack on Pearl Harbor, Hawaii. Japanese bombers have caused heavy damage to battleships and cruisers at the U.S. Naval Base. The extent of damage is still being assessed and the full story will not be known for hours. It has been reported that counterattacks have been launched by the United States Air and Naval Forces. . . ."

Chapter 3

The Division Goes South

In May of 1942, 5th Field, along with the entire 1st Division, was ordered to Camp Blanding, Florida, for hot-weather training.

After we had been there a week, we were betting we would be shipped out to the South Pacific. We sweated under a blazing sun along sandy roads and in cypress swamps that steamed like Turkish baths, while we went through our final artillery firing tests, known as General Headquarters, or GHQ, tests. Every outfit had to take them just before going overseas.

The 5th had three firing batteries, each with four 155-mm, or six-inch, howitzers that fired a 95-lb shell. When aimed for high-angle fire so the shells would clear a high hill, the howitzers were pointing almost straight up in the air.

Rex Rawie, a tall, hard-driving regular army captain, commanded A Battery with a booming bass voice and a cocky self-confidence that got maximum performance and respect from his men.

Len Warren, commanding B, was Rawie's antithesis: a head shorter and with the quiet, analytical assurance of the skilled attorney he had been in civilian life. Without all the showmanship, he had attained a "superior" unit rating.

I commanded Battery D, which had been organized by Alexander Hamilton, then a captain, at Watertown, New York, 1 March 1776; it was the oldest regular unit in the U.S. Army. It had fired its first rounds at British warships off Manhattan's Battery and had fought at the battles of Princeton, Monmouth, Trenton, and Yorktown. We named our four howitzers after those battles.

Each battery carried a red guidon, or flag, with its unit designation and crossed cannons in gold. But in a formal ceremony back at Fort Devens I had been presented, on behalf of the battery, with a distinctive white and red silk guidon like the one carried by Hamilton's unit. The staff bore a silver ring for each battle in which the unit had fought and was the only one of its kind in the U.S. Army.

The men were fiercely, occasionally violently, proud of this honor, and they worked their asses off. The other batteries were envious, going so far as to emphasize that D was *two* steps, not just one, behind B. They worked as hard as they could to beat us at every chance. D passed its GHQ tests about even with B and only a hair behind A.

From Florida, we were ordered for Division maneuvers to Fort Benning, Georgia, where we would fire over the heads of our infantry with live ammunition. We trudged through the sticky red clay of Georgia in boiling June heat, checking and rechecking every minute detail of survey and fire direction. Since a 155-mm shell could obliterate everything in an area 90 yards wide, a mistake in gunnery could be disastrous.

One gray morning, Col. Warren Stout, who had become our battalion CO early in 1942, Rawie, Warren, and I were hunched down in a forward observation post, or OP. A Battery was firing, and since we knew the range and time of flight we could actually see our own black projectiles passing overhead. Artillery gunfire was coordinated with low-level bombing runs by A-20's, the Air Corps light bombers. We watched them go over and could tell the difference between the flat, heavy thump of their bombs and the crack of exploding shells. One A-20 came over very low and began its run over the target. Suddenly, its whole tail section disintegrated. The aircraft spun into a nose dive and plunged straight to the ground. Its full bomb load detonated, sending acrid smoke hundreds of feet into the air.

No one at the OP said a word. We carefully rechecked our firing data and found we'd had no shells in the air at that time. Though we never discovered the cause of the plane crash, it gave me a brutal jolt. It was the first time I had seen Americans killed.

The hot-weather training dragged on, and the fall of Corregidor and the Bataan "Death March" hung over America like a funeral pall. Most of the time we were tight-lipped, every man a tinderbox of suppressed emotions, but we sang "God Bless America" every chance we got — and meant it.

Men lost their tempers easily. Some slight in a barroom, real or fancied, and suddenly the floor was a shambles of broken chairs and teeth and blood. Men picked up by the MP's or local police were sent to me for disciplinary action, but unless there had been some other offense besides brawling, I gave them a few days of KP and a blistering lecture that we were in this thing to fight the Japs and the Germans, not each other.

In early July we were ordered from Benning to Indiantown Gap Military Reservation at Hershey, in the Blue Mountains of Pennsylvania. This was the staging area for army units leaving for Europe. The camp was a veritable city.

Row upon row of white wooden barracks in rectangular patterns stretched to the rim of mountains on the horizon. Unpaved roads and parade grounds separated buildings. Everywhere, the brown, clinging dust blew in the glare of a roasting July sun.

Indiantown was a gloomy place; I felt the doomsday mood, the grim specter hanging over the tens of thousands of men waiting for the sentence of banishment that would come with orders to the port of embarkation.

The warnings came in sequence: first, all leaves were canceled. Then wives and families had to go home, and men living off the post moved into barracks.

In the last week of July Emily had come to Indiantown to stay at the old Hershey Hotel so we could steal a few of the remaining hours together. High on a hill above the town, the hotel's *fin-de-siècle* magnificence and flowered gardens dominated the landscape, and the air was rich with the aroma of chocolate.

The entrance of the hotel still had a high *porte cochère* with white columns, where once carriages had unloaded men in frock coats and top hats and ladies in long silk dresses. Now, men in light tan khaki uniforms escorted women with shoulder-length hair, wearing shirtwaist dresses with short skirts.

The Hershey Hotel was a crazy extravagance for us, but we had saved some allotment money and, for those few precious hours at least, tomorrow didn't exist. Still, this was no casual spree for us. Ours was no sudden, wartime marriage. We had gone around together for five years and had been married for five and a half. In our late twenties before the shadows of war, we had thought our lives were well settled. Now in our thirties, with two children, we had survived the bitter strains of a year apart. Though we hated and dreaded the prospect, we never feared that our relationship would be lightly forgotten in a longer separation.

Emily was in the room when I got back from the post at 7:00. I was hot, sweaty, and caked with grime, but we clung to each other. She was fresh, clean with a faint scent of Arpege, and wearing a pale blue dress that was my favorite. Light brown curls hung to her shoulders, and her eyes were very full.

I let her go reluctantly. "I've got to get a shower."

Her eyes followed me across the room. "Okay," she whispered, "but please hurry."

Days at Indiantown were grueling: training, loading equipment for POE, inspections, inventories. And the few evenings Emily and I had together vanished in a poignant, bittersweet whirl. The last day before she left, I was scheduled for the battalion officers medical exam, which now was requiring merely two minutes per man. Dr. Henry Albrecht, Captain, USMC, sat at a desk behind a pile of mimeographed U.S. Army forms.

Last leave at home before going overseas, June 1942. Emily, Joe, Jr., Margaret, and JSF.

"What's the procedure, Henry?" I asked.

He shoved a form at me. "How do you feel?"

"Fine, why?"

"Good! You've passed. Now read the form and sign here," he said, chuckling, somehow able to find an amusing side to this charade.

I read: "I hereby certify that I have given Joseph S. Frelinghuysen, Capt. 5th FA Bn. 0-313280, a complete physical examination and find him in excellent condition. He is qualified for full combat duty." It was signed, "Henry Albrecht, M.D. Capt. USMA."

Beneath his signature I was to certify that all the above was true and correct and that I had no knowledge of any illness or infirmity.

"Are all the others signing this, Henry?"

"For Christ's sake, Joe, I wouldn't dare find anything wrong with you. They'd shoot me and you too." As I signed it I found myself grinning. I felt kind of swashbuckling and devil-may-care. But the feeling was short-lived.

On my last night with Emily, she wore an evening dress with a full green- and rose-colored skirt, and I put on my best garrison uniform. I reserved a table in the main dining room with its two-story ceiling, balcony, and high arched windows looking out over the upper gardens, a rainbow of colors in the dying sun. An orchestra alternated background and dance music.

We had California champagne, lobster, and flaming crepes with ice cream. We danced to some old ones: Cole Porter's "Night and Day," and Irving Berlin's tunes from "Top Hat." Then they played a new one slowly, and a young girl sang:

> There'll be bluebirds over
> The white cliffs of Dover,
> Tomorrow just you wait and see.
> There'll be love and laughter,
> And peace ever after,
> Tomorrow when the world is free.

England had been at war for three years.

We finished the dance in an embrace. She took my hand, and we walked out through the lobby onto the terrace for a last look at the gardens in the pale light of a quarter moon.

At 5:00 I shut off the alarm and got up, instantly alert. I'd learned how. Emily looked asleep in the dim light from the bathroom, but I knew she wasn't. It took a huge effort to lift an arm, a leg; my body seemed made of lead. The ache spread from my chest down through my whole body. I checked my uniform and equipment. "The car keys are on the bureau," I said. It was time to go.

She was already up and dressed. "I always know," she whispered and flung her arms around me. We held each other, and I felt her tears on my face.

"I'll pray, I'll write. Now don't say anything," she said softly. She knew I couldn't. Finally I got the strength to break away and we went out into the hall. Along the corridor doors opened and closed; there were murmured farewells; we tried not to listen.

With her clinging to my arm, I drove out to the post in silence. When I stopped at the 5th Field area, she looked up at me, her face white and tense. Kissing her quickly, I jumped out of the car, unable even to whisper, "Goodbye." This was the second time we'd been parted. How many more would there be before it was all over?

I strode firmly over toward the mess hall, but before I turned the corner into Battery Street I stole a quick glance back. She was still sitting in the car watching me. I gave a little wave and walked on, head up, returning salutes with a stiff "Good Morning," playing soldier again. But the pain didn't go away. I felt as if I had been kicked in the stomach.

From then on it was hard-nosed business: tough calisthenics in the morning, which I enjoyed but the men hated; long, hard hikes with full field equipment, dripping with sweat in the everlasting dust and only a small canteen of water to drink. The army lived in dust. Except when it rained. Then it lived in mud. When I was out in the field with no place to wash, I thought enviously of those Navy guys with their showers. But then I also thought of the cramped quarters and steel bulkhead doors below water line, where they sweated out the menace of a U-boat attack.

Colonel Stout, our battalion CO, was a small, slight man with a trim, military mustache, a cleft chin, graying hair, and steel-rimmed glasses. He'd fought in World War I and had then entered the U.S. Military Academy, from which he graduated in 1923. Precise, scholarly in appearance, he obeyed orders to the letter and expected the same from his subordinates. He was devoted to his men, and they to him.

After the wives had departed, Colonel Stout invited his senior officers to dinner at the Hershey Hotel. I surmised that this was a personal thing that probably followed some ancient tradition. But the regal dignity of the place — oriental carpets, 30-foot ceilings, the whole atmosphere — had other associations for me, and I was reluctant to go back to it.

The table was set in an alcove separated from the main dining room by rows of potted palms and orange trees. Shining silver gleamed and glasses sparkled against the starched white tablecloth. An aroma of wines and rich sauces filled the air. In the distance, the orchestra was playing a medley: "Don't Sit under the Apple Tree," "Tipperary," and "I've Got Spurs that Jingle, Jangle,

Jingle."

I had arrived early in a newly pressed, full garrison uniform, with my leather Sam Browne belt like polished mahogany. On his left shoulder each man in the 1st Division wore the Big Red "1" and the braided Fourragère, the citation awarded by France in World War I.

Len Warren, looking formal and thoughtful, walked in with his slow, deliberate stride and nodded to me. We were good friends and had worked together on various problems over the past year. And he was an excellent chess player, as I had discovered to my chagrin whenever we had an opportunity for a game. Marty Lawler followed him in with a brisk, springy walk. Marty was a tall, intense man, with curly brown hair and strong sharp features.

Some of the officers couldn't be present, and those who could were there by the mere chance that their night duty schedule permitted it. This was a most heterogeneous group of men. They had been drawn to the 1st Division by its prestige, but had finally been selected from among many because of their ability. More than any other unit, the 1st demanded uniformity in dress and conduct, obedience to orders, toughness of attitude, suppression of feelings. But no matter how hard the reserves played soldier, the differences ran deep. The U.S. Military Academy men were the *real* soldiers. The regulars who earned permanent commissions in other ways were close behind and most respected. Reserve officers from college ROTC's were classed with men from officer training schools, and were generally looked down on by the regulars.

Soldiering for those of us in the reserves was not a way of life, nor would it become one, except for a very few. For me, it was something I knew I had to do, but still I couldn't wait to get it over with, no matter how patriotic I felt. And whenever I tried to imitate the regulars, I was acting, though for most of us the spirit was genuine enough. I was sure that Colonel Stout and his senior officers knew all this, and they gave us credit for working hard; no matter how they deplored our inexperience and lack of soldierliness, they were completely aware that there was no way they could train an expanding wartime army without us.

The conversation was stilted and military as we dined on soup and steak, and drank red wine. I longed for a couple of stiff bourbons. After the main course, the colonel asked for our attention.

"Gentlemen," he began without rising, "I'm very pleased you could be with me this evening. I regret that the other officers could not join us, but, obviously, it was impossible for everyone to be here.

"You've all worked very hard. The state of training of the battalion shown on our General Headquarters tests was rated 'Excellent' and in some 'Superior.' " I was careful not to look at anyone else. Training had been fiercely competitive and some feelings had been rubbed raw.

The colonel continued, "But now we are about to undertake the type of service for which you've all been prepared: combat. It is, and will be, very different indeed from any kind of training you've experienced. But I have great confidence in all of you and know you will serve with leadership and courage in the highest tradition of the 1st Division and the 5th Field. Good luck and Godspeed." He raised his glass and took a sip.

There were murmurs of, "Thank you, sir," "Thank you, Colonel Stout."

Capt. Gordon Bilat, a brilliant, at times acerbic, regular officer and the next senior present, turned to face the colonel. "Colonel Stout, sir, I know I speak for all the officers of the 5th when I say we feel honored to serve under your command and will do our utmost to live up to the standards you have set for us. We thank you for your splendid hospitality this evening and for your words of encouragement." Gordon raised his glass: "Gentlemen, Colonel Stout."

Everyone except the colonel rose and quickly took a sip of wine.

Although the dinner was a stuffy, formal affair, I would not have wanted to miss it. Now I realized that all the soldiering hadn't been phony. I had done it for a purpose, one that now seemed at last to make some sense, no matter what my fears and apprehensions were. But I had no idea what an incredible meaning this dinner would hold for us in the future.

On 31 July 1942 the 5th and the rest of the 1st Division, 17,000-strong, went by rail to the New York Port of Embarkation, where we boarded the now battle-gray Cunard-White Star liner, *Queen Mary*.

And a "queen" she was, all 100,000 tons of her, as she sailed majestically down the Hudson River and headed out past Ambrose Light into a rolling, cobalt-blue Atlantic. Too swift for any escort, she swept on alone with foam-crested bows, pursuing a bizarre, zig-zag course. All that any of us knew was that we were racing east at an incredible 34 knots, with nothing between us and our destination but the U-boat "wolf pack" of the German navy.

The *Queen* would land at Gurock in Scotland, where, after intensive training in England, we would embark on a tiny Ulster Line ship for the 8 November invasion of North Africa.

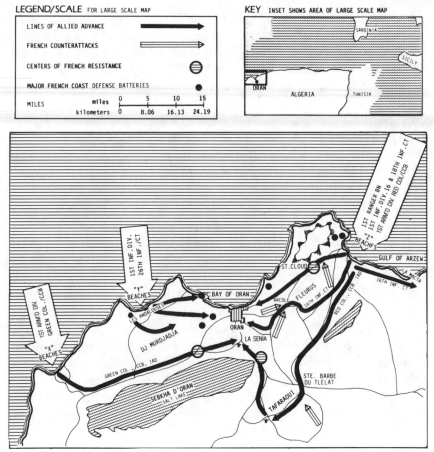

Seizure of Oran, 8-10 November 1942. (Adapted from Map V, Northwest Africa: *Seizing the Initiative in the West,* by George F. Howe, courtesy of the U.S. Army Center of Military History, and from map of the capture of Oran, courtesy of the Society of the First Division.)

Chapter 4

OPERATION TORCH, 8 November 1942: D-Day on the Northwest African Coast

In the dark of the moon, a few miles off the shores of northwestern Africa, three blacked-out Allied Task Forces lay dead in the water. Every man aboard was waiting in taut, brittle silence for the command, "All hands to invasion stations!"

Just before midnight of 7 November 1942, thousands of heavily armed troops scrambled down from their transports, on cargo nets, into landing craft. Organized in waves, they sped away to assault the beaches of French Morocco and Algeria along a thousand-mile front and begin a drive deep into the coastal plain. In a matter of hours these troops, the first massive American commitment in World War II, had secured beachheads in the Casablanca area in the western sector, at Oran and Arzew in the center, and, along with a powerful British force, at Algiers in the east.

This was the first time in the European Theater that any American fighting men had plunged into battle. In this part of North Africa some 75,000 French infantry and supporting units, plus scores of coast artillery batteries, stood poised in the balance: on the one hand they might back the French Vichy government, which had collaborated with Nazi Germany since the fall of France; or, on the other, they might swing over and welcome the Americans as comrades-in-arms. If they chose to back Vichy, these French forces could give the 80,000 Americans on the beaches a very bad time.

At this stage of the war, Germany had gained control of most of the European Continent, in addition to the hegemony she exercised over North

Africa through Vichy France. On all of the Continent the only countries not under German domination were Switzerland, Spain, and Portugal. This three-pronged invasion, which had been named OPERATION TORCH, was designed to wrest control of the Mediterranean from Nazi Germany and Fascist Italy, and to allow the Allies to sweep eastward through Tunisia and strike Rommel's army in the rear. This would crush the "Desert Fox" in a giant pincer as he faced British Field Marshal Montgomery's beleaguered Eighth Army in the sands west of Cairo.

On the western flank of the Center Task Force, which was astride the Oran-Arzew sector, the 26th Infantry Combat Team of the U.S. 1st Infantry Division, commanded by the charismatic Brig. Gen. Theodore Roosevelt, Jr., was attacking the beach at Les Andalouses, west of Oran. On the eastern flank of the force, the 16th and 18th Combat Teams of the U.S. 1st were making progress inland, commanded by Maj. Gen. Terry Allen, whom General George C. Marshall had called the "Firebrand." Together with Lt. Col. Bill Darby's renowned 1st Ranger Battalion, General Allen led ashore the two 1st Division Combat Teams, thus spearheading the amphibious assault on the town of Arzew.

Darby's Rangers had stormed ashore at 1:00 a.m., scaled the steep cliffs at the harbor's edge, and captured the French guns guarding Arzew. But in the process they had dashed our 5th Field Artillery's landing craft on the rocks, leaving us stranded on the transport and forcing us to attempt a landing direct from ship to shore.

A gusting wind swung the ship and sent her crunching and scraping against the concrete bulkhead. Burly British sailors quickly flung out heavy hemp lines, looping iron stanchions, winching the ship taut to the quay. Some other men from the 5th, on a different ship, had in the meantime made an assault landing while we were going down a gangplank — an ignominious arrival they would never let us forget.

Bursts of rifle and machine-gun fire whizzed through the ship's rigging and clanged against her steel superstructure. The men ran for the gangplank. As I scrambled off with them, I caught sight of the action on land: a building disintegrated in reddish dirt; black smoke roiled up from burning trucks; detonating explosives reverberated in the town.

The firing had stopped when I marched the men up from the waterfront, past pink and white stucco houses huddled over narrow streets. Over the crest of a rise, the Algerian countryside stretched out in sand-colored hills, dotted with farmhouses hidden among olive groves and palmettos. The cold morning air smelled of coal smoke and fresh vegetation; above the far horizon, the towering Tel-Atlas Mountains hung in the sky like a mirage. Strongly moved by this brief impression of Africa, I sensed a land so huge and diverse that it defied all comprehending. I longed to see it without this damned war.

An ancient Arab in a dirty burnoose, hunched over in a crooked doorway, stared at us out of red-rimmed eyes. At the next corner, an American soldier staggered along, waving a half-empty bottle of red wine. His other arm was around a young Arab, a swarthy fellow, flashing a toothless grin. A noncom in my D Battery column glared at the pair and spat a brown stream of tobacco juice in their direction.

Just beyond Arzew two American infantrymen lay sprawled out at the side of the road, their faces a grayish green, the ground around them pooled with drying blood. Then it hit me like a physical blow: I could be one of them; this was the thing that happened in war, conveyed to the wife in a five-star, "Deeply regret" telegram. *This* was death.

I marched up a long grade like an automaton, my mind 4,000 miles away, remembering the last time I'd seen Emily, reflecting on our final nights at Hershey — bittersweet escape from grueling army life just before the Division had sailed for Europe. But the contrast with the present was too cruel, and I strove to blot out the memory.

Shouts from men on a passing column of vehicles snapped me out of my reverie, and I looked back to make sure our men were getting off the road, at the same time trying to adjust to the exhausting, dusty, menacing realities of this invasion.

By 4:00 p.m. on 9 November, the 5th Field had rounded up its full complement of light 105-mm howitzers, which had been specially assigned for the landing. Now ready for action, the battalion had been ordered west to support the 16th Infantry in its attack on Oran, a French Algerian city some 25 miles to the west.

My car moved out at the head of Battery D. Orders were to keep 50-yard intervals between vehicles as we rolled through open country, where flat-roofed farmhouses of brick and stucco were islands in bright green fields of winter wheat.

Night fell, and the column edged its way west in total blackout. Drivers grew jittery and tended to close up their intervals, afraid of losing contact with the vehicle ahead. Toward midnight, we turned left into a narrow road between two high stone walls — a real trap. Shading my flashlight, I determined our location on the map. We were traveling at a right angle to the line of advance, and, as an artilleryman, I knew we were a juicy target for those expert French gunners in Oran. I had heard that those gunners might even have Nazi agents pointing pistols at their backs.

Each man in our landing force had a small but visible American flag on his left shoulder to remind people who we were. But we also knew from bulletins we had read on shipboard that we would be bucking the powerful influence here of the aged French hero, Marshal Pétain, who insisted he had collaborated with the Germans solely to save his country from destruction. It was said that he, along with Pierre Laval, the Nazi puppet head of Vichy France, controlled elements of the French military as well as segments of the population. Bulletins on the ship had warned us that we could be in for some very strong resistance, to which Colonel Darby of the U.S. 1st Rangers had added, "If the French support Vichy, we could have the fight of our lives."

At about 1:00 a.m. the battalion halted, and the truck behind me closed up. Ticked off, I ran back and shouted at the drivers to keep their intervals, but, in their alarm, they still crowded together. Though I kept after them, they remained jammed up and wouldn't be able to move till the battalion started up again.

Halfway down the column, I heard a distant rumble of artillery fire. A second later, a shell hit the stone wall with a blinding flash and a crack that shook my whole body. I dove for the ditch. Shadowy figures scrambled under the ammo truck in front of me. Beyond the wall another shell exploded, its fragments shredding the truck's canvas top. I said nothing.

Two more shells landed short of the road. Acid fear: they had us bracketed! Then fear turned to anger — what kind of a half-ass order had put us on a transverse road? And why in hell were those stupid Frenchmen shelling us? They detested the bloody Germans. These wild thoughts were routed when another shell burst against the wall, sending bits of rock whistling over my head.

They were coming in at 20-second intervals now; I hit the ditch, hugging the ground and waiting for the four-round volley I was certain would put us out of existence. I'd expected risks. Had thought a lot about getting killed. But never because of a mess-up like this.

Then the shelling stopped. I glanced at my watch, waited two minutes, and knew that for some reason they'd canceled their fire mission. I got up shaking, trying to convince myself it was from those cold stones I'd been lying on. I took a few deep breaths and went back up the column, speaking to the chiefs of section, telling them to come out now. And I reminded them again to stay at least 50 yards behind the truck in front.

By 3:30 that cold morning, we'd regained intervals and were moving over an open area, when a heavy artillery shell roared overhead like an express train. Exploding about 200 yards beyond us, it shook the ground and flashed in the sky like sheet lightning. "Dismount and dig in!" I shouted. Men leaped out, picks and shovels clanged on the iron-hard ground. Two shells burst short of the road — they had us bracketed again! Resisting an impulse to run, I dropped flat on the ground.

The bombardment lasted 15 minutes, minutes that seemed like hours. But the rounds that landed in our area didn't explode — and I realized the French cannoneers hadn't been fuzing their shells. I heaved a sigh of relief and stood shivering, my clothes soaked with sweat. The sudden relief soon left me, however, and I wandered around feeling frustrated and guilty: it was my duty to look out for these men, yet I hadn't been able to do one damn thing to get them under cover.

10 November 1942

Light was starting to show in the east when our Battalion Exec, Maj. Bob Tyson, stopped my command car and pointed. "Frelinghuysen," he sounded off in his southern accent, "D Battery gun positions in that low ground; you're in direct support 2nd Battalion, 16th Infantry, advancing westward on Oran. Now get up to the front fast and report to Colonel Crawford, Battalion Commander!"

I saluted and rapped out, "Yes, sir!" This was my first combat order, and it was with the elite 16th Infantry, the first U.S. outfit to march into Paris in World War I.

We raced toward the low-ground gun positions. My Battery Exec, Lt. George McNeill, his long face thin and drawn, ran over to get my order to go into action. He assigned a man to mark each of the four gun positions and signaled the firing battery to follow us in. Four GMC trucks, each pulling a 105-mm howitzer, swung around to the markers, throwing up thick clouds of dust. Even before the trucks pulled to a stop, the cannoneers came vaulting out, lowered the guns into position, and sent the vehicles off. All this had taken less than a minute. I signaled Jackson, my driver, and jumped into the moving car. A lanky, bronze-complexioned Oklahoman, presumably of American Indian ancestry, Jackson was an expert at the wheel. For three miles he drove all-out.

We dodged broken-down trucks, returning jeeps, command cars, signal trucks, and ambulances. Just ahead, a line of eucalyptus trees ran across the road at right angles to it. Two platoons of 2nd Battalion infantrymen lay splayed out in a ditch parallel to the trees, firing a staccato barrage. As we swung up to the line, a platoon sergeant came on the dead run, waving angrily at us. "Get that damn vehicle off the road, you're drawing fire. And take cover till I give clearance."

Jackson spun off the road and careened over the ditch behind some trees. When machine-gun fire pierced the car's top, we dove out on opposite sides into the ditch. After catching my breath, I poked my head up to assess the situation.

Gunfire cracked out from several houses and another line of trees half a mile ahead, spraying dirt geysers in a wheatfield and whining over us. At the same time, heavy machine-guns from the 16th Infantry raked the houses and trees. In order to deliver accurate artillery fire wherever Crawford might want it, I needed a fast precision registration of the battery. I dropped back into the ditch. Pascuzzi — my signal sergeant, who had come forward with the wire truck — was watching me. "You want radio, Captain? Wire won't be in for a few minutes." I nodded. At only 20, the sergeant was husky, bright, and brutally hard-working. Already he had the gun position on the radio, and just minutes later, I'd "shot in the battery," recorded base deflection, and could shift quickly to other targets.

"Hey, Cap'n," Jackson complained, his dark face concerned, "Pascuzzi tells me that target you fired on's a brewery. Why'd you have to pick that?"

"Take it easy, Jackson, I swear I didn't bust a single keg," I said laughing, but he still looked annoyed.

The platoon sergeant waved us forward, and 300 yards toward the front I saw a tall officer standing at the side of the road. Helmet cocked at an angle and feet wide apart, he searched the trees through his field glasses. Even before I saw his silver leaf, the stance and hard line of his body told me this must be the battalion commander. I jumped down from the car and saluted. "Colonel Crawford, Frelinghuysen, D Battery, 5th Field, reporting, sir."

I hadn't finished when he rasped, "OK, see that line of trees? Snipers in there got my men pinned down. They're in those buildings too. With machine-guns! I want fire on them. Fast!"

Rifle bullets began to zing past us, one nicking my car and ricocheting off behind us. Jackson, Pascuzzi, and I took cover in the ditch, but Crawford just stood there with his hands on his hips laughing. "That stuff won't hurt you," he said cockily. "Now at least you know where they are, so get moving!" He sauntered over to his jeep, waved his driver out of the ditch, and sped off.

Pascuzzi had the phone hooked up. Jackson took it muttering. "Sir, I don't think I agree with that colonel."

Fifty feet in front, more rifle fire. First a puff of smoke in the trees, then a spurt of soil on a line with my head. I hunched down and called, "Jackson, got the battery?"

"Yes, sir."

"Fire mission, base deflection left one-five-zero, open five, fuze quick, battery one round six thousand, fire when ready!"

Jackson, helmet off, lay with his face on the ground and repeated each command into the handset. In a moment, he exclaimed, "On the way! Time of flight 22 seconds."

I glued my eye to the second hand on my wristwatch. "Splash!" he called over. I yanked my head up to see four 80-foot blasts erupt behind the line of eucalyptus, shaking the earth beneath us.

When a bullet spat dirt in my face, I banged my head down and called, "five-four hundred!" We were dangerously close to the impact area — an erratic round could land on our position, but I couldn't wait. I had to run the risk.

Jackson reported, "On the way!"

Four bursts exploded just 200 yards ahead, throwing dirt over the road. A limb directly above me fell, sliced off clean. I called, "Two rounds — Zone five-four-hundred— six thousand!" Seconds later four shells burst in unison just in front of the houses. A roof cornice and wall crumbled in a shower of debris. Volley after volley pounded up and down through the zone, as bursts followed without further command. Half of one house simply disappeared. Trees stood split and broken, bare of leaves in clouds of ominous chalk-gray dust.

One more volley. I called, "Cease firing!" and looked up. Crawford was standing over me.

"Come with me, Frelinghuysen," he ordered. "Let's see what's going on up there. Bring only one vehicle beyond this point."

Crawford stood up in his jeep and waved an arm forward. The infantry leaped out of the hedges and advanced swiftly across the field, rifles at port. An advance squad prodded some bleeding *tirailleurs Algériens* out of the wrecked buildings at bayonet point. Thin, dark-skinned men in torn uniforms and dirty Arabic headdresses filed out onto the road, hands high in the air.

We drove on toward the city slowly, while the infantry moved up cautiously across the fields. I slumped down in the rear seat of Crawford's jeep, while he talked on the radio. Half an hour later, the colonel stopped at a thick hedgerow where the highway crossed a field of corn stubble. A thousand yards beyond, the high apartment houses of the city looked luxurious and inviting. I hoped like hell I wouldn't have to fire a mission in there.

I scanned the streets immediately ahead through my field glasses; a heavy tank with a yellow star and code insignia of Combat Command B, 1st Armored Division, was grinding toward us. U.S. and French colors, mounted on its turret, whipped in the breeze. All down the line, platoon leaders bellowed, "Cease firing! It's one of ours."

Rather incongruously, a round-bellied man in a black felt hat and business suit was clinging to the top of the tank. In a few minutes the huge vehicle lurched up and jerked to a halt. Crawford and I walked over to it, watching its leather-helmeted commander come up out of the hatch. "This guy wants to make a deal, or somethin'," the commander informed us in a Deep-South drawl. "But I can't quite understand what the hell he's talkin' about."

The civilian slid off the tank, brushed himself off, made a bow and announced, "*Messieurs, je suis le maire de la cité d'Oran. Je viens vous offrir accès libre à notre cité avec un accord que vous montriez plein égard au Tricolor et l'honneur de la France.*"

All the Americans looked blank. I translated quickly and Crawford growled, "He damn well better surrender! All right, Frelinghuysen, tell him to come with me in my jeep. You follow the infantry CO's command car. Every vehicle will fly the Color."

I stumbled a little when I explained to the mayor that "*Monsieur le colonel*" had accepted his condition, because I wasn't at all sure Crawford had. But the mayor looked pleased to be riding with the colonel in the lead vehicle — I suspected it would help in the next election — while I offered a silent prayer that the colonel would calm down. All the mayor had asked for was military courtesy.

We had landed with American flags in all our vehicles, and Jackson had mounted ours at the corner of the windshield. We moved out, third in column, with the "Color" flying. Up ahead, "*Monsieur le colonel*" and "*Monsieur le maire*" appeared to be chatting amiably and, from time to time, Crawford would even let out a laugh. (I concluded that the Frenchman had found some schoolboy English he hadn't dared risk in his negotiation.)

As Jackson drove into Oran, windows and balconies of 10- and 12-story buildings bulged with people waving French and American flags. Arab men in traditional dress, women in veils, and smartly dressed French civilians thronged the streets, and a deep-throated roar began to swell through the city. A strange feeling of excitement and a sense of power took hold of me as I mused: was this how the Romans had felt when they captured the ancient African cities?

We turned into the main thoroughfare of Oran, where the background sound rose into an overwhelming *vox populi* that I could feel in my gut. Jackson drove at a crawl behind the two infantry vehicles, threading his way through tightly packed people who poured from buildings and pressed against the truck.

The sound became a chant: "*Vive la France! Vive l'Amérique!*" Jackson squinched up one side of his face. "Say, Cap'n, I can't figure it. Some of them guys were shootin' at us an hour ago." I was just as confused. It did seem that they changed alliances kind of fast. Why had they fought? I thought of the wounded infantrymen and *tirailleurs* back there. War didn't make sense.

That night my pup tent stood on a hill above our bivouac, and beyond it the sentries on the perimeter guard walked past their posts. Brilliant stars silvered the mountains and valleys and the rectangular outlines of farms. Far to the south a muted silhouette of the Tel-Atlas range rose against a bluish-purple sky. And I dreamed of a small white house in the green hills of western New Jersey, recalling that painful day there more than a year ago when I'd said goodbye to Emily and set off for Fort Devens and the 5th Field. I'd had no word from her since we had left the south of England six weeks before.

Chapter 5

The November Race for Tunis

Our main strategic purpose was, therefore, the speedy capture of northern Tunisia.   Dwight D. Eisenhower, *Crusade in Europe*

<u>21 November 1942</u>

Division Headquarters had ordered the 5th Field Artillery Battalion to move out of its bivouac southwest of Oran, Algeria. D Battery came down the hill in "march order," with its white and red guidon flying. At the corner where we turned east on the highway, the 1st Division Artillery Band was playing, "When the Caissons Go Rolling Along." Their instruments glittered in the bright morning sunlight, the flags rippled in the breeze as we passed the Division Color Guard, and each battery in turn presented arms.

The 5th Field, now fully equipped with its big 155-mm howitzers, had been detached from the 1st Infantry Division and ordered to cross North Africa alone. We would be attached to the British 78th Division, which was fighting the Germans in Tunisia, 600 miles to the east.

As the battalion rolled southeast of Algiers into the foothills of the eastern Atlas Mountains, we climbed up narrow, winding roads. Drivers cramped their long rigs around precarious switchback turns, the engines of our Diamond-T prime movers roaring in low gear. Looking back along the column, I could see our 155-mm howitzers out on the curves, their huge wheels almost at the edge of the cliffs. Off to the south, snowcapped peaks, reaching up to 13,000 feet, appeared white and purple in the distant haze.

I breathed a sigh of relief when we descended into the lower areas of dry wadis cut deep by the torrential rains of the winter season. Still further down, broad valleys were dotted with oases, fringed with orange and olive trees and a few stunted palms.

Near the valley floor a green grove of trees stood out in refreshing contrast to the dusty brown desert. But when we approached the grove, clouds of smoke billowed up from a column of burning vehicles strung out along the road. Shattered and overturned personnel carriers, bearing British insignia, belched flames and oily black fumes. The outfit must have lost a lot of men.

An arm signal was repeated down the column. I halted the battery off the road and drove forward. Captain Rawie, A Battery CO, and Captain Warren of B Battery were there. Both men, white-faced and grim, were waiting in the trees. A British major was standing apart, declaiming loudly to Colonel Stout, who beckoned to us. We went over and saluted. Several angry-looking British officers ignored our arrival. The major was saying: "Simply this, two of your aircraft, clearly identifiable as twin-fuselage P-38's with American markings, came down and strafed us with cannon and machine-gun fire, not once, but three times, despite the fact that our carriers, transport, and equipment are well marked with British insignia." He paused, then ground out through clenched teeth, "Six men killed and 30 wounded; I'm out of action!" And he stood glaring at Colonel Stout.

"I deeply regret this, Major. What else can I say?"

"You bloody well better think of something and get your men properly trained."

Colonel Stout stiffened. "I understand your feelings, Major, and deeply sympathize with them. How can we be of assistance?"

The major relaxed slightly. "We could use some first aid kits and your medical officer, if you have one."

Stout nodded to his adjutant, who went off on the double.

Back at the head of our column, the colonel addressed his officers: "Gentlemen, this is what happens when two armies, however friendly, are thrown together in the field without joint training. In three days we'll report to British 78th Division, which, as you know, is in combat in Tunisia. You must be constantly on guard against incorrect identification, against failure to know the location of both friendly and enemy units, and against lack of proper communication. This is of paramount importance if disasters such as this are to be avoided." None of us spoke. We saluted and walked back to our vehicles in shocked silence.

Early on 24 November the battalion reached Souk Ahras, the last city in eastern Algeria before the Tunisian border. This was the main British supply base in the "Race for Tunis," which meant Get There Before the Germans Make the Area Impregnable. We threaded our way through hordes of supply troops, ammunition lorries, and light tanks revving up their engines. Shouts and commands rang out in Cockney and every other kind of British and Scottish accent.

Beyond the city we climbed the steep road leading to the mountains of

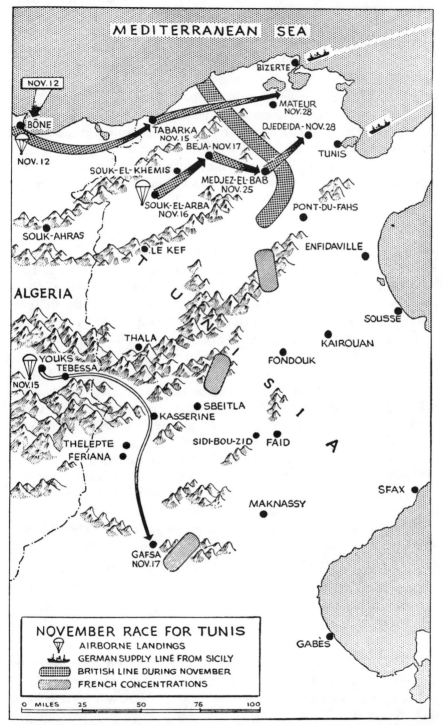

The November "Race for Tunis." (From *Crusade in Europe*, by Dwight D. Eisenhower [Doubleday & Co., 1948]. Reprinted with permission.)

Medjerda, on the border between Algeria and Tunisia. At the top of the pass the air was icy as we began the descent into western Tunisia, where French and Arab farms were scattered widely across the broad valley floor. By noon we reached the shattered town of Beja and passed through its rubble-strewn streets. Buildings were pockmarked with bullet holes. The faded red canopy of an outdoor cafe hung cheerlessly from its frame, while beneath it little sidewalk tables lay jumbled amid broken plaster and stucco.

After Colonel Stout had reported to the British commander, for the next two days we were sent in and out of bivouacs and gun positions, without any apparent battle plan. On the afternoon of the 26th I got orders to report for a night reconnaissance with a command car, driver, and radio operator. Following the column, with Colonel Stout leading, we traveled for three hours through wild, arid hills on primitive dirt roads.

I scrutinized my map as we came into a little town called Pont-du-Fahs. Here, too, buildings had been smashed by gunfire and wreckage was all about, almost blocking the streets. And a foreboding stillness hung in the air. In the center of the town Colonel Stout's car suddenly turned and started back out on another street. All at once, my driver and I were left alone, struggling to get through the rubble. The back of my neck began to prickle, and I ordered Carlson, my driver today, to plow through the stuff somehow and get us out of there fast. He spun the wheel and we careened across mounds of debris, at one point almost overturning, until I saw a command car up ahead. "Thank God," I thought. What a place for an ambush! We pulled up behind Len Warren's car, where in the dim light I again studied the map; we had to be 25 miles from our bivouac and at least 15 beyond the last British units we had seen.

I went on forward and told Rex Rawie I was worried that we were well beyond the south flank of the British army. As if my remark was out of order, he scowled and grunted, "Maybe so, maybe so," without turning his head.

On the way back we lost our way several times in the darkness and didn't arrive at our bivouac until dawn. I worked hard all through the day, and it was after 6:00 when I finally was able to quit and get some supper.

7:00 p.m., 27 November

John Asher, my first sergeant, had to shout and shake my arm to wake me — Battalion had just ordered me to report for the second night recon in a row. I looked at my luminous wristwatch and groaned — I'd been asleep ten minutes. I struggled up to a sitting position.

Asher said, "Same equipment as last night, sir. Detail will be ready by the time you get there."

I stood up, feeling dizzy, and pulled on my field jacket. My stomach burned from too much coffee, my clothes stuck to my body with five-days' dust and dried sweat. In total blackout, my command car and jeep pulled out into column behind B Battery vehicles, and we headed southeast for somewhere below Tunis. With Colonel Stout leading, we bumped and twisted over rocky mountain roads for four hours. We'd made only 35 miles when the column stopped, and I ran forward. Rawie and Warren were already there waiting in the bright moonlight.

On the side of a steep valley with 3,000-foot mountains to the east, Stout pointed out the general area for the battalion gun positions. He walked in from the road with us past a silent white farmhouse. I thought, if anyone is in there, we make easy targets.

The colonel showed me an area for D Battery gun positions near a deep ravine. But the place proved too steep for our equipment, so I ran up the road ahead of our column to look for a better one.

"Halt!" a voice rasped at me out of the shadows.

I stopped and snapped out the password, startled, but not too worried — he sounded American.

"Put up your hands, high up! Who're you?"

I told him we were artillery on reconnaissance. A man stepped out, pointing a sub-machine-gun at me. A jeep behind him bore U.S. 1st Armored markings. My God! I hoped these guys weren't trigger happy.

"Your name and unit?" I gladly gave him what he wanted.

He lowered the sub-machine-gun. "OK," he said, "you know what's in those mountains?"

I said I had no idea.

"The German army, that's all! You're 15 miles in front of the British Infantry. Whoever sent you out here on a night recon don't know shit from Shinola. You nearly got your head shot off."

All this I reported to Colonel Stout, minus the allusion to brown shoe polish, of course. He volunteered that British HQ didn't seem to know the location of their troops or anyone else's. We turned around, headed for our gun positions, and reached them by daylight of 28 November.

All that day I was on a treadmill: gun-cleaning, inspections, training with British grenades, cannoneer drills, camouflage inspections, and, when darkness fell, perimeter guard inspection. I tramped up and down the rocky hills, worrying about being attached to a British division and wishing the hell we'd come over here with the U.S. 1st.

The British had ordered our battalion recon party out into no-man's land — where a unit with no armor and only a few small arms did not belong — on the nights of both the 26th and 27th. Those operations had risked the personnel, and exhausted them, without achieving anything. I'd conferred with Rex Rawie and Len Warren, the other two battery CO's. As a regular officer, Rex Rawie was highly experienced and had managed to acquire some knowledge of the British artillery; he said that our 155-mm howitzers were heavier than anything they had. With Len and me, he had questioned whether they knew how to handle 12 howitzers that could each hurl a 95-lb shell nine miles and blast a hole as big as a house.

By 9:00 on the night of the 28th, I was just about able to stagger up to the mess truck. The mess sergeant had saved some hot stew and coffee for the battery officers. "Figured you'd need a hot feed, sir, after two nights on the road." He pulled out a wooden table and set up two places. In a few minutes, George McNeill, my Battery Exec, joined me.

The mess sergeant brought us more stew, and we each polished off a second plate. In a rather animated discussion, George and I came down hard on the recons of the last two nights. The lack of information about enemy locations appalled us.

I was having coffee when Asher ran up. "Message from Battalion, sir: recon party, same vehicles and personnel." And he added in a tone that only an old combat veteran could get away with, "You better hurry, Captain, that messenger had been to A Battery first —"

"Good God!" McNeill broke in, "three in a row. Can't I go in your place, Captain?"

Asher broke in quickly, "Sir, the message said, 'Captain Frelinghuysen.' New detail and vehicles'll be ready about now." He saluted and disappeared.

Chapter 6

Captain Rawie's Decision

<u>9:00 p.m., 28 November</u>

I grabbed helmet, gas mask, binoculars, and map case, and strapped on my Colt .45. McNeill stood up, his long face solemn. Suddenly, he wrung my hand and said, "Goodbye, Captain." The words gave me an uneasy feeling — usually we parted with just a casual salute.

Now, well behind B Battery, Carlson, today's driver, drove fast down the hill to the command post tent, where I ducked low to go through the flaps. The inside of the CP reminded me of an old Frederic Remington painting my father had of the Civil War, all done in black and gray, of tense, hard-faced officers poring over a map.

Colonel Stout looked up and gave his order: "We are to report to CO, Lancashire Fusilliers at Djedeida." He described route and order of march, and added, "Radio silence. Come forward on foot at all halts. This is our first mission under British command. Be extremely alert. Enemy patrols in the area."

We moved in column down a hill, with the moon high in the direction of Tunis. Long shadows lay in the valleys, but on the eastern slopes, trees, orchards, and occasional farmhouses stood out clearly. It would have been beautiful, another time, another year.

Five miles north and east of our gun positions, a challenge rang out in a Cockney accent. The column stopped, and I ran forward. Stout was listening to a lance-corporal next to a light machine-gun. The man was saying, "But my orders, sir, was not to let no one north and east of 'ere. Enemy activity in the area, sir."

"What activity, Corporal?"

"Tank battle at the next turn. Bad show, sir. Your chaps took a beatin', they did, sir."

Stout instructed his officers, "Move forward according to plan," then got into his command car, his thick glasses flashing in the moonlight.

A mile beyond, the column halted again, this time at three medium tanks strewn at crazy angles across the road. Wisps of smoke still curled up from them, and the big yellow stars of the U.S. 1st Armored Division were barely visible on the fire-blackened armor plate. When I got up forward, Stout commented, "This must have occurred four or five hours ago. I'm surprised the British artillery commander didn't mention it."

Gordon Bilat, our battalion S-3 and a highly capable senior captain, who had been in the command car with the colonel, shifted uneasily as he listened to Stout. "If the colonel will permit me," he said with a tinge of sarcasm, "it looks as if there's been a major change in the situation."

The colonel snapped back testily, "I'll permit you, Bilat, but I still have my orders." Bilat stared at the ground, pushing a toe in the dust and shaking his head almost imperceptibly. In the clear light, I could see the angry set of his jaw as he boarded the command car. Our column moved on ahead.

While we were rounding a turn to the east, two British motorcycles overtook us, whining past. Directly in front of us, the road to Djedeida stretched out for two miles, a straight white strip, until it disappeared into the black shadows of a clump of trees.

The motorcycles vanished only seconds before flashes burst from the trees and yellow tracer bullets arced into the sky. The recon party stopped abruptly about half a mile from Djedeida. Some of the tracers came toward us, curving to our right — that meant they were drifting left — and sounds of explosions and machine-gun fire reached us. Thinking aloud, I burst out, "What the hell! Have those dumb limeys shot up their own people?" It struck me that we'd have to be damn careful or we'd get the same treatment, since we hadn't been given their passwords or other means of identification.

The instant the firing started, all vehicles had swung off onto the shoulder of the road as I did my 220-yard-dash up to the head of the column. Bilat stopped me just behind the colonel's car. "*Now*, how damn much convincing does he need, Frelinghuysen?"

"Have you told him what you think?"

"Hell, yes, but I can't give him written proof."

When we joined Stout, the colonel conceded, "I realize the situation looks peculiar, but I have orders to go to Djedeida. I'll take my car with driver and radio operator, Bilat, S-3, and Stafflebach, S-2. Rest of party will wait here. If no one returns with further orders, come forward to rejoin me in 30 minutes. Break radio silence; sets on battalion command channel. Any questions?"

Bilat sighed. "I've said I thought there's been a radical change in the situation, Colonel."

"I'm quite aware of your opinion, Bilat."

The S-3 went on anyway: "Sir, it appears that the town has either been retaken or there's fighting up there — no place for a battalion party. In addition, we have the British outpost's warning."

"Bilat, I've heard enough. This is our first mission here and I'm not taking the word of a lance-corporal over that of regimental headquarters. We're wasting time. Now mount up!"

Bilat saluted woodenly, then he and Tom Stafflebach climbed up into the rear seat and slid in behind the huge Signal Corps radio set that stretched the entire width of the vehicle. Tom, tall and lanky, could barely squeeze his long legs under the set. Stout got in front with the driver, and off they moved moved toward Djedeida.

I said aloud to myself, "God help those guys in back if they ever have to get out of there fast."

11:30 p.m.

The car crept slowly forward from our position toward the black clump of trees half a mile ahead. What a hell of a decision Stout had had to make. A night reconnaissance in enemy territory was like jumping off a cliff into unknown waters. He had to know it was crazy; yet he was damned if he'd cop out on his first mission. His unarmored car was a sitting duck out there.

I shivered. A dozen miles to the east, flashes resembling sheet lightning lit up the sky over Tunis. Seconds later, the thunder of high explosive blasts reached us, while far above the city chains of red tracer from American bombers curved lazily toward the earth.

Stout's car reached the trees and abruptly disappeared in the darkness. Instantly, the spot where I'd last seen it erupted in blue-white sheets of flame. Antitank guns cracked out, and from both sides of the road machine-guns ripped blazing crossfires. Yellow tracer bullets streaked in fiery arcs across the clear November sky.

When the tracers swung toward us, I dove straight out to the right and landed on stony ground. "Carlson," I called to my driver, "you OK?"

"Think so, sir."

"Crawl over here fast and get in the ditch." Tracers were still curving down the road, drifting left. I agonized, trying to remember — where had I heard about "yellow tracer that drifts left?"

With Stout missing, Rex Rawie was now in command, and in short order he left no doubt about it. "Frelinghuysen," he barked, "we got too damn much equipment out in this moonlight! Follow B Battery vehicles back to the orchard at that last turn in the highway!"

I jumped into my command car. Carlson made a U-turn and followed the artillery recon party, a bunch of survey and communication trucks with only a few small arms. Our big howitzers back in the gun positions were the most powerful killing force the British had in their First Army. I wondered when they would realize that fact.

Rawie was on the road, watching the black outline of a command car approaching from the rear. He waved us off the highway. Marty Lawler of Headquarters Battery called out from the car, "Is Colonel Stout here?"

"All vehicles off the road," Rawie growled.

Lawler followed me. Rawie joined us in the orchard. Len Warren, in command of B Battery, was already there, his face hidden in the shadow of his helmet. The others looked green in the moonlight.

"Where the hell's Stout?" Lawler demanded. "His orders to report to British CO at Djedeida have been canceled. I've got to tell him fast!"

"There was gunfire at Djedeida when he went forward," Rawie said, "so I brought the party back here."

"For God's sake, Rex," Lawler insisted, getting more agitated, "we've got to stop him. The Top Secret Division codes are in that car, plus all our FM frequencies. A couple of them are jammed already."

"Cut the bullshit and let's get moving," Warren shot back. "We've got two orders to get up there — Stout's and British HQ's."

"Anyone know why those yellow tracers —" I tried to ask.

Rawie cut me off. "Situation's changed. Stout's order to go up there is obsolete. I won't stop you, but I'm going to report back fast in Stout's place."

Warren, Lawler, and I agreed to go after Stout, each with a jeep, driver, and radio-operator/machine-gunner. I would go first, Warren would follow 200 yards back, Lawler 400 yards behind him. If we ran into trouble, Lawler was to report enemy locations, with all radios on D Battery channel.

Rawie groaned, shaking his head. "I wish you luck, but I sure as hell disagree with you."

Gray moonlight flickered through the olive trees as I ran for my jeep. I jumped in and told Herschel Ash, who was to drive the jeep while Carlson stayed with the command car, to go back to the highway. The luminous dial of my wristwatch read precisely midnight. We turned north and shortly swung east, headed for Djedeida. Left of the shining ribbon of road lay an open plain, shrouded in a light mist. To our right, mountains rose to 2,000 feet. Scattered clouds passed over the moon, making the land features murky and indistinct.

Equipment had been slow in coming, so we had welded a .50 caliber machine-gun mount in the rear of the jeep. Sid Delanoy hunched behind the gun, earphones on and a hand on the radio. Leaning forward, he whispered, "Channel jammed, sir. I can hear B Battery but I can't read him."

I signaled Ash to halt and turn off the motor. In the utter silence, the dark mass of trees at Djedeida was foreboding. "Whose troops were in there?" I wondered. Were they British, as their HQ had told us? If so, what was the strange gunfire we'd seen earlier?

"Go ahead — but this time dead slow," I whispered.

By now the light cloud cover had dissipated, revealing thick trees along the road to the left, one big one to the right. Behind us, Warren's jeep was a black rectangle on the dimly lit pavement. Again inching forward, we crossed into the shadow of the trees.

For one blinding second, the world exploded in my face. Machine-guns blazed from three directions; yellow tracers ripped across from both flanks and ricocheted off the macadam. Delanoy fired back a burst right past my head. Brilliant white flares went off in the air, bathing our death-trap in an otherworldly light.

Dazed by the concussion, I started out of the jeep and had a foot on the ground when a stick grenade exploded a few feet from my face. Unable to see, I crouched down briefly till my sight came back. Ash and Delanoy had disappeared.

Suddenly all firing stopped. After a few unnerving seconds of silence, an exchange of shouts in German yanked me to my senses. Water dripped from the jeep's radiator, a front tire was in shreds, and the air reeked with raw gasoline mixed with cordite and TNT.

Machine-gun fire from the west shattered the brief calm; our red tracers blazed up the road from the west; I dove for a shallow ditch on the right, crawling fast away from the town. The Germans fired back, and I found myself caught in an enfilade of gunfire from four directions.

Bursting flares exposed two men lying in the ditch. Assuming them dead, I scrambled on by. Now a second machine-gun opened up from the west. Bullets ricocheted off the road in both directions. Here it dawned on me — the first gun had been Warren and the second, Lawler, who had closed up his interval.

I was 50 feet further along the ditch when German soldiers began closing in from the west. In the weird light, their deep-flanged helmets and gray faces had a death's head aspect. Some 30 or 40 were in the ambush. In the brilliance of the flares, any movement on my part could be fatal, so I hugged the ground, watching, waiting for the light to die down. As I lay there, familiar images flashed across my mind: hemlock-wooded hills, a white cottage in a valley where we had lived — yet the images seemed to be from a strange world, all black and white and gray.

I snapped back to the present when the hail of gunfire again slammed to a stop, echoing in my ears in the treacherous silence. Len Warren was walking toward me, his hands in the air, a stream of blood running down his forehead. Then I saw the black hole in his helment. Was he one of the walking dead?

A minute later the flares subsided, and in one last desperate attempt to escape I crawled wildly along the ditch. But in the eerie, dying light, I saw a ring of German paratroopers closing around me. I lay motionless, praying they might miss me in the shadows. But after only a brief moment a couple of them prodded me out with rifles. When I hauled myself to my feet, their sergeant stuck his pistol in my stomach. *"Fur Sie ist der Krieg beendigt!"* he sneered, then translated into heavily accented English: "So now for you the war is over!" Adding derisively, "Not even can we catch rabbits so easily," he reached over and grabbed my Colt .45 from its holster.

I was totally shattered, with a crushing sensation in my chest almost like a physical pain. Just five minutes ago, I'd been in command of 150 men; now I'd lost everything — I was nothing. I cursed myself: What in hell had we been doing, anyway, an artillery recon outfit, five miles beyond the last British outpost?

Fighting to steady my voice, I said to the sergeant, "Let me go to my friends." He escorted me over to them, but wouldn't let us speak until we were surrounded by Germans pointing rifles.

Len Warren had been frisked, too, and allowed to lower his hands, but I couldn't take my eyes off the hole in his helmet. "Are you OK?" I asked.

"What do you mean, OK?"

"You've a hole in your helmet."

He put his hand up, felt it, then took it off and saw the hole. He wiped his head with his handkerchief — the bullet had creased his scalp and blown out the back of the helmet. Marty Lawler, also a captain, hadn't been hit, but he was as stunned as the rest of us.

Corp. Sid Delanoy, my machine-gunner, and Herschel Ash, my driver, came walking up with their hands in the air. I couldn't look at them. When I tried to say something, all that came out was a jumble of words. I was totally overwhelmed with guilt at my stupidity: The Intelligence report had said, "Yellow tracer drifting left is German." Had I only remembered, this would never have happened.

The Germans marched us toward the town, through the small woods at the rear of the ambush, past the antitank gun that had fired at me just minutes before. When he saw us looking at it, the sergeant hustled us on by. As they were herding us into a courtyard behind a two-story building, Marty Lawler suddenly nudged my arm. "My God! Look at that!" he whispered. In the shadows next to the building lay the shattered hulk of a command car with Colonel Stout's code insignia. The antitank gun had blown huge ragged holes through the windshield and radiator. The rest of the vehicle was a honeycomb of bullet holes from rifle and machine-gun fire.

"Marty, there's no way —" I began, then said no more. For Gordon Bilat had been in that car, and he and Marty were married to sisters.

Marty hadn't heard me anyway. He was already on his way over to look at it, when one of the guards shouted, *"Nein! Nein!"* and pushed him back toward us. Then the Germans yelled some more and waved their rifles, shoving us into a building which was apparently the command post for this unit. There they put us in a bare room, its walls faced with unpainted tongue-and-groove boards that could easily be pried off. Two British officers were sitting on the floor, propped against the wall. We sat down next to them.

"Oh, you chaps too," one of them said casually. "You know, that's the third bike I've had shot out from under me this week. I imagine you were also advised the British were firmly ensconced in this lovely town of Djedeida?"

I nodded.

A bored German soldier aimed his rifle at us while we chatted with the British officers, a bit diffidently until we no longer doubted they were authentic. They were Lts. Jack Mosses, artillery, and Hilary Rogers, from an infantry regiment. As had we, they had been ordered to report to "British" Headquarters in Djedeida.

After a while I too slumped down against the wall. The *élan*, the *esprit de corps* we'd had was gone. I was at the bottom of the pit, berating myself, the Germans, the idiots who had sent us into a German-occupied town, and everyone else I could think of.

Two hours later, we were awakened, each from his own private purgatory, by cries of *" 'Raus! 'Raus! Alle heraus!"* The guards bundled us out to the courtyard and ordered us to climb aboard an armored carrier. I stood in the back, shaking with cold, as it rumbled down the road in the waning moonlight. In the front of the vehicle a guard faced us, helmet hung low over his neck. In the spectral light he had the look of a cadaver, but the careless familiarity with which he fondled his machine-pistol gave away his experience with a weapon that could rip a man in half.

I agonized over the devastating loss of freedom, identity, and self-respect. Yet this was no time to wallow in self pity, for now I was faced with the frightening duty to escape. Fighting physical and mental numbness, I tried to figure the chances of success in jumping down six feet, at 35 miles an hour, to a hard-surface road. One voice inside of me repeated the old army saying about escaping, "The longer you wait the tougher it'll get," while another warned of at least a broken leg and at worst being machine-gunned to death on the pavement. It would be just like these bastards to set an example. I muttered to the British officer next to me, "Can't get any tougher than this; the hell with it."

He looked at me scornfully and said to his fellow prisoner, "Let's have a go at it." But neither made a move, which was a relief. Suddenly, I didn't feel as guilty about not trying it myself.

No one moved or spoke again for the rest of this ominous ride. I watched them for a while; they seemed somewhat embarrassed at their failure to act.

Finally, I slid to the floor and huddled back against the cold steel side of the vehicle.

At any rate, I was out of the wind, though I couldn't retreat from the torment of self-recrimination that flooded my mind. In all my life, I had never wished so hard that I might live something over again. Why hadn't I planned it better? Why hadn't I remembered those goddam tracers? Then I tried disbelief: This hadn't happened; it would all go away like a bad dream.

Visions of violent escapes began to race through my thoughts. Sometimes these ended in bloody disaster. More often, I would shoot half a dozen Germans, then run like hell, and eventually arrive heroically back at the battalion CP, dirty and exhausted but with the locations of all the German units burned in my brain. Then under the protection of night we would sneak the battalion up within range and, acting as forward observer, I would rain the fires of hell on the unsuspecting Germans.

Whatever temporary relief this provided, there came the moment when this fantasy had exhausted me emotionally, and I had to come back to the unspeakable reality: I was a *Kriegsgefangener*, a German prisoner of war. I sank even deeper into the despondency of self-reproach.

Chapter 7

Kriegsgefangener

Gray light shone in the eastern sky as our carrier rumbled along the shadowy streets of Tunis, where city smells of garbage and animal dung mingled with the familiar odor of soft coal smoke. Widely spaced houses nestled in clumps of trees along avenues lined with shrubbery.

As I sat shivering in that carrier, I realized the bitter irony of our situation: We had achieved General Eisenhower's objective of reaching Tunis as fast as possible; we had won his "Race for Tunis." There was only one slight hitch: We had lost our freedom in the process.

The carrier finally stopped at a row of low buildings with narrow-barred windows. "Christ, they're taking us to a bloody wog jail," one Britisher remarked. Two iron gates creaked open, and the vehicle ground into a courtyard. The high walls were topped with broken glass embedded in concrete. Six of us were shoved down a dark hall that stank of mildew, urine, and feces, and into a bare ten-by-ten-foot cell with a thick door and one narrow window with rusty bars.

The guard went out, the door clanged shut behind him. I remembered a time as a child when I was tied up in a quilt and locked in a closet. For a moment, that trauma now swept over me. I struggled with it, trying to rationalize a dreamlike terror. Gradually a certain apathy overcame me, and I stretched out on the cracked cement floor. I glanced at the others and turned away, too tired to talk or even think. I was only an inch from the man on each side, but I needed even that little separation to create an illusion of privacy. I pulled off my gas mask to use for a pillow. Having been on my feet for three days, I fell asleep in seconds.

A leaden sky showed through the barred window when a German guard stuck his head in the door the next morning. *"Aufstehen! Aufstehen! Alle heraus!"* he shouted. I got up slowly and stretched my rigid, numb limbs, feeling the grime and stickiness from days of dust and dried sweat. He marched us to the putrid latrine, where we used pits in the floor and were allowed to rinse our hands and faces in icy water.

"Trinken das Wasser?" I tried on him.

"Nein! Nein!" he shouted back. I drank some anyway and he shrugged his shoulders. Back in our cell, the guard ladled out a half-pint of watery soup into each prisoner's canteen cup.

An hour later, at about eight, a young German officer in a light-blue uniform pulled open the heavy cell door. He was thin, erect, with blonde hair, china-blue eyes, and a frozen smile. What a typical Nazi bastard, I thought. "Now, Gentlemen, I have a nice surprise for you," he said in heavily accented English. "Today you will have the pleasure of meeting one of our senior officers. I remind you that military courtesy must be observed."

Someone behind me whispered, "Fuck you!" If the German officer heard it, he didn't react.

We knew the rules: name, rank, and serial number in response to every question; don't try to be clever, just repeat the routine again and again. We knew, too, that it would not work, and that they had their methods. The guards called only one prisoner at a time. Without their saying so, I knew Len and Marty were also wondering how long they could hold out.

When none of the prisoners came back, Len observed, "Obviously, they don't want us to compare notes until all their interrogations are over."

"For God's sake, Len," Marty Lawler growled, "this isn't a cross-examination in a courtroom." Len frowned and stared at the floor. In a few minutes a guard came in and called my name.

Chapter 8

Birds of Prey

<u>11:00 a.m.</u>

When I returned to our cell, still shaken from the interrogation by the German colonel, neither Len nor Marty was there. The other prisoners eyed me inquisitively, but I sat down without speaking, not trusting my composure. An hour or so later, Len and Marty were brought back separately. In comparing notes with them, I realized German Intelligence had indeed put together accurately the order of battle.

I thanked God when we did not hear from the German staff colonel again.

<u>8:00 a.m., 1 December 1942</u>

After we had been in the Arab jail two days, an old Wehrmacht *Feldwebel* (sergeant) lined us up outside the building. He was about 45, with a bad limp, and he had a purple scar across his pallid cheek that distorted his mouth and gave him a sinister squint. We speculated that he had been wounded and assigned to limited duty, but Jack Mosses said it wouldn't stop him from shooting an escaping prisoner.

The *Feldwebel* called us to attention with an *"Achtung!"* and began to speak slowly in broken English: "You are now in trucks going, but do not be mistaken. If anyone tries to escape, I will cut him down before he gets two meters away. Then I will line up all the others and shoot them also." He demonstrated his skill with his machine-pistol by swinging it and aiming it in different directions, but chiefly at us. *"Sie kannst Verstehen?"* (Can you understand?), he said. With that, he loaded us into a truck that headed north out of Tunis and joined a convoy of open vehicles, crammed with British prisoners.

Beyond the city a flight of 50 black, trimotored Junkers Ju-52's roared over our convoy like huge birds of prey against a serene blue sky. As our trucks halted in front of some ancient hangars at El Aouïna, the main Tunis airport, the planes swung westward. Sunlight on their wings and fuselages caught the black and white crosses and the macabre swastika emblems.

Powered by three 830 hp BMW's, the Ju-52 was the workhorse of the Luftwaffe and, we had heard, the prime factor in the swift movement of German troops to Tunisia. They reminded me a little of the old Ford Trimotor with a fuselage like a small boxcar. I realized now that the Germans had retaken Djedeida with troops flown over in 52's and had used these reinforcements effectively to halt the Allied Forces in their race to capture the city of Tunis.

The 52's touched down about 200 yards apart, bouncing clumsily on the bumpy metal strips of the runway. After braking hard, they swung alternately right and left onto the dirt aprons between the runways. As each plane came to a halt, doors flew open and a unit of heavily armed paratroopers leaped to the ground; I counted 17 getting off one plane. Flanged helmets low over their faces, they slung rifles and machine-pistols over their shoulders and ran across to waiting camouflaged trucks.

Pyramid-shaped piles of bombs were deposited around the field, one right in front of the hangar where we were now lined up. A few yards from it I noticed a huge stack of rectangular metal cans gleaming in the sunlight. Bored guards in visored field caps slouched around us, casually holding their weapons.

An American pilot glanced at the sky, then at the guards, and whispered something to a Britisher standing near me. A high-pitched drone directly over the airport caused one German to look at three specks glistening in the sky. *"Da kommen, unsere Stukas,"* he said gloating.

The pilot muttered under his breath, "In a pig's ass they're Stukas. They're A-20 Bostons. Now, watch out!"

No alert was sounded. No prisoner moved. The 52's were rolling in and skidding off the runway in continuous succession when a shift of wind brought the whistling screech of falling bombs. Across the field, as the first bombs exploded, huge columns of black dust burst into the air and hung there for an instant. A split second later, the concussion waves and flat, heavy thuds blasted over us.

Prisoners scattered in all directions, while the Germans screamed commands. Another stick of bombs hit the runway much nearer, on a direct line with me. I stood there transfixed, forgetting to move, as a 52 flipped on its back, belching orange flames and oily black smoke. With that, I came to and dove behind the stack of big shiny metal cans.

Flak guns thundered, dotting the sky with white puffs like balls of cotton, almost drowning out the third stick of bombs, exploding alongside the hangar behind us.

Then it was over, the hush hard to believe. Guards rounded up the prisoners and herded them into a group. Jack Mosses grinned at me, obviously pleased with himself. "I say, old boy, you must like the warmth. Can't you read German?"

"Just *trinken und pissen und scheissen.*"

"Well, you'll be happy to know it says, 'High Octane Petrol,' on those tins where you were hiding."

I watched in silence as firemen set hooks into the burning 52 and bulldozers dragged it off the runway. In minutes the flights were landing again. Only then did an ambulance draw up and asbestos-clad firemen start pulling men from the wrecked plane. Mosses observed softly, "People who fight a war like that will be hard to beat."

Chapter 9

The Concentration Camp
at Capua

Evening, 1 December 1942

The darkened Ju-52 skidded to a halt at the Naples airport on the west coast of Italy, 65 miles south of Rome. In the faint glow cast by the plane's dimmed blackout lights, I saw shiny black boots and gray uniforms. I climbed out the fuselage door to the sound of Italian and noticed with relief that the German troops were leaving. We were now entering the heartland of Mussolini's Fascist Italy, the far weaker and unenthusiastic southern partner of Hitler's Nazi Germany.

An Italian officer counted us off, selected a random group of British and Americans, and marched us out to some waiting trucks. I was crammed into one of them between Jack Mosses and the tailgate, and the rickety canvas-covered vehicle roared off through the deserted streets of Naples. I looked around at the other men, leaning against each other or slumped forward with their heads on their hands. At this time, we had been prisoners for only three days, but it seemed more like three weeks.

One Italian guard sat up in front with his back to us, smoking and talking to the driver. I estimated my chances of survival if I jumped out onto the tarmac, but the driver picked up even more speed. I said in Jack's ear, "At this point, it would be plain crazy."

He laughed. "I certainly agree, old boy, especially since I imagine your Italian isn't any better than your German."

"I'm afraid you're right," I moaned, appalled at the idea of having to learn Italian — I knew about three words of it.

"These people won't be very friendly, you know," Jack warned. "Your Liberators have been giving the city a bad time from bases in Libya."

Two hours later, the truck slowed down and passed through a gate that led through five rows of brilliantly lit barbed wire. X-frames, concertinas, and seven-strand fences crisscrossed like fishnets surrounded a group of low wooden buildings. Pairs of black-uniformed sentries patrolled between the rows under glaring floodlights. Every hundred yards or so was a tower with a machine-gun. Everything there was calculated to keep us locked in, to kill us if we tried to escape.

Jack slapped me on the knee and burst out laughing. "I say, old boy," he said, "it's just like coming to a new public school."

"Are they that bad?"

"Ra-ther!" Jack answered, chuckling.

In a muddy compound an officer marched us to an unheated wooden barracks. One bulb glowed dimly in the middle of a long room that was dark at the ends and chilled by the damp December night. Each prisoner was handed a gray army blanket. Bare iron cots with rusty wire netting stood along the walls. Jack Mosses examined the squares in the netting and said to me, "Good show, we can play checkers on your back in the morning."

I shook my head, totally unable to comprehend how Jack could think that all this was funny. But shortly I learned that this way of coping with hardship, danger, and disaster was deeply ingrained in the British character.

Len, Marty, and I picked out cots next to Jack. I rolled up in my blanket and dozed intermittently in a shivering sleep, awakening to a cold, foggy dawn.

2 December

From the moment I woke up I had been ravenously hungry, but by evening I was convinced I was starving. This camp was at Capua, 20 miles north of Naples, a city already short of food. The Italians gave us two "meals" that day, at 11:00 and 4:00, in a barracks room with rough-cut wooden tables and splintery benches. Each meal consisted of a roll half the size of a hamburger bun, and a small plate of tomato soup and rice. By nightfall my stomach was growling and giving me strange twinges. I gulped lots of water, which blunted the hunger for a while.

During the following day I learned the bugle notes for the Italian reveille, which was at 6:30 a.m. Roll call, or *appell'*, was at 7:00. We all lined up behind the senior British officer, known as the SBO. He reported, "All present and accounted for," to Lieutenant, or *Tenente*, Russo, the Italian officer in command of our compound. Russo was tough, but bright. He spoke six languages. And, whether or not he was a true Fascist, he followed the party line. I didn't think he'd take too much crap from the British or anyone else, and I wondered what the SBO would tell him if someone escaped.

4 December

At morning roll call, a British officer hid in the barracks. The men in ranks did a neat little shift so one man was counted twice. It worked, but only because the Italian soldier who was counting wasn't alert. They didn't risk it again though, knowing that if Russo had taken the count he would have noticed what was going on.

From *appell'* to the soup-and-roll lunch was four hours — a span long enough to make me bitchy and short-tempered. To counteract my irritability, I walked, talked, wrote diary notes on pieces of paper scrounged from the garbage pile. I stalked around on the dirt paths in the compound, trying to figure out how to steal some food. On the northern side of the camp I discovered a small kitchen hidden in the corner of the enclosure, used to prepare meals for some of the guards. I watched the cook working. As he prepared potatoes and onions, leaving some of the vegetable on the skin, he noticed me staring at him and roared, *"Via! Via!"*

He scowled angrily, so I walked away. But when he went into the cookhouse, I poked around in the garbage dump, picked up handfuls of the scraps and stuffed them in my pockets. This time two guards noticed me. One shouted, *No! No! No! È vietato!"* and waved his carbine. I nodded and strolled back to barracks, trying to look casual.

In front of our building, I spotted Len, who was kneeling, trying to light a fire of paper trash. His field jacket collar was buttoned up tight, and he looked half-frozen. Though he'd always had a pale complexion, his face was now alarmingly gray, and his eyes were slightly bloodshot. He looked up with a hint of a smile. "Trying to get a little warmed up." Len seldom complained and, when he did, it was in a quiet, thoughtful voice. Even on the night we were captured, he hadn't seemed to lose his cool.

When I showed him my canteen cup, into which I'd put the scraps, he peered into it and laughed. "I need a magnifying glass," he said, "but right now, I'm not looking a gift horse in the mouth." He poured a little water from his canteen over the scraps and started cooking them on his fire.

A British "leftenant" came over. "You chaps can't do that!" he fumed. "You'll cause the Allies to lose face with the Eyeties." We ignored the admonition.

The following morning, Len and I were sitting on our bunks, making ourselves even more miserable talking about food. Marty was stretched out, staring at the ceiling. He quickly sat up when a very erect British captain strolled over, his heels clacking on the wooden floor. A man about 35, whom we hadn't seen on the trucks, the officer inquired, "Didn't you men just come in with the last bunch?"

"Yes," Len answered, giving me a sideways glance.

"The food situation is a bit difficult right now, but after a week or so you'll get used to it," our new acquaintance assured us. "We're accustomed to rationing in England and know how to plan. You people eat everything at once, but we save the roll and eat it later when we get hungry."

I managed a polite, "I guess that's a good suggestion, thank you." But when he left I began to bristle.

Len cautioned, "Take it easy, Joe, that's just their 'new boy' stuff, from those precious public schools of theirs. Another limey tried that kind of thing with me in London — seemed to think we were just a bunch of illiterate colonials they'd have to tolerate for a while."

I looked around nervously. "You better not let them hear you say that —"

Marty broke in, "Don't worry about it. Just keep your distance and do whatever you have to. I admire their guts, but if you let them, they'll walk all over you." He was silent for a few moments, then burst out, "I wish the hell I knew what happened to Gordon!"

At this comment, the image of Colonel Stout's shattered command car flashed into my mind; I was afraid I knew only too well what had happened to Gordon Bilat. Lord, how those guys in the 5th would miss him. His minimum standard was "Superior," nothing less, and he'd never given me credit for any capability until one day in England. I was firing a problem with the guns way off to my right. It was called "Large T," and the angles and computations I had to do in my head were difficult indeed. Two other officers muffed the same problem, whereas I'd hit it on the nose. I'd never seen Gordon look so incredulous; this was to be the beginning — finally — of a good relationship between us.

I glanced quickly at Marty and then away, because now I sensed what was weighing on the minds of all three of us: Every officer present at Colonel Stout's dinner that night back in July had been either killed or captured in the ambush at Djedeida.

"That dinner at the Hershey Hotel —" I began in a whisper.

Len, who must have been reading my thoughts, finished the thought for me. "I know, I know," he said, shaking his head sadly. "It was a kind of Last Supper."

On 6 December, five days after we had arrived in Capua, we were visited by an elderly Italian. He wore an army cap with gold braid, yet was dressed in an unusual black surplice with military insignia and two crosses. "I am from the Vatican," he said in clear, though accented, English. "I have some telegraphic forms on which you may send a message to your families."

I hesitated, while Len just shrugged. But Marty said, "It drives me crazy not being able to get some word to Joan."

The priest smiled at us. "I see you are worried," he said, lowering his voice. "I don't like this uniform either, but I must wear it." He resumed his normal voice. "The Holy Father makes it possible for you to send this message.

Perhaps some of you have been reported missing, and at least your families will know you are alive and not wounded."

Marty said he thought the guy was on the level, so I began struggling to devise a message that would bring my family some measure of relief. As we racked our brains over what to write, the priest feigned impatience. "Hurry up," he said loudly, "I haven't all day to stay here. I must see hundreds of others." With an Italian officer watching us, I told the priest I appreciated what he was doing. The kindly old man smiled at me but only after his back was turned to the guard.

Later on, I thought about the message I'd written. If it did get through, it might be the first word Emily would receive indicating I was alive and a prisoner, since I was sure that Rex Rawie had reported me "Missing in Action." It made me shudder to think how she would feel if some dumb clerk in the War Department chose to interpret that as "Presumed Killed in Action." I thanked God for the old priest and prayed that the new information would reach her. And I remembered the last letter I'd had from her in England with the obvious tears and protestations between the lines. Why had I done it?

Joey was proving to be a troubled child. As the doctor at home had explained, when the father goes away this often happens to a boy — he feels deserted. The thought occurred to me that I wouldn't be able to recognize my own son when I got out. Then another thought intruded, and I said to myself *if* I get out. I forced my mind back to Capua and to how in hell I could steal some food from that damn kitchen.

Early the next morning, a British chaplain who had been captured at Tobruk came over and spoke to the Americans. He had managed to hang onto his prayer book, and the Italian priest had loaned him some rather ancient hymn books. The chaplain, an immensely tall young man, about six feet six, with a long sunken face and a big projecting lower jaw, was like a statue of heroic dimensions. While his eyes had a gentle look, I had the distinct feeling he would have guarded those books with his life.

"Would any of you chaps like to sing in a choir?" he asked. "We practice every day, and then sing in the services on Sunday. The Italians have given us permission to use the mess hall just after lunch."

We laughed at the word "lunch."

"I'm not looking for opera stars, but it might help a bit if one has done some singing."

Several replied, "OK." I muttered, "Maybe. At least I'd like to try." Don Waful, an American tank commander from the 1st Armored, gave me a funny look, knowing I wasn't very musical. In civilian life this curly haired, affable guy had had his own band and had sung professionally. He just shrugged his shoulders and said, "Well, Padre, I guess it won't be a cathedral choir, but — uh — let's have a go at it."

We had choir practice right after lunch that day. It was a diversion for most of us and got our minds off the constant hunger. For Don, it may have been more like a distraction, for a couple of times he sighed and rolled his eyes up toward the ceiling. We dragged the practice out as long as possible, poring over the hymn books as we tried to learn our parts. At least it made a big dent in the afternoon.

Sunday morning, 8 December, dawned dark, with a heavy overcast, and there was even less light than usual in the cold, damp mess hall with its small windows. The chaplain had arranged the benches in rows, the tables shoved to the back, and made an altar of boxes with a little wooden cross on the top. The service, which lasted an hour, reminded me of an El Greco painting: the long, grim, white faces of the shivering prisoners, the skin taut and drawn around the chins and necks of the men who had been in concentration camps since the fall of Tobruk six months earlier.

The chaplain had an excellent ear, leading the singing right on pitch, and the choir did better than we had expected. Whether a prisoner was an agnostic, a little atheistic, or anything else different from a member of the Church of England, the service was, if nothing else, a calming, meditative experience.

The weather in Capua was much colder than in North Africa; winter had arrived and we were now some 300 miles further north. We were lucky to have been issued wool uniforms for the landing at Arzew, as there had been some talk about issuing us cotton. Two days after we had sent the Vatican messages to our families, the International Red Cross gave us long OD overcoats. We thought that the Italian priest and our chaplain had had something to do with it. In any case, I wore mine every day and even slept in it. It was truly a godsend.

From dusk each evening to the following morning we were confined in barracks. One man at a time was allowed to go to the latrines, but a two-man patrol watched him every second.

Although there were times during the day when I was momentarily diverted by a joke, an interesting story, or choir practice, basic life as a prisoner soon grew into an endless struggle against gnawing hunger and against nerves that felt as if they'd been rubbed with sandpaper. There were other discomforts too: a small cut from the rusty springs on the cot wouldn't heal; my lower GI tract was in turmoil, alternating between concrete and diarrhea.

10 December

One day I overhead Don Waful saying he wished he had some sheet music. When I told him I would write some for him, his jaw dropped. Then he started to laugh. I was serious, however, and told him he would see.

"OK, Joe, OK," he said. "You just go ahead and write it out for me. And I want four-part harmony too."

"Four-part harmony?" It began as a question, but I tried to make it sound like a statement. I said, "OK, Don, four-part harmony."

I sat down with a note pad and a pencil. There were smiles around the room and a few giggles, but I paid no attention. My selection was "Old Man River." I'd heard Paul Robeson sing it many times and had seen the original "Show Boat." I'd had piano lessons from age five to age ten, at which point my busty music teacher declared to my parents that I was hopeless.

Nevertheless, I had managed to learn the scales and a few simple chords, and now I dug these up for Don, mainly from the key of C. I drew two sets of five lines with a straight edge and added the treble and bass clefs. Then I hummed the tune, and put down each note — where I thought it should go. That would always be the top note of the chord. I added the little "flag-pole" for the high notes and a "tail" for the low ones. I tapped the beat — more funny looks. Then I put in the rests, where they looked right. After that, I worked out the harmony: just plain old chords from the music teacher. Suddenly I remembered to fill in the quarter and eighth notes in the center. Remembering the words was easy. It had all taken hours, but at last the score was ready for Don.

He looked at the sheet, appearing puzzled. He scowled, smiled, said, "Oh, my God!" and "Joe, you can't —," sighed and sank down on a cot. This did little for my musical confidence. He fixed me with a gloomy stare. "Joe, I'm sorry, but it doesn't work this way. Couldn't you find something else to do?"

My musical career rather ingloriously ended, I returned to reality. I wandered around the camp for hours, staring at the wire, looking out beyond it at distant houses with red tile roofs. A carillon tower dominated the skyline of a little town, and russet hills rose on the far horizon. I said to myself, "People live there and work there. Wouldn't it be great if I could go there and chat with them over a glass of wine? Yet, even if I could, they would hate me." Right then an overwhelming sense of confinement came over me like an invisible net, pinning my arms and legs.

Gradually, from a long way off, I heard the wail of the Naples air-raid sirens, rising from east of the city, increasing in volume; then from all over the area came a strident cacophony of sound. In a moment bombs whistled and thunderous blasts shook the ground. Prisoners across in another compound began to cheer, and the men in ours took it up. Amid the tumult, guards shouted, "Silenzio! Silenzio! Andate nei quartieri! Subito! Subito!"

They dashed into our compound, rifles pointed. I started to run for our barracks, but a British voice behind me cracked, "Walk! Walk! Don't let the buggers see you run."

I walked with an eye over my shoulder — those guards were furious and acted as if they really wanted to shoot someone.

11 December

Just ten days after we'd reached Capua another visitor arrived, immaculate in long gray overcoat with brass buttons, shiny black boots, and high peaked cap. He strutted in and addressed us as a group. "I have a questionnaire that each of you will fill out. This you are required to do as a prisoner of war."

A British "leftenant" said audibly: "Damned if we are! Not under the Geneva Convention."

"*Silenzio!*" the man stormed. "Disobedience and discourtesy will be punished. No more interruptions, or your rations will be reduced."

"Bloody fascist!" someone behind me said in a stage whisper.

I shivered, feeling the seething anger among the British in the room; I had no desire whatsoever to bait this man any further.

The questionnaire asked for race and religion, in addition to name and residence. Some prisoners simply left the first two items blank, but a captain who had been an infantry company CO in the U.S. 1st Division said to me, "I'm Jewish, and I don't like these questions one bit."

Wanting to advise him correctly, I mulled over the problem, because we were alert to the special danger to Jewish prisoners of war. Finally I suggested, "Look, I can't tell you what to put down, but if I were you I wouldn't write anything that looked evasive, like atheist or agnostic. They might seem like red flags. Caucasian covers all of us, and as for religion, I wrote Episcopalian, which should prove harmless."

I never did learn what he wrote, but later on he came and sang with our little group. He had had some training in a choir and had an excellent voice. In fact, largely because of him and Don Waful, choir practice and singing at the service improved greatly.

That afternoon the SBO, a major, called us all together and addressed us: "I am the senior officer present, and under regulations and Articles of War you are all, *de facto*, under my command, regardless of branch, unit, or nationality. There will be a complete set of regulations passed along by word of mouth, and they will be obeyed by all present." We had heard rumors about this, but the way he said it irritated me. We growled and protested among ourselves, but in general we decided it was better to go along with it.

The SBO assigned various officers to specific duties. The Americans were given some vacuous chores, while all the tough and dangerous assignments went to the British. These involved membership on the Escape Committee, made up of a chairman and several officers. No prisoner was permitted to attempt an escape without first submitting his plan for approval. If approved, the plan received the help and support of everyone else.

13 December

In mid-morning I passed an Italian soldier walking across our compound. Other than his gait, which appeared rather determined for an Italian, I noticed nothing unusual. But when I looked into his face I had a start. He was an officer named Buchanan, from the British 1st Parachute Regiment. One member of the committee saw me staring at Bucky, as he was called, and peremptorily ordered me to forget what I'd seen and get back in barracks. But he couldn't stop me from thinking. I guessed Bucky had been conducting a dry run to see if any of the guards would spot him. His appearance had been almost authentic, though a bit overdone. He was short enough to pass as an Italian, and his hair and mustache had been dyed black with stolen India ink.

On an afternoon two days later, a member of the committee told us to stay in barracks and not go near any windows. I stood well back in the room and looked out. It was almost dusk. A British prisoner was sitting on some steps across the compound reading a book. Two Italians, whose duty it was to heat the soup for the prisoners, came out of the cookhouse and left the compound. The man on the steps turned a page in his book and yawned. Bucky, wearing his Italian uniform, appeared around the corner and headed down the compound toward the main gate.

I said nothing about what I saw. Bucky didn't show up again for the next two days. Then he reappeared, in British uniform this time, looking paler than usual and with a bruise on one cheek. When I said hello to him, he just nodded and walked on by.

For several days, I tried to find out what had happened. Then one day I got him alone. "Hey, Bucky," I said, "can't you give me some idea what happened? Might help if we want to try something later on."

"No doubt it would. But this type of 'gen' is classified, you know. Bloody bad show if it got in wrong hands. You understand?"

I nodded. Indeed I did. We sat on a couple of cots. Bucky waited a moment, then began:

> Getting out with that Italian uniform wasn't anything. I waited in the mess till one of our chaps gave me a signal that the coast was clear at this end. The main gate was open, so I said, *"Buona sera"* to the guard, and it was "quick march" right out to the road to the railway station.
>
> Nice walk, that. Got there at 4:20 and had a look around. The agent's window was closed so I went over to a schedule on the wall. Two old crones sitting on the bench next to it began to stare at me. One of them spoke to me but I understood not a word.
>
> Had a bit of a turn when I saw the next train wasn't due for over an hour. I had to wait somewhere, so I headed for a sign that said *"Cesso."* I was halfway in the door when the two old girls screeched something about *"Donne,"* so I guessed it was the women's loo.

I found the men's and spent a whole bloody hour in the stinking place, never peed so many times in my life. When I came out, the old dames were at the window talking to the agent. They pointed at me and ran out the door. I wasn't too happy about that.

Anyway, I went to the window and said in my best Italian that I wanted a ticket to Reggio Calabria. The sod just glared at me and said, *"Documenti!"*

I took a guess that meant ID card, so I pulled mine out and showed it to him. Since then, I've had a word with the chap who made it up, as it wasn't exactly a success. The agent took a look at it and bellowed for the *carabinieri*. With that, it seemed things weren't going too well. Even so, when the *carabinieri* lads came and grabbed my arms, I told them I was a soldier going on leave.

One of them had the nerve to tell me in jolly good English I was an escaped British prisoner and if I resisted he would shoot me.

They dragged me off to their local police station, which stank about like the *cesso*. Three blokes put me in a chair and trussed me up, and banged me around a bit in the process. I found all that rather disagreeable. Then a *tenente*, who spoke English, put a hell of a great light in my eyes. I couldn't see much else, except a little off to the sides. Suddenly, the bastard put a revolver to my head. I bloody well saw that all right. He announced we were going to play a little game. He would ask a question, and if my answer wasn't to his liking, he would pull the trigger. At that, he slid a cartridge into the chamber as he was holding it to my head.

First, he asked if I was Leftenant Buchanan. At that point it seemed silly to deny it. But when he asked me my regiment, that was another matter. I sat there and said nothing, so he pulled the trigger. Naturally, I was glad enough when it clicked, though I knew he wasn't going to shoot me on the first question.

The next questions were on subjects that are under wraps, but each time I told him some nonsense or refused to answer, he pulled the trigger. When it clicked he would say, "Ah, *Tenente*, you were lucky that time."

Bucky's face tightened. A slight wrinkle appeared on his forehead, and his voice grew a shade quieter as he continued:

This charade went on for a bloody long time. I wasn't sure whether he might shoot me or himself. Finally, I decided he had a trick. Either he pulled the trigger on an empty chamber, or the cartridge was a dummy. Still it wasn't my idea of an evening's sport.

In the aftermath of this abortive escape attempt, the Italians locked us all up and held roll call so often that further attempts to escape from Capua were now out of the question. Still, Bucky's effort had planted in my mind the idea of escaping. It also reinforced my admiration for British initiative and courage, though sometimes their disregard of the risks and possible consequences made me shudder.

I made mental notes of the mistakes in plan and execution: Bucky's Italian hadn't been nearly good enough; his knowledge of what an Italian soldier could and could not do had been nil, and the ID card had been quite inadequate. Bucky's failure notwithstanding, I was impressed by the fact that the British had organized this operation and set it in motion within a very short time after their arrival at Capua.

On the morning of 20 December two British officers, Marty Lawler, and I were selected by the SBO and marched off to the camp commissary behind *Tenente* Russo. We waited in line for half an hour and then finally were issued one small basket of oranges. The SBO complained to Russo, "Is that all? We have 40 men in that building."

"Major," Russo barked back at him, "our people in Naples are near starvation."

From there we marched through a compound holding British prisoners captured in the Libyan Desert in 1941. Some had been kept in cages in North Africa, and their scrawny necks stuck out of their collars like pipe stems. By comparison, we were robust, even fat, and the poor fellows stared at us through sunken eyes, savage with hostility.

Suddenly, two of them dove for the basket and a few oranges rolled on the ground. The SBO snapped, "Carry on!" but the other desert prisoners broke out of their group and scrambled for the oranges like wild dogs after a piece of meat. I felt sick. Would we be looking and acting like that in another year?

Len and I shared three bitter little oranges, even ate the peels. I told him about the men who had been in the cages, but he'd already heard about them from a British prisoner who had been in one. The prisoner had told Len about how a German guard had laughed at him and thrown him a dry bone between the bars, and how he had chewed on it all night and finished it by morning.

The story haunted me for the rest of the day, and when "lights out" came, I couldn't sleep. For hours, I lay on the wire cot, tossing and turning and grinding over in my mind the long sequence of events that had brought me to this crisis in my life.

In late December a few parcels began to arrive from the Red Cross in Switzerland. Then one day Russo walked in and announced angrily, "I have to inform you that the entire city of Naples is under constant air attack by *your* B-24 bombers. Surely you know that from the air-raid sirens blowing all night. As a result, many parcels have been destroyed, streets are torn up. We can't get anything through, so this delay is no fault of ours."

We all had a brief respite from the shortage when a few parcels appeared at Christmastime — the Italians even issued us a small ration of sour red wine. But the supply tightened up again right after that, and toward the end of December the parcels were so scarce that we had to divide one per week four ways. This was such a small supplement to the two miserable Italian "meals" of tomato soup and a small roll that we grew snappish with each other. Some men even took to their beds during the daytime, as we struggled through hours of hunger and frustration.

On a frigid, cloudy New Year's Day 1943, the air-raid sirens started howling at 8:00, and the guards chased us back into barracks on the double. Our building rocked with the thunder of the monster six-inch flak guns that ringed Naples. An hour later, when we were released from barracks, I paced up and down, wondering if some bombs intended for the railroad marshaling yards might be dropped over or short of their target and land squarely on the camp. Later I asked two U.S. Army Air Forces pilots about the possibility.

"Be a damn good idea," one of them cracked. "Give us a chance to get out of this fuckin' place."

Disturbed, I walked on with them, envisioning what it would be like running among falling bombs. One of the airmen glanced casually at the sky. "Don't look up," he said, hardly moving his lips. "The Ites haven't spotted them."

Forcing myself to look straight ahead, I strolled along. Then, in a moment or two, came the whistle of falling bombs, their explosions thudding on the south side of camp. Seconds afterwards, from all over the city, we heard the howl of air-raid sirens.

Guards shouted, "Inside! Inside! *Subito* or we shoot! Why are you not inside?" Running and sneaking a look at the same time, I saw white-plumed vapor trails streaming out behind the planes, which were black specks like insects silhouetted against the sky.

As we crowded into our barracks, I was panting and shaking a little. "What's got those guards in such a flap?" I asked the pilot.

"Because we saw those B-24's before the camp's air-raid warning personnel and the whole damn warning system in Naples," he answered, and he and his friend roared with laughter.

The Italians doubled the guards at all posts. When their sergeant spotted us peering out the windows he yelled, "Get away from the windows or we shoot." The pilot who had been doing all the talking shrugged. "What the hell do you expect? Those are our bombers, and those guards have families and friends in Naples."

After the "all clear" we were let out once more. It wasn't long before the sirens went off again, but this time the British flatly refused to go in. Cursing in Italian, the guards suddenly wheeled toward them and fired, but the shots went overhead. To tell the truth, I was relieved when they locked us in for the rest of the day.

4 January 1943

Russo strode into the building, saluted, and gave a characteristic heel-click.

"Ufficiali, attenzione!" he called. We shuffled over and formed a ragged line, slumping in our dirty, wrinkled clothes, smelling of stale sweat.

Faintly smiling, Russo stated, "Gentlemen, we have word that your Intelligence mistakenly identified this camp from the air photos as an ammunition dump. So for your own safety, we are moving you to another location."

We broke ranks and swarmed around him demanding to know, "Where are we going? How soon will we be leaving?"

Russo clicked his heels and left without a word.

Len and I lay on our wire cots, talking in low tones until midnight. He was concerned that the Italians might send us to Germany because they had too many people of their own to feed. Yet, on the other hand, he reasoned, they needed us as hostages, and a man on the Escape Committee had told him that British Intelligence had located several other prisoner-of-war camps in Italy.

I hoped he was right, because a winter in Germany could be torture. If they sent us to a permanent camp in Italy, we would be a damn sight better off, especially if the Allies invaded somewhere in the south. Even before that happened, however, I felt we should try to establish the best possible relations with the Italian guards. A good relationship wouldn't be easy to achieve, but at least it wouldn't have to be the cat and dog situation we had had here in Capua. The way the British baited the Italians at almost every roll call had always bothered me. "Wouldn't it make more sense if they buttered them up rather than calling them 'bloody Eyeties' all the time?" I asked Len. "Perhaps that would give the guards a false sense of security. Then if there should be a landing, we could make a break."

"You're not about to sell that idea, Joe. The British have a bug up their ass about the atrocities those black-shirt Fascists committed in Africa. Troops of a modern army, with sophisticated automatic weapons and artillery, slaughtered tens of thousands of Ethiopian tribesmen, armed with nothing but crude spears. From that point on, the British considered it beneath their dignity to be friendly with the Italians."

That annoyed the hell out of me, and I told Len so, for it completely overlooked the fact that all Italians weren't rabid Fascists like the black-shirts. Our problem at this point was to find out which Italians were friendly toward Americans and to work on them. In spite of my arguments, however, I knew Len was right as far as the British were concerned. We never would make a dent in their bitterness over the war in Ethiopia.

The next afternoon Russo paraded in with several guards. The *tenente* saluted briskly and announced, "Pack all your belongings, we leave in an hour." At 5:00 the SBO lined us up outside the building. It was 11 January, and we had been in Capua six weeks — long enough for us to have grown scrawny and bedraggled, like hoboes, with long hair and torn clothes. I stood clutching a cardboard box containing bits of food I'd saved, some string, and pieces of a gas mask cover I had managed to hang on to. All along, I had been convinced that these things would some day be of vital use to me.

"Mount up!" the SBO sang out, and each man heaved himself up into one of the familiar banged-up, canvas-covered trucks. It seemed very strange to be driving out into the growing dusk through the rows of barbed-wire fencing. Even the air was different; it bore the scent of freedom within reach. I felt I might even throw off the oppressive sense of confinement, but this elation was mingled with fear at what might happen if I should get loose out there: I recalled the American pilots' remarks that the townspeople were thoroughly bloody-minded about Americans right now. I recalled, too, their macabre tales of grounded pilots who were beaten and torn limb from limb by frenzied mobs. I peered along the dark streets and shivered.

Miserable as the camp at Capua had been, I had had there a sense of protection, of a structure in which I didn't have to make decisions. Now we were back in the war again, passing through a bombing zone full of vengeful people. Escape, the soldier's duty that could not be avoided, became again a nagging, frightening demand.

Upon our arrival we found the Caserta railway station already packed solid with gray-clad Italian troops, a few civilians, and a scattering of Germans in the black uniforms of the hated *Schutzstaffeln*. Throughout this mass of people, huddled in uncomfortable clusters, were other prisoners. When we tried to catch their eyes, our guards shunted us off in another direction.

For five hours we stood there, crowded against one another, tired, hungry, and breathing fetid air that smelled of sweat, sour wine, and garlic. Near midnight the guards took us out onto a cold, windy platform, where we gulped long drafts of fresh air. After waiting outside for nearly an hour, we were ordered to climb up into an old wooden passenger car marked *"Terza Classe."* It had no heat, its slatted seats were viciously uncomfortable, it reeked of urine.

Chapter 10

Chieti, an Old Fascist Prison

12 January 1943

At 4:00 in the afternoon we arrived at a deserted brick station, called "Chieti Scalo." I learned from a British officer who had traveled through here before the war that we were just below the "calf" of Italy and about eight miles southwest of Pescara, a major city on the Adriatic.

To the west, for about 30 miles, stretched an open plain beyond which rose rugged mountains, deep purple and gray against the afternoon sunlight. Above them all the snowcapped Gran Sasso d'Italia, the Apennines' highest peak, shone in a dazzling sunset. Off toward the southwest the massif of the Maiella, a dark, mysterious mountain, extended down the spine of Italy. The ancient city of Chieti perched in tiers upon a high hill east of the station, its thick walls, churches, and bell towers painted a sunlit gold. Waiting at the station, I breathed in the spirit of the medieval culture and history of the place. It had an enchanting beauty, yet it was alien: it belonged to that hostile, forbidden land beyond my world of confinement.

The Italian guards marched us east, across the main highway and through high, wrought-iron gates into a courtyard about as long as two football fields, where a sign read: *Campo Concentramento, Prigionieri di Guerra No. 21.* At the rear of the courtyard an eight-foot fasces emblem on a brick tower vaunted the camp's origin as a Fascist political prison. The security here looked tighter than at Capua, which had been a transient camp with an air of impermanence. Chieti boasted nine-foot brick walls topped with barbed wire; every 200 feet, sentries on machine-gun platforms scrutinized the entire prison area, while other guards with rifles patrolled the outermost perimeter within the enclave.

The big open area was flanked on either side by six rows of rectangular masonry buildings, coated with peeling stucco that revealed a reddish brick understructure. The uncompromising walls and forbidding buildings seemed to announce, "You'll be here for the duration." How long that duration might be and how it might end were awesome unknowns. What I did know definitely was that Chieti, for the immediate future, would be a tightly run, locked-in community of men, struggling to live by certain rules and civilized codes. Yet being imprisoned was still new to me, and suddenly I was again battling with the sense of confinement seizing me. I took one more look westward at the magnificent Gran Sasso reaching into the sky, but such beauty was a mockery in my present state and I turned from it in disgust.

The guards separated the Americans from the British, and then put ten of us in the back room of a building on the south side. With no heating and a tile floor, this big oblong space was pervaded with an icy dampness. Lined up against the walls were crudely made double-decker bunks. For mattresses, straw-filled burlap bags were laid across loose, wooden slats.

An elderly Italian sergeant showed us a washroom in the rear with walls of old cracked tile. Two long troughs, each with a single faucet, stretched down the room. The sergeant turned the tap. Nothing came out. "Water in morning," he said. "*Lavare* — to wash, not to drink." He frowned, waving his finger sideways and saying, "Tsk! Tsk! Tsk!"

Out in the hall, he pointed to a door and said, "*Cesso.*" I peeked in and was buffeted by the stink of feces. It was strictly a stand-up, hole-in-the-ground latrine with no plumbing. Still I thought, at least it's in the same building — no dreary walk through snow at night.

Len Warren and I grabbed a double-decker. Marty Lawler claimed one across the room. Also housed here were several men from the crew of a B-24 bomber that had been shot down off the Italian coast near Salerno. The navigator was David Westheimer, who occupied the bunk next to us with an Associated Press correspondent, Larry Allen.

Larry spoke a fast, ungrammatical version of Italian, which he was showing off to us when we heard voices down the hall. Someone coming into the building was being greeted in all kinds of British and Scottish accents, friendly, humorous, and cordial, but all with a note of deference.

"Where's the new bunch of Yanks that just came in?" I heard from the next room. The voice was American and sounded familiar.

"Next room, Alan, about ten of them," someone answered.

A man about 40 came in, followed by three Britishers. He was slightly bald, with a turned-up nose, a clean-shaven upper lip, and a thick beard sprinkled with gray. His bright red cheeks and laughing eyes gave an impression of a slim but very merry Santa Claus.

"Hey, Alan," Westheimer said, "there's another guy here from New Jersey you might know, but I can't pronounce his name."

I jumped up and went over to him. "Alan? Alan Stuyvesant, is that really you?" I exclaimed in astonishment. "It's Joe Frelinghuysen."

He inhaled sharply, "My God, Joe, what the *hell* are you doing here? I didn't recognize you with that mustache!" He spoke with an educated American accent, but with overtones of someone who had also spent considerable time in Europe.

"Your beard threw me too," I said, laughing at the way it bobbed when he talked — he'd always been clean-shaven during the 15 years that I had known him. My delight at seeing him was tempered by the disconcerting thought that I would soon have to tell him the absurd way I'd been captured.

I'd met Alan when I was in college, and he was living in a lovely place in western New Jersey called Tranquillity. The meandering old family house nestled between two mountains in a hidden valley like the one in *Lorna Doone*. I'd spent many pleasant weekends in that valley with members of his family.

Alan had an old stone hunting lodge up on the mountain, where deer, fox, and wildcat roamed the miles of woodland. For Alan, a shoot was as much a reason for seeing a friend as it was for sport. He had many friends throughout the U.S. and in Europe as well, where his fluency in French and his lighthearted graciousness made him especially popular. I remembered a lunch he had given at the lodge for a group of his friends after a shoot. We had feasted on hasenpfeffer, roast duck, and wild rice, along with a vintage Bordeaux.

Now Alan and I sat on an empty bunk. "How did you get here?" I asked.

"Oh, hell, it's a long story. Just briefly, I was driving an ambulance in the American Field Service with the Free French and was captured at Bir Hacheim. Because I was unarmed, I'm eligible to be exchanged for a German prisoner. Now let me tell you something about the camp before they sound a roll call." He paused, glancing across at the other Americans. "Do you know about Escape Committees?"

"Sure, they had one at Capua."

Alan said the prisoner organization at Capua was nothing compared to that at Chieti. The SBO here was a very senior British colonel with full staff and unit commanders — an entire military hierarchy. There were about 1,500 British now, but only 100 Americans. The senior American officer was Lt. Col. Max Gooler, an old regular, who had been caught while he was liaison to the British Eighth Army. He was trying to run the U.S. "show," as Alan put it, but the Americans were an unruly bunch.

"Where do you come in, having been with the French?" I asked.

"I'm under the British as a noncombatant. They're doing one hell of a job here, but with a little too much spit and polish for our compatriots."

Alan chatted with the other Americans, who crowded around asking questions. He'd been a natural with the Free French because of his command of their language and because he knew some Italian.

After an hour or so, he got up, wished me luck, and said he had to get back before roll call to the British sector where he was quartered. When he left, the Americans told me he was liked and respected throughout the camp.

But I quickly learned that the SBO wasn't liked or respected, at least with the Americans. Apparently he was very reserved and was rarely seen except at roll call. They said he had been a prisoner for three years and that some of the people felt he was "a touch around the bend."

We had arrived too late for the afternoon "meal," so we had to sweat out the evening without anything to eat. By curfew, I was so tired that I rolled up on the burlap sack and slept until morning.

The British prisoners lined up at the morning roll call formation like the Coldstream Guards and clicked the steel inserts in their heels in unison when called to attention. Such a trick was impossible in American boots with rubber heels. We just slouched around in unkempt clothes, our hair unruly. We had no hats. This unmilitary appearance brought a tirade from the SBO right at the formation. He fit my idea of the typical British professional officer: tall, straight as a steel rod, the weathered face of an aging army colonel — perfect for the regimental CO in a film about India.

Colonel Gooler promptly called the Americans together for their own formation. He was a slim man in his mid-forties, with close-cropped gray hair and thick, steel-rimmed glasses, his face tanned a deep brown from his months in the desert. He gave it to us unadorned: From here on we were to stand at attention properly at all formations, to dress neatly, and to keep our room from looking as if it had just hosted a riot. After we were dismissed, I backed him up because I'd been embarrassed by our appearance. For my pains, I was called a bootlicker and asked, "You bucking for a promotion or something?" I got this from a couple of younger men. It left me angry and defensive — they could go to hell.

15-31 January 1943

The routine in Chieti was similar in some ways to that in Capua. Roll calls were the same, as were reveille and curfew. We had the same miserable ration of a plate of soup and a roll at about the same time of day. In contrast to Capua, though, the mess at Chieti was run by British OR's ("other ranks," *i.e.,* enlisted men) under a British mess officer. Although some OR's had been POW's a long time, those who brought in the food were round-faced and husky, looking far from starved. The Americans said nothing. Even if they did make out better than we, it was not a big deal in the camp as a whole.

During this period I began to study Italian. Each day I would sit bundled up in a blanket on my lower-deck bunk poring over a grammar I got from an officer of the guard. But the straw-filled burlap sack on the slats was miserably uncomfortable. I couldn't lie on it to read or study, so I would hunch over with my feet on the cold tile floor. First my feet got chilled, then I would grow cold all through my body. Eventually, I would have to get up and walk around to get warm.

Despite the cold, I forced myself to study that grammar; Bucky's misfortune from not knowing Italian still tormented me. Fluency in the language could be the key to a successful escape. I was determined to learn it.

With a lot of help from Frank Gallo, an American medical officer who had been captured in North Africa, I memorized 30 words a day. With a broad face and dark hair and eyes, "Doc" looked Italian and had spoken the language since childhood. Nearly six feet tall, he was a squarely built, husky man, who had lived in Winsted, Connecticut, with his wife and children before entering the U.S. Army Medical Corps. In his deep, rough voice, he spoke several Italian dialects, as well as pure, Florentine Italian. He was a painstaking teacher, and frequently he would listen to Larry Allen spouting his version, wink at me and laugh.

Soon Doc and I were conversing steadily. This brought protest from our roommates. I found it easy to understand him, with his precise diction, but the Radio Roma news programs that came over the camp PA system were very difficult. Though my ability to imitate the pronunciation was good enough for me to speak with a fair accent, it didn't help me understand the machine-gun delivery of a professional newscaster. Each time I listened, I ended up cursing, shaking my head, and more discouraged. In time, I managed to scribble down key words and ask Larry about them. A word like *sgomberare* meant literally to "clear away." One report made it sound as if the Axis troops had cleared away from the Allies, when, in fact, it meant that the Axis had cleared out and evacuated an occupied town.

To combat the cold, I started doing some exercises. But it was a lonely business, so I looked for someone to do them with and came across an American B-26 pilot named Conrad Kreps. A friendly guy in his early twenties, Connie was blond and curly-haired. I discovered that he had been a capable gymnast and weight-lifter before the war. I wasn't remotely in his class, but I knew enough about gymnastics and weight training to talk his language.

In spite of the months of meager diet, Connie had a back and shoulders knotted with muscles, a taut, ridged abdomen, narrow waist, and powerful legs. Along with this imposing array, he had a thoughtful, mild-mannered way about him and an unflappable disposition. He had been shot down flying his B-26 Martin medium bomber over the Libyan desert. After crash-landing safely, he had walked for hours under a broiling sun on just one canteenful of water, only to be picked up by a German patrol. I liked him immediately and felt sure we could work together.

One Sunday morning Connie and I went out into the courtyard next to our building, known as the "American bungalow," where he showed me his favorite exercises. He could do push-ups standing on his hands, handsprings, front and back flips, and a flying front-roll, which he did on a couple of burlap sacks filled with straw.

We worked out a routine together: sound, basic calisthenics, at my speed, however, not his. He agreed with me that such a program was necessary to help preserve our sanity, while keeping us fit enough to escape, should we ever get the chance.

On one occasion when we were exercising together, two British parachutists came over and asked if they could join our "PT," or physical training. Next day a few more showed up. Once or twice we had a problem with a man who wanted to tell us what exercises to do. If the suggestions were appropriate, we included them in the routine, which seemed to head off any problems.

The classes grew, and Connie took one group, while I took another. Soon we had three classes a day, mostly for our British clientele. Connie was an iron man, but sometimes I got very tired. Nevertheless, a workout warmed me up, and I felt great for several hours. Gradually I got into good shape and was better able to handle cold, discomfort, poor diet, and that oppressing sense of confinement.

That invisible barrier was inescapable, constantly there between me and the outside world. Sometimes, halfway between sleep and waking, I would get a strange sensation of being down in a smooth steel cylinder, and I would fight to claw my way up the sides until I wanted to scream. One man who had experienced something like this, though far more intensely, wound up slashing his wrists. They got to him in time, but he stayed over in the MO's (medical officer) area for four weeks.

An American named Tom Holt, who had enlisted in the British commandos, had been captured at Dunkirk. One bitter-cold day, I saw him walking round and round in little circles in a courtyard right under the Fascist emblem on the water tower. His thick British "greatcoat" was wrapped tightly around him, and his face was half-hidden behind its upturned collar. I liked Tom, and we had grown very friendly, so I eased over toward him to see if I could help. When he saw me approaching, he shook his head, while he continued walking in those little circles. Some days afterwards, I asked him what the trouble had been. His face twisted as if he were in physical pain, and he said, "Joe, I guess I was just having trouble being a prisoner of war."

February 1943

All the exercising in the courtyard next to our bungalow didn't increase my popularity with the other Americans. Nor did it help when Colonel Gooler got involved in our PT program, and then told them they should get in shape by joining too.

Since he hadn't put it in the form of a direct order, most of the men paid little or no attention to it. During classes some of them hung out the windows letting out hoots and catcalls: we were crazy, we were sucking up to the British, we would collapse from lack of food. We disappointed them on all counts.

As winter wore on, our diet worsened. Deep snows in the Alps delayed and sometimes blocked the supply trains. The Germans certainly did not give precedence to food for prisoners over their own troops, so our supply of Red Cross parcels dwindled. But the prison ration remained the same: a small roll and a plate of soup twice a day. Each man got only a fraction of a Red Cross parcel per week, and, like the others, I lost weight steadily. On some mornings it was hard to get out in the courtyard for the first PT class. Knowing that every single one of those British would be present, however, forced me to get out there. Connie, on the other hand, was always ready, though now paler and thinner around the face. He never even hinted that he might not make it.

The PT, plus striding around the camp and doing gymnastics with Connie, helped me counter the loss of initiative. We did hand-springs, backshoots, nip-ups, hand-to-hand balances. Occasionally, I even got off a front flip when Connie was doing them. But the gnawing hunger was always there.

In time, I became very touchy, imagining slights that didn't exist. One day I blew off at Len Warren, really upsetting him — and me too. During the worst of the hunger, I noticed that some people became paranoid about their "territory." If another POW came too close or left an article in what they conceived to be their domain, they would shout at the trespasser in angry, quivering voices. A disagreement that normally could be resolved with friendly debate and goodnatured kidding would get so heated that participants almost came to blows. I felt these same emotions myself. A few men actually thought a fistfight was a good idea, that it would clear the air. I didn't agree, because the guy who lost would be looking for revenge, turning matters into a vendetta. And if anyone were seriously injured and the Italians got onto it, the Fascist officers would court-martial both men. Neither would stand a chance.

This loss of control reminded me of the men with pipe-stem necks running after the oranges like wild dogs — I was damned if I would let it happen to me.

By now it was obvious that the sense of confinement and hunger were causing the loss of initiative and the irritability. Though I had proved that vigorous exercise helped with both problems, it still wasn't enough. Each day I felt myself steadily losing the battle to maintain some measure of control.

In my youth, my father had often talked to me about "stick-to-itiveness." He had been with the U.S. Cavalry in Cuba in '99, and his favorite example was from Elbert Hubbard's best-selling essay, *A Message to Garcia*. From early childhood, I'd heard how Lt. Andrew Summers Rowan had once been given a message for General Garcia, the Cuban insurgent who was helping the Americans chase the Spanish out of Cuba, and how — despite mountains, jungles, desperadoes, snakes, and alligators — Rowan had prevailed against insurmountable odds and delivered his message. The obvious moral was: No matter what odds you face, you must carry out the assigned task, you must fulfill your duty, you must carry *your* message to Garcia.

One scorching day in early June of 1927, my family was moving to a new house. I was 15, and had the job of loading library books in the 1924 Buick roadster. Loading half of the front seat was easy; but in stacking books in the rumble seat, I skinned my ankles and knees. When I couldn't squeeze in a single other volume, my older sister took off in a cloud of dust on an old dirt road, while I sat down to rest, just as my mother drove up with our old Lafayette touring car. The huge tonneau would hold a dozen shelves of books. I glanced at the porch thermomenter — it read 98° — and I told my mother I had to get a drink of water. I'd been gone 15 minutes when she came fuming into the kitchen where I was finishing my fifth glass.

She laced into me: "Are you coming to load the car, or aren't you? Do you want me to call your father at the office?"

I stalled: "Why does my sister get to drive all the time while I have to work?"

"Anyone knows that ladies don't do this kind of work, the men do it. Besides, your sister's old enough to have a license," Mother reminded me.

I rebelled, got red in the face, flatly refused — for a while, that is, until Mother reached for the phone and gave the operator Dad's office number. Quickly relenting, I shouted, "I'll do it!" She hung up.

That night I caught it for 30 minutes: "Lieutenant Rowan never refused, never lay down on the job, and it was a damn sight hotter in Cuba than in New Jersey."

The British seemed to know instinctively that in circumstances such as ours, activity was a critical necessity. Very few of them yielded to the inclination to lie on the burlap sack and stare at a spot on the wall, whereas many of the Americans fell into a minimum routine: get up two minutes before roll call; after it, back on the sack till time for soup; avoid PT as if it would poison them; avoid all classes set up by the British.

I swore I wouldn't get sucked into such a rut. The exercise did help, and, if it came to it, I would starve on my feet, not lying on the sack. Most important of all, if we ever had a chance to escape, I knew it would take every ounce of willpower I could muster to make myself do it. I didn't think those guys would be able to. And if they did get out, they would never make it over the 9,000-foot Apennines off to the southwest.

March-April 1943

The British sector of the camp instituted a schedule of daily classes so well organized that we called it "Chieti College." Courses were given in music, drama, history of art, creative art, French. There were also contract bridge lessons, some of which I taught. The officer of the guard who had provided me with the grammar, offered lessons in Italian. I went to his classes so regularly that one wry Englishman said, "Why, you may even get a doctorate." By now studying was almost effortless for me, since I always kept Bucky in mind and never tired of learning Italian. Later on, I gave instruction in the language myself.

At the "college," one British major offered a course entitled "The Military History of the World," which he conducted entirely from memory. He began with the Battle of Cannae in 216 BC and took his students across the centuries to and through the battle in Libya during which he'd been captured. I took that course, too, and learned more tactical maneuvers — including those in the American Civil War — than had ever been touched on in Military Science at Princeton.

Alan Stuyvesant gave me lessons in French. On a nice day we would go out into the courtyard and sit on a blanket in a quiet corner, propped against the stucco wall of the bungalow. Alan always wore a cherubic smile and, with his piquant sense of humor, his eyes twinkled as he explained to me certain expressions: it was *"une brodelle,"* as contrasted to the Italian *"bordello."* The lady in charge was known as *"Madame"* with exaggerated *politesse* — never forgetting that *un tout petit cadeau*, a gift of perfume or even francs, slipped in her hand with charming compliments would assure you of the youngest and prettiest girls.

Each lesson was an amusing *pièce* in itself, especially the one based on the true story of a good friend of ours who had once been chased out of *une brodelle* in Paris *sans* his clothes. It seems our friend had been found hiding in a doorway and been taken on his personal credit to his exclusive men's club by a compassionate taxidriver. The *concierge*, not expecting anyone at 6:00 a.m., looked over his *pince nez* at the stark naked man and remarked as if everything were perfectly normal, "Ah, good morning Monsieur le Marquis, lovely day, isn't it? Now, here is my coat. After I show you to a room, I shall take care of the taxidriver, then arrange for breakfast, clothing, and toilet articles." The tale, of course, was much more colorful and amusing when my teacher related it in his Parisian French.

Alan had obtained a few French novels from the Red Cross, and some others had reached him from home in the course of the year and a half he had been in Chieti. As the weeks passed, the food ration decreased and I grew more fractious by the day. But my French language appetite was refreshed, and I was diverted by spicy De Maupassant novels, the most entertaining of which was *Les Soeurs Rondoli*. It was a Frenchman's account of how a loving but realistic Italian mother establishes her three daughters as mistresses of wealthy Frenchmen. Flaubert's *Madame Bovary* was fascinating, but her blood-vomiting death was far from cheerful. I alternated these with books in Italian. One of the latter was a translation of Howard Spring's *My Son! My Son!* into *Figlio, Figlio Mio!* The scene where the father sees his son executed left me devastated. The other Italian novels I came by were almost all Fascist and universally deadly.

Alan had dozens of English friends in the camp. He introduced me to many of them and arranged for me to go to some of their "bring-your-own" dinners, which had all the pomp and style of a London men's club, even if we ate our own carefully hoarded food and drank the vinegary wine of the lees that the Italians gave us. This *vino* was a muddy, maroon substance from the bottom of the vat, which was usually thrown out. Still, it did have some alcohol, and you could get drunk on it.

At these dinners they discussed art, literature, drama, and music. All of this was a bit beyond me, and I felt somewhat uneasy. Alan relished the human-ities, however, since he had always had a flair for them, particularly French literature. Although the topic was usually forbidden, one evening the conver-sation swung to the war. One Englishman began to criticize the Americans, with some bitterness, for sending so much help to the Russians and to the war in the South Pacific. He felt they should have sent more help to the British sooner in Egypt and Libya. Alan looked at me sharply, but I failed to catch his warning not to get drawn into the discussion.

Although these men had been in battle for four years and were near-professionals, I tried to explain, rather nervously, our disastrous position after Pearl Harbor, the need to keep Russia fighting in the east. Our British companions skillfully countered every point I made, and I felt my control slipping. Alan noticed and looked sharply at me again. This time I got the message and shut up. The group began talking on camp subjects, but the warm, friendly mood had been shattered.

Even so, Alan got me out gracefully, soothing their ruffled feelings — and mine — without weakening my position. We headed back to our room in the dark, long after curfew, peering down the long walkways and around the corner of each building, looking for patrols.

Alan laughed, swaying slightly. "Oh, relax, Joe. These guards won't shoot you. Just give them some of your beautiful Italian." (The adjective sounded like "booful.")

"You're crazy," I said, then added quickly, "I'm sorry, Alan, I really did enjoy the evening in spite of messing it up a bit. Those are great fellows."

We came to a guard post on the wall. Alan nudged me. I said quietly, *"Buona sera."*

The guard merely grunted, *"Via, via, é troppo tardi. Entrate immediatamente!"*

"Si, si signore, subito."

"You see," Alan whispered, "nothing to it."

Around the corner of the building, we walked head on into a patrol. This time I nudged Alan.

In halting, though comprehensible Italian, he said, "Good evening, good evening. I know we are out late. However, we have permission from our commandant, who wanted to see us. Now we wish you goodnight." They said nothing, just stood there, watching us until we were out of sight.

When the door of our bungalow had closed silently behind us, I sighed, "Alan, we were damn lucky. Six months ago we would have been shot."

"Of course, *mon cher Joseph.* And what a useful piece of knowledge you have now for your next escape attempt."

What a way to find out, I thought. Yet Alan was right. It was an invaluable piece of "intelligence" — in itself and in the more friendly trend it implied.

A few of the men who didn't go in for classes or exercise programs cordially hated our guts and caused a lot of friction. Once, the mounting tension from this got me into a nasty dispute with an American fighter pilot.

He had been shot down flying cover for B-24 bombers in the Middle East and had been a prisoner for more than a year. He was somewhat of a mystery man to the rest of us, who never even learned where he came from. At 35 he was a lot older than the other pilots; he had thick curly hair and a drooping mustache. His drawl sounded as if he had lived all over the West and Southwest, and his shifty eyes reminded me of pictures I had seen of Mississippi riverboat gamblers. Or he could have been a hired gun in a Western. No one seemed to know much about him, except that his surname was Brooks, and that he was called "Stony." Occasionally, he refused to get up for roll call, then covered it up somehow. Since he was always morose and surly, I tried to avoid him.

One night he tried to pick a fight with me over some of the muddy red wine the Italians gave us. By swapping Red Cross cigarettes, I had stored up a gallon or so of it in a wooden box I kept by the open window next to my bunk. It was already dark, and I was sitting on my bunk, when I heard some scuffling outside on the walkway. I looked around quickly. Stony's face was framed in the window, and below it was a hand clutching a pint canteen cup dripping red wine. His bloodshot eyes fixed me with a stare that sent a shiver down my spine.

I knew I was in for trouble. Stony, a cantankerous man on a starvation diet, had probably drunk a quart of the stuff. Now the son of a bitch was spoiling for a fight. I cursed myself. The open box had been an invitation. I wished to hell I had never messed with the damn wine.

Twenty minutes later, I heard the scuffling again. The bright red face and half-closed eyes peered in. He looked as if he wanted to kill me. I said, "Come on, Stony, knock it off. You've had too damn much already."

"You fuckin' cheap-skate son of a bitch. Who the shit do you think you are? You think you're too good for me, don't you?"

"Oh, for God's sake, Stony," I said. "Shut up and go to bed."

He mimicked my words exactly, adding, "You and your goddam PT, you think you're so fuckin' great. Why don't you get off your ass and show how tough you are? Because you know I can lick the shit out of you —"

"Screw off, Stony, you're drunk."

Stony crawled in through the window and sqatted on the tiles next to the container of wine. He filled his cup again and swallowed most of it in one gulp. A red trickle seeped out of the corner of his mouth and ran down his chin. He took a deep breath and spewed out such a string of curses that it brought exclamations from around the room. Several men jumped to their feet, watching tensely.

An Air Forces major, in Chieti only a month, sidled over to me. "How can you control yourself?" he said quietly. "I couldn't." I looked at him: five-nine, scrawny white arms, a face almost like a girl's. I could have laughed.

A guy called across the room, "For Christ's sake, Joe, you gonna take that? Guess he's right after all." The men stood by their bunks waiting for me to react. Stony took more wine and lunged towards me. I measured the distance and figured. My old army boots had worn out. Now I wore British ones; their steel plates would slip like glass on the red tiles. I had no wish to land on that tile and really didn't want Stony to either. A hard fall here could kill a guy. A hard right to the gut would do the trick without the mess.

Stony stood facing me, pouring out invective. His speech was slurred, but he was still clever and kept challenging me to make the first move. Still I resisted, making excuses. (Something like this happened when I was in college, and I got into a bloody brawl. That time, I took the blame anyway, and learned that any guy who gets into a street fight or a drunken donnybrook always comes out a loser.)

I perched on the edge of the bunk, ready for him if he came at me. But I would not risk getting seriously injured, or a one-sided Italian court-martial. I could miss a chance to escape. Stony lost his balance and reeled into the post of a double-decker, mumbling. I didn't know if he was talking to me or the post.

I said, "Stony, if you feel the same way in the morning, you can fight me then, but I'm damned if I'll fight a guy as drunk as you are." Surprisingly, he turned and went back to his bunk.

As a result of all this turmoil, I couldn't sleep much that night, so I got up early and just stood around waiting. Stony lay on his burlap sack with his face to the wall and never moved. Later he staggered out for roll call and again went back to his bunk. We did not speak again.

The pilot's problem was gone as soon as his hangover, but I ground my teeth over it for weeks afterwards, mostly wishing I had taken a chance and slugged the guy.

Before this stupid confrontation, I had felt I was coping fairly well with camp existence. Now, in an effort to distract myself from a tormenting memory, I began to collect things: every scrap of paper, piece of string, any kind of woven material. The Italian officer had taken my gas mask when I was searched at Capua, but I had talked him into letting me keep the case. It was made of tough, gray canvas with a thick inner lining of cotton. I unraveled the canvas carefully, then the cotton, and wound the thread on paper spools. In this I had an ulterior motive, almost an obsession. I had known all along we would never get out of Chieti without some dangerous and frightening action, like getting trapped in the midst of a battle between Allies and retreating Germans, or caught in a hail of gunfire from jittery and capricious guards; or we might have to make a run for it in a bombing raid. Whatever it was, it would not be easy, and we would need every conceivable material thing that might prove handy in an emergency or an escape attempt.

At the Italian lessons the officer of the guard had given me some lined notepaper. By sewing up the center of the stacked sheets, I made a crude paperback book with 140 pages. Each day I would set aside time to write down my experiences with the 5th Field from August 1941 to November 1942, the date I'd been captured. When I'd finished the account a couple of weeks later, it totaled 138 pages. A large part of what I'd written was classified material, so I kept the little book with me all during the day and even slept with it under my pillow at night. Like a magic symbol, it tied me to the past.

My next project was to put a proper collar on a British shirt I had gotten through the Red Cross. I cut a piece of the shirt-tail and by folding it over, stitched it into a double collar. Then I sewed on two bars for the U.S. captain's insignia with the cotton thread. In my more honest moments, I knew I was looking for a way to bolster my confidence, but I kept telling myself that all this was for another reason. The remaining pieces of my U.S. Army uniform were worn ragged. If I ever did get out, I would have to rely on civilian clothes. This troubled me, for I had heard that there was an unwritten rule that if you were recaptured and still had on any piece of military clothing, you might get away with claiming you were in uniform, a slim reason not to be shot as a spy.

I kept up the PT classes with Connie and tried to work even harder. Most of the participants were British, and I often chatted with them after the workouts. The conversations were, for me at least, refreshing. Our Allies had a keen awareness that to survive you had to have more than the gall to scrounge extra food. You needed the will and the ability to establish a separate identity. From Bucky's story, I had learned how much guts and determination it would take to attempt an escape, and I knew I'd never have either if I let myself become another sheep in a flock of indistinguishable prisoners.

In the British sector across the camp, the Escape Committee ran its show. The tunnel-builders had their crews. Some of the prisoners concentrated on keeping themselves good soldiers, like the 1st Parachute Regiment men. One of these was James Cleminson, a tough and resourceful young lieutenant who never lost sight of his objective to return as fast as possible to the British Army.

James and some other 1st Parachute men came to two and occasionally three PT classes a day. At other times, they marched, heels clicking in unison, on the paved walkways, wearing the crimson balmoral at a jaunty angle. The balmoral was a little like a trim tam o'shanter, but had the silver regimental emblem on the upper side. They swung their arms in perfect cadence, put their chests out, wore tough but cheerful expressions. In the left breast pocket of his jacket each man displayed prominently a stylish handkerchief, with colors that complimented the OD uniform, the crimson balmoral, the gold buttons, and the black boots. The handkerchief, however, was in fact a map of Italy on rubberized silk, which could be stretched to get a fairly consistent, large scale. Some of the men had come through interrogation with it sticking out of their pockets and saw no reason to stop doing so.

Differences in attitude stood out between men like the parachutists, who struggled to maintain identity, and those who retreated from reality. The longer I was a prisoner the more I realized that, in addition to everything else, natural courage and initiative tended to deteriorate.

In early April the Italians began giving us something they called "meat," because it seemed to have come from either a bovine or an equine creature. It was the color of dark oak and rubbery in texture, with a sour smell and sweetish taste. The principal part of it was strips of tendonous tissue, and after several minutes of chewing this "meat," my jaw would ache. Finally, I'd succeed in swallowing a piece, washing it down with some water from my canteen. Others, however, would spit it out on their plate. One day a man gagged on the stuff and ran for the door. But I always forced myself to eat as much as I could, and it would sit in my stomach, a solid, immutable lump. It stopped the hunger for a while, but I felt like throwing up and subsequently wondered if I had come out even. After a number of tries, the Italians, with the consent of the British staff, ceased to offer it to us. Rumor had it that the rest of the supply on hand went to the glue factory. For sometimes afterwards, the debate continued: had it been gristle and tendons from the shank of a horse, a mule, or a draft ox that had dropped dead in the traces?

As the icy winter crawled toward spring, outbreaks of dysentery ran rampant through the camp. One attack put me on the burlap sack for six weeks. It was a miserable, bone-chilling business, going into the stinking pit-in-the-floor latrines, where I didn't know which end to let go first. When I was through, I would have just enough strength to get back to my bunk. To shorten the distance, Marty Lawler, who was right next to the latrine door, mercifully swapped bunks with me. Throughout the ordeal, I lay on the sack, in every piece of clothing I owned, including the Red Cross overcoat from Capua. I was cold for so long that I felt as if my body had frozen. For a couple of days, I began to wonder if I was going to make it. It scared me in one sense; yet, in another, I was almost past caring what happened. If I died, at least I wouldn't have to face those bouts of cramps in that filthy latrine any more.

One day Colonel Gooler sent word that I was to go across to the British sector to see one of their medical officers. The 200 yards was a difficult trip, because I was anything but steady on my feet. The sky was overcast, the air icy, and I was shaking when I got to the MO's building. At the door I drew myself up and strode into his cubicle office, determined not to let him see my distress. That simply wouldn't do before a British officer.

If he noticed anything, he didn't let on and, to my surprise, was very friendly. He had known the problem and treated it for years. He prescribed a white rice diet, with nothing else except boiled water for five days. The mess personnel arranged this by pulling the rice out of the Red Cross parcels and saving it. At first I thought I was going to starve, but after two days, I began to feel much better and was no longer hungry. After the five days I was well enough to go back to the usual routine. On my last visit, the MO weighed me on some ancient balance scales. I was 66 kilos, about 146 pounds, down from 215 since I was captured. I was immensely grateful to the doctor for his treatment and recommended him to everyone who had the same complaint.

While recovering, I tried to read. Whenever I found the energy, I talked with prisoners who related stories of how they were captured. One of these was a young man named Claude Weaver, who had left his native Oklahoma early in the war to enlist in the Royal Canadian Air Force. They needed men so badly then, they weren't fussy about their age.

Claude was a mere 17 when he joined up, but he must have had abnormally sharp eyesight and the reflexes of a lynx, because he quickly got his pilot's wings. About a year later he transferred to the RAF. After some training in Britain, he flew a Spitfire into Malta from a carrier in one of the convoys. By the time I met him in Chieti he had been credited with six kills and wore the Distinguished Flying Medal on his blue RAF uniform.

The defense of Malta was a vital element in the battle to gain control of the

Claude Weaver at Chieti, at about age 19, wearing RAF uniform with wings and the Distinguished Flying Medal. (Drawn by Gordon Horner at Chieti and later taken to England via Germany. From *For You the War is Over,* by Gordon Horner [London: Falcon Press, 1948]. Reprinted with the kind permission of the author.)

Mediterranean, since the loss of the island to the Axis powers would have been disastrous to the Tunisian campaign and would have delayed the invasion of Sicily indefinitely. In the logical sequence of events, the invasion of mainland

Italy and the ultimate arrival of Allied troops in the Chieti region also depended on the successful defense of Malta.

Claude Weaver told how, two or three times daily, waves of Stukas and Junkers 88's dove down out of the sky to blast and strafe the Malta defenders in their shelters. Adding to this, flights of Me-109 fighters skimmed low across the water, jumped the island's cliffs and screamed across its three airdromes to destroy any aircraft still on the ground.

Every Allied plane, every bullet that reached Malta came on the shattered convoys. And every pilot had to count, because each day these men had to soar up in their Spitfires to battle overwhelming numbers of Me-109's in order to get at the attacking German bombers.

One morning Claude awoke nauseated and dizzy, and reported to his unit medical officer. The MO took one look at his yellow eyeballs and grounded him. Jaundice was too contagious to take a chance. Weaver protested — other men in his section could be lost if he didn't show. But the MO was adamant. After a spirited argument, Claude finally agreed to go to the hospital. When he left the MO's office, however, he sneaked off to his flight briefing. The bond among these men who faced death daily in the skies above Malta was too strong to be denied.

That morning Claude's section got an emergency takeoff order, or "scramble," to intercept enemy planes: Stukas and Junkers 88's were heading from Palermo to Malta. Secondary targets were Junkers 52's, bringing troops from Sicily for the defense of Tunisia (but not 52's going back to Sicily, as the British knew well that returning flights carried prisoners of war).

The section roared down the airstrip, climbed to 8,000 feet on radio silence, where they went into heavy cloud cover. Claude kept his eyes glued to the instrument panel, his head throbbing with a vicious headache that made him feel like vomiting. Flashing out of the clouds, he banked the Spitfire, but couldn't see his section or any of the rest of his squadron. Then he spotted Ju-88's headed for Malta. An Me-109 fighter swept by with its machine-guns blazing.

The Spitfire's right wing dipped and oil streaked back from its engine cowling. Claude's windscreen was suddenly oily black, the roar of the big Rolls Royce engine dropped, oil pressure went to zero. The only sound was the shriek of the wind, as he put the plane into a dive. It lost altitude fast, and in seconds, Claude was leveling it out to bring it in just above stall speed, as a turbulent blue sea with foaming whitecaps sprang upward.

Heading into the wind with the flaps down, he pushed his canopy back and flattened the plane out over waves that looked ten feet high. It hit the first one with a shuddering crash, bounced off, then plowed into solid green water that surged over the cockpit. Then, as Claude felt the fuselage ripping apart and with a tearing noise in his ears, his world went black. He came to, clawing and spitting out water. As he rose high on a wave, he saw through the spray the black bridge and conning tower of a German submarine. He made a desperate effort to swim away before two husky German submariners hauled him aboard a rubber dinghy.

Chapter 11

Harbingers of an Armistice

Larry Allen was about 36 when I met him. He had been an AP correspondent in the U.S., Europe, Asia, and Central and South America, and now called himself the "Chieti AP representative." He was bright, quick, a fast talker; and somehow after a year and a half on a prison diet he still had a pudgy, unathletic figure and a slight double chin. His last official assignment had been with the Royal Navy, where he'd been on three ships that had gone down. In the last sinking, the Germans had fished him out of the ocean and sent him to Chieti. King George VI awarded him the Order of the British Empire, *in absentia,* for his outstanding news coverage of the war at sea.

Generally, the British liked him and were amused by his "AP bulletins" with their tart humor and sarcasm. But he was strictly on the SBO's shit list. He was an agitator, disobedient to orders, and was known to have said he'd be damned if he'd put out phony news to suit the SBO. As a noncombatant, Larry was subject to court-martial only for very serious offenses. The old man would have to wait his chance before he could slap Larry in solitary.

During March and April Larry and I listened to the news on Radio Roma, which we were allowed to hear presumably for its propaganda value. Each morning we stood shivering in the main courtyard at 7:58, until the big, rusty loudspeaker boomed out, "*Abbiamo i signali delle ore otto.*" Eight electronic bells rang out and the news began. At this stage in my study of Italian, I understood about 70 percent of these broadcasts.

"Today the Supreme Command reports that the courageous troops of the Italian and German armies have made notable advances. They have consolidated their positions in Tunisia near El Hamma and Gabes and west of the Mareth line in the south."

Larry jabbed me in the ribs and wrote furiously. The positions to which they had "advanced" were 20 to 50 miles to the rear of their last reported positions. I was learning from Larry and Doc the key Italian words that gave clues to the Axis retreats or "strategic withdrawals." "Our courageous troops have cleared the way to new fortified positions," meant they had withdrawn to positions prepared in anticipation of a retreat.

In mid-April Alan Stuyvesant had heard that his orders were coming through for repatriation as a noncombatant. In early May a Swiss Red Cross representative came to the camp and told him to pack up.

Alan was nine years older than I and had turned 40 at Chieti; we had had the chance to renew a warm friendship. He had guided me in French language and literature and in getting to know the intricacies of the British network in the camp. He had been in Chieti so long that Care packages from his family had begun to arrive, even though they took six to eight months in transit. It was significant that the Italians let them come through, because the Germans would not have. Alan "willed" me any more that might come through after he left. From these packages I shared the food and clothing, but kept all the vitamins simply because no one else wanted them. I had a hunch these put me way out in front in the struggle to survive.

I'd said goodbye to Alan with mixed feelings. Certainly I was delighted for him, but at the same time I was envious. He was getting out from under the oppressive sense of confinement without having to risk an escape. It didn't seem fair to the rest of us. I was puzzled, too, when he told me he was going to enlist in an airborne outfit and get parachuted into France to fight with the Resistance. I assumed that he had felt the same kind of guilt I had about not being in combat when everyone else was. But how could a man of 40 go to jump school? And how the hell could he get out of this damn prison and take a chance of getting caught again? It was common knowledge that when the Germans got you the second time you went before a firing squad.

After Alan pulled out, I plunged back into exercising and into cramming on Italian. All my energies were focused toward getting out. One day Len and I and Larry Allen got into a discussion about where the Allies would land on the Italian peninsula. My feeling was that they could come directly over from North Africa and land in the plains of Puglia on the east coast, then establish a bridgehead until they got control of the port of Bari and the airport at Foggia.

Len sat cross-legged on his bunk, looking like an inscrutable Buddha. Larry leaned against the post of his bunk, a pungent Italian cigarette hanging out of his mouth. He squinted as its smoke curled up, smelling like burning skunk cabbage.

Len observed in his quiet, methodical voice, "They'd never get up the Adriatic. The Germans would hit them from air bases in Yugoslavia and Foggia, as well as from Sicily."

"Well, they made the crossing from the States and came down from England. This isn't nearly that far," I said.

Meanwhile, a B-24 pilot named Dan Storey had wandered over. From Corsicana, Texas, he was stocky and bald, with a crinkly, infectious smile and a broad Lonestar drawl. "Those buggers got bases on both sides of the straits," he said. "A convoy would have to run past a shooting gallery along the coast of Sicily and the bottom of the boot; then through a gauntlet in the straits between Otranto in the 'heel' and Vione over in Greece. Christ, they'd get the shit knocked out of them. You guys don't know what the map looks like. I've flown over that area so many times, I could go there with a bag over my head."

Len asked, "OK, Dan, where do you think they're going to make the landing?"

"In Sicily, for God's sake. It's only a hundred miles across from Tunisia — they'd have air cover the whole way. They'd take a Christ-awful beating on landing, but I think they could make it at Sciacca or as far east as Licata."

I didn't even know where those places were.

David Westheimer had come into the room and had been listening intently. "Westy," as he was called, had been nicknamed "Little Caesar" because of a fancied resemblance to Edward G. Robinson, who had played Al Capone in that film. But at this moment Westy looked more like a cat ready to pounce than the infamous gangster — he was an expert navigator and knew his geography better than anyone present. "Dan, you're right as far as that goes," he said, "but you're missing the point. The Italians have an island called Pantelleria, a hundred miles east of Tunis. It's got an air base and is loaded with flak batteries. The Allies have to take that first, and then they'll have air cover from there, Malta, and Tunis as well."

Larry, who had been watching through a haze of smoke, yelled, "Yeah," clapped his hands and began singing, "Deep in the Heart of Texas," in his version of an Italian translation. He sang it off key and was even further off when I joined him. The other guys put their hands over their ears. Westy was from Texas as well as Dan.

Late in the afternoon the sky clouded over, and we had somewhat of a letdown after our daydreaming session. Larry came in and told us the parcel distribution would be delayed. "A fuck-up with the Italians," he moaned. Dan sat on his top bunk glowering out the window. By nightfall he was generally pissed off about everything and wasn't talking to anyone. So we just left him alone. Long after lights out, I saw him still sitting on his upper bunk. He must have stared for hours out that window in the moonlit courtyard.

Sometime during the night footsteps sounded on the cement walkway outside, as a two-man patrol walked past our room. Dan sprang up on his knees with his hands on the frame of the open window. Suddenly, he stuck his head out and bellowed, *"Bastardi Italiani!"*

Before the second word was out, a blinding flash and explosion erupted into the room. Three bullets from a scatter shot rifle whizzed by Dan's head and were buried in the ceiling. A numb silence followed; bits of plaster plopped to the floor. Someone hissed, "For Christ's sake, Dan, shut up!" This was unnecessary. Dan had lost his appetite for invective.

Spirits improved when we were treated to a few days of warm May weather, and we lay out, baking in the sun. Some men took off their shoes and went barefoot. One morning a guy in the room next to us, named Charlie Remsen, ran down the hallway to the latrine. In his haste he left the door open, and we heard him retching. Doc Winston, an MO who'd been captured when he was with the 1st Armored, ran in after him. Doc was a friendly, low-key guy with an easygoing manner.

Half an hour later he came out of the latrine, holding Charlie up. The guy's face was ashen and his head rolled forward. Doc muttered something about the camp infirmary and took Charlie on out. When Doc returned he would say only that Charlie was very sick, but not in danger.

Two days later, Doc came into our room again, holding a brown paper bag. "Hey fellows," he said, "come over here, this is important."

The men sauntered over, a couple of them yawning. Doc took a glass jelly jar with a screw top out of the bag and held it up in front of them. "Look at this," he said. "Charlie Remsen threw this up this morning." Lying on a piece of white tissue, a seven-inch gray worm squirmed and wriggled.

"How the hell did that get inside him?" I asked.

"It comes in through your feet as a larva. From there, it goes up through your body and grows until it becomes a long worm. Then it crawls into your stomach."

At this, I felt like throwing up too. Len wanted to know, "Didn't Charlie have a hell of a lot of pain with that thing in his gut?"

"He was in terrible pain. That's partly why he vomited so much. You can get this larva right here in Chieti if you go around barefoot," Doc warned us. "So you guys better damn well get your shoes on and keep them on. And while I'm at it, don't drink that cistern water we get for washing. You can get a disease called schistosomiasis — little flukes that will eat out your liver. It's incurable."

A man next to me from an armored outfit asked in alarm, "For Christ's sake, Doc, is that on the level? You're not kidding, are you?"

"The hell I'm kidding; you men better listen for once!" With that statement, about as strong as any I'd ever heard Doc make, he walked off and headed down the hall on his way to check on Charlie.

Long before this I had wondered about drinking the cistern water. The approved supply for the camp came from one faucet in the main courtyard, which put out a thin stream. That was for 2,000 men. Sometimes there'd be 100 in the line. All my life, I'd been accustomed to drinking a lot of water, so hot days were particularly rough.

One day during the heat, I went over with a two-gallon tin to get a supply for the room. Among 30 men, this amounted to one glass each. For nearly an hour, I stood sweating in the hot sun. When at last I got back to the room, exhausted and crazy with thirst, I took my ration of one glass and gulped it down. Fifteen minutes later, I had to take PT class and was still damn thirsty. The cistern water immediately popped into my head.

I went into the washroom. Over on the side, a naked Englishman sat on the tile floor under a gushing wall faucet. Water poured onto his head and cascaded down his body while he soaped his arms and legs. He caught some water in his mouth and squirted it in the air.

After watching him for a moment, I opened a sink faucet and gulped about three glasses from my cupped hand, wiped my face, and walked out to warm up for PT class. I felt great. Screw the damn bugs anyway, I thought.

By 15 May Radio Roma could not possibly conceal the magnitude of the German and Italian defeat in North Africa, but the Italian camp commandant and his executive, though Fascists, pretended not to be affected by it. The rank and file guards were afraid of these two. If the officers weren't around, the *carabinieri* were less hostile to us, and the Italian army guards actually showed signs of wanting to be friendly.

One evening about 20 May I was still out after curfew and sauntered past a patrol consisting of two Italian privates. One of them came up to me rather diffidently. *"Siete Americano, signore?"* he asked, his voice soft and ingratiating.

"Si, si, signore," I answered. *"Sono capitano nell' artiglieria. La mia casa é in Nuova Jersey."* Your home location was always a good opener. This fellow came from Reggio Calabria, down in the toe of Italy; he had a cousin in Pennsylvania and asked if I knew him because it was near New Jersey. We talked some more, agreed the war should end soon, wished each other good luck, and said goodnight.

Similar exchanges with the guards became possible for any prisoner who spoke Italian. They seemed to have cousins, brothers, relatives of all kinds, scattered across New Jersey, Pennsylvania, and Ohio, who had around the turn of the century migrated in waves to work in the coal mines and steel mills.

The Italian sun grew steadily warmer, and I had long recovered from the bout with flu and dysentery. Although I was still hungry, the improving news and the arrival of two letters made my spirits rise. The feeling, though, was short-lived. In one letter, all the censor had left was, "Much love, Dad." So I was willing to bet that my father had been trying to tell me some "important military secret."

The other, a letter from Emily, came through more intact. She was well, as were Margaret and Joey. But our friend Anna Page, who had been so helpful, was giving Emily problems, and Stan Olson had become completely uncooperative. I puzzled for a minute, then got it — the A & P rationing was getting tough, and Stan Olson (for Standard Oil) meant she couldn't get gas for the car.

I read on: "Frankly, they have grown so difficult, I have had to move to Long Island. Louise, Nancy, and I have rented a huge house on the beach in Southhampton, and all our kids can go everywhere on bicycles. We have big baskets for marketing."

I stopped reading. My God, I thought, she's moved out of our house! Every time I had envisioned her and the children, it had been in the little white house in Far Hills. It was the one place I dreamed of returning to. I was stunned, shattered. How could she do it? The problems couldn't be that severe. Suddenly, I felt lost, betrayed. Then I grew irate.

Len was studying me. "Did you get some disturbing news, Joe?" I sat still for a moment, seeing his look of concern. Then I suddenly blurted out the whole story in Emily's letter.

"I think of home the same way," he said. "But perhaps she had no other choice? Do you know these other gals? Are they OK?"

"Oh, sure, they're fine people and old friends. Their husbands are in the Navy in the Pacific. But Emily came from Long Island, and now she's going to want to move back there permanently after the war."

Len had a questioning smile on his face. "Didn't she indicate it was a temporary thing?"

"Yes."

"Look, Joe, you and she are 4,000 miles apart, like me and my wife. We have to take what they say at face value. We haven't a clue what problems they have to deal with back there, so trust her. Rely on her judgment; my guess is it was the only thing she could do."

I thanked Len. If not emotionally, at least intellectually, I understood. But I could no longer dream of that white cottage as a haven. It was merely an empty shell, cold and lifeless. Now I also felt like an empty shell.

June 1943

The island of Pantelleria, as Westy had explained, was a key Axis bastion 100 miles east of Tunis and about 70 miles from the coast of Sicily. On the evening of 11 June Radio Roma reported that it had been evacuated by the Italian garrison without a fight. The news was so startling, especially since the official radio had been so frank, that it set off a wild celebration in the camp. The SBO issued an order that in the future any such demonstrations would be met with courts-martial. Then he became more morose and stranger than ever.

Working on the escape tunnel, Chieti. (Drawn by Gordon Horner at Chieti and later taken to England via Germany. From *For You the War is Over*, by Gordon Horner [London: Falcon Press, 1948]. Reprinted with the kind permission of the author.)

Word was passed around quietly that he claimed to be receiving secret orders from British Intelligence, saying there was to be no breakout of prisoners and no disturbances in the camp. No one was to escape, under threat of court-martial. The British high command simply did not want them running around behind the German lines. To me the story seemed suspect; and the Air Forces men, including Claude Weaver, agreed it was bullshit, invented by the SBO to bolster his authority.

By the 15th the British had stepped up their tunnel digging to a new level. Claude Weaver began disappearing in the morning and not showing up until just before afternoon roll call. Once I asked him where he was going, but he just frowned and turned away. Another morning after roll call he put on an old torn shirt, frayed shorts, and an ancient pair of sneakers, then slipped on his blue RAF uniform and hurried out. Len gave me a funny smile and said, "He makes it damn clear he wants no questions, doesn't he?"

About 4:00 that afternoon, the camp PA system blared: *"Attenzione! Attenzione! Appell'! Appell'! Immediatamente nei quartieri."*

The announcement was repeated three times. Each man stood beside his bunk while the guards made their inspection. Such an inspection usually consisted of tapping the floors with little hammers to detect the hollow sound of a tunnel. Our men would project a mock seriousness, and struggle not to start giggling. This time, though, two prisoners were missing, and I knew it wasn't funny. If a tunnel worker was caught, the Fascist commandant had him thrown in solitary.

I could hear the guards tapping two rooms away when Weaver and another pilot came from the opposite direction, dragging in a B-24 bombardier named Russ Gardinier. His face was gray with brown streaks and his hair and clothes were covered with dirt. They hoisted him onto his upper-deck bunk, pulled his blanket up to his head, and ran to their places.

His bunk mate asked him quietly, "Russ, you OK?"

"Yeah," he answered faintly, "But get this dirt out of my hair and wipe off my face."

The other man grabbed a comb, whisked out the dirt and wiped Russ's face with a filthy handkerchief seconds before the tappers marched in.

"Ufficiali, attenzione!" the guard officer called. We snapped to attention more smartly than usual. The officer looked at Russ. "What is the matter? Why is he not at attention?"

Larry stepped forward and said in his best Italian, "Please excuse it, *Tenente*. He is sick today. If he stands up he vomits."

The officer scowled, raising his eyebrows. He shrugged, turning his palms up, and told his men to hurry up. When they had left, we made stilted small talk till they were in the next building. "All clear, Russ," Larry advised.

Russ grinned. "Thanks, Larry, you even convinced me."

Russ had been "at the face" of his tunnel too long, and the alert came just in time. He had nearly passed out from severe lack of oxygen when they pulled him hurriedly from the tunnel. Russ's experience gave me nightmares, but he was a pragmatic engineer and regarded it merely as a problem to be solved. Two weeks later he had built a pipe out of old Red Cross food cans fitted together. One end of the pipe was put at the face, and at the other a man turned a fan made of flattened cans. Those tunnel workers had no more troubles from hypoxia.

One elaborate tunnel actually reached outside the barbed wire concertinas surrounding the brick walls. Many wooden bed slats disappeared and turned up as shoring for the tunnel roof. A British engineer, or sapper, stole some of the wires that were bound around the Red Cross parcels and with them rigged a line down the tunnel. He then installed a stolen light socket and bulb and made a connection to the camp electrical system. But the supreme achievement of the tunnel was its entrance: the sapper had removed the cement around one of the huge granite steps that led into one of the British bungalows. After hollowing out behind the step, he balanced it on a pivot at its center of gravity. Thus it could be rotated horizontally when a wedge was removed. This revealed a wide, flat aperture just high enough for the thin prisoners to slide through. When it closed in place, the granite block looked exactly like all the rest. The effort those Englishmen were making and the risks they took each day were extraordinary, and I hoped that tunnel would serve its purpose. Or was this *tour de force* an end in itself?

During this period of frenetic tunnel-digging, the level of the camp vegetable garden rose two feet. Because of the constant replanting, however, the vegetables were not as successful as the deluxe tunnel.

28 June 1943

Weaver had disappeared again on the morning after the surprise roll call. When he came back that night, he had gray smudges under his eyes, and he staggered over to his bunk and flopped down on it without speaking to anyone.

Two days later, Len and I asked him what was going on, letting him know we were as interested in escaping as anyone. If he had any information that would help, Len and I would consider it top secret, we assured him.

He nodded toward the door and we followed him out into the courtyard next to our building. For the moment, it was deserted. We sat in a corner leaning against the wall in a warm June sun. In the distance, we could hear shouts from a game the British had organized in the main courtyard.

"You guys swear this will not be repeated?" he pleaded. "The committee would have my neck." We each gave our word.

Claude said a British enlisted man named Watkins had heard a sound of running water under the stove where he worked in the mess. A sapper had investigated, located an auxiliary sewer, and knocked a hole into it through the bottom of the stove. He had estimated it ran laterally about 30 feet to the sewer main. The committee asked Weaver to go down and explore it. He had been on his way to do it the day he left our room with his old clothes under his uniform.

Claude told us that when he put his head in the hole, he heard the water running, then the smell of sewage hit him. He wriggled down, scraping his arms and knees, and entered a pipe 16 inches wide and 9 inches high. It was barely the width of his shoulders. He inched along, pushing with his fingers and toes.

He had with him a rubber bag tied around his neck. It held matches and an improvised miner's lamp made from a sardine can. The lamp had a string wick and contained sardine oil. It was fitted with a band to go around his head.

I broke in, "For God's sake, didn't they tell you about sewer damp?"

He smiled. "Yeah, sure, but you know the old British understatement. I'll come to that part."

Claude pushed himself along in the pipe, breathing in the stench of sewage and getting cut from rusty forks and knives that were caught in cracks. About 40 feet along, his head and shoulders slid out into an open space. He freed his arms from the pipe just in time to avoid going headfirst into sewage in a main that was about four feet deep. Edging forward, he managed to get his hands on the far wall of the main, slide his legs out of the small pipe, and crouch on the bottom, up to his knees in reeking, slimy ooze.

When he looked back up the pipe, he could see Watkins' head hanging down through the stove. He called back to tell him he was going to light up the lamp. Wiping his hands on his shirt, he opened the bag around his neck and pulled out the lamp and the matches. After a few tries a match lit and the tiny wick took hold. Then, adjusting the band around his forehead, he edged his way down the main in a half squat. In the flickering light, he saw something move on the surface. It was a long gray worm. The surface was covered with them.

Without warning, a blinding flash and explosion sucked the air out of his lungs and seared his face. With the oxygen gone, he gasped, trying to get this breath. He turned around in the total darkness and fought his way back up the sewer gradient. When he reached the smaller pipe, he felt a slight draft and gulped in the fresher air.

He got himself into the smaller pipe by putting his feet on the opposite wall of the sewer main and pushing. Only then did he realize how steep a grade he had come down. He scraped with his toes and pushed with his fingers for 45 exhausting minutes until Watkins grabbed him under the chin and hauled him out.

As Claude told us that part, he frowned, a muscle in his jaw twitching. But when he described the cleansing hot water and iodine bath that the MO had given him, he smiled and said he was thinking of trying the sewer again as soon as his cuts were healed.

The two Britishers gave his body a complete going over. The MO put more iodine on his cuts, dressed them, and helped him into fresh clothes. Then Claude had a cup of tea and went off to his debriefing with the Escape Committee.

When he finished the story, Len asked him how he felt about his adventure. He said he felt fine, but that before the next try he would need better equipment. The problem was to find a light that wouldn't explode.

I glanced at Len, who was slowly shaking his head. I said to Claude, "Look, we all want to get out of here, but I don't think that's the way."

Claude shot back, "You know what Watkins said to me? 'Ye wouldn't get me bleedin' arse in that fookin' poipe!' "

Len and I laughed, but I inwardly shivered. "You've been in the RAF a while. Maybe you understand the British better than we do, but at times I think they have courage to a fault."

"So, what're you getting at, Joe?"

"Things are changing fast with this North African victory, Claude, so keep in shape, learn a lot more Italian, and I'd sure as hell stay out of that damn sewer."

Claude watched me with a peculiar smile. He knew I couldn't have made myself go down that pipe. And I knew I wasn't willing and, perhaps, wasn't emotionally equipped to escape with Claude Weaver. Much as I might kid myself that I wanted to take advantage of the opportunity this resourceful guy would sooner or later create, deep in my heart I was aware that he was not for me.

After that time, dreams came again and again. In one, I was in the old vertical cylinder, looking up at the glistening sides. At the top, the piston had started to descend. There was an escape hole near the bottom about the size of my head and shoulders, but just as I put them into it, it began to shrink until they stuck. The fear grew — wild, uncontrollable terror. I struggled, but still it shrank and the piston kept coming down. I was suffocating. I tried to scream, but no sound came out. Suddenly I awoke fighting the blanket and soaked with sweat.

Len murmured, "For God's sake, Joe, what the hell's the matter?"

Then he rolled over and was snoring, while I remained awake for hours, afraid to sleep.

July 1943

The sewer was soon forgotten when Allied air raids started on the rail yards at Pescara, only eight miles northeast of Chieti. During the day the American pilots in the camp quickly recognized the B-24 Liberator vapor trails, even though the planes themselves were barely visible. Whenever the sirens went off, guards would send us back into our bungalows at gunpoint.

On the afternoon of the 15th, news of the Allied invasion of Sicily hit the camp like a thunderbolt. Larry and I rushed out to the courtyard to listen to the news fillers behind the headlines. I marveled at how his hand flew across the pad. Suddenly, he muttered, "That's it!"

I had heard something like, *"Cinque giorni fa. . . ."* The Allies must have landed five days ago, on 10 July!

Larry knew the map of Sicily well enough for us to trace their progress. Evidently, they had been held up in those first days after the initial landings and had then broken out of the perimeter. "My God," I thought, "I wonder if the 1st Division went in there? Right at this moment, Rex Rawie could be up with the infantry as a forward observer."

As Allied forces advanced through Sicily, our guards became increasingly friendly, though they'd get jittery and irritable whenever the excitement among the prisoners threatened to get out of control. One morning I was sitting on my bunk when three shots rang out a few seconds apart. An Englishman from the colonel's staff rushed in. "Just sit tight, fellahs," he said, imitating an American accent. "No one's hurt. But no more disturbances, SBO's orders." He stalked out, his heels clicking on the tile floor. Evidently, some of our guys had been raising quite a ruckus out in the courtyard.

The incident set me to thinking that the men were damn fools to provoke our captors like that, since it would just put the guards on edge. They would surely be tense over the prospects of an uprising in the camp, fully realizing that, should they be overwhelmed, they could take a terrible physical beating, or worse. The British had made abundantly clear their bitterness against the Italians. Nevertheless, it seemed stupid for them to transfer this animosity to our Italian army guards, who were obviously limited-duty garrison troops.

With things breaking as they were, I decided to go and see Colonel Gooler, who was still our Senior American Officer. Captured at the fall of Tobruk in eastern Libya on 21 June 1942, he had been in five months longer than I had. My stay here, though, had been long enough for me to have grown careless with formalities, so I reminded myself to sharpen up my military courtesy. Colonel Gooler was a very senior regular army officer.

The colonel used a little cubicle in the front end of our bungalow as his office. A slim man of medium height with a tanned face and grizzled hair, he peered at me through steel-rimmed glasses with heavy lenses, greeted me affably, and waved me to a seat. "I suppose you want to talk about escaping, Frelinghuysen," he said, smiling.

"Among other things, if I may, sir."

"Shoot!"

I described the gradual change in the guards' attitude, starting with the time they caught Alan and me out after curfew. The colonel smiled, and I concluded that he hadn't heard the story before. Nor did he seem to realize the extent of the change since the invasion of Sicily. At the risk of irritating him, I suggested it was foolish to bait the Italians and call them "bloody Eyeties" the way the British did, and also pointed out that if there was a landing on the Italian mainland, our jailers might look the other way.

The colonel shrugged a shoulder and looked out the window. "Well, maybe," he said. "But what about the Italian camp adjutant, Captain Croce?"

I reminded him that, although Croce liked to pose as a diehard Fascist, there was apparently a lot of bluff to it. For example, three months before, he had tried to break up a Sunday Mass by ordering a roll call. Father Brach, the American priest, ignored the *appell'* and continued to say Mass. Croce then barged in with four guards, threatening to shoot the priest, who had refused to move. In the end, it was Croce who backed down, despite the serious loss of face.

"Frelinghuysen, that hasn't a damn thing to do with it," he argued. "You may be right about some of the guards, but you can't expect them just to let you walk out."

I was losing my case and getting irritated. Gooler had served with the British and decided he had to back up the SBO, but I kept on just the same. "Anyone who tries to escape has to take his chances. If any of us do get out, we'll have to walk over a hundred miles to Allied lines; we'll need food, money, and Italian clothes. Besides, I'd never pass as an Italian, nor would many of the others. We'd have to make it on foot across the Apennines with the help of the local *paesani*."

The colonel scowled, then sighed and seemed to relax a little. "It is an interesting problem," he said. "Very well, Frelinghuysen, make your plans; get a partner, if you wish, and talk it over. You have the language and may get an opportunity, but right now it's out of the question."

I walked out into the main courtyard, puzzled and frustrated. Gooler was certainly sticking to the British line. Yet we were both in the U.S. Army, and I had expected a good deal more discussion. Now I was worried and frightened; for the first time, it began to dawn on me — we could get trapped in Chieti and never get out.

August 1943

Occasionally, when he was not too upset about the tunnels, the Fascist commandant allowed the guards to show us an ancient movie. Usually, it was a piece of rabid Fascist propaganda, and "Thunder Over Mexico" with Warner

Baxter was no exception. The theme of the film was the Southern California ranchers' persecution of the Mexican-Americans. To the Italians, this was symbolic of the "barbarous North Americans bombing our cities." Translation of the Italian subtitles was handled by a British officer who was proficient in Italian.

Baxter played the Mexican-American leader who was attempting to get his people better wages and living conditions. A sheriff's posse arrested him on flimsy charges. He made a running break, dove over a steep bank, and rolled end-over-end, as the posse fired six-shooters down the hill at him. Each time he was hit, he fell again, his face contorting in a grimace. He half stood up, crawling and limping. Crouching low, his whole body an expression of agony, he finally stumbled to a lower bank and rolled down into the river. At the story's end he was seen floating face down in the water, while the ranchers pumped more bullets into his inert form.

After the film was over, I pondered that scene of Baxter's running break and surmised that it might have an analogy to an escaping prisoner. In spite of the warm evening, I shivered.

A few days afterward, I found an old Italian poem, which I translated:

> I am the blind ballad singer
> At the corner of the street,
> Read these words and change your ways:
> Don't wait for fortune at your door,
> She may not come your way.
> Don't quench your thirst at every spring,
> Nor let mirth lead you astray,
> From misfortune do not hide,
> For she will find you;
> Here today or there tomorrow,
> She may be written in your fate.
> If pain taps you on the shoulder,
> Always answer: Here am I.

Some good advice there, too: "Don't wait for fortune at your door. . . ." Many times in the weeks ahead I was to think of the blind ballad singer.

Chapter 12

The Badoglio Armistice

As air-raid sirens in the city of Chieti howled night and day throughout August, all 2,000 prisoners were held for long hours in their bungalows, cursing and sweating. By the 1st of September, when the raids had become less frequent, the men poured out to listen every time Radio Roma blasted the news across the camp. I was there for each broadcast amid noisy, shoving men, who wanted instant translation: "What's he saying, Joe?" "Come on, get busy! What the hell you been studying all the 'Eyetie' for?"

I translated what I could for one group, Doc Gallo took another, and sometimes Larry Allen a third. But usually Larry would break off to write his bulletin. His listeners then swarmed over to Doc, who translated much better than I did.

My shortcoming in Italian notwithstanding, there was no difficulty in ascertaining that the German defense of Sicily was about to collapse. Larry Allen began to drop broad hints, picked up from Radio Roma's double talk: The Axis defenders were evacuating Sicily. Then on 25 August word came over the air that the "glorious defense of Sicily had ended" and that the "courageous Axis troops" were setting up "impregnable defenses on the Italian mainland." Larry estimated that the surrender had actually occurred about a week earlier. From that announcement on, every man in the camp believed in his heart, if not in his head, that it would take but a week or two for the Allies to invade the "boot" of Italy.

September 1943

Colonel Gooler instructed Larry and me and two others to move into the front room of the bungalow. New prisoners were still coming in and space was needed in the old American room. Our new quarters were long and narrow, opening out onto the front portico where Larry had his bulletin board, so I was closer to the radio broadcasts. As a result of the move, I also had more room for stuff I had collected: sweaters, socks, warm underwear from Alan Stuyvesant's packages, an old suitcase I had been given somewhere along the way, and a small store of canned food I had hoarded as an escape kit. The *pièce de résistance* of this store was three tins of New Zealand chocolate bars. Setting aside the escape kit had demanded all my discipline, because our total daily rations, including shares of the Red Cross parcels, were so meager. I was resolved to use the chocolate only when I was at the end of my rope — absolutely at the bottom.

Though I was physically more comfortable in the new room, I was for some reason more tense and uneasy, and I began to wonder if men who are locked away from the violent activity and brutal impact of war may acquire a special intuitiveness. A verse from Tennyson's *Palace of Art* would often come to mind:

> A still salt pool, lock'd in with bars of sand,
> Left on the shore, that hears all night
> The plunging seas draw backward from the land
> Their moon-led waters white.

Now our "still salt pool" was about to be washed away by the rising seas of the war. The false feeling of security would soon be shattered. As far as escaping was concerned, we were going to have to "shit or get off the pot."

On the evening of 8 September I was standing in our long narrow room, looking over Larry's shoulder as he sat on his bunk writing a bulletin. The headline read: *YOU ARE FREE*. In a moment he ripped the page from his pad, scurried out to the portico, and posted it on his bulletin board.

Everyone in the room poured out after him, jockied for position, and shoved each other, trying to read the subheadlines: "Badoglio announces Italy has signed armistice with Allies! American troops have landed on west coast of Italy, just below Naples and Salerno. Italian press states Americans are being driven back into the sea, but informed Allied sources term that Fascist propaganda."

For the first time since I'd been captured, I was elated, charged up to the skies. Yet something inside gnawed like a rat: *YOU ARE FREE* was simply too good to be true.

These doubts didn't seem to affect the others, however, for soon the wild howls and yelling around the bulletin board began to get out of control. Men shouted obscenities at the Germans, at the Italians, at the SBO who had told people they weren't allowed to escape. One group went so far as to form a snake dance, prancing through our bungalow and out the other end, while the patrols watched. Some of the guards laughed, others fingered their rifles and shifted from one foot to the other. I studied them all carefully, trying to memorize the faces of those who seemed to think the demonstration was more amusing than threatening.

Badoglio's announcement had explosive implications. It could help us by bringing the Italians over to our side. On the other hand, additional German divisions could pour into Italy as they had in North Africa after the Allied invasions there. The difference was that here they would not need the Ju-52's. They could stream in by rail and truck.

It took only a few minutes to realize that Larry had overstated the situation drastically. Because even if the Allies didn't get driven into the sea, they were still 150 road miles away, with the whole Apennine Mountain range and a growing German army between us and them. A number of the other men must have sensed the same thing, because shortly the exuberance tapered off.

I lost interest in reading the rest of the dispatch and walked around to the front of our bungalow, where I met an American officer known as "January" Long. Only about five feet tall but thickly muscled, with the sloping shoulders of a born athlete, January moved with a lithe grace. Someone had informed me he was a judo expert from some special, top-secret unit. With his round face and easygoing Western drawl, he seemed an unlikely cloak-and-dagger spy. January, garbed in combat coveralls with no insignia of rank or branch, was carrying an old suitcase.

Half laughing, I inquired, "Where the hell are you going with that?"

But he was dead serious. "I'm going to walk out the main gate," he asserted and started off. I still thought it was a gag, as I watched him approach the gate. The two guards were facing away from the main courtyard when he turned the handle of the gate. To my surprise, it opened, and he proceeded out toward the main road until a guard yelled in Italian, "Come back! Come back! It is too soon to leave."

January hesitated, then kept on walking, with the guard running after him, gesturing and babbling incoherently. The Italian was too far away for me to hear what he was saying, but after a brief discussion with him January sauntered back, the guard trailing and waving his carbine.

When January got back into camp, he had a minor argument with the Escape Committee for not getting clearance and was ordered not to try again under threat of court-martial. This both unnerved and infuriated me. From subsequent brief talks with the guards, it seemed clear to me that had January been fluent in Italian and able to offer the guard help when the Allies arrived, the man who stopped him might have let the American continue on his way. A decision of that kind by an Italian soldier hung on a thread; he was uncertain of his position, not anxious to offend an Allied officer, yet afraid of getting into trouble with his superiors. Claude Weaver had witnessed the whole incident, too, and after that I saw him talking to the guards whenever he got the chance.

The next day a major of the guard came slinking into our room. Since he'd been responsible for getting several men thrown into the cooler, no one liked him. When Larry got up and inquired in Italian what he could do for him, the major pulled out some cigarettes and asked if we wanted some. Larry took a couple, as did two or three of the other smokers in the room. In a moment the whole pack disappeared, but the major still managed to smile. He paused awkwardly, then shook hands with the men standing next to him, said "Goodbye," and departed.

"Larry, what do you make of that?" I asked.

"For God's sake, Joe, don't you see the guy's petrified? He's trying to make a few friends."

By the morning of 10 September the social and military framework of the camp, at least the American part of it, began to crumble. Men refused to go to roll call. Colonel Gooler warned us to act like soldiers or be prepared for the consequences. This got people to behave — for a while anyway.

Larry posted bulletins throughout that day as they came in over Radio Roma. The statements seemed very conciliatory and purported to give the progress of the Allied forces that had landed at Salerno. By afternoon the men, highly agitated, stood around in groups. talking, and at times shouting. Occasionally, a scuffle would start up. The tension ran so high among all the prisoners that no one slept much that night.

11 September

The following day the SBO had an order tacked on all the bulletin boards in the camp: "There will be no rowdyism, and officers will not form in large groups. Any attempts to escape will be the subject of military discipline. The Allies will arrive shortly, and in the meantime, all personnel will keep cool, calm, and collected."

Colonel Gooler sent an order, through his senior officers, that we were to obey the SBO's orders to the letter, and that violators would be subject to disciplinary action. A rumor followed all this, again saying that the SBO claimed to have received "secret orders" from the British War Office to see to it that prisoners were not running around behind the lines, for the British Eighth Army would be arriving in three days.

Within an hour Larry Allen had posted a bulletin refuting the SBO's notice and insisting that it was wrong to wait any longer. The news was clear, Larry concluded, that it would be *months* before the British or any other Allies would arrive. His statement ended with, "Keep cool, calm, and *get* collected by the Germans."

The SBO went wild. Larry was told he was going to be court-martialed, but

Gooler intervened and got him released on the promise that he would make him behave — a tough job, because Larry was a journalist first, and in addition was scared stiff that we might all get trapped in Chieti by the Germans. He had several times talked to me about escaping with him. That was why I had tried to get him to exercise. One day he walked about half a mile and came in and collapsed on his bunk. Fond as I was of him, he was as soft as a bowl of Jello, and I had no intention of trying to carry him over the Apennines.

The false premise behind the SBO's order was clear to me. He had simply swallowed the German propaganda. The Germans were the ones who didn't want us running around behind the lines. Soon some of the prisoners were in revolt, most of them American pilots. I talked to Claude Weaver, who laughed openly. "My orders in the RAF have always been to escape if captured and yours are too. I haven't the faintest intention of obeying that stir-crazy crackpot, and Max Gooler shouldn't either."

I thought long and hard about Weaver's position, and for a moment was tempted — what a chance to go with a clever, aggressive guy! But I still couldn't agree with him. Ignoring the SBO's order was one thing, but disobeying a direct command from a U.S. regular army officer wasn't in my book. Yet even as I went over the issue in my mind, I was aware that I was rationalizing, convinced that I'd never be able to make myself do the crazy things Weaver would do.

That evening at early dusk I was sitting on some steps at the back of our bungalow when a bulky Italian in a private's uniform swaggered over and stood looking down at me. I'd never seen such an Italian. The massive shoulders threatened to burst the jacket. The jet-black hair and mustache were at odds with the lightly tanned skin. Without fanfare, the man said simply, "Goodbye, Joe, I'm leaving."

First I gasped, then howled, "My God, Claude, it's terrific! How the hell did you get that uniform?"

"Never mind. You see how this works and then try it yourself. Mouse Rideout's going with me; sorry you're not. Want to change your mind?"

"Thanks just the same, Claude. I admit I'm as uneasy as hell about it, but I've made my decision. I'm going to obey the order."

He put out his hand. "Good luck, Joe, but I think you're making a damn dumb mistake."

"Maybe. Anyway, good luck to you and Mouse."

Rideout, an American fighter pilot, now dressed like Weaver as an Italian private, came around the corner carrying a ladder made of boards from the double-decker bunks. I watched them cross the courtyard and lean it against the high brick wall. Claude went first. Mouse followed and hauled up the ladder. They dropped it on the far side, and in seconds both disappeared into the night.

The after-dark curfew had become so relaxed that I was not in the least concerned when a two-man patrol of the Italian guard wandered by. If they had seen Weaver and Rideout, they gave no indication.

I stood up and greeted them with a cheerful, *"Buona sera."*

After the two whispered to each other for a moment, one of them walked over to me. *"Buona sera, signore. Vorrei parlare con voi"* (I would like to speak with you).

"Very well," I answered in Italian.

"You are an American officer from this block?"

"Yes."

"Where are you from in the United States, *signore*? I have cousins in Pennsylvania." This made me wonder if all cousins lived there.

"I come from New Jersey, but I'm glad to know you have relatives near where I live. Where is your home in Italy?"

"I come from Bari. It is far to the south."

"Would you like to go there?"

"As quickly as possible, *signore*. I know the way and I can walk for many hours. I can arrange things for us along the way, but I am afraid I will be shot when I reach the Allies — your friends."

"I see. You guide me and I guarantee your safe conduct through the lines."

The man grabbed my hand and shook it. His voice trembled with excitement and he said, *"D'accordo! D'accordo!"*

"One moment, I must find out," I said cautiously. "I would like to go right now, but I have orders. I will meet you here later and tell you if I can go. Otherwise, you better go alone." The man pumped my hand more enthusiastically than before and walked off with his companion. I went inside and found Colonel Gooler sitting gloomily in his office.

"I'm sorry as hell, Joe, but those are orders," he said when I'd explained why I was there. "I know I may be making a mistake, but that's final." The aging colonel had lost some of his army formality in the last few months, but his tone of voice left no doubt he meant what he said.

Angry enough to hit somebody, I walked back to our room to find Len Warren sitting on his bunk. "Where the devil have you been all this time?" he asked. "I thought maybe you'd taken off."

"No, but I've been watching somebody else."

"I'll bet it was Weaver. I heard he was going tonight, and also that Dennis Newman had left."

"He did? Rideout was with Weaver when I saw him. These Air Forces guys don't give a damn about orders."

"Maybe they're smart. By the way, how did they look?"

"Great!"

"Wait'll they start to sweat and that India ink begins to run."

I told Len about the guard who offered to guide me down to Bari.

"Hell, that's just above the heel. What'd you tell him?"

"That I'd give him my answer tomorrow night. But I just asked Gooler again."

Len leaned forward. "What did he say?"

"In effect — not a chance. I think he's out of his head."

"I know, Joe, but I've come this far obeying orders, and I'm not going to start disobeying them now."

"God help us if Gooler's wrong."

"What do you think's at stake?" he asked me.

"Maybe three years in Germany — that is, if we make it for that long."

Len groaned and shook his head. "Christ, you're gloomy. We better get some sleep." He rolled over in his bunk.

Wearily, I crawled into mine and stared up at the slats under Len's straw and burlap mattress. Sleep was impossible. A nasty doubt nagged me: Was my reluctance to ignore the order an excuse to avoid making a dangerous, frightening decision? I tossed it back and forth amid a morass of self-accusation. Three years of near or real starvation in Germany? Chieti was probably a country club compared to what that would be like. Then I envisioned Weaver and Rideout walking through the hills in the night. They had performed magic. They were free!

Suddenly I thought of the Italian guard I'd spoken to an hour before. I'd promised to let him know; besides I wanted to keep the door open in case Gooler changed his mind. But I detested the thought of telling the man I couldn't go — one more chance thrown away!

I sneaked out and waited just inside the back door of our bungalow, not wanting to get picked up by the British patrol — they'd throw me in the cooler for curfew violation and screw everything up. I checked my watch — 10:30 — the guard would still be on; they didn't change till midnight.

Half an hour later I heard a patrol coming. I went out and spoke to them in Italian, "Is one of you the man I talked with before? I'm the American captain."

"*Si, si, signore*, are you ready to go now? My friend Pietro, here, has found a ladder — he will go also."

It was the hardest thing to say, but I managed: "No, I cannot go. I have been ordered to stay by the American colonel."

"*Santa Maria, Signor Capitano*, you are making one horrible mistake! I am disappointed and sorry for you, because you will be in German hands any moment now."

"My friend, I am a soldier — those are my orders." It just about killed me to say it. The man turned away angrily, talking to his friend Pietro, loud enough for me to overhear: "I can't believe how stupid these Americans are."

Pietro exploded, "It is you who are stupid, they are afraid to go." And the voices trailed off as they walked away. I slunk back into our building, feeling like a beaten dog.

The next few days were utter confusion. The entire military garrison (as distinguished from the *carabinieri*, who also did guard duty) escaped or deserted by going over the wall at night. One evening, after talking to a couple of *carabinieri*, I realized they knew the Germans would take over shortly and didn't want to be caught in the middle when they arrived. In order to get some Italian *lire*, I sold to a sergeant of the guard some surplus clothing I'd inherited from Alan Stuyvesant. Two hundred dollars had been sent to me from America, through the Vatican, but since we were allowed only a few *lire* a week, the entire sum had been confiscated promptly by *Capitano* Croce, the Fascist adjutant. From this sale, I collected 600 *lire*, which I felt was sure to be handy later on.

One of the funniest and yet most ironic sights I saw during this period was a British private helping an Italian sergeant climb up a ladder to escape over the wall. Of course, the private was dutifully obeying the order to stay put.

Continuous false reports were fed to us by the Italian commandant and Croce: The Allies were in Genoa, Livorno, Bologna, even in Ancona, which was not far north on the Adriatic coast. We were extremely suspicious of those reports, but it was only too easy to swallow something we wanted to believe so badly. I lived in a state of utter frustration: Hoping those reports were true, I knew in my heart they weren't; I was driven to escape, which went against my resolve to obey the order to stay put; and I vacillated between the fear of risking escape and the fear of getting picked up and sent to Germany.

Chapter 13

Rossbach

14 September 1943

The mood of the men at Chieti alternated between ecstatic elation and smoldering resentment. And it was certainly the latter when I came out in front of our bungalow around midmorning. About a dozen Americans and two or three British stood in a group, arguing loudly. An American pilot yelled, "I'm damned if I'll let my ass get hooked in here by the Krauts just because that jackass, limey colonel doesn't know his ass from a hole in the ground. We got to organize the Americans and any British who want to join us —"

This set off cries of "To hell with the British!"

"OK, without 'em then, but with Gooler, if he'll go along. Then we'll just tell that limey colonel to shove it."

Someone jeered, "Attaboy, George, you tell 'em!"

A British voice piped up, "I say, you chaps, that's inciting to mutiny — you can get a firing squad for that!"

When more enraged shouts burst out, and things got to the pushing and shoving stage, I beat it around the corner into our courtyard, where I ran into David Westheimer. "Did you get a load of that, Westy?" I asked.

"Sure, but forget that, it's idiotic. There are 2,000 Britishers here who'll go along with the SBO. Let me tell you something really important; there's a new guy here I want you to meet. He was captured in Sicily with an armored outfit, and I hear he's made two escape attempts already. In one of them, he jumped off a train in the Brenner Pass and was out a week before they picked him up again." Westy added with a sly grin, "His name is Dick Rossbach, and since he comes from New York, you just have to meet him."

"The sooner the better," I told Westy.

Around 2:00 I was soaking up a little sun on the steps of our building when

Westy brought over a guy about half a head taller than he, maybe six-one. This new guy had broad, sloping shoulders, a thickset build, and a widely rolling gait. His thinning, ashblond hair gave him a high forehead. Hardly the image I'd had of a lithe, gymnastic escape expert. But when I rose to meet him, I noticed the uncompromising expression in his gray eyes and thought, definitely not a guy to fool around with.

He put out his hand and began to speak as Westy was introducing us. "Hi," he said, "I'm Dick Rossbach. I've wanted to meet you."

"Same here," I replied. "When did you get to Chieti?"

"September 9th, the day after the Badoglio announcement, when all of you were celebrating your 'freedom.'" He spoke with an educated New York accent, with that characteristic silent "r" after a vowel.

Rossbach and I sat down on the steps in the warm sunshine. "I heard you went to Princeton," he said, "I was '36 at Yale."

"Yes, I was '34 at Princeton, so we can have a bet on the Yale-Princeton game — if we're still here then."

His face grew serious and his voice quiet. "I haven't the slightest intention of still being here in early November."

I blinked a little at the certainty that there'd be no "if" about it. He had made a statement of fact beyond question — I made my second mental note to be careful.

The conversation turned lighter as we compared notes on people we knew in the New York area and found we had so many acquaintances in common that we wondered why we hadn't met before. It was exciting to hear that his father had been born in Germany and that Dick had learned the language as a child and still spoke it fluently. It came out, too, that he also spoke reasonably good French. With my Italian, we had four languages between us, a fact which made us well suited as an escape team. Furthermore, as Dick's story began to unfold, I realized he was adjusted to the idea of escaping, since he'd already made two attempts. It crossed my mind that I might have one hell of a job keeping up with this guy — I'd been a prisoner now for some nine and a half months, and despite my effort to fight deterioration my energy and aggressiveness had been undermined.

As we discussed North Africa and the Sicilian campaign, I gazed across the courtyard; off to our right a softball game was going on, thanks to some bats and balls from the Red Cross. On the central walkway, long-haired British prisoners strolled in twos and threes, wearing their battledress, on which the Italians had made them sew large red and blue squares. Along the outer walkway, four 1st Parachute men strode briskly in cadence. They had shed their jackets, and their trim white T-shirts showed husky arms and shoulders.

Dick stopped talking and took in the scene, too. "Those guys look as if they could make it," he commented.

Capt. Richard M. Rossbach.

"Yes, they've been training like that all winter. Incidentally, most of the British parachute men here got picked up in an ambush about the same time I did." I leaned forward toward him, lowering my voice. "I have an idea those guys will go out a tunnel — when they get ready. We're not in on it, so we have to figure out our own way. Maybe you can tell me how you worked it."

He laughed. "Neither of my ventures worked, but they might have, and I'll come to that. But first I want to tell you how I got captured, because it has to do with screwed-up orders, which is what we have here with this horse's ass SBO." He began his story:

I was in command of A Battery of the 58th Armored Field Artillery, which was self-propelled 105's. General Patton sent us out on the night of 8 August on a pinch landing near Santo Stefano, 70 miles east of Palermo. We landed in the midst of a bivouac of about 200 sleeping Germans, captured them, and blew up their vehicles.

But Patton got too smart for himself and tried to do the same thing two nights later, further east at Brolo. His junior officers raised hell — as much as anyone could with that guy — and complained that the troops were exhausted, that proper ammo resupply hadn't come through, and that there wasn't time to get our plans straight with the Navy and Air Forces. Despite all that, Patton ordered us to proceed. Our mission? To seize the coastal road and the flatlands near the beach, a railroad embankment, and the high ground of Mount Brolo.

I went off with my battery on an LST, along with several other LST's carrying an assault battalion consisting of the 30th Infantry, C Battery of the 58th, and a detachment of four tanks.

That night the Mediterranean was very calm and the Germans would surely hear us approach the beach. This time my men were unusually tense, and I was more uneasy than before any battle in Tunisia or Sicily. I went around the ship, checked the battery, and talked to some of the men.

At 2:00 a.m., all the infantry left their various ships in amphibious vehicles, led by beach engineers in small landing boats. They'd gone only a few hundred yards when the Germans opened up with rifles, machine-pistols, and heavy machine-guns.

I got the battery ashore OK, but ran into the railroad embankment. It was too steep for our self-propelled 105's, so I went off in my jeep toward Brolo and found a railroad bridge over a dry river bed. It seemed solid enough, so I brought the gun sections through there. By 4:00 a.m. I had them in position in a citrus grove, ready to fire east.

In the ammunition mixup, all they'd given me was a high explosive shell, not worth a damn for antitank. We needed armor-piercing, and they hadn't given us a single round of it.

A little while later, U.S. planes staged a massive dive-bombing attack off to the west of us; shortly afterwards, a messenger from my CO reported that our tanks had all been destroyed in the raid. We were totally without antitank protection.

As Dick talked his voice grew solemn and took on a harder tone, while he looked across the big parade ground.

After that we had a German attack from the east. We pounded them, or thought we did, but the HE (high explosive) didn't faze them. Then my Executive, who was my second in command, moved two gun sections west, fired on the enemy tanks from the side, destroying their tracks and breaking up their attack. The Navy had a forward observer liaison in our area, and shelling from the heavy cruiser *Augusta* drove off the rest of the German tanks.

Most of the German attacks throughout the day were from the east and were beaten off. At 3:00, I climbed up on the embankment. The whole side of the mountain was ablaze with brush fires which cut our telephone lines to our HQ on Mount Brolo. Then a mortar shell exploded a few yards away and knocked me flat. All I got was a broken finger and a cut-up knee. But I got off that embankment in a hurry.

My Recon Officer phoned in that C Company of the U.S. Infantry protecting our eastern flank was being run over by German tanks. My Exec already had two gun sections up straddling the road. Their HE shell seemed to shatter the tanks, but the tanks kept coming, apparently undamaged. Suddenly, a German shell blew the track off my second gun section, putting it out of action. Then my first section took a direct hit. Two or three cannoneers scrambled out of the flames. The others didn't make it.

My Exec kept his head. He moved the two other sections up on the side where they hit the German tanks from the flank and knocked them out. Then there was a brief lull. That lull was the last chance I had to evacuate the battery area and take my remaining men and equipment to better positions up on Mount Brolo. But I couldn't leave the men who were on the ground everywhere. I sent some off in my jeep to try to get them to an aid station in a railroad underpass. We helped the others to shelter and bandaged them up the best we could.

Next, a messenger reported that the Germans were overrunning our units to the west. A few minutes later, I got an order from my CO to abandon gun positions and bring the remaining men and equipment up to Mount Brolo. But by then it was too late; the Germans were swarming along the road between us and the mountain.

Our infantry reported that the forward observer from the *Augusta* had left the flatlands and gone to his ship. I guessed what he had told *Augusta's* fire control when she opened up on our position with her eight-inch guns.

The few men I had left ran for the irrigation ditches and foxholes, but you can't get away from that heavy stuff. The other two gun sections were knocked out and the casualties were disastrous. To top it all, the Air Forces must have seen the *Augusta* shelling the flatlands, so they came in and dive-bombed and strafed our entire area. When the firing was over, I had eight men left, Marty Keiser and myself — out of about 150.

We started to make a run for the mountain, but a unit of Panzer-Grenadiers swung in, and we had to take cover in a ditch. They set up a machine-gun about a hundred yards away and sprayed the top of the ditch whenever anyone stuck his head up. For a while I thought we might hold out until dark, but we were outnumbered ten to one and hopelessly outgunned. We fired back with carbines, and I emptied my pistol at a German 20 yards away. When we ran out of ammunition, we had no choice but to surrender.

After they took us over to the Italian mainland, we spent four miserable days traveling north toward Naples. Finally we stopped at a headquarters of their 1st Parachute Division, where Marty Keiser, who'd been my RO, and Frank Diggs, an infantry lieutenant, were the only officers in a group of 40 men from different outfits.

"Those German parachute troops were from the same outfit that captured us," I said. Dick frowned and gave a quick shake of his head, impatient at my interruption. Then he went on:

I had an idea that in the confusion of moving, elite troops like those wouldn't waste time chasing one escaped prisoner.

We'd had this rather efficient *Feldwebel* with us all the way up from Sicily, and for some reason he suddenly turned us over to a *carabinieri* sergeant and three other Italians. At that moment, I had to take a crap in a hurry and asked the sergeant where to go; he tossed his head over toward the roadside. I went over and squatted down. Out of the corner of my eye, I could see the *carabinieri* looking casually the other way. Then I glanced off to the east of the road. There the land fell away in a series of olive groves, planted on terraces held up with old stone retaining walls.

After tending to my business, I began to button my overalls. Suddenly, I sprang around and raced for the first terrace. As I jumped over the edge, a fusillade of shots whistled past me. I landed sprinting, reached the top of the next terrace, and leaped. My foot caught some vines on the wall, and I pitched over it headfirst. (He paused and smiled.) If anyone had a picture of that, it would look as if Rossbach was trying to fly — by clawing the air. I had a hell of a jolt when I saw it was an eight-foot drop. I landed headfirst, but luckily in soft earth. My neck cracked, and I passed out in a shower of fireworks.

When I came to, my head was spinning, and I was surrounded by *carabinieri* pointing rifles down at me. As I turned my head, I saw the *Feldwebel* racing down, waving his machine-pistol; I knew the guy might very well shoot me. Then I realized I was so damn fed up with the whole fucking business that I didn't really give a shit whether he shot me or not.

I was still dizzy when the *Feldwebel* got there puffing and blowing. But he looked down at me, burst out laughing, and said in this weird accent, "You cwazy Amewican, you cwazy Amewican. Now get up and get back to your twuck!"

"May I ask you a question now?" I said.

With a mock arch of his eyebrows, Dick chuckled, "Yes, you may."

"Did you have any repercussions at all from the guards?"

"No, I think it was just plain luck: the kind of person you're dealing with,

the mood he's in. I don't think you'd get that reaction often." Then he uttered one more, "You cwazy Amewican," and laughed.
"Where did they take you then?"

To Capua. For about ten days. There were only six officers at that point, but soon three more joined us. One was a guy who'd been an RAF antiaircraft officer, Ricky Prosser. He wore one of those guard's mustaches and was the most British-looking bloke you ever saw. Another was a very young second lieutenant named Tom Ellzey, who had been with the 1st Division Infantry.

We were kept at Capua till August 27th, when all nine of us were taken to the train station, ostensibly bound for Germany. All at once it was a different ball game: efficient *Wehrmacht* troops, no more easygoing Italian guards. We climbed into a beat-up railway carriage and trudged down a filthy side corridor with a German guard posted at each end of the car. The *Feldwebel* in charge told us another guard would be in each of the eight-passenger compartments. He counted off seven of us into one compartment, two in the other, and announced in a loud voice, "Five enlisted men will fill the compartment with the two officers."

Right then I decided it was time for Rossbach to make his move. I shouted angrily in German, "This is an outrage! No American officer will tolerate sitting with enlisted men! I demand you make better arrangements."

I wasn't sure where that act would get me, but I knew the Germans were used to arrogance — in fact, they had come to expect it from officers. The other British and American officers looked at me as if I were out of my head . . . except for Ricky, who was watching me with a funny smile.

As I hoped, the *Feldwebel* answered respectfully enough. *"Jawohl, Herr Hauptmann,* I understand your position, but I do not have the authority to change the arrangements. Only the train commander can do that."

I snapped back at him, "Then get him here immediately."

Believe it or not, he went and got him. I had a hell of an argument with that one and carried the bluff as far as I dared till he finally agreed nine officers could squeeze into one compartment. The guard would stand out in the corridor. This was just what I wanted, and Ricky and Tom got the idea, too. But the other officers were so damn mad at me, I was afraid for a while they might blow it. Finally, they settled down. The train headed north toward Florence, Bologna, and the Brenner Pass into Austria.

Around 11:00 in the evening it slowed down noticeably as we began to climb the steep mountain grades. By midnight we seemed to be down to about 20 miles an hour, and I calculated that we were nearing the Austrian border. All the prisoners were dozing in cramped positions, except Ricky and Tom, who were watching me. When I said, "All set?" they nodded.

The guard out in the corridor was slumped back against the glass door, his head rolling with the movement of the train — a picture of boredom.

I lowered the outside window. Even though the noise level in the compartment changed, the guard didn't move. I still had my steel helmet, and jammed it down on my head and tightened the strap. Ricky helped me get my feet out the window, so I was facing the compartment. I clung to the windowsill for a second. The cold air hit me, and I heard the clacking of the wheels. Then I gave a sudden, hard push away from the train and dropped into space.

It was a hell of a sight farther down than I'd thought, but my knees were bent when my feet hit the ground. I was flung onto the crushed rock of the embankment and spun over, scraping my hands and knees. In the bargain, my helmet sailed off in the darkness.

Oh God, I got this terrific feeling of elation as I watched the red blackout lights on the end of the train disappear in the distance. I got up slowly and checked to see if I was all in one piece. I gave the "bobwhite" whistle of a Carolina quail, and got a realistic answer. In a moment Tom Ellzey scrambled up the embankment and said calmly, "How ya doin' Cap'n?"

I told him I was OK, just a few scratches, and whistled again. This time Ricky came over from across the tracks laughing and ribbing me, "That bird of yours doesn't sound very Italian."

I estimated we were 60 to 80 miles from the Swiss border, which had to be off to the west. To get there, our main problem would be food and water, though we had enough of both for that night.

The next day, as we watched German convoys rolling south on a *Strada Nazionale* down in the valley, I made Ricky swap his RAF jacket for Tom's U.S. Army jacket. This created two hybrid combinations that looked less like either an American uniform or a British one. To make Ricky look even less British, I shaved off his handsome mustache dry — to conserve precious water. On top of it, the razer was dull, but I think he minded losing his mustache more than the painful scraping.

That night we went down the valley to a river, where we drank our fill and replenished our canteens. We continued along a main road and in the darkness ran into some Italian soldiers. We pretended we were German and, by God, we got away with it. I was delighted.

About 2:00 in the morning, I was leading our trio down the highway, when I suddenly came up to a parked truck. I decided to brazen it out, and walked right by it. Then I went by another and fast realized with horror I'd walked into the middle of a German convoy that was parked for the night.

I waited for the others to catch up. We agreed to bluff it out as slightly drunk Italian soldiers. We linked arms, slouched over, and kept going. At the fourth truck a voice growled in German, "Halt! Who's there?"

Instantly, every Italian name I ever knew flew out of my head, except last season's Notre Dame quarterback. In my most obsequious voice, I said, "Angelo Bertelli."

That German spat out disgustedly, *"Ach, gehen Sie Weiter!"* (Go along with you!) I was glad he wasn't a Notre Dame fan. We three "Italians" walked happily past the entire convoy.

"Why didn't you go around them in the woods or out in the field?" I inquired.

Here Dick's voice sounded a little strained. "For the simple reason there was a big river on one side and 10,000-foot cliffs on the other."

While at this point I admired his nerve, I questioned his judgment. It sounded like an unnecessary risk to take, regardless of terrain. He went on with his story.

By this time, food and water were critical. I knew we'd have to take a chance and get some soon at a house or a village. By the fourth day, we were at the end of our rope and agreed to risk going into a good-sized town off to the west. When we were about half a mile from it, we passed four Italian soldiers, who eyed us.

Once in town, we followed the sound of a carillon and came to a church built right up to the sidewalk. I thought the priest might help us, so I pushed open a wooden door in a wall next to the church and crossed a courtyard. The priest, who was putting on his vestments, stuck his head out a door. I asked him in German if he could help me. He said he was about to celebrate Mass and would speak to me after the service.

Then the three of us went into the church, because we had to get off that street. When my eyes got used to the darkness, I could see only women kneeling. Up a side aisle, there were candles flickering at a shrine, but there were no seats anywhere. Immediately, I began to feel trapped.

We were shifting around uneasily in the back, when the four soldiers we had passed burst into the church and pointed their rifles at us. I tried in my most haughty German to tell them they had no business coming into the church after us; we were German soldiers, our truck had broken down and we'd just stopped in to see the church for a moment.

These guys were tough. The sergeant told me just as haughtily he was taking us to see his lieutenant, who would find ways to help us. The guns were still pointing, so we went.

He took us to the lieutenant's house, where we were greeted by two fashionably dressed ladies. I got badly shook when one of them addressed us in perfect German. I repeated to her the same story I'd told the sergeant, about our truck breaking down.

Then she asked Ricky who he was. He gave a stumbling answer in German, and she swung around and questioned Tom. He pointed to his throat; I told her he'd been wounded in the throat on the Russian front and was on limited duty as he was unable to talk. Then the lieutenant arrived and offered to take us back to our truck. At that, I knew he was calling my bluff.

From then on, I was sparring to stay in Italy; I knew there were Italian camps for Air Forces prisoners, so I took a deep breath and said in English, "Oh, hell, lieutenant, I guess you know we're not German. We're American flyers. Our aircraft was shot down on a raid over northern Italy. We were forced to parachute and land in a field somewhere near Trento. We've been walking ever since."

You should have seen the change in those people — they all broke into smiles. The older of the two women, it turned out, had a son who was a POW in

America, so I assured her he would be treated well, because the Americans really like the Italians. After that, to my utter surprise, the woman invited us into the house for breakfast.

They actually gave us some toast and marmalade, which we gobbled down, much to the ladies' amusement. But in spite of their treating us so well, it was clear we were prisoners of the Italians. After breakfast, we were sent off in a truck to Trento.

From then on we had a rough time with the interrogations. They continually tried to break down our story that we were American flyers. We managed to keep up the bluff in spite of Tom, who almost got caught with his ID card. Fortunately, I found out, and made him tear it up and flush it down the toilet.

Being "flyers" did have one bad result. We were sent to the Italian Air Force Interrogation Center at Poggio Mirteto and thrown in a dungeon in solitary confinement. I had a particularly nasty time, because I had very bad dysentery and the guard wouldn't let me go to the crapper. The son of a bitch kept telling me it was *"Occupato,"* but I never believed him. They kept us at Poggio nine days and brought us directly to Chieti.

"What happened to Ricky and Tom?" I asked.

"Oh, they're here, too. Ricky was assigned to the British sector, and Tom is in another American building on this side. I haven't seen much of them since. However, I was rather pleased with the results of our escape, and I think they were, too. For one thing, we avoided going to Germany. We're back under Italian administration, and with this armistice we should have another chance to get out. That is, if this SBO doesn't screw us up with his goddam crap about not being allowed to escape."

"The only way I can explain it is that he's bought the commandant's propaganda," I said. "In some crazy way, it got interpreted as an order from British Headquarters."

Larry Allen, who'd been watching us, drifted over. *"Il Colonnello Gooler vuole verdervi, tutti e due,"* he said, imitating the voice of the Radio Roma announcer, and added, *"Immediatamente!"*

"What's he want?" I asked. Larry shrugged and strolled off. Dick smiled. "I suppose that meant he wants to see 'all two' of us right away. I'm as curious as you are."

Dick propped himself against the windowsill in the colonel's little office, and I sat on a wooden box. The colonel was in a formal mood. "Gentlemen," he said, "you two are in an excellent position to make an escape — at the appropriate time. Rossbach, I understand you speak German, and Frelinghuysen, Italian. The combination is an obvious asset."

"And Dick speaks French," I said, "if we get that far."

Ignoring my interruption, the colonel continued: "Now we don't always get orders we agree with. But what *we* think hasn't anything to do with it. Since we are, at the moment, under British command, I have no choice but to tell you as of now, that you do not have permission to escape. Is that perfectly clear?"

I murmured, "Yes, sir," but Dick was seething.

"One more thing," the colonel insisted, "I assume you've discussed Rossbach's escapes as examples. All that may prove useful later on. I'm sorry, but that's it."

Dick and I walked out on the portico. "For Christ's sake, Joe," he said, "you didn't tell me Gooler had bought that shit from the SBO!"

"He's been regular army for over 20 years," I said as evenly as I could. "He was the liaison with the British Eighth Army and, right or wrong, that's the way he's interpreted this one."

"My God, you guys go along with it? Is that what —" He broke off.

I looked at him, feeling my face flush. When he spoke again his voice was almost gentle. "Perhaps we should both think about this some more. It involves some vital decisions for both of us, so let's sleep on matters for the time being."

I had a tormenting conflict within myself: I had a compulsion to follow my training and obey orders. Also, I had the old suspicion that I was still using all this as a crutch to avoid the dangerous risks of making an escape; and behind it all, I had a frightening feeling that if I didn't take my chances and go now, I would miss an opportunity and regret it for the rest of my life.

Dick and I had talked about the Djedeida disaster and the absurd orders that preceded it. Rex Rawie had known what to do about them, and here at Chieti Claude Weaver had also known. And Dick had been caustic and blunt, in four-letter words, about the stupid screw-ups by the U.S. Army, Navy, and Air Forces to which he'd been subjected in North Africa and Sicily. So what had I been doing in my talks with Dick except trying to convince myself I should ignore the SBO's order?

Still, I had some doubts: I was afraid I couldn't keep up with Dick. Suppose he wanted to take a course of action I thought was crazy. Would I be able to go through with it? And his casual attitude toward ways of escaping that I thought were plain suicidal didn't do much for my confidence. I wondered if I could crank myself up to his level of drive in the war against Hitler. What brought home my doubts above all, though, was his willingness to accept the conditions of war, its total brutality, dangers, and hardships. Those were interesting and exciting facts of life to him. Fear seemed to stimulate him — he had asserted, in fact, that it was better than a martini.

This military toughness blended so closely with his essential personality that it was hard for me to distinguish between the two. How was I to get along with him if we were traveling together? To make the partnership work, I would probably have to be willing to accept his leadership in planning and executing a maneuver to get us back to Allied lines. The idea of complete acquiescence to his judgment stuck in my craw.

As Dick had related the story of his escape attempts, he had emerged as a very unusual man. He was clearly more aggressive than I, with a kind of nerve I had never had even before I was captured. As we continued our discussions, whether I wanted him to or not, he soon became my mentor in my obsession to find an escape plan that would be feasible. Under the increasing tension and appalling uncertainty of life in the camp we came to know each other rapidly.

Almost unconsciously I began to attach myself to this newcomer and began to move away from friends I had been with for all these months. Somehow I knew this was the man I wanted to go with, convinced as I was that he had both the techniques and the experience for escaping. Yet still there were those nagging doubts: Could I summon the nerve to attempt an escape? And after that, could I keep up with this man?

Chapter 14

To Obey, or Disobey

15 September 1943

About 11:00 a.m. a German observation plane, a "Fieseler Storch," with black and white crosses and a swastika, buzzed straight over the prison, 100 feet up. Catching a glimpse of it, I felt a nasty sensation shoot up my back. Some prisoners ran out into the courtyard; others hurried into the buildings to grab their escape kits, then came back out. Exasperated with the SBO for ordering them not to escape, they raged at him in bitter obscenities.

A few *carabinieri* came out, resplendent in black uniforms and white gloves, and asked us to go back into our barracks. A number of the prisoners complied, but most of us stayed and argued with the guards. A *carabinieri* sergeant, apparently fearful of losing control, asked several British officers to command us to return to quarters. Later the SBO reaffirmed his directive: no demonstrations and "keep cool, calm, and collected."

That same evening I heard that two British officers had wedged a ladder up against the outside wall. One man was halfway to the top, when a British "patrol" came around a corner, raced to the ladder and knocked it to the ground, and forcibly took the two escapers into "custody." Later, word was circulated that the SBO had had the two men thrown in the cooler to await court-martial when the "approaching" Allies arrived. For the rest of us, the implications were clear: either take the chance on the cooler or go to Germany. And just in case the SBO happened to be wrong about the Allies, work on an uncompleted tunnel was begun again with feverish haste. The "deluxe" tunnel, meanwhile, was prepared as a hiding place.

For five days, we were whipsawed between hopes of freedom and fear of being shipped off to Germany. One day I saw some German trucks stop at the main gate. Two officers got out and entered the camp, one with a face like the colonel who'd interrogated me in Tunis. That incident all came back in a rush: the desperate feeling of being trapped, the plain, cold hatred. Blood pounded in my head, and a kind of electric shock raced through my stomach and chest.

Here and there men would gather in clusters and shout wildly, continuing their tirades against the SBO. Westy had built a device out of wood with a cardboard pointer that he called a "flapmeter." It had a dial with gradations that went from "Calm" to "Hysteria," according to his estimate of the situation. Most of the time he fixed the pointer at "Hysteria," which caused the British to say the Americans had the "wind up." It was true, and it only underscored the idiocy of the order not to escape.

On the 20th, Dick and I watched two British parachute men stepping out around the outer walkway, in full uniform with the crimson balmoral, and with those jaunty, colored handkerchiefs sticking out of the pockets of their battledress jackets.

"Have you seen those handkerchiefs the parachute guys wear?" I asked.

"Yes, and I think I can borrow one for a while. Can you get some paper and a pencil and meet me here in a few minutes?"

We went to a secluded corner in the courtyard next to our bungalow. The handkerchief was a scale map of 1:200,000, but Dick stretched the rubberized silk in order to get a larger scale. Then I selected an area southeast of Chieti and held it while Dick began tracing. When it was finished, our "map" included a rectangle of the Abruzzo region, from the Adriatic 35 miles west to a town called Popoli, which was beyond two ranges of the Apennines. The western boundary of our handkerchief-map also went west of the city of Sulmona, while the southern boundary was below the Trigno River, 50 miles to the south.

That afternoon, I grew apprehensive when it was announced that the SBO would address us over the camp PA system — he could have gotten permission for that only if the Fascist commandant had approved what he was going to say. In a sense, he was actually helping the commandant.

The SBO began with some estimates of the positions of the Allies, and of when they would arrive. During this speech, Larry Allen stood all slumped over, shaking his head. He had changed in the last few days. Admittedly, he had never been the neatest dresser, but now his shirt tails were out, his feet were half in a pair of torn bedroom slippers, his hair hung down over his face. When the SBO finished with his ususal line about "cool, calm, and collected," Larry let out a shriek and started writing on a pad. Seconds later, he put up a notice on his by now very popular bulletin board: "You will be collected in a very few days." In short order, Larry was reprimanded for the third time for "causing a panic among the prisoners."

Rossbach, Warren, and I called an emergency meeting that night, a meeting that turned into a griping session over the same frustrations, and into a debate over whether or not to disobey the SBO's edict. After much haggling, Dick got fed up and stalked out to ask Gooler to change his mind.

He came back very quickly, as angry as I'd yet seen him. "That guy had the crust to remind me of World War I prisoners who were court-martialed for disobeying orders," he said. "I'm telling you guys, I saw another truck with German markings parked outside the front gate today. When I tried to see what the men in it were doing, that Fascist bastard Croce hustled me away and threatened to throw me in the cooler. We go tonight, my friends. Or never."

My response was that I'd been in the military one way or another for 13 years and wasn't about to disobey a direct order. But the sense of being trapped grew worse even as I mouthed the old platitude, and I wondered why I was still clinging to it.

Dick exhaled sharply. "I couldn't be more uneasy about staying in this damn place. Every instinct I have tells me it's dead wrong, but for tonight I guess I'll go along."

By this time, tired enough to fall asleep on my feet, I left the others and went off to my bunk. In spite of my fatigue, I dozed fitfully. Weird forms and colors spun around in my mind. Once I thought I heard trucks nearby, grinding in low gear, but decided it was part of the dream and turned over, lapsing finally into a deep sleep.

21 September

I suddenly awoke, jolted as if I'd been told I was going to die. It was 4:45 a.m., still black outside. Someone called angrily, *"Posten! Posten! Was ist geschehen? Warum bist du nicht hier?"*

"Oh, my God," I groaned aloud. "We should have gone last night!" Maybe it had been a nightmare. But the German voices shouting from the walls around the camp snapped me back to reality. My spirits were at their lowest level since I'd been captured.

For these last crucial days I'd sat in Chieti, living each day for itself, denying the part of me that knew the inevitable. Despite the growing sense of doom, I had done nothing, and I now cursed myself with every name I could think of. I was a tortured soul in hell, who had had his chance but lacked the courage to challenge a system that had become an end in itself, without mind or reason.

At the first streaks of daylight, I saw them: tough, precise German paratroopers, manning every guard station on top of the walls, armed with pistols, rifles, machine-guns. Yesterday I could have had freedom for the taking of a minor risk. Today I was once again a *Kriegsgefangener*, a prisoner of war.

That morning Larry Allen shuffled around the camp in his bedroom

Right: 20 September 1943. A relaxed and friendly Italian guard. Below: 21 September 1943. Alert troops of a German parachute division. (Drawn by Gordon Horner at Chieti and later taken to England via Germany. From *For You The War is Over*, by Gordon Horner [London: Falcon Press, 1948]. Reprinted with the kind permission of the author.)

slippers, his eyes staring glassily ahead. When I asked him how soon he thought we might be moved, he answered with a jumble of words — half in English, half in German. Later, I heard him give an imitation of a train announcer calling out stations along the route through northern Italy, Austria, and into Germany. His voice was shrill, somewhat hysterical, eerie.

For the next 48 hours I continued to feel as rotten as I had in those first moments following my capture. These two days found me wandering around the courtyard, numbed by the knowledge that we were headed for Germany. British officers strode by quickly, as if on important business, with their flushed, tense faces turned the other way.

23 September

Someone shaking my shoulder woke me abruptly. A dim bulb was glowing in the room, but it was still dark outside. Sentries around the building were shouting in German, and Colonel Gooler was standing over me.

"This is it, Joe," he said, in a voice like a weary old man's. "The Germans are taking us away in two hours. They claim it's only to a dispersal area, but you can't believe a word of it. There'll be breakfast in 30 minutes, but it won't be much. Tell the rest of the men in the bungalow."

As he walked out, I had a flash of resentment. Why wasn't he going to do it? I looked at my watch — 3:45. The men cursed at me: I had backed the colonel and this was what they'd got; they sounded as if I were taking them to Germany.

I'd already packed all the kit I could carry in my old Italian suitcase made of brown cardboard, even jammed in an extra set of clothes and Alan's heavy sweater. I'd saved enough Red Cross food for one good meal, which I'd also squeezed in. Now I stuffed my three precious tins of New Zealand chocolate in my pockets, along with some razorblades and a rusty safety razor. On my belt I hung my canteen. Lying on my bunk, I stared at my diary and thought of all those hours I'd put into it, carefully recording events while they were fresh in my mind. But I'd written it all in ink, and it was sure to get wet. So I tried shoving it under my shirt, but it was far too bulky for any kind of a tight squeeze. Then, reluctantly, I threw it in the trash can, feeling as if I'd lost a friend. Dick, looking like a bear waked up in the winter, joined Len and me in the mess hall.

A German trooper stuck his head in the door and bellowed, " 'Raus! 'Raus! Alle heraus!" We straggled out into the central courtyard, swearing at the Germans, at the SBO, at ourselves. Crowds of prisoners stood about, holding boxes, rolls of clothing, homemade knapsacks, and overcoats from the Red Cross. On the central walkway 150 British prisoners who were going with us had already started to line up, but all the Americans were still milling around. We grudgingly began to shuffle into line when a Feldwebel shouted at us, "Achtung! Achtung! Schnell! Schnell!"

While lining up, a few Americans muttered at him; one said quite audibly,

"Christ, tell that bastard to shut up!" A British officer spoke hurriedly to an American major, who turned around and barked at us, "Don't fool around with these men. They're not Italian guards, you know." After that we lined up on the double. After the Germans had counted us three times, one of our officers took over and marched us out the main gate. I plodded on, struggling with my suitcase, which kept banging against people's legs.

It was strange and scary, exiting from the prison, and I remembered the sensation I'd had leaving Capua. Every moment from here on would have to be weighed for its escape potential. No more ducking the issue with excuses. This was a time of reckoning.

A column of seven antiquated German and Italian trucks stood on the far side of the highway, facing southeast. That puzzled me. The map had shown the main road northward as leading up from Pescara, northeast of us on the coast. These trucks were headed in the opposite direction.

As the Germans started counting us again, this time into groups of 50, I looked across the road and observed how different the season was from when we had arrived in January. Now, fields of vegetables were bordered with bushes and thick green undergrowth — plenty of places for a man to get under cover.

Our group of 50 was ordered to mount up in the back of an open-bodied truck with a cargo space about 15 feet long. We clambered up, pushing and shoving as if in a football scrimmage and, once in the truck, bumped and fell into each other, trying to get a place to stand. Eventually I got to the side of the truck and wedged myself against it, while several in the group kicked at my suitcase and bitched about it, and about me, too.

No sooner were we all aboard when the Germans ordered us to dismount, then to mount up again. The tailgate was high, so this time we boosted each other up, and the men in the truck helped haul the rest aboard. Again the Germans ordered us to dismount, and I heard a British prisoner grumble, "Fucking Krauts are plain bloody-minded." This harassment was taking place up and down the whole convoy.

When all 350 prisoners were loaded one last time, a *Feldwebel* shouted an order. Two troopers leaped from the last truck, raced to the side of the road, set up a machine-gun, and fired bursts into bushes around the fields. From command to first round took about 20 seconds. Italian civilians, mostly women in long black skirts and bare-legged children, ran from the fields in all directions. A few old men hobbled away stiffly, one of them shaking his fist at the Germans as he went. From the front of our truck, an American pilot growled, "OK, Krauts, knock it off! We get the message."

The two troopers then mounted up as fast as they had jumped down. The Germans never bothered to find out whether any of those Italians had been hit.

The trucks headed southeast down the *Strada Nazionale*. After about a mile, they swung west through the valley of the Pescara River, toward Popoli. Len Warren and Connie Kreps were in my group. We squirmed and wriggled until we got near enough to talk about where we might be going.

To the west the massif of the Gran Sasso appeared to be suspended in the sky. South of it, below the gorge cut by the Pescara River, the great hogback of the Maiella stretched southward to the horizon, its upper reaches fissured by long, rocky ravines. These were the high Apennines, rising in places to nearly 10,000 feet. They lay between us and the Allied armies.

The wind was frigid as we rumbled down the highway doing about 50. For a second or two I thought of jumping, then decided it would be suicide; if I wasn't killed by the fall, the guards in the following trucks would riddle me before I got away. When we entered the river gorge, I completely dismissed the idea. Mountains that appeared to be 4,000 to 5,000 thousand feet high rose on both sides.

An hour out of Chieti we entered a long valley that ran south past Popoli. As we rolled through the main *piazza* of the town, crowds of stony-faced people stared at us. A few prisoners waved, but no one waved back.

From my studies of the map I recalled that below the town the *Strada Nazionale* headed straight down the lower part of Italy. To our left, towering above us, was the forbidding Monte Morrone, its massive flanks dotted with dun-colored boulders and cut by long rock slides and crevasses. Far above, brown crags disappeared into clouds. In places the mountain's cliffs looked too steep to scale without equipment. How the hell would I climb that? I wondered. Below, an ancient town, in defiance of gravity, clung to the side of the declivity.

Len glanced up at the mountain and shook his head slowly, a hopeless expression on his face. He told me that an Englishman up in front had found out from the guard that we were going to Camp 78 at Fonte d'Amore (Fountain of Love), near Sulmona, which had a railhead. That explained why we had come this way; otherwise, it wouldn't have made any sense, because we were headed almost south, toward the Allied lines.

The leading truck slowed down and turned onto a narrow road between two hedges. A guard in front scrambled up on the roof of the cab and scanned his truckload of prisoners, his knuckles white as he gripped his rifle.

Just as our truck swung off the road, something moved violently among the men in the truck ahead of us. Our guard and the one ahead swung around and fired into the hedge on our right. A prisoner snapped, "Don't look! Someone jumped!"

"Christ, I hope he made it," Len said, prayerfully.

My heart had skipped when those rifles went off. For a moment, I was the man in the bushes — hiding, ducking, perhaps wounded. Chilled by the image, I shook myself and tried to think of something else.

We drove through a small town called Badia, with little tile-roofed stone houses. A quarter of a mile further we passed in through gates in the barbed-wire enclosure around a concentration camp. German guards with machine-guns manned high wooden towers at the corner of the camp, while patrols walked between rows of wire.

We dismounted and were lined up across an open area, ankle-deep in powdery dirt, while a few prisoners in ragged clothes looked on. In reasonably good English a German officer told us that we would be assigned to quarters later, and that in the meantime we were dismissed. It was a relief, at least, to see that the officer was not a paratrooper.

Len and Connie and I walked over to one of the Camp 78 prisoners. Len asked him how long he'd been in 78. "About two weeks," he said. "Two days after the Armistice, the Italian guards disappeared. Three thousand of us went off up into those mountains."

"When were you recaptured?" Len asked.

"Well we weren't," the man said, looking at the ground. "But they would have caught us anyway. We couldn't stand it. We nearly died of cold and starvation up in those mountains, so a bunch of us walked in."

At this incredible utterance, I wanted to get away from this guy. Len, however, kept on in a soft, relaxed voice: "Must have been pretty bad up there. Did the local Italians help you?"

"They tried to, but there were too many of us. Most were rounded up by German patrols and shipped out to Germany. This is the railhead, you know."

We stepped back, feeling awkward and embarrassed. Now I was glad Len had followed up on the man's story. The lessons we had learned as a result were vital: don't go in crowds, get away from the camp as fast as possible, look out for German patrols.

Chapter 15

Fonte d'Amore

At noon Connie Kreps and I sat on the barracks steps and ate bits of food we had brought from Chieti. Mine was horsemeat and stale bread. Connie glanced right and left and said, "Hey, Joe, what do think about this place?"

"At least it doesn't have ten-foot brick walls. Let's have a look before the Germans decide to lock us in for the night."

We pretended to be exercising as we walked the perimeter just inside the fences. They were all barbed wire, very different from Chieti. But here the towers also had machine-guns manned by German guards, who stood at the railings of the platforms, gazing at the prisoners.

Barracks ran north and south across the camp, with a wide center walkway down the middle. Five parallel fences of barbed wire — some straight, some concertinas, a few X-frames — lined the north side. An overhead lightbulb hung at midpoint in the barrier, but the guards seemed to patrol there less frequently. The German command post building stood next to the north walkway near the midpoint.

The fences on the west side were beyond the dusty parade gound. These had just three rows of wire, but the guard in the highest tower could fire along them in either direction. In one spot a prisoner had cut an opening, which was only loosely repaired. Connie said, "That's tempting but much too obvious."

The south side was heavily guarded, and German billets stood immediately outside the fences, so we wasted no more time over it. We ruled out the east side too, with its four strong, brand-new barriers. It was the most heavily patrolled of all.

We had walked for two hours when we were ordered to report for building and room assignments. I left Connie and went to collect my suitcase and what was left of my food. I was surprised to find my room assignment was with

Dick Rossbach. Since we were alone, I asked, "What are you thinking of doing?"

"Me? I'm seriously considering going through the section where the wire's cut. You want to come?" he said as if we were talking about having a cup of tea.

"In broad daylight?"

"Possibly," in the same calm tone.

I gasped, floundering for an excuse. "You know we have to get permission from Colonel Gooler." My voice sounded kind of high-pitched.

"Of course, let's go and ask him again. This time he may have changed his mind." Rossbach gave me a sidelong glance that made me shiver.

Colonel Gooler was sitting hunched over on a bare wire cot in a room he was sharing with an Air Forces colonel. Their clothes were rumpled, both men unshaven. Gooler managed a sheepish smile. "I know what you fellows are here for. I gave you a bum steer about leaving back at Chieti."

I felt embarrassed. "That's over and done with, Colonel. What we want to know is, do we have your permission to go *now*?"

"Frelinghuysen, so far as I'm concerned, you're free to go any time. I'll accept responsibility for any repercussions from the Senior British Officer when he arrives from Chieti. But first of all, we know it's not going to be any picnic out there. In addition, two Britishers from the Chieti Escape Committee told me the guards here have gone bloody-minded. One of the prisoners who jumped from the truck this morning tried to surrender and was shot dead with his hands in the air."

Dick's voice was impatient. "We understand all that, Colonel." He turned to me. "Joe, we have plans to make. Let's get moving." We saluted and left.

As we set out on our reconnaissance, the second one for me, Dick announced, "Escaping is like doing your Christmas shopping; you've got to do it early to avoid the crowds." I had a sudden memory of laughing people hurrying along a darkened street lit by red, white, and green lights, a choir somewhere singing, "O Holy Night —"

I yanked myself back to reality and said, "I'm willing to agree with your selection of that section of broken fence as the place to go, but for God's sake, I won't go along with doing it in broad daylight." Despite my protests, I knew I was going to have to make an agonizing decision; Gooler's warnings still rang in my ears. Dick continued, "I've definitely decided I'm going to try it in half an hour. You can come along or not, but you'll have to make up your mind soon, because I'm going anyway."

Plain suicide. All that the guard in the tower had to do was glance our way, swing his machine-gun, and shoot straight along that wire. He could hit us with his eyes closed. I went on being evasive. "I'm not going to make up my mind now; I'll decide later when I see how the situation looks. I think you're crazy." Totally unperturbed, he turned away and went on stuffing little pieces of food in his battledress jacket.

Just before 5:00, I went to find Connie and Len Warren. They were sitting on their cots, looking as if they were already on the train to Germany. In spite of my doubts, I said, "We're going in a few minutes, do you want to come along?"

"In broad daylight?" Connie said. "You got to be out of your mind. Why don't you wait till dark? I might go with you then, but I'm doggoned if I'll go in daylight right under that machine-gun."

"I agree with you, but Dick is convinced there'll be so damn many trying it tonight the guards will have a shooting gallery. I still haven't made up my mind, but I'll say goodbye now." As we shook hands, I couldn't tell whether Len and Connie felt hurt or were just sorry for us.

Dick and I walked down toward the parade ground, where some off-duty Germans were playing soccer. A group of prisoners had gathered near the field to watch. The sentry up in the tower occasionally laughed or cheered for a good play.

A certain Major Parsons, who had been involved in some escape attempts at Chieti, walked over to us. From his expression, I assumed he already knew of our intentions.

"You two are going?" he asked.

Dick nodded.

"I can help you with a diversion. Give me a couple of minutes to get it started."

"Take five," Dick said. "We're going over near the wire in that corner behind me. Warn everybody not to look in that direction."

"OK, I know," Parsons said and strolled back to the group of prisoners.

Dick glanced out of the corner of his eye at the place where the wire had been cut. While looking at me, he explained, "After we get through the first fence, we'll have to move sideways about 15 feet before we can get through the second and third."

A cheer went up from the group watching the soccer game, as a player was dribbling the length of the field. When he neared the goal, they let out a thunderous roar and the guard leaned forward over the wooden railing and yelled something in German at a player. His machine-gun sat on a swivel mount next to him. A half turn to his right, and he would be in position to fire along the fences at us.

Then I was dimly aware some fist fights had broken out among the prisoners. Guards were shouting. My stomach churned, my chest tightened; I felt as if I might choke. Dick seemed impervious to the whole thing. Suddenly, he said under his breath, "All right, here goes!"

I heard myself say, "OK, I'm with you!"

Dick plunged down into the wire, making a hell of a racket. I snatched a look at the guard, but he was busy shouting commands at the brawling men. Dick ran sideways and slipped through the second row. I dropped forward, shoving hard between the bottom strands. I flailed, scrambled, fought off the wire, jumped up, ran left, flopped down again, wrestled more wire. This can't be me here, I thought. It must be someone else. Suddenly, I was on the road outside the camp.

Dick began to walk sedately along this road, tripped on more wire, fell hard on his face and knees, cursing. "For Christ's sake, shut up," I snapped.

Hoping we looked like off-duty German soliders, I followed close on his heels. But something warm and wet was running down my face, my OD shirt was torn, my pants ripped from seat to ankle, and with Dick in British battledress, we did not look much like off-duty German soldiers.

Cautiously we skirted the edge of Fonte d'Amore, passing German billets. Now a building stood between us and the camp, blocking the tower sentry's view. We turned away from it onto a street leading into town. A few townspeople eyed us suspiciously.

Further along, a man's face covered with shaving soap peered out a window above us. Dick stared straight ahead, kept walking. The face disappeared. A second later, a muscular arm thrust out the window, pointing a pistol down at us. It was a Luger. The man shouted, *"Halt! Was ist den das? Halt! Oder ich schiesse!"*

Some townspeople raced for the nearest doorways, but Dick stood his ground, arguing with the man in fluent German. Now the street was deserted. Dick interpreted, "He tells me he'll shoot us if we don't go back in. What do you want to do?"

I thought, Christ, what a crazy thing to ask, that son-of-a-bitch couldn't miss! But I fought down a panicky answer and tried to act nonchalant. "We're damn easy targets," I said quietly.

Dick turned back up the road toward the camp. When no guards appeared, he reversed direction and walked off on a small road running parallel to the camp. I followed, staring straight ahead. Soon we came abreast of another German billet, where, out in front, some Germans were drinking wine. When they saw us, they began to roar with laughter. One put down his glass and strode over, shouted in German, and pointed toward the south gate of the camp. I understood clearly: "Go back or we shoot."

When his comrades made sneering remarks about us and the U.S. Army, Dick shouted back in German. Two guards with rifles ran out of the camp and waved toward the gate. We were shunted back into PG 78. Dick whispered, "Now we got to make damn sure they don't throw us in the cooler."

I should have felt horrible, but somehow I did not. In fact, I was elated. Perhaps it was because, at the very least, Dick and I had managed to get outside this blasted concentration camp, if only for a few minutes. No one else in our group had done it, and certainly not under the nose of a German guard with a machine-gun. Some of the stored-up guilt I had felt from being captured began to lift.

As we were being marched back past the parade ground, I was not at all ashamed that we had been caught — rather I felt proud we had escaped, even for a few minutes. The soccer game was over, and the third contingent of Chieti prisoners was unloading from trucks near the north gate, about to be lined up for a head count. Not one of them looked directly at us. I caught some furtive glances, but the prisoners took their eyes off us fast. That told me they knew what had happened.

Gradually they began to shuffle their feet in the heavy dust, which rose in dirty gray clouds and spread through the whole formation. German guards ran around the flanks screaming, *"Halt! Halt! Stillstehen!"*

A loud murmuring sound arose from the men and swelled in volume. Some howled. Clouds of dust enveloped us. We slipped into the mass of prisoners, ducking and twisting through them to the side toward our barracks, while guards continued running and yelling over by the parade ground.

We emerged slowly on the east side, Dick with his sedate walk, as though out for an afternoon stroll. Every step away was a victory. In seconds we found ourselves around the corner of a building. I glanced over my shoulder; the parade ground was still in an uproar, dust clouds hanging in the air, prisoners shouting, the captors barking commands. The thought kept repeating in my mind: "We've done it! We've done it! Been first out through wire under German guns!" Dick and I ambled up to our quarters, but I was flying.

As we walked up outside our building, American prisoners surrounded us, all talking at once, wanting the story. "The air is much fresher and cleaner outside," I informed them. "It has more oxygen. Why don't you try it?" I laughed to cover the odd sound of my voice, which had cracked a little. I decided I wanted no more questioning, and Dick and I ducked into our room.

Connie was waiting there for me, hands on hips, battered Air Forces cap on the back of his head. He was wearing only a pair of frayed trunks, and the muscles of his tanned shoulders stood out like thick ropes. All he said was, "I'm glad you guys didn't get hurt." Yet I knew he was upset we had gone without him, and said, "Come on, Connie, get your stuff together, we're going again in an hour or two."

"No, Joe, I don't think it's propitious." His voice was clipped. And he added tersely, "I'm not going tonight, I'm going tomorrow." He left, looking unhappy, but Dick and I bounded back to the euphoric mood, laughing and joking about the wonderful smell of the free air out there. I felt as if I had had a triple shot of adrenaline. "Dick," I said, "I insist we shave for our next escape attempt. We must look our best, you know."

While we shaved with water from our canteens, Frank Gallo and Larry Allen came and sat on the steps outside our room. I described to them, in Italian, how wonderful it was outside and suggested that they might want to come back some fine day after the war and spend a vacation in this region. I embellished the suggestion by inventing beautiful girls we had seen in the village.

Doc Gallo muttered, *"Non esistono in quel villaggio, tali creature."*

I said, "We didn't have time for them then, but we enjoyed it so much on the other side of the wire we'll be going back there soon."

We finished shaving, and I changed my torn clothes, putting on my shirt with captain's insignia I had sewed on, an OD sweater, and a pair of OD pants. It would pass, I hoped, as U.S. Army uniform. Then I pocketed my New Zealand tins and some other chocolate I had saved and went outside where Larry and Doc were still waiting. Doc said, "We want to go with you very badly. You and Dick have the imagination and ability to carry it out. Just let us know when you're going and we'll be ready."

I said, "I'm not sure yet." But I was embarrassed and very unhappy. Back at Chieti, I had been after Larry for months to get in shape, but he had not done a damn thing about it. Still soft and pudgy, he would not stand a chance. Doc Gallo was a different matter. He was in far better shape and, besides, he had black hair: he looked like a native of Southern Italy and spoke Italian like one. Frankly, I thought he would be better off going alone. Continuing to stall, I told them I would let them know later. Their expressions told me they saw right through it. As they wandered off, I knew I had hurt them too.

7:30 p.m.

The sun had fallen below the mountains to the west, and the dusk had settled in the long valley we had come down that morning. But the towering rock promontories north of the camp were still tinged with brilliant orange.

Dick and I refilled our canteens and began to prowl the outer walkway, just inside the wire. Curfew was at 9:30, so we still had nearly two hours. Even though I had been on my feet most of the time since noon, I was not at all tired. I was too pumped up at the thought of freedom.

We studied the wire. The hole where we had gone through on the west side was no good — the Germans had set up a machine-gun right at the spot. On my earlier tour of the camp with Connie I had already ruled out the south side as too heavily patrolled, and the east likewise. That left the north, with its five rows of wire.

The north, toward the huge mountain, was now the darkest section Dick and I had seen. As we were scrutinizing it, a man emerged from the shadows and said with a cockney accent, "I've dimmed the light with a bit of foil from my fags. Had to be careful not to put it out, or Jerry would be on it in no time."

"Good show," I remarked, and he left.

In the twilight we could make out the five wire fences, less tight than the south and east, and not as heavily patrolled. At one point the wire ran only a few feet from the command post. Dick whispered, "The Germans wouldn't dream anyone would try it right by their CP."

Staring up at the black mountain above us, he continued, "When we get out, we'll be heading north, which is good — remember those guys told us Jerry's patrolling to the south? My idea is to go up the western ridge of that thing six or eight miles, then cut across it and head south in the next valley. How high is it anyway?"

"About 5,000 feet, according to a guard back at Chieti. It's called Monte Morrone."

A British OR came down from the top of the camp and informed us, "Four just got out up there. So far they're clean away." He walked off quickly.

"Joe, all hell's going to break loose any minute. Let's haul our ass out of here!"

This time I didn't hesitate. "OK, I'll go first."

Right opposite the command post I selected an X-frame sawhorse strung in loops. It was actually a gate, fastened with twists of wire, where sentries went through to patrol between the fences. I had a quick look up the hill: almost completely dark, patrol out of sight.

Unwinding the wire, I shoved the frame hard, moving it about eight inches. I slipped through it sideways and dropped into a slit trench next to fence two. Lying prone, I tried to crawl under the strands close to the ground, but they snagged my sweater and canteen.

Dick whispered angrily, "You damn fool, go through on your back and hold it away with your hands."

I twisted, picked off the barbs, squirmed over on my back. Holding the wire away, I wriggled under, stood up between fences two and three, ran to a wired gate off to my left, untied the wire and squeezed through. At fence four, I flopped down on my back and was under it in seconds, heart pounding. Dick was right with me.

We crawled about 20 yards to fence five: actually a stone wall with wire on top. I got up and climbed over carefully, trying not to dislodge any rocks, but a couple fell, sounding like a landslide. I dropped down on my stomach. "OK so far?" I whispered. I was sweating all over.

"Stop gabbing, keep moving!"

I was startled when I heard someone crawling off to our left and nudged Dick. "Hell, that's no German," he said aloud. "They don't bother to be quiet around a prison camp at night."

Relieved, I jumped up, and ran in a crouch for about 300 yards, well away from the sound, then crept on hands and knees past a black, silent house. In

100 yards more, we came to another fence, stood up, and picked our way over it.

This time, an American voice called softly, "Who's over there?"

I heard him walking toward us. He turned out to be a pilot from Chieti, waiting for a group of buddies, and he asked if we'd seen them. I told him no, and wished him luck.

Dick muttered, "Wish *us* luck for Christ's sake, and get going." We moved on, fast, wanting no more contact. Up over rocks we scrambled, crossing gullies, heading north along the western shoulder of the Morrone. Below, to our left, rows of lights blinked from a building that looked like a huge factory. Climbing steeper and steeper ridges, we measured our progress by the distance we had gone beyond that building.

I tripped and fell into a ditch full of brambles, tearing my pants and skinning my knees. Behind me, Dick fell too, let out a "Fuck it!" as he picked himself up. All at once, brilliant flares burst in the sky above the camp, and we froze in position, half way down in the gully.

Dazzling blue-white light cast gray and black outlines on the buildings, rifle and automatic weapons fire cracked in an irregular staccato. Hunching low in the shadows, I thought about what I would have done if the flares had gone up when we were in the wire. They died out slowly and I clambered out of the ditch, feeling shaken. "I wonder who that was for?" I asked.

In the faint light, I saw Dick shake his head and look away.

A bright three-quarter moon rose as we kept on climbing. By this time, I had sweated through my clothes, as much from tripping and falling as from the climb. Crazy with thirst, I drank half the water in my canteen. Dick scolded me, "You'll never make it if you don't discipline yourself better than that." Now I grew desperate, not knowing how I would get along without a lot more.

At about 10:00 we crossed an open field, passing some houses down to our left. In the distance, dogs barked, and while I was peering at the dark shadows between the houses, I tripped and fell flat on top of a huge square stone. Dick got on his hands and knees and began feeling the top of it. Countersunk into the large stone was a small round one with an iron ring. He lifted it up and dropped in a pebble. It splashed — a miracle! Almost delirious with relief, I reached down, gripping my canteen tightly in my fingers. As the water sucked in, I remembered Doc Winston's warnings about cisterns and springs but laughed at the thought.

I filled and refilled our canteens as we gulped the water down. From here we stepped off more briskly, proceeding steadily higher and higher. "I hope the Germans don't hear your stomach gurgling," Dick said.

From the North Star, I guessed our route to be northwest. This took us to within 50 yards of a small hamlet. When more dogs began to bark wildly, I suddenly wanted to run. "Dick," I said urgently, "they'll wake the dead — we

Roccacasale, with a shoulder of Monte Morrone in the background. (Reprinted with permission from Pepi Merisio and under license from the Touring Club Italiano, Milan, Italy.)

have to get away from that racket."

"That'd be a waste of time. Those mutts probably howl like that if they hear a rabbit." Nevertheless I insisted, and we swung wide, watching the houses for signs of movement. We were half a mile beyond before the dogs stopped their clamor.

Toward 1:00 in the morning, we stumbled into a broken-down, weed-filled vineyard where some of the stakes had collapsed and dried-up vines lay all about. Though most of the grapes had been picked, Dick hunted and found some small wrinkled ones that tasted like raisins. Grateful for even the smallest things, we cleaned off several vines, had a sparing drink, and went on feeling revived.

By 2:30 I could see ahead the white outline of buildings in a town perched on the side of a cliff, toward which a narrow trail led. I said, "My feeling is that this is the town we saw yesterday morning off to our left, after our trucks had passed Popoli."

"So what about it?" Dick asked, not really interested.

"Well, I think it's Roccacasale, and we've come six or seven kilometers as the crow flies."

"For God's sake, is that all? I feel as if we'd made at least three times that."

Sheer rock walls, shining in the moonlight, rose to the right of the town, while to our left, the mountain dropped off steeply below the houses. Straight ahead, they huddled against the mountain as if they had been piled on top of one another. Between us and the town some cattle moved restlessly and began a steady lowing.

Bewildered, I questioned, "Where the hell do we go now?"

"Obviously we can't go around the town, so we'll have to go right through it," he said. I had come to recognize his soft, tense voice that signaled impatience and irritation with me, and I felt like a kid who'd asked a dumb question. Still, I blurted out, "That's crazy. How do we know it isn't full of Germans?"

His voice grew tenser. "I'll go ahead this time, but dammit, don't drag so far behind you lose sight of me."

He walked along the trail, straight toward the town. And though I was convinced we were making a mistake, I followed at a distance of some 50 yards. He reached a paved roadway in the town while I was still stumbling over rocks. Dick walked fast, with a rolling gait; his broad back started to draw away from me. I tried to run, but tripped and stubbed my toes in the uneven light. When I reached the pavement, he was merely a vague form a hundred yards ahead, and each time he turned a corner in the narrow streets, I lost sight of him for a few moments. I was starting to get out of breath.

At one juncture, I called as loudly as I dared: "Hey, slow down!" Evidently it wasn't loud enough, for he disappeared around a corner. Quickly, I ran up to it on my toes and looked down the street. Not there! Then I turned back and went up a narrow alley, trying not to make a sound. The alley ended in a half-circle of doorways with no exit. In a near panic, I hurried back, knowing that each moment he was getting farther and farther away.

Now I was thoroughly frightened. The houses made weird geometric

The *piazza* at Roccacasale.

figures in the moonlight. I heard voices inside the houses, and lights showed through cracks in boarded-up windows. The occupants must have been getting up to feed their animals and had surely heard me, and any moment now would be calling the German sentries.

It was nearly 4:00 when I came upon a tiny *piazza*, hurried across the open area, and ran up a flight of steps. At the top, three alleys led off; one went up, one down, one straight ahead. Gasping for breath, I debated: Which way had he gone? For a moment I couldn't think; then I realized we would have to climb the Morrone anyway, so he must have gone that way. I took the right-hand alley, up the mountain.

As the tiny cobbled street grew steeper and steeper, the houses thinned out and were finally left behind. Eventually the road became a vague trail, winding up the cliffs in the shadows and moonlight — Dick couldn't have gone that way.

At this point I felt it was too dangerous to go back into town, and since it would be getting light soon I turned off to the the left of the trail and started down the mountain over the rocks. After a few minutes, I came to a near-perpendicular drop, where I lay on the ground, hung backwards over the edge, and probed blindly with my feet till they got a firm hold. I crouched on a ledge, peered over, and found myself looking down at a 70° slope to yet another ledge. I slithered down, landed on a pile of shale, and sent it clattering over the brink, the pieces bounding hundreds of feet below. Yet I kept on descending — I couldn't have gone up if I'd wanted to.

When I'd slid down some 300 feet, I came to a narrow trail running parallel to the mountain and crept along it. A voice called out to me softly in Italian, "Who are you? Where are you going?"

It was only a shepherd out early with his flock, I assured myself; I answered in Italian, remembering the guard at Chieti. Surely I could appeal to this man; he would be friendly. The reaction to my agreeable answer was a low and familiar chuckle. Dick was around a corner, leaning back against the cliff. Though I had a surge of delight, I was ashamed of my panic and furious at him for not waiting for me earlier.

"How the hell did you know who it was?"

"Oh, it wasn't all that difficult. When I heard you coming down those cliffs, it had to be either you or a herd of elephants."

I wanted to laugh and cry all at once. Dick just roared, but after a moment he said, "Don't worry, I was every bit as glad to see you as you were to see me. Now we're far enough from that camp, and I've just about had it. Let's find a place to sleep." High up to our right faint streaks of gray showed in the sky.

We followed the trail for perhaps half a mile, when it leveled off into a field, the ground gently sloping away to our left. Straight ahead a huge dark tree stood at the foot of a rise. We might sleep under it, I thought. But when we walked around back of it, we found a large black hole that bored into the hillside. I crouched down and started into the pitch-dark aperture, immediately cracking my head. Cursing the protruding rock, I went down on my hands and knees and crawled in. I found a cave roughly four feet high, running into the hill for about 15 feet.

All at once I was too exhausted to worry about hunger or the jagged rocks on the floor of the cave. Dawn showed clearly through the opening as we stretched out and fell asleep.

Chapter 16

Uneasy Freedom

24 September

In the late morning I awoke with a vicious headache, shook my head,
wished I hadn't, and sat up. Dick was sitting at the mouth of the cave, gazing
out over the valley to the west. He was leaning forward, the back of his
battledress jacket covered with bits of dirt and stones.

"Have you got a headache?" he asked, without turning around.

"How did you know I was awake?"

"I heard you groan. I've been watching convoys of trucks on that highway
down there. Come out and breathe some of this free air. It'll clear your head."

I crept up beside him. A thousand yards or so west and down in the valley,
on the *Strada Nazionale* that ran from Popoli to Sulmona, a steady stream of
vehicles was moving south just as we had done the day before.

"They're German trucks," I said. "And by God, the men in them look like
prisoners." Their slouched positions and ragged appearance were unmistakable.

Dick said, "They're probably the last contingent from Chieti on their way
to Fonte d'Amore and ultimately to Germany."

At the mention of Germany I felt again that ghastly trapped feeling I had
had in the truck with Len and Connie, knowing I was going to *Deutschland* for
God knows how many years. Now those guys down there felt that way —
Christ, was I glad I wasn't one of them! As I watched the column of trucks
until the last one had disappeared, a thrill of excitement surged through me —
I was free . . . in a fashion, that is.

We talked about the military situation for the next hour. The British Eighth
Army was here on the east side of Italy; the Americans were over to the west.
Our first idea was to travel toward our own troops, but that wouldn't make

sense. We would have to cross the rest of the Apennines and move through all of Italy's heavily guarded rail and highway arteries, which were carrying supplies and ammunition to the German divisions fighting in the south.

I reminded Dick that back at Chieti a Scottish officer had told us that the British army would arrive in "two or three days." Dick let out a guffaw, "Oh, for God's sake. Those guys were just kidding themselves. The British can't possibly get this far north in less than two or three weeks. Before you woke up, I saw convoys of German infantry, armor, and artillery, going south. With that kind of build-up and these mountains, it could be more like a few months."

Rummaging in his pockets, he pulled out a couple of half-eaten cans of Red Cross food; one held ham paste, the other offered a fish concoction with an aroma like cod liver oil. It was 30 hours since I'd had anything like a meal and the smells, both good and bad, sent my appetite out of control.

Into my own pockets I had stuffed my "last reserve" of three tins of New Zealand chocolate. These couldn't be touched. But I had one and a half bars of chocolate-flavored U.S. D ration that had been issued back in the States, to be used only for emergencies. They were too much like candy, however, and the men consumed them even when they were having regular meals. Someone in the quartermaster corps had gotten the brilliant idea of impregnating the bars with kerosene to prevent the men from eating them except in a true emergency. The QM, however, hadn't taken the time to investigate the effect of ingested kerosene, and a lot of men wound up in the hospital. Fortunately the Red Cross hadn't been that imaginative, so mine were OK. I took a hefty bite out of the half-bar.

Dick gave me a hard look, his eyebrows up, his forehead furrowed. He asked indignantly, "Is that part of your reserve ration?"

Feeling a little guilty and at the same time a little angry, I shot back, "No! It certainly is not. I haven't touched my New Zealand stuff."

"Well, I want to warn you, things are going to be extremely tough — worse than anything you ever dreamed of at Capua or Chieti. It's going to require the greatest self-restraint not to eat our reserve rations when we get really hungry."

I didn't answer all that, feeling somewhat the way I had when Colonel Hunt dressed me down that night in Carolina when one of my howitzers was wrecked.

I had begun to realize that Dick was proving difficult at times but, dammit, so was I. In my more reflective moments I recognized my genuine fondness for him and my great respect for his judgment. The last thing in the world I wanted was an angry exchange that might break up our escape team. I was certain he didn't want it either.

He pulled out the map he had drawn from the parachutist's handkerchief. Together we estimated our position to be about eight miles north of Sulmona and five miles from a town called Corfinio. We looked west and thought we could identify the latter in the distant haze across the valley. Far off to our right we could see a corner of a big town of Popoli, just around the shoulder of Monte Morrone.

"Look down there in the fields," Dick suggested. "I think there are actually some women working there."

"Now, don't get any ideas."

"Well, I already have, but not what you think. Take a look at that little house."

The warm afternoon sunlight was bathing the valley in an orange gold. A quarter of a mile from the highway a small stone dwelling nestled among some trees that still retained most of their leaves. Men and women in dark clothes were threshing the grain in the fields next to the house, and I could hear the swish of the sheaves as they struck the ground. The young girls Dick had been watching were singing and whistling as they worked. The strains of a lighthearted tune, along with peals of laughter, wafted up to us.

"That's a good sign," Dick observed. "They'd never be so happy-go-lucky if there were any Germans around. In fact, the women wouldn't even be out there at all. I was thinking that might be a good house to approach for some food."

Why does there have to be a war going on? I asked myself. This valley is right in the path of the British Eighth Army. It's sure to be a battleground soon and those people will be driven out of their homes — if they aren't killed first. As I so often did in my captivity, I daydreamed for a moment about my own house, in a valley 4,000 miles away, and wondered if the war would ever reach there. The idea appalled me so much that I hauled myself back to reality, telling Dick I agreed with his suggestion, but that it would have to be after dark.

At dusk I gathered up my meager kit — canteen cup, an old fork and spoon — donned Alan's sweater, which had a couple of bad tears from the wire, checked the precious tins of chocolate, and was ready to go. Dick had left a bundle of his stuff in a corner of the cave. Drawing his attention to it, I pointed out, "Dick, that has got to be a mistake. We have no idea what's going to happen next; some Germans might swoop down on that house, and we'd have to take off across country and never see this cave again."

He frowned. "We're coming right back here —"

"Don't be so damn sure. Now I want an agreement with you that wherever we go we take every single thing we own. I insist on it."

Waiting for his reply, I wondered if I'd gone too far. Then in the dim light I could see he was grinning. "OK, I'll be good," he promised.

We started cautiously down the slope, trying at each level to stay behind hedges and trees so as not to be spotted from the house, which was only about a quarter of a mile from the highway where we'd seen the German trucks.

Before long two figures appeared in the darkness, walking rapidly uphill. I overheard one of them say, "*prigionieri*," and "*caverna.*" We paused, giving them an opportunity to approach us, but they kept on going.

When we were some 50 yards from the house, a black and white terrier raced out, barking crazily. With this, I was on the verge of running for the house to get out of sight, but quickly a small, thin man rushed out and told the dog to shut up. The man seemed young, and even in the fading light I could see he was terrified by our presence. Quickly I explained to him in Italian that we were American prisoners.

"I am Mario," he said. "Don't stay out here, come into the house immediately."

There was no light in the house, and I could see nothing when we entered. Gradually my eyes adjusted, and I could discern on a wooden table a bowl of tiny apples, a piece of bread, and a carafe of wine.

Slowly, out of the darkness on the far side of the room, drifted a tall man's figure. "Good God!" I gasped, "Is this a trap?" Dick made a quick movement, while I half-turned, ready to fly out the door.

"I've been staying here," the man said in an educated British accent. "Mario tells me you two are Americans."

"How the hell does he know that?" Dick whispered. "Mario hasn't spoken to him."

I went over to the man, put out my hand and cited my name and rank. Dick did the same and asked him where he'd come from.

"Oh, with that big lot from down below about two weeks ago." His tone was guarded.

I was growing uneasy. "Are you a POW?" I asked.

"Why, of course, I'd assumed that was obvious," he answered rather arrogantly.

Dick told him carefully how we'd come to Fonte d'Amore, but the man still didn't reveal his identity. During this exchange, Mario had stood, watching us and listening to every word. Only now did he shake hands and offer us some bread and apples. I took a handful of the apples and bit into one. It was no bigger than a grape and very sour, but I ate it anyway, and with relish. Mario held the bread against his body and cut off two slices, then poured out some wine into two little jelly jars.

Our host talked to me in Italian while I finished the apples and the slice of bread. Mario had been in the Italian army and had been given a medical discharge. The word "lungs" came into the conversation and I gathered the problem had been tuberculosis. His father and mother lived up in Roccacasale, the town we'd come through the night before. When he told me his father was an American citizen who had lived in the States for 20 years, I got excited. The father had come back to Italy in 1939; he had been caught by the war and prevented from returning. "Where have you been hiding from the Germans?" Mario suddenly asked.

Hesitating at first, I decided to tell him. "Last night we found a cave up there on the hillside, and that's where we've been."

"Oh, I know that cave·well. My grandfather hollowed it out digging for limestone many years ago. Now that we know where you are, my father will bring you some food tomorrow around noon."

Our generous friend then pressed on us more food to take along: a small chunk of bread, a few apples, some grapes. We trudged back up the hill, delighted with the kindness of our Italian friend, although Dick remained somewhat skeptical about the whole situation. He stated very firmly that the bread was going into our reserve, and that he would ration it out when he felt it was absolutely necessary. He got no argument from me. Areas of authority were being defined. Matters of rationing settled for the time, I asked Dick about the strange Englishman down at Mario's.

"He didn't seem to me all that strange," Dick said. "Maybe just youthful — told me he's 23 and a sergeant. I admit he was a bit reserved about his former unit, just said he'd been in the infantry."

"What's his name?"

"Charles Rydesdale, or Charlie. He was a little reluctant about telling me his last name, but I finally got it out of him. I think he was just trying to be careful."

I made a mental reservation about Charlie.

Arriving at the cave, I crept cautiously inside, found it empty, and lay down. Dick stretched out on the ground just outside the mouth. It was far colder than the night before but, because I was still exhausted, somehow my body adjusted to the discomfort, and I slept through the long night.

25 September

When I got up in the morning my hands looked a little blue, but I warmed up as soon as I moved about. Though I was still overjoyed by the treatment we had received, Dick continued to be wary, insisting they'd change their tune in a hurry if the Germans came around and told them anyone would be shot who helped escaped prisoners.

Near midday Dick was sitting out at the front of the cave when I saw a man coming up the hill. "Come on, get back out of sight. We don't know who that is," I called out nervously.

He grumbled, "Oh, for God's sake," but crawled back in, and I sighed with relief. The man continued climbing. He wore a dark brown suit and an old fedora and was carrying a bundle wrapped in a red and white gingham cloth. He looked like many Italian-Americans I'd seen back home.

He bent low and entered the cave, clutching his bundle. "I am Saverio Santo D'Ascanio," he announced in fairly good English. "I live in States 20 years and have American citizenship papers. I help you." He was a spry, thin man with sparse gray hair, about 70. The band on his ancient hat was stained dark with sweat, and his frayed striped shirt was fastened at the neck with a gold collar button. Saverio half squatted and half sat on a rock, pulled out some papers from his coat pocket, and unfolded them. Wrapped in the papers, which bore an imprint of a huge American eagle, was a small American flag, which he waved back and forth. We applauded, but quietly. He handed me the papers and wasn't satisfied until I told him I recognized the citizenship papers and congratulated him on being an American like us. He grinned and said, "You boys hungry?"

He opened the bundle without waiting for an answer. It contained a blue and white crockery bowl, two big chunks of homemade bread, and a half-liter of red wine. An aroma of garlic, olive oil, peppers, and some kind of cooked meat instantly filled the cave. When I peeked into the bowl, my stomach went around like an old butter churn.

"Trippa," Saverio announced.

Dick mumbled to himself, "I don't give a damn if it's the dog."

Saverio handed us a couple of forks and the wine, and wished us buoyantly, *"Buon' appetit'! Mangia! Mangia!"*

Admiring the citizenship papers and trying to eat at the same time, I memorized his full name: "Saverio Santo D'Ascanio." (We had made a rule against writing anything down.) The food was still warm from the stove, very hot from the peppers, and it — especially the tripe — was utterly delicious. At home such a dish would have given me indigestion for a week, but here I could have eaten anything, and the meal was gone very quickly.

Saverio asked us our plans. We said we had thought of staying in the area for a while. He told us he would give us more food and in fact produced more bread, which he handed to Dick. I knew right where that was going. As Saverio was leaving, he pointed to his son's house down below and said, "You go down there again tonight. My son will give you fine, hot meal." Unexpectedly his manner became brisk, and he said rapidly, "You meet Charlie down there?"

"Yes." Dick answered. "We had quite a long talk."

Saverio hesitated for a moment, as if he was trying to make up his mind, then said, "Charlie been working in our fields and sleeping in my son's house — very dangerous. Sometimes Germans stop there for water."

Dick gave me a "leave-this-to-me" look and suggested to the old man, "Maybe we could persuade him to come up here tonight."

Saverio smiled and nodded rapidly. "Good! I'd be very happy if you do that. I'm very fond of Charlie, he's a good boy, just like my son."

"Don't worry," Dick assured him. "we'll take good care of him."

When the old man had left, I asked, "I wonder how Charlie is going to feel about that?"

"Let's not borrow trouble. That was quite a talk we had last night. He seemed reasonable. I think I can persuade him. But that old man's cagey. You notice how he maneuvered that? They knew all the time we were up here, and he had a good enough look to tell we were Americans. That's how Mario knew."

The meal that night included hot meat and vegetables, but I guessed they didn't have much themselves, because the portions were less than heaping. After the Spartan meal Mario and I remained at the table talking. When he got up to gather the dishes, I tuned in to Dick's conversation with the young Englishman. Charlie Rydesdale, I learned, had been a platoon sergeant with a British territorial regiment, roughly comparable to a U.S. National Guard unit. Because of the blackout, Mario had the shutters closed, and in the candlelight Charlie appeared about six-one, with neatly brushed, curly brown hair, a scrubbed-looking, rosy-cheeked face. Handsome enough to have had an easy time with the girls.

To my surprise, I heard him agree to return with us to the cave that night, where in spite of temperatures barely above freezing, we all slept reasonably well.

26 September

The next morning Dick, who had persuaded Mario to give him three burlap sacks, announced that he was going to make knapsacks for each of us, for carrying our kit and reserve — that way we couldn't get at them so rapidly. The idea was fine with me, since it took a lot of willpower not to nibble when I was hungry. Saverio and his son had been very generous with us according to their standards, but it hadn't made a dent; I was still ravenous.

Charlie declined. "I don't need one of those 'knapsacks,' as you call them. I shall get along very well as I am." His haughty statement seemed final, and neither Dick nor I argued the point.

Later that morning, a grinding roar and the unmistakable sound of shifting gears broke the stillness. Dick crawled to the corner of the cave to peek out. "That's a big German truck," he said. "I wonder what he's doing up in Roccacasale?"

This development gave me a case of the jitters, and I was all set to make a getaway in the other direction. Already I could envision myself trying to stay below the shoulder of the hill, ducking behind hedges to keep out of sight. "That can't be more than 300 yards from us," I lamented, "and I don't like any damn part of this."

Charlie looked amused. "No need to get so excited about it." The urge to slug him was almost irresistible.

Our cocky pal went on, "The Germans came by the house frequently when I was staying there. I see no cause for alarm."

Dick avoided my eyes. His voice was low and calm: "Well, Charlie, I don't know. Joe's all for trusting these Italians, too, but if Jerry wants to pull a raid and puts pressure on them for information, I'm not sure how long they'd hold out."

Not enjoying getting caught in the middle, I contended, "We can't stay here forever. We're much too close to that damn camp, and it's not part of our plan anyway. It's time we got out of this valley and over into the next one."

We argued for an hour. Finally I got an agreement that it was indeed time to move on, and that we would go that night. I was pleased that they had listened to me, because Charlie scared me — for my taste, he was far too cavalier.

Around midday Saverio brought us some lunch, but now his attitude had changed considerably. He seemed agitated. His speech was rapid. At times he lapsed into his native Italian. From an upstairs window of his house he'd seen two German officers with that truck. The officers had asked people in that town if they knew of any prisoners in the area, and warned that if they did, and failed to report them, or if they helped prisoners in any way, they would be shot. A notice to that effect had been posted by the Germans in the *piazza* that Dick and I had crossed two nights before.

We told Saverio we intended to move out that night. He offered generously, "You boys stop by my house on the way. My wife give you good feed to send you on your way. I come back at 8:30 when it's dark and safer. If it's too dangerous, I guide you around town and show you trail up mountain." Saverio left, clearly relieved that we were getting out of the cave and the whole area.

At 8:30, however, Saverio hadn't returned. Dick thought he might have decided it was too dangerous, but I was confident he would come, and so was Charlie — for once he and I were on the same wavelength. At any rate, we all agreed to wait until 10:00; then, if he still hadn't shown, we'd start up the mountain on our own. The idea was frightening, but not half as much as staying in the cave while the Germans were a few hundred yards away. By this time I realized that probably every man in town had explored the cave in childhood and had probably sneaked his girlfriend in there for some torrid lovemaking. In short, our cave was about as clandestine as the town hall.

Half an hour later I nearly leaped to the roof when a shadowy figure suddenly appeared against the faint light at the entrance. *"Non avete paura"* (Don't be afraid), the man said hurriedly. "I am Saverio. Now come very quickly. Make no sound. Stay right behind me!"

In spite of his age Saverio walked so fast we could hardly keep up with him. He led us to a small, narrow house, squeezed into the middle of a block right in the town. Glancing anxiously up and down the deserted street, we followed him through a darkened doorway. Inside, a curtain shielded the dim light that came down a steep flight of stairs.

Saverio's wife was a very short woman, with a weathered and heavily wrinkled face. Dressed in a long gray skirt, a scarf around her head, she took my hand perfunctorily, then almost shoved it back at me, her expression angry and suspicious. I felt far from welcome. To my further dismay, I quickly discovered that Signora D'Ascanio spoke only the Abruzzese dialect. At first I could barely understand anything she said. It made little difference anyway; to her, POW's were obviously as popular as pit vipers.

We were led upstairs into a small room with an open fireplace and a narrow table set with five places. The only illumination came from the fire and from a candle in a bottle, which threw tall shadows up the walls and ceiling, giving everything an impression of height.

Saverio motioned us to the benches along the table, with a *"Si accomodi"* (Make yourselves comfortable). We sat down, cramped in. I was right next to the *signora's* place. She brought over a pot of thick *minestra*, along with chunks of bread, while Saverio produced a bottle of red wine. After the *minestra*, served in cracked bowls the size of coffee cups, she brought us homemade pasta, which we washed down with the wine.

The *signora* sat down and began to talk. By that time, I had nearly finished my meal and was able to listen more attentively. The dialect words, I discovered, weren't completely different from the pure language, but for the most part were simply chopped off. I started to catch the old lady's meaning.

Our hostess's talk was largely a diatribe on the troubles the escaped prisoners were causing her and everyone else in Roccacasale. She was terrified; in her view, most of the escapers were nothing but a bunch of lazy freeloaders — I gathered that statement was aimed more at Charlie than at Dick and me. She moaned that the Germans would crack down sooner or later, that Saverio's food wasn't going to last all winter at the rate he was handing it out, that Charlie had been with them ten days, and she wasn't about to have us with them that long. She ended her tirade with, "Why don't you go and join your friends the British?"

"Oh yes, that's an excellent idea," I said in Italian. "In fact, we're going tonight."

This time I distinctly heard, *"Tu no' capisc'"* (You don't understand). She was out of her mind with fear. Their house could be destroyed by the Germans, and all her family killed. With Fascist spies in the town, she trusted no one. The Germans could be on their way this very minute. "You and your friends should leave, *subito!*"

The last word was rather shrill. Dick stared down the table at me, and even Charlie glanced up from his pasta. The *signora's* fears also alarmed me, and I wondered just what she knew. At that moment, Saverio began to talk heatedly to his wife. While I didn't understand exactly what he said, it was clear enough that she got a tongue-lashing for being rude to his guests.

When the rumpus subsided, Dick asked, "What was that all about?"

I explained to him and Charlie, and said I thought we should leave at once.

"Never heard anything so bloody silly in my life," Charlie volunteered. "You chaps do get the wind up, don't you?"

"That's enough out of you!" I exploded. "That damn stupid attitude of yours is going to get you recaptured —"

Dick broke in, "Oh, for God's sake, Joe, simmer down and have some more wine, it'll cool you off."

But I kept on. "You're both out of your heads. She says there're spies in the town and this house could be raided any minute; and damn it, if you guys don't get going, I'm going to get up and leave by myself. I'm not going to sit here and get trapped."

Unruffled by my outburst, Dick merely snorted and went on talking to Saverio. Fear didn't mean much to him anyway, and with a little *vino* it was nonexistent. Knowing I'd had some wine, though, made me more apprehensive than ever. Still I was distracted momentarily when *signora* produced a chunk of prosciutto. It must have been a peace offering, for prosciutto was like gold to these people. We all had some, then Saverio insisted we take with us whatever was left.

By this time my apprehension was such that I could hardly keep myself from running out the door. My imagination began to take wing: Germans were surrounding the house, coming in the front and back doors with guns drawn. I'd had this same sense of being thwarted and frustrated the night before the Germans took over Chieti.

When Saverio produced a bottle of *grappa*, a fiery, raw country brandy, I again nearly exploded. He poured us drinks and then stood up and proposed a toast to the United States. Reluctantly, I drank a little; it went down like hot acid and started a small fire in my stomach. Then we drank to England, to a free Italy, to all our families. Now the fire was really raging.

I said, "OK, Dick, enough is enough, before we have another round of toasts, I'm as scared as she is. Let's get on the road."

Dick was furious with me. Charlie shook his head. But by this time, I didn't give a damn. Finally, Saverio got to his feet swaying. I thanked the *signora* with a profusion of compliments. She responded with wishes of good luck and a blessing. Dick grumbled angrily, "So who's holding up the show now? For Christ's sake, cut out the Old-World courtesy!"

Saverio stepped outside with us to point out the trail up the mountain. Now he didn't seem nervous at all, as he teetered up the street in the light of a newly risen moon, a wiry, stooped-over disheveled old man in his shirtsleeves and suspenders, despite the cold mountain air.

Roccacasale was silent as we climbed up steadily through narrow alleys. The mountain fell off steeply to our left, and the buildings below us were squares and angles of gray and black. The night was brilliantly clear and beginning to turn very cold. We continued to labor up a sharp rise on a narrow trail cut into the side of the cliffs, where the footing was strewn with rocks, causing us to stumble frequently and to hug the precipice wall. Almost miraculously, Saverio didn't stumble at all, but he did from time to time sway out close to the edge of the trail. At one point, I went up behind him and put out my arm just in case he lost his balance.

Dick laughed. "Don't worry, pal, he's been doing this so long he's probably a hell of a lot safer up here than we are."

We had climbed for 45 minutes when Saverio suddenly halted. "This far as I go. You completely safe now — no Germans anymore. You climb one more hour and you find some woods. It's beautiful night, and you sleep there. Tomorrow, you go on and you come to big *masseria* (farmhouse) called Santa Croce. Tell people there Saverio send you and they help you. Then cross *il Morrone* and go to town called Salle. You be safe there too."

Saverio bade goodbye to Dick and me very warmly, then kissed Charlie on each cheek, and made us promise to take care of him. We vowed dutifully, but Charlie muttered, "Hmph!" As we turned to go, Charlie said firmly, "I'll bloody well take care of myself, thanks very much."

Dick led the way on up the slopes along a trail that was almost impossible to follow in the confusing light. Shadows and moonlight combined to distort the topography and the distances. We had climbed for two more hours, over rocks and through pine woods, when we came to a fork in the trail. The two diverging paths appeared to be sheep trails, and I thought that the lower one would take us too far down the mountain. But Dick didn't agree.

I insisted, "We have to go up that mountain at some time, and there's no point in losing altitude now that we're up this far. The lower trail can't be right."

Dick started to get ticked off at my stubbornness. I looked at Charlie in desperation. For a moment, I thought he was going to side with me, but then he said, "I don't think it's all that important. We can take one, and if it doesn't work out we can always come back here and try the other, but let's not have a fuss over it."

Dick relaxed slightly. "I have a suggestion; let's take a route half-way between the two trails and see if that answers the question for us." Within a couple of hundred yards, we found a well-defined path, so we trudged on, soon emerging from the woods onto a misty plain, covered with long waving grass. High above us loomed the western massif of the Morrone, as intimidating as the Alps. We selected a point on the shoulder of the mountain and headed

The rocky crags on the way up to the Guado di Coccia.

straight for it. On the far side of the plain, however, we came upon a dense forest of pines sloping steeply upward, and concluded these must be the woods Saverio had mentioned. The trek to this juncture had taken three hours instead of one.

Despite that unhappy comparison, we had at least been able to settle a dispute regarding the route. But I was still upset about the shenanigans back at

Saverio's and determined not to let it happen again. Perhaps my apprehension and caution would serve to keep the three of us out of trouble from now on.

After we'd selected a fairly level place, we bedded down uncomfortably. Pine needles stuck through our clothes, the air was stinging cold; my shirt, damp and sweaty from the long climb, clung like an icy wet sheet. It was 2:00 in the morning of 27 September, and I reckoned we were halfway up Monte Morrone.

"Dammit, we'll freeze if we don't huddle up together," Dick said. "We'll play 'Lucky Eddie.' He's the guy in the middle, who keeps the warmest."

So we huddled against one another, taking turns at being "Lucky Eddie." I never could make up my mind whether the cramped position in the middle was worth the miniscule extra warmth.

Chapter 17

Santa Croce

27 September

At daybreak I came to, shivering, with my legs feeling like logs. A brief recon disclosed that the tall woods where we'd slept were an island in a sea of verdant grass, while off to the west sprawled the vast Peligna Valley with little, toylike villages nestling half-hidden in the haze. Above us to the east rose the rocky crags of Monte Morrone. How in hell would we ever scale those cliffs near the crest?

Far out on the plain a lone shepherd with a flock of brown goats seemed to glide slowly through the high grass. Occasionally a dog's head bounded up, as if surfacing for air. Dick got up silently and stumbled around. Charlie stretched the stiffness out of his legs and inquired, "Who's for some grub?"

"What grub?" Dick answered hoarsely. "Nobody's eating any of the reserve." He glared at each of us in turn. No one argued. Then he added, more cheerfully, "So I nominate Professor Frelinghuysen, the Italian scholar, to go over to those shepherds and get us some breakfast." When I groaned at the idea, Dick winked. "Don't mind him, Charlie, he always groans in the morning."

I gave my needlers a frozen smile and started to collect my things. Dick didn't let up. "I want to remind you," he declared, "that wherever we go we must always take our entire kits along."

Charlie grinned, looking bright-eyed and rosy-faced, as if he'd just enjoyed a hot bath. He didn't even need a shave. Glancing at Dick, then over at me, he placed his order: "Porridge and kippers for me, old chap, if you don't mind."

"OK, you guys, I'll go, but don't try to be so damned comical."

Slowly, I picked up my kit and slipped on the knapsack Dick had made. Then I decided to take my jacket off, so I wriggled out of the knapsack. When I had the jacket off, it seemed chilly, so I put it on again. They were both staring at me. Each moment it became harder to set out on my mission.

Then, all at once, I forced myself to stride out into the grass, and before long I came down into a gully, where I heard the sound of trickling water. Kneeling by a sparkling rivulet, I scooped out the sand and, when the water cleared, dipped in my canteen and drank my fill. Then I rolled up my sleeves and pulled back my collar.

But just then a surge of anxiety gripped me, and I stood up cautiously. I could see the spot where I'd left the others, while ahead of me the shepherd and his flock seemed quiet and peaceful. Not another living thing moved in the awesome panorama of sky and mountain and valley. For an instant I felt very small and very much alone.

After soaking my head and face, I rubbed my neck with cold water. The relief was so intense that I wanted to strip and wash all over, but then the thought of the risk involved in taking off my clothes made me shudder — a German with field glasses could see my bare ass for miles! Furthermore, if I had my shoes off and a patrol burst on the scene, I'd never be able to run — I dismissed the thought and made a resolution: From now on, we must remove our clothes only when under cover, and we must never take off our shoes without someone standing guard so as not to be taken by surprise.

Patting my full canteen, I walked on, feeling much better about my assignment. Just beyond another ridge, I found an ancient shepherd and a boy with a donkey watching over the brown goats, who were up to their bellies grazing in the lush forage.

The old man's long white hair hung to his shoulders, and a flowing white mustache curved down to his chin. His trousers were in tatters, but a thick set of sheepskins sewn together in the form of a poncho was thrown over his shoulders. This woolly, virtually weatherproof garment made him look four feet wide.

"Hey, Bud, where you goin'?" he greeted me in English, with an American accent.

Pleasantly surprised, I replied, "I'm an American, traveling with two friends — we're all escaped prisoners. Could you possibly give us some food?"

The old man smiled. "I know, I give you goat's milk and bread." Pointing to the canteen on my belt, he asked, "You got a cup in there?" Then he reached down to pluck a handful of green ferns and took a leather-covered jug from the pack on the donkey's back.

"What are the ferns for?" I asked in Italian.

"They purify the milk. Now drink it," he answered, also in Italian. Then he quickly added, "I was in the States for several years, but where did you learn to speak Italian?"

"In the prison camp at Chieti."

Apparently satisfied with my explanation and no longer suspicious, he reached into a knapsack and pulled out a piece of bread, so small that I was too embarrassed to accept it. Moreover, I had no idea how I could divide it three ways.

"Why don't you drink your milk?" he said gruffly.

"I'm going to take it back and share it with my friends."

"You drink that milk here!" he shouted angrily. "You try to walk over there and you spill it. I got no milk to waste for such stupidity. I tell you, drink it here!"

What the devil could I do? Other than give the milk back, which would be even stupider, I decided I better drink it, knowing full well what would happen when I got back. Any thought of lying about it was out of the question.

I drank slowly, stalling to delay my return. "Is Santa Croce near here?"

"Where did you hear that?" he asked suspiciously.

"From Saverio in Roccacasale. He helped us right after we escaped from the prison camp."

Mollified by my response, the old man pointed across the plain in a direction I calculated to be northward. "You go over there," he said. "It's about half-an-hour walk for us, but more for you. The big *masseria* — farmhouse — they good people. They help you."

"Thank you. After that, if we want to cross the mountain to Salle, how would we go?"

"Ho! Ho! Ho!" he roared, nodding vigorously and pointing straight up the Morrone. "Very long, hard climb up that mountain. Trail is narrow and hard to follow and goes up across the rocks at the summit. For us it takes four, five hours. For you —" he paused and shook his head, "maybe seven. It's very cold and often snows up there this time of year. You no got this!" he said, yanking the edge of his sheepskin.

I changed the subject. "How high is that mountain?"

"Two thousand and sixty meters."

I converted and got an ugly surprise — 6,800 feet, 500 feet higher than Mount Washington. This brought to mind a frigid climb on a winter day some years before up the northern headwall of that New Hampshire mountain: glacial winds and driving snow, weird ice patterns on stunted pines.

Swallowing hard, I asked, "Have you seen any Germans up there?"

He made a gesture Saverio used: index finger waggled back and forth, while he went, "Tsk! Tsk! Tsk!" meaning, in short, "No!"

When I returned, Dick and Charlie looked up at me, eager and expectant. Now I had to try to explain what had happened. After my account Dick said in that quiet voice of his, "Why didn't you dump the water from your canteen and put the milk in there?"

"How did I know he was going to object to my carrying it back?"

"What the hell! You could've figured *some* way to bring it back." He paused and let out a sound that was half sigh and half growl. "Trouble with you is you're trying to be so damn polite all the time, you're afraid to open your trap."

"Dammit, Dick, I said I was sorry. I simply didn't know what to do."

All this while, Charlie had been silent, watching me. "I agree 'sorry' is a thin breakfast, but there's bloody fuck all we can do about it now. Dick, how about a bit from that precious reserve before we chew each other up?"

Grimacing, Dick reached for the knapsack where he kept the reserve and gave us each a slice of bread, plus a piece of prosciutto about the size of a quarter. Sitting on a nearby rock, I ate it slowly, a few yards away from them, mentally kicking myself for the way I had handled the whole thing.

Ten awkward minutes later, I ventured a look at Dick, who was grinning back at me. I walked over to him and began hesitantly, "You know, Dick, I think we ought to get going up that mountain."

He turned and looked up at it. "How high did you say that thing was?"

"Well, I told you the other day it was 5,000 feet, but according to that shepherd it's more like 6,800."

This time Dick groaned, and I thought I was going to get another blast, but he just turned and said, "Come on, Charlie, let's get going."

We crossed the rest of the *pianura* fairly easily and found a trail leading toward the mountain. As we climbed, the slope became steeper and steeper, rising between craggy outcrops and huge boulders. Soon I took off my jacket and tied it around my waist. The others did the same, and in half an hour we were all stripped to our undershirts. Sweat poured, and we gulped in air. As we went higher, I noticed every now and then that Dick's face contorted in pain, and he seemed to favor his left leg. When we came to a spring, I suggested we stop and fill up. With a sigh, Dick sank down on a rock. Charlie stood and stared out over the valley, looking so serene he could have been out for a stroll on an English lane. I slugged the cold water down to kill the hunger pangs.

The shoulder of the mountain at this point was so steep we could no longer see the top. I climbed up an outcrop for a look around and saw an old woman chopping wood. Wisps of gray hair straggled out from under the soiled bandana on her head, and her deeply lined skin was mottled red as she stared at me through bloodshot, rheumy eyes.

"*Buongiorno,*" I began, and continued in Italian, "*Signora*, we're escaped prisoners and want to know if it's safe to go to Salle. Are there any Germans there?"

In the meantime, Dick had limped over and was standing next to me as she waved her finger back and forth, clucking her tongue: "*N' sci stav' no li*" (No, there are none there). Though she spoke mostly in dialect, I understood her to say Salle would be a good place for us to head for.

"I'm beginning to get the drift," Dick remarked. "Any place is good as long as it takes us away from these locals — we're a danger to them. Anyway, she obviously can't spare any food. We'll be running into more of this as we go along." I couldn't go along with his skepticism. It might be valid in the case of this poor old girl, but it certainly hadn't been of Saverio.

We had climbed about 1,500 feet from the grassy plain when a man appeared high above us, bounding down the trail. We ducked behind some rocks until we were sure he was an Italian, and then I ran over to intercept him. But when he saw me, he started back up the mountain. I called out who we were, and he hesitated, then crept down, cautiously.

Dressed better than anyone I'd yet seen in this area, the man wore Italian army trousers, black boots, and a gray jacket. I asked him why he was in such a hurry.

"I escaped from Salle when the Germans surrounded it for a *rastrellamento*. They capture young Italians to use as slaves to build the German fortifications in the mountains." Ominously, he added that they had also recaptured some *prigionieri Britannici*.

Again, I felt the tightness in my chest — suddenly I didn't want any part of the town. "What time did you leave Salle?"

"Two hours ago. I came over the mountain pretty fast, too fast for any Germans."

"Did they try to follow you?"

He shook his head, then took off down the mountain at a dead run.

Saverio and Mario had also mentioned *rastrellamenti*, but this was the first actual raid we had heard of. Just over this mountain, where we had to go sooner or later, prisoners were being rounded up and shipped off to Germany. Both Charlie and Dick were peering up the mountain as if they expected a patrol any minute. Suddenly, I was perversely pleased: I had been "old windy Joe" and "nervous Nellie," but now they were as edgy as I was. My gloating helped with the constriction in my throat and chest that I lived with constantly.

When we stopped and rested at another spring, Dick explained that he had injured his left knee in a skiing accident a few years before and that it was still bothering him. Later, I watched him out of the corner of my eye — when he moved that leg, his face twisted and he exhaled audibly.

As we sat by the bubbling spring, the sun came up over the mountain and the brilliant light revealed a great house amid a cluster of farm buildings off to the northwest. It had to be Santa Croce, big enough to draw the Germans' attention. Since I didn't want to give back the height we had reached, I suggested we build a lean-to up here. We gathered branches, broke them in four-foot lengths, and placed them around as vertical supports. Finding it impossible to drive them into the rocky ground, we propped them up with rocks. The sides were a rough weaving job and would provide no more than a windbreak. The roof was a flimsy crosshatched affair. When we finally found time to rest, the sun was already low and it had turned chilly. "That house down there looks pretty inviting," Dick hinted. "It's got to be a damn sight warmer than sleeping out on this mountain; and we might even get something to eat."

"It's ridiculous to spend another night out in the cold," Charlie chimed in. "Jerry'll never come up this high. Let's see what the place is like."

The mere possibility of some food was too much for me. "Screw the blasted Hun," I blurted. "Let's get the hell down there before I start gnawing on someone's leg." Dick began to gather up his kit.

An hour later we had recrossed the *pianura* and were only half a mile from the house. At dusk we entered a courtyard behind it, where a dozen young Italians were hiding in back of a stone wall. One of them shouted, and they scurried off in all directions.

A man about five feet tall, and nearly as wide, waddled out to meet us, talking volubly. I identified us and mentioned Saverio's name. "Saverio's a good friend of mine," he shouted. "Did he send you?"

When I told him our story, he seemed satisfied and grabbed my hand firmly. "I am Cesare, the *padrone* of this *masseria*. Come in! Come in! Americans are friends."

I introduced Dick and Charlie, stating each one's rank. The welcome Charlie got was civil enough, but the farmer slapped Dick and me on the back heartily, bellowing with laughter, and telling us we would have a big meal later on.

Cesare marched us hastily into a big, low-ceilinged room, lit with flickering candlelight. The place hummed with Italian voices and reeked with sweat and cigarette smoke. Jammed in here were some 40 to 50 men, who now fell silent, staring at us.

"*Si accomodi*" (Make yourselves comfortable), Cesare said to us and disappeared. I introduced myself to the nearest man, who smiled and shook my hand. Most of the others in the room appeared to be former soldiers, since they were wearing parts of uniforms. All were dirty-bearded and uneasy.

They chattered, "*Americani*," "*Inglesi*," and proffered their first names quickly as I walked around shaking hands. I kept going until I found a pair who were willing to give me some information.

These men, all refugees of one kind or another, had mainly been in the army. After the Badoglio Armistice, they had thrown away their arms and headed for homes scattered throughout the provinces of southern Italy. If caught, they would be shot as deserters or forced into slave labor.

After an hour and a half Cesare returned and shouted, "*Venit'! Venit'! Ragazz', Mangia! Mangia!*" (Come boys, eat!)

He steered us into a small room furnished with a long wooden table and benches. He motioned Dick to a seat on his left and me to one on his right. Charlie was seated down the table a ways with some Italians. Half a dozen others were left hovering in the background, while the rest had to remain out in the big room.

A woman, the size and shape of Cesare, put a huge cauldron on the table, and the smell of pasta and vegetables made my stomach rumble. As she passed Cesare, he slapped her ample buttocks and shouted, "My wife, Concetta, see how well I take care of her!" The two howled with laughter.

"Buona sera," I said to her in my most charming manner, but she completely ignored me. She brought bowls and spoons and shouted in dialect, *"Magna! Magna!"*

The bowls were small, and I wolfed down my helping in a couple of minutes. After we had a second round, Concetta whisked our bowls away, refilled them, and handed them to the other men waiting.

After consuming some bread, a sour wine, and a small piece of sheep's liver, I began to wonder where Cesare managed to get all this food. He couldn't possibly be producing all this from his own farm.

Dick found one man who could speak French, so I had Cesare to myself. He announced that we would soon kill all the Germans, they were nothing anyway, not people to be afraid of. *"Tedeschi"* (Germans), he said, and made a gesture of drawing a knife across his throat. That brought the loudest laughter yet.

Smelling of wine and garlic, Cesare leaned over and whispered in my ear, "You see all this food?"

"Yes, we're grateful for your help."

He waved impatiently. "I know, I know. I have a big farm, but not this big. I get outside help." He rolled his eyes heavenward, and I wondered what he meant by "outside help."

He looked around the room, checking on the people who were within earshot, then leaned over again and in a whisper, said, "If I had to feed this crowd of people from my own farm, we would be starving in two weeks. There are certain people who collect the food and bring it up here." He took another drink of wine. Dick had stopped talking and caught my eye, giving me a steely-eyed look that meant: *be careful.*

Cesare went on, "The food is sent here by the people of the Communist Party, who will rule Italy after the war."

Dick cautioned me in English, "No political arguments, Joe!"

"I understand." I said to Cesare in Italian. "What's important is that we are allies, and we all want the total defeat of Germany."

Cesare grinned and slapped me on the back. He and Concetta, carrying a lighted candle, then took us upstairs to a room with three wire cots, each covered with two blankets and a thin mattress. He pointed to them and said, *"Per voi."*

I protested — we didn't need beds, we'd been sleeping on the ground. "Oh, for God's sake, Joe, cut it out, will you?" Dick growled. "At least we'll get one night's sleep."

This was the first semblance of a bed I'd slept in for nearly a year, but it meant I had to take my shoes off, which I refused to do. So I pulled the mattress and blankets up on the wire springs and stuck my feet out below. I twisted and turned in the darkness, trying to get comfortable, until the blankets and I were the shape of a pretzel. I stood up, unwound them, and started out again. All at once, I longed to sleep in a real bed with box springs, clean sheets, and warm woolen blankets. And then for an instant, I yearned for the safety and love that were half a world away. But I drove the thought away and plunged back into the world of cold, filth, and everlasting fear.

Finally I drifted off into a half-sleep, plagued with fantasies of Germans surrounding the house; if I were caught, should I try to pretend I was an Italian and then escape while working on the fortifications?

28 September

Dick and Charlie were snoring when I got up at 5:30 and went downstairs. Cesare and Concetta, rolled up in blankets, were sleeping on the wooden floor of the big room — they had given us their bedroom. I found a door leading into the courtyard and walked up and down in the chill morning air, swinging my arms to get warm.

An hour later I was cold and stiff when Cesare stuck his head out the door. *"Caffè?"* he offered and disappeared back in the building. I followed him in. Concetta was at the stove, grumbling and snapping at him. She didn't answer my *"Buongiorno."* Cesare poured a little ersatz coffee in my canteen cup and gave me a small chunk of bread. He cast an eye at the men crowding in the door and nodded to me. I thanked him quickly and went back upstairs.

When I roused my two companions, I caught a barrage of flak, but finally persuaded them that we had to get out of the house early and spend the day back up at our lean-to. Santa Croce had too many refugees hanging around. The men who brought the food lived in the town where we'd been told there were Fascist spies; Cesare's *masseria* was a set-up for a *rastrellamento*.

That night, back at Santa Croce, I insisted that we let our two *padroni* have their own room. Although I staked out a corner away from the Italians, I passed a wretched, tossing night. By now I had begun to figure the percentages: Each night we slept in a house increased our chances of being caught in a raid.

<u>29 September</u>

On the third night at Santa Croce I had an anxiety attack like the ones I'd had at Chieti — I was back in the steel cylinder, the piston was coming down! Suddenly, I couldn't stand the house another second.

"Dick," I nearly shouted, grabbing his arm, "we've got to get out of here! They could do it tonight."

"Who? Cesare and Concetta?"

"Oh, for God's sake! The Germans could raid Santa Croce."

Charlie was smiling and shaking his head. "I've never seen a chap get the wind up like that one. It's ridiculous, we're as safe as a church up here."

"Damn you guys, now shut up and listen! This place is like a juicy piece of bait: all the food disappearing from town loaded on these donkeys; it's just a question of time."

Dick had stopped laughing. "What do you want to do?"

"Go out and sleep in the woods."

Dick emitted sounds like an angry bear, but he began to pick up his kit. In a few moments we were both ready, but Charlie hadn't moved a finger. "Sleep tight out there, lads," he said. "I'll go to a chemist shop in the morning and get you something for your lumbago." I let it pass.

We had to grope our way out of the courtyard, but gradually, the dark sky became visible above the jet-black outline of the Morrone. I looked back toward the house. Dim light shone from cracks in the shuttered windows. We felt our way along gingerly until it disappeared from sight.

"Joe, you know what the hell is the matter?" Dick said. "There's a pea soup fog out here. Unless the Germans have been waiting here since dusk, there's no way they could find that house. Now, which way do you want to go?"

In desperation, I looked back to where I thought the house had been, turned directly away from it and started out. "Now we're heading east," I said.

"Five bucks says you're wrong."

I tripped on a stone, fell to my knees and began feeling around with my hands. Nothing in any direction. A sensation of dizziness overcame me, and I remembered the expression, "He doesn't know which end is up."

After wandering about 50 yards farther we stumbled into a rocky area where it was impossible to take two steps in a row. Dick had been quiet for too long. Suddenly, he exploded with, "Why the hell did we have to do this? The whole goddam German army couldn't find us up here."

That did it. I was on the spot. I had to do something. In desperation, to try to make contact with some object, I swung my arms in wide circles, turning round and round, till I lost my balance and fell on my knees. One hand cracked against a rocky surface that felt like a curved stone wall. I followed it with my hands and discovered an aperture in the wall that was like a small door. I crawled in and found myself in some kind of stone shelter that was built like a beehive. "Dick, come in here; this is one of those stone shelters for the shepherds."

"I'll come in, if I can find you. I suppose you had this planned all along."

There was just enough room for two people to stretch out. The floor was rocky, but at least it was the first night we had had with absolutely no fear of a German raid. I slept as if I had been drugged.

Chapter 18

The Communist Party

30 September

Charlie was waiting outside the *masseria* when we returned in the morning. Standing there, with his curly brown hair and flawless fair complexion, he looked perfect for the lead in a British film about the war. Though we had been together now for a week, an air of mystery still hung over him — I knew only his name, and that he was an Englishman. He never mentioned what camp he'd been in, what his unit was, or even where he came from in England.

"How was it out on the mountain?" he greeted us.

"Not bad, after Joe lucked out on a real screw-up."

"Lucked out? I had it planned that way all along."

"You chaps have a point about not sleeping at Santa Croce," Charlie conceded. "I'm bloody browned off at that lot in there."

He told us that the Italians had kept him awake most of the night, gabbing loudly and playing cards until he had to move out into the hall and sleep on the stone floor. "I'm not as windy as you chaps," he added. "Nevertheless, I wouldn't mind sleeping out from now on."

As we headed back toward the mountain, I was so relieved I even offered to go over to a group of shepherds and ask them for some food. The other two laughed, a bit too hard, I thought. Dick very quickly remarked that he would be glad to go along this time, so I wouldn't get lonely.

These sheepherders seemed different from the one who had given me the milk. They stared at me with hard, dark faces, hats pulled down over their eyes, and their arms hidden by sheepskin capes. When I produced my most cheerful *"Buongiorno,"* their eyes flickered and they said nothing. "We're very hungry." I went on, "Would you give us something to eat?"

They exchanged glances, and one man nodded, reached into a wicker basket on a donkey's back, and pulled out a pound-sized piece of cheese that looked like gorgonzola. As he handed it to me, his expression was a mixture of cynical humor and contempt.

I accepted the cheese with the usual expressions of gratitude, but the men turned away abruptly and began chattering unintelligibly. We quickly walked off.

"Let me see that cheese," Dick demanded. When I handed it to him, I saw that it was crawling with yellow maggots. I flicked a few off my hand.

"My God," Dick said, "look at the damn thing, it's absolutely vibrating!" But he divided it into three chunks, and every man consumed his portion — maggots and all.

30 September-2 October

Each evening we went back to Santa Croce for food. Then, after a meager supper, we headed out to one of a series of caves and shelters we had located on the mountain, being careful never to sleep in the same one two consecutive nights.

On 2 October Cesare spoke to us: "There's a man I want you to meet. He's the *capo* of the *partigiani* (partisans) in this area and will be most important after the war." Cesare lowered his voice and added, "Chief of the Communist Party of the province. A man named Giancarlo will come to get you tomorrow at 9:00 and take you to the Chief, who is anxious to meet the two American captains." I didn't translate that last part, in deference to Charlie. Cesare described a shelter where we were to wait for this man.

Before we left Santa Croce on that crisp autumn morning, I asked Cesare if he could give us some paper — any kind. Although the food had not bothered Charlie, something we had eaten recently had given Dick and me severe cramps and diarrhea. Our small supply of newsprint and wrapping paper was painful and irritating, but I didn't have much hope for anything else.

Cesare looked puzzled, then said, *"Ah, carta igienica."* He disappeared and, to my surprise, returned shortly with a small roll of toilet paper. "This is the last we have," he said. "And no more will be available till after the war. Soon you will be using leaves."

The next morning, Giancarlo was waiting for us at the shelter. He appeared to be in his early twenties, and had black hair and rather white skin, high cheekbones, and a long slim nose. Though friendly enough, he was in a hurry and moved off with a vigorous, swinging stride that left us panting a hundred yards behind.

He stopped and grinned. "You aren't accustomed to walk as we are. You'll get used to it soon." Dick limped up. "Christ, I hope so," he said — he had understood Giancarlo perfectly.

We reached a clearing in a stand of tall mountain pines where a group of men were gathered around one central figure sitting on a log. He turned and stared at us. A man about 50, he had a face so dark he could have passed for an American Indian. As we approached, his black eyes fastened on each of us in turn. "This guy doesn't look as if he'd be scared of anything," I said under my breath.

He shook hands with us without getting up and addressed us in rough Italian. "I am Giuseppe D'Acciaio, and Giancarlo is my second in command. He'll take care of your needs while you're around here, but if you want to go south to join your friends the British, we'll tell you how to go. However, you must first get some civilian clothes; those uniforms are too conspicuous."

The Chief nodded to us and didn't shake hands again — we appeared to be getting the brush-off. He resumed talking to the *partigiani* even before we had followed Giancarlo up the trail to another clearing.

Waiting for us there, next to a donkey with two baskets slung across its back, was a taciturn fellow. Without a word he pulled out a blanket and spread some civilian clothes on it. Dick got a frayed tweed jacket, a work cap, and a work jacket; Charlie, a pair of pants and a jacket. The only thing that fitted me was a tweed cap with a visor, but it felt comfortable and would help with the cold and the rain.

Giancarlo told us they would try to get me some larger clothes, and he asked if we would join their band of *partigiani*. The Chief and he had 70 men altogether and were trying to obtain arms. "Now, you two are officers. You have had combat experience. We would like you to command our group."

Before Dick could answer, I interjected, "The people at Santa Croce don't stand guard even at night, so it's not safe there. We'd like to stay with you temporarily, but certainly not to command. It's our duty to return to our own army as quickly as possible."

Giancarlo said, "We will be glad to have you with us for now; we have received a report that the British were stalled somewhere far to the south." This was the second reference to our leaving. Dick had understood Giancarlo, and he asked me to say that we were anxious to leave and would go as soon as we had obtained some larger clothes, some food, and information on the best route to take.

That night we said goodbye to Cesare. He blinked hard and said he was sorry to see us go, but that we were making the right decision. Concetta wished us luck. This time Dick let me thank our hosts without any complaints about "Old-World courtesy."

As we started out for our shelter under a clear, starlit sky, Dick commented, "I'm not sure that Cesare's emotion wasn't because he was so damn glad to get rid of us."

"No doubt," I replied, "but you must admit that without them we'd be in bad shape."

The next morning we climbed up and met the partisans. They were a dirty, unshaven, and noisy lot, but they fell silent while Giancarlo spoke briefly to them. Then they broke up, talking volubly and peering in our direction.

"These are only half of us," Giancarlo said. "We keep another group in a separate camp for security reasons."

"Good idea," I agreed.

"Now, this is Francesco," he said, introducing us to a man in his forties, not exactly a fashion plate in his rumpled city clothes. "He'll stay with you and set up your tours on guard duty."

"Va bene!" Dick replied.

Charlie complained that this was all a damn waste of time, that we ought to "bloody well get on the road." Ignoring him, I said to Giancarlo, *"D'accordo,* we'll work with Francesco."

"One more thing, Giuseppe," Giancarlo said, "we know an Italian Captain of Engineers, who's living up here, waiting to go south. He has some large-scale maps of this zone, which we are tracing. When we're through, you can take a look at them." He said goodbye and strode off up the mountain.

Dick looked pleased. "For the first time, all this is beginning to make sense. The more I see of these *partigiani*, the less I want to get involved. You made a good decision, Giuseppe, not to 'command' them — God help us. We'll stay here only long enough to get the civvies, see those maps, then get the hell out."

Charlie sighed, "It's about time you Yanks came to your senses. I don't like being too close to the *partigiani*." Nor did I. We spent the next two days building a log shelter a quarter of a mile above their camp.

9 October

At 8:30 in the morning, the second after we completed our "log cabin," there arrived a young Italian who announced, "I have orders to bring you up to the Chief; he wishes to talk again to the two American captains. We must start immediately, because it's a very long walk."

Lately, Dick had been limping a little more on his left leg; he was not too anxious to go, but he didn't want to miss the engineer's maps. Charlie flatly refused to leave. "I don't care for this," he stated. "I understand the word for 'orders.' Who does this *capo* fancy he is?" We left him muttering something about *"capitani Americani."*

Dick and I followed the young Italian, plodding our way up the rock-strewn slope of the Morrone, until we went from a warm October sun into the chill darkness of a tall pine forest, where moss underfoot made a soft, springy cushion. Periodically, our guide would stop and listen, but there was only the rustle of the wind in the treetops. After climbing for two hours, we emerged above timberline onto bare rocky slopes, a wild and desolate place, where the shoulder of the mountain hid the valley far below. I felt as if we were nearing the top of the world.

Soon the sky clouded over, and a cold wind came up as we crossed several miles of sheer rock surface. Beyond a crest, hidden in a gully on the mountaintop, was a big stone shelter, its dry-rock walls covered with lichen and worn smooth by fierce mountain storms. A few partisans whom we had never seen before came out of the rugged structure and greeted us. They looked like brigands.

Giuseppe D'Acciaio met us at the door and ushered us into a 50-foot room that smelled of wood smoke, stewing meat, and wine. Two men were tending an enormous copper-lined kettle that was bubbling over a bed of coals. The Chief pointed to some log benches, and we sat down with him. His manner was affable and not at all as it had been at our first meeting. Dick whispered in English, "I wonder what he wants from us?"

Overhearing him, the Chief frowned. "We're trying to determine," he said, "when your friends, the British, will arrive. It's of vital importance to me, and it will be helpful if you tell me something about your military experiences." I began to think he understood a little English.

After telling him my combat time had been brief, I quickly recounted the North African landings and my capture in Tunisia. Then I said that Riccardo, my companion, had seen a lot of action in Tunisia and Sicily, and perhaps he could be more helpful than I.

The Chief turned to Dick with a new interest. "Tell me," he said, "about the Sicilian campaign and why it was you were captured."

Dick said, "I understood what you said, but I will give my response to my friend here and let him translate it for you." Then he turned to me. "I'm going to be pretty frank; he wants to know where he stands."

Dick launched into a concise but complete description of his landings in Sicily and the disaster that ensued on the second landing. He pulled no punches about the blunders among the American supporting units.

The Chief leaned forward, trying to catch the English words before I translated. As Dick came near the end, his voice became somber, and I realized again that this was a hard story for him to tell. When he had finished, the Chief was silent for a moment, then spoke rapidly to me in dialect as if he did not want Dick to understand. This much I got clearly: "If you Americans have many more like this one, the Germans are in for a hard time." I did not translate and Dick did not ask me to.

D'Acciaio paused and spoke in Italian, "You have told me what I wanted to know. You have the equipment and a big army. Your troops are courageous, but they lack experience. It will be months before your American comrades in the west get this far north. And the British on the east coast will be just as slow. They fought well in the desert, where it's flat, but they have no experience in these mountains. It will be spring before they get here, and I must plan accordingly."

Dick nudged me. "I understand most of that. Tell him I also think it will be several months, and that he mustn't start guerrilla action too soon. The Germans would wipe them out, along with their families, who are still living down in the villages."

When I translated for D'Acciaio, he scowled. "You're telling me what I already know only too well. Your friends had better hurry if we're still to be around to help them."

"And if we stay here any longer eating up your food, we won't be any help either," Dick answered him.

"I agree, you must leave right away. Now, here's something you can do for us: Memorize the location of this camp, which the engineer will point out to you on his map. Then, when you reach the British, tell them to drop us guns, ammunition, food, radios. These are things we need very badly, and I'm asking your help, but for God's sake, don't write this down anywhere."

"Of course not," I assured him.

"Giancarlo has the rest of your civilian clothes and will give you food for your trip." Giuseppe paused and pulled out a small caliber automatic pistol. "And in addition, I can give you this."

My heart skipped a beat — to be caught in civilian clothes carrying a gun was sheer suicide. Dick watched for my reaction, but I looked the other way and said quickly, "We'll deliver your message, or the first one who arrives will do it. We can use the clothing and food, but you keep the pistol. You'll need it more than we will."

"Why did you say that?" Rossbach snapped. "It just might make the difference."

"Yeah, the difference between getting shot as a spy and not getting shot," I flung back at him.

The Chief looked over at the two cooks; one of them waved to him. "The food is ready," he said. "We have something very good today."

The two men brought over three bowls of *minestra*. Barely waiting for our host to begin, Dick and I quickly polished off our portions, while the Chief talked about the problems the war had brought to Italy. He paused and said, "Now today we are having rabbit stew." I looked at Dick, remembering his comment about Mario's dog. This time, however, he was circumpsect. The Chief gestured expansively toward the steaming kettle and said, "And while we are eating, I'll give you some background on your route south so you will understand it."

The men arrived with plates of stew and the Chief continued, "From ancient times, the shepherds of Italy have had an undisputed right to take their herds south in the fall and north in the spring. Their traditional route, called the *tratturo*, follows the best pastures of the high Apennine plateau. Here the sheep manure has fertilized the ground for centuries, so in the spring, if one flies over Italy, one can see a bright green stripe down the entire length of our country. The grass you have seen around Santa Croce is a part of this stripe."

The Chief poured some wine and went on: "The Germans lie along the *tratturo*, where they round up the sheep and slaughter them for their troops. If the shepherds help, they let them go. But they machine-gun any who tries to hide his flock. Some *pastori* report the location of *partigiani* and prisoners, just so the Germans won't take all their sheep. Be wary of the shepherds, even though you must follow the *tratturo*. It's the only route to take, because in other places the mountains are impassable."

I said, "We plan to cross the Morrone, go south in the next valley, and then cross the Maiella."

"That's good, but go soon. There's only one pass over the Maiella, Guado di Coccia, opposite the town of Campo di Giove at the foot of the valley. No one ever crosses the Guado after the first snows, which could come any day now." I told the Chief we would like to see the Italian engineer the next day, and would definitely leave the following morning. He agreed to arrange it all with Giancarlo.

We thanked the old man for his help and the splendid meal, and promised to deliver his message to the British. I said goodbye to him with regrets. Regardless of politics, he had treated us royally.

On the way back to our shelter we met Giancarlo, who gave me new clothing. I squeezed into "civvies" for the first time in two years, and he looked me over and smiled. "Those come with the compliments of the biggest man in Popoli. You don't appear exactly Italian, but at a distance you'll be all right."

While Dick put on his civilian garb, I asked Giancarlo about his family. He was 24 and unmarried, and his mother and father were living in Popoli. I told him about my wife and children. He fell silent for a moment and said, "I can imagine how you must have felt leaving them. I was two years in the army, and I know how it was when I left my parents at my home." I looked out over the valley, lost for a moment in a dream.

Dick paraded by in his civvies and said, "I wish I had a mirror." Then he showed off his Italian: *"Non sembro molto Italiano?"* (Don't I look really Italian?) Giancarlo winked at me and laughed.

My old ragged uniform went into my knapsack, along with Charlie's battledress jacket. Though a bit snug, my new outfit was clean and comfortable enough and, to tell the truth, I felt rather dashing.

Late that afternoon we rejoined Charlie at our log shelter. To my surprise, he was interested in our trip and listened closely as we described our meeting with the old Chief. From his keen interest, I saw that Charlie was glad to be back with us again.

10 October

About midday we went to meet the Italian engineer, or *Ingegnere*, a short, stocky man with a slight paunch and a most unmilitary manner. A young refugee named Lorenzo, who had come across from Rome, had attached himself to the engineer and, I surmised, liked the idea of the maps as well as we did.

The older man hadn't volunteered any name, so I just called him "Ingegnere," because it is customary in Italy to call a man by his professional degree. Unmilitary or not, he became very precise when he spread out some excellent 1 : 100,000-scale maps on the grass. With the three of us hovering over him, he explained our prospective route in detail: After crossing the Morrone, we would go south in the Valle dell'Orta, which ran for 17 miles into a V-shaped cul-de-sac, walled by 7,000-foot peaks. Our only way to cross out of the cul-de-sac was on the eastern periphery via the Guado di Coccia, a 5,600-foot pass.

Ingegnere agreed to travel with us, which pleased me very much, as did his firm statement that we would leave the next day at 9:00 a.m. sharp. That afternoon, Giancarlo brought us some canned meat, big pieces of bread, a little jam, and a rare gift of sheep's milk cheese, all of which Dick immediately transferred to the reserve. Before Giancarlo left, he assigned the guard shifts for the night. We were to stand them in pairs for added security.

I went on a three-hour shift at midnight with Francesco. He was in a talkative mood. "Giuseppe, isn't it true that the poor in America are worse off than the poor in Italy?"

Smelling the wine on his breath, I smiled in the darkness. "No, that isn't true now. It has been bad in some places in the past, but right now everyone is either in military service or working in a factory."

"But aren't your workers slaves, laboring 16 to 18 hours a day?"

"No, they are not slaves. We are at war, and they may work as much as 10 hours a day, 12 at most."

He laughed. "Twelve hours is easy. But I don't believe it's so little. Don't Mr. Ford and Mr. General Motors run your government?"

"No, those are the names of the big companies that make tanks and trucks for the war. Our government is run by President Roosevelt and an upper and lower chamber of deputies," I corrected him.

"Ah, yes, I've heard Mr. Roosevelt is not such a bad man, but he hasn't been able to stop the oppression of the masses."

There was a long moan from inside the shelter. "For Christ's sake, Frelinghuysen, knock it off! You can't win that. What a hell of a pair of guards."

Chapter 19

The Escarpment

Giancarlo came by in the morning to say goodbye. I thanked him as warmly as I could for all that he and the others had done. I considered it far more than just Communist Party strategy. I felt grateful to Giancarlo, and told him that if I made it through, I would try to get in touch with him after the war.

"Buona fortuna, Giuseppe," he said. "In my heart I feel you'll be successful in reaching your comrades and eventually your family." As we shook hands, I was sure we would never have helped anyone that much back at home had our situations been reversed.

Giancarlo was barely out of sight, when Dick issued an edict: "This is the beginning of austerity. Ingegnere and Lorenzo have their own food. The ration for the three of us will be one slice of bread each for breakfast, lunch, and supper." Feeling hollow already, I didn't welcome this news. Dick added, "But, Joe, you'll be glad to know I'm not rationing you on spring water." I grunted and began to eat my breakfast slice — very slowly.

Dick seemed relaxed and was smiling cheerfully as he looked up at the clear blue sky. "Wouldn't it be wonderful if the Lord would grant us ten days of perfect weather?" That would take us to 21 October. To Dick's wish I added my silent prayer, thankful for the help we'd had so far.

Good to his word, at precisely 9:00 Ingegnere announced our departure and pointed out a route up the main ridge of the Morrone. Charlie led the way, pursuing a steep but plainly marked trail over boulders and through the everlasting scrub oak and stunted pine. Despite his rotundity and a flimsy pair of sport shoes with rubber soles, the old engineer climbed easily; and Lorenzo, who had good boots as did the rest of us, gave the impression that he could have run up the Morrone like a mountain goat. Still, both Italians seemed content to go at our pace. Ingegnere kept his eye on Charlie, and where the trail became vague he would tell *Carlo* to stay a little more right or a little more left. Charlie was amused at Ingegnere's orders, but understood and followed directions.

The first time I stopped to gulp down icy spring water, I peeked over at Rossbach and noticed him laughing at me. Though I was sweating freely, I kept both my jacket and sweater on — the temperature was probably in the mid-thirties at most. After two and a half hours of hard climbing, I still felt fresh and was glad our days on the mountain had conditioned us so well. Dick seemed to be doing nicely, too, though at times he had to favor that left leg.

A cloud drifted over the Morrone, and the valley to the west was lost in a bluish-purple haze. We reached timberline and struggled up a steep slope of huge, jagged rocks. I tried to remember where timberline was in the White Mountains back in New England and decided that we now were at around 5,300 to 5,500 feet. Almost straight above us, the mountain was shrouded in clouds and fog.

Ingegnere called to us, and we stopped to listen. "After we cross the rocks, we'll come to the western escarpment, where there are trails, but they're apparent only to trained climbers. I suggest each one select his own way to get up and then wait on the summit."

A short while later, near-perpendicular cliffs loomed above us for 200 or 300 feet and disappeared into the mist. Charlie and I scouted back and forth, trying to find a route for our ascent. I found only more cliffs, each one steeper than the last, but Charlie picked out a spot and began crawling up the face of the rock, looking like a big brown spider as he went. I couldn't see how in hell he was able to hold on. In a few minutes he was swallowed up by the fog.

Off to my left, Ingegnere and Lorenzo began their ascent, then Dick started to climb. Unable to stall any longer, I also began scrambling up. After about ten feet, I looked up but couldn't see anything further to grab onto. Nevertheless, I clung somehow to the flinty surface with a strength I didn't know I had, my fingers in the tiniest of cracks and my toes pushing on the narrowest of projections. At a certain point, immersed in fog, I looked down into an oppressive blinding whiteness and was stricken with a sudden vertigo. I flattened out against the rock and forced myself to keep looking up.

In time, I began to get the hang of it: reach up with one hand, claw for a grip a couple of feet above; then reach up with one toe and probe for some projection to push from; then heave myself up, hoping like hell the support wouldn't break off.

At another point I paused, gasping for breath, lost in an opaque world of mist. I sensed that the cliff had become considerably less steep, and, gaining confidence, I picked up a little speed and soon found that the slope had leveled off. Spotting a ledge above me, I was able to get both hands over it and haul myself up with an enormous feeling of relief, like a fogbound pilot who has just barely made the runway.

Lying sprawled out on the flat rock summit, I found that Charlie was looking down at me — I was never so glad to see anyone in my life. "That wasn't too graceful," he laughed, "but it certainly worked. What's happened to Dick?"

"Why I must have passed him in the fog." I leaned out over the cliff and called, "Dick!" It was like shouting into a feather pillow. I bellowed, "DICK!"

A muffled voice rumbled out of the white blanket below, "Here, god-damit!"

Minutes later Rossbach crawled slowly up into sight. Charlie and I each grabbed an arm and helped him up on top. For a few seconds he sat on the rock, catching his breath and rubbing his knee; then he asked, "Where's Ingegnere?"

"*Eccomi,*" announced the old man, emerging calmly out of the fog with Lorenzo. "We thought we'd lost all of you till I heard you calling Riccardo."

"Come on, you blokes," Charlie said. "You're wasting time again. Let's get cracking before we freeze!" Dick tried, but he couldn't mask his pain and exhaustion. Angry at Charlie, I looked over and caught Dick's eye — his tacit message, "Ignore it."

After estimating our position with relation to Salle, Ingegnere led us north along a knifelike ridge of solid rock for about half a mile, when the ridge dropped off in a perpendicular cliff. I hunted back and forth along the precipice but could find no way around it.

The drop appeared to be about 12 feet. Ingegnere and Lorenzo hung over the edge by their fingertips and let go. Lorenzo landed on his feet; Ingegnere rolled over and scrambled up, brushing himself off; Charlie made it easily. Then I hung over and let go. The drop was further than I thought. My feet struck the ground very hard, but I fell on all fours and wasn't hurt. Dick jumped to get away from the cliff and fell to the left, with one leg twisted under him. He landed with a loud "oomph!" With his wind knocked out, he lay on his side, again rubbing his left knee.

"You OK?" I asked. He didn't answer right away, so I went over to him. "I twisted this bloody leg ten years ago," he answered, "and now I've done the same damn thing again." In a few minutes he got up and tried to walk. It was painful even to watch.

We made our way over rocky terrain for another half-hour until we came out on a trail leading down the eastern slope. Our route up the mountain had been a mile too far south, and that had put us behind the cliff where we had to jump.

Toward 1:00, we stopped by a spring for a rest. Dick again rationed out to each of us just one slice of bread, this time with a thin smear of jam. I wondered how long I could keep going on this skimpy diet. I recalled that shortly after Rossbach, Prosser, and Ellzey had jumped out of the train in northern Italy, they hadn't been able to keep going because of lack of food — and their hunger had driven them into a town where they were quickly picked up. After I had devoured the bread and drunk two cups of water, I was as ravenous as before.

We were still very high up, and we were chilled from sitting down, so it was actually a relief to get going again. When I looked back at Dick limping along, he gave a little shake of his head. It meant, "Leave me alone, I'll make it." Our descent was gradual, the air warmer at every step. Soon the cold fog had lifted, and we paused just above a thick pine forest. Ingegnere pointed out the spectacular Valle dell'Orta, wedged between the Morrone and the Maiella. The lower valley was picturesque, dotted with tiny hamlets, and farther south, halfway up the eastern slope, perched the town of Caramanico, dominated by two church spires and bordered with terraced vineyards. The picturesqueness swiftly vanished, however, when Ingegnere revealed that the place was crawling with German troops. Above Caramanico, the Maiella rose in rocky, snow-filled ravines, a 9,500-foot barrier that we would have to cross at the pass.

Peering out over the valley, Dick asked, "Where the hell is Salle?"

Ingegnere consulted his map. "Off to our left below the shoulder of the mountain."

A little farther on, we came upon an old man in a field, turning the soil with a hoe. He was the first *contadino* (farmer) I'd seen since I got my civilian clothes, and I told the others I'd fool this guy into thinking I was an Italian. "*Buongiorno!*" I called. He just looked up at me and smiled. Then in my finest Abruzzesi, I asked him what the situation was in Salle. Grinning broadly, he said, "Hello, fellahs, I live in Peetsaburg long time. You live near there?" There were guffaws behind me — I even recognized Ingegnere's chuckle among them.

The man was delighted when I told him I hailed from New Jersey, which he knew was not far from Pittsburgh. Then he explained that there was an "Old Salle" and a "New Salle," and that the people of both places, nearly all Communists, were hospitable. We bade him goodbye and went on, intrigued by the fact that the Communists were coming off as the good guys in all this.

"I have my doubts about all that," declared Ingegnere. "There have been conflicting reports on that town."

Dick and I were just as skeptical. The man from "Peetsaburg" had been a little too glib. We decided to forget about Salle and, instead, look for a farmhouse down the valley. It was only mid-afternoon, and Dick felt he could keep going, since the trail would be mostly downhill from here on.

Turning south to avoid the town, we came to a long, deeply eroded ravine. Dick said he would have to walk around it in the open fields on the lower side; there was simply no way he could crawl down one steep side and up the other.

Up on the mountain, I had felt aloof, remote. Fog and solitude had afforded a kind of shelter, and I'd felt more secure. But now the old tightness came back in even greater intensity. How I hated coming back to German-occupied towns, patrols, and raids! Powerless to control my anxiety, I argued with Dick: "You can't go out there in the open! You'll attract a patrol, you'll be like a red flag."

He shouted back, "Goddamit, I have no choice! Now for Christ's sake simmer down." I glanced over at Ingegnere. He and Lorenzo were walking on oblivious of our outburst. Charlie was ahead of them, so I slid down into the ravine alone. Something stirring off to my left scared hell out of me. Four men in brown uniforms were staring at me — my heart went up in my throat. Then I recognized the cut of their uniforms. They were British! I heaved a sigh of relief.

After I identified our little group, one of them said, with a nervous grin, "Gave us a bit of a turn, Yank, ye did."

"Same here — thought you were Jerries for a minute."

"Bloody lot of them around. They came into Salle a while ago."

"A raid?"

"No, just a patrol. We got out easily. We're waiting for the British army to arrive."

Again, that trapped feeling! I'd heard that line too many times in the recent past and had an idea where the men were who had sat in Chieti, waiting "for the British to arrive." Saying a hasty goodbye to the four soldiers, I scrambled up out of the ravine. Whenever I felt that people were careless or cavalier, I couldn't get away fast enough.

Within a few minutes I caught up with the others. My relief was intense when Dick smiled as if nothing had happened. "I gather you didn't care for your limey friends," he said.

"Whew, they gave me the creeps! Jerry'll get those guys on his next raid. Now, let's have a look at the map and figure out where we're going."

The land below us fell away into a gorge cut by the Orte River. Winding south through the gorge, a secondary highway branched off the *Strada Nazionale* that we'd taken from Chieti to Popoli. It continued on through German-occupied Caramanico all the way to Campo di Giove at the foot of the valley. Further south, on our side, was a town called Roccacaramanico, which was connected to the highway by an old country road.

Ingegnere explained that Giancarlo had warned him that Germans were all over these roads, and that their patrols had picked up prisoners on the east side of the valley. It was obvious that we had to continue on, hugging the western side.

Here, crumbling stone walls separated small pastures that were grazed down to the bare soil. We continued walking along a stony path for an hour and a half, and by the time we reached a big stone house perched on the side of a hill the light was fading. There was no one around and the place was shuttered. I crept up some steps to a terrace and knocked on the door. Nothing happened. I pounded on it. An angry voice broke the stillness, "Who are you?"

"Siamo prigioneri Americani," I answered gently.

The door opened a crack, but there was a big rusty chain across inside. "I got nothing," he said gruffly. "What the Germans haven't taken your people want. Go somewhere else." The door started to close.

"Signore," I wailed, "we have to have a place to sleep. One of my companions had an accident and is lame, we can't go anywhere else. He can't walk any further."

He didn't answer, but the door opened a crack more. "Five! *Santa Maria!"* he cried.

Looking around, I could see ourselves through his eyes: five filthy, starving men, with scraggly beards and ragged clothes. For an instant I imagined myself opening the front door back home and looking out in the dusk at five hoboes peering at me — I'd slam the door in their faces and run to call the cops. Was there something wrong with us back in the States? Already, six sets of people here had helped us since we had gotten out. Now one wretched soul was resisting, and I couldn't blame him.

I tried him once more: We and the Italians were allies now; we had all left our homes and families to help free Europe; I had many, many Italian friends at home.

When I finished my pitch, there was a deep sigh; the chain clanked down, and the door opened. We entered, blinking, into a dark hall and went on into a big open room. A huge fireplace stood on the left, an iron cookpot hanging over some coals. A semicircle of slatted wooden boxes stood in front of the fire.

We squatted down on the boxes to wait, eyes glued to the cookpot, and for an hour I forced a desultory conversation with the *padrone*. Finally I looked at the pot over the fire and said to him bluntly, "We're very hungry. We climbed the Morrone from Santa Croce and have eaten only a small piece of bread since this morning."

"You don't understand, you people," he responded. "That's the way *we* have to live. You must get used to it."

Desperate, I looked at Dick. "Keep working on him, Joe, I think he's weakening." To avoid irritating the *padrone*, I changed the subject, hoping he'd hear my stomach growling. "What is the next town?"

"Roccacaramanico, then you go through the San Leonardo Pass to Campo di Giove. It is a long way, though easy going for you; but also easy for the German patrols — unfortunately." Reaching down into a small basket, he displayed a handful of dirty brown balls, the size of marbles.

"What are they?"

"Those, my friend, are potato culls, all the Germans left in my field. I can give you a few of these and nothing more." He swung the cookpot out and threw in a couple of handfuls of the culls.

For another hour, we waited, shifting on the uncomfortable boxes. After what seemed an eternity, he pulled off the pot, fished out the culls, and put them in a tin basin, which he handed to me without a word. Our little group divided the culls five ways — four or five each — and ate the tiny potatoes, including the skins with the dirt still on them.

"Is there somewhere we can sleep?" I inquired, crunching grit.

"Not in this house. Too dangerous. All the farms have been raided, and the Germans come in the night. Now you've got to get out. It's already too late."

"Haven't you got a barn where we can stay?" I persisted.

Spitting out a string of curses, the farmer drew a deep breath and said, impatiently, "I have some corn cribs out there full of husks. Bury yourselves in them and you'll be warm enough and safe for the night. But you must leave well before daylight, and you must give your word that if the Germans find you, you'll say you crawled in there on your own."

After we had sworn to all his conditions, he opened the door, looked around, and listened. A faint light shone from a waning moon, and frost glistened on the short grass. We followed him through the farmyard to some corn cribs about ten feet high. The slats slanted outward toward the top, so we would have to climb up a reverse angle. Ingegnere selected a crib, and he and Lorenzo moved up easily, hand over hand.

Charlie, having scaled another one like a monkey, began thrashing around in the husks. I followed, gripping the slats and getting my toes on the cross-pieces. When I stepped into the crib, I sank up to my knees. Then I leaned over the side to help Dick up. With considerable effort, he finally pulled himself over and fell in.

When I burrowed down in the husks, I discovered they had sawtooth edges and sharp points that stuck through my clothes like needles. Pulling my cap down and turning up my collar, I put my hands inside my jacket and twisted until the points didn't stick into me any more. Still those edges rubbed my skin, reminding me of the time the class wise guy in my grade school rubbed my arm with itching powder. In spite of my exhaustion, I tossed restlessly for hours. Somewhere around 2:00, I mercifully fell into a dead sleep, and when I awoke it was broad daylight. I looked at my watch — it was nearly 8:30.

"Rossbach," I called, "we got to get out of here right away, it's way past 8:00." He made a noise somewhere between a sigh and a groan. "My God, my knee feels dislocated."

In a couple of minutes, I was out of the crib. Ingegnere, Lorenzo, and Charlie were waiting beside the next one. "I think we should get moving quickly," Ingegnere urged.

"I agree, but Riccardo's having trouble." Ingegnere raised his eyebrows and shrugged.

Dick at last climbed out and slid down, landing hard and rolling over. Clenching his teeth, he sat up and began to rub his knee. It was a cold gray morning with no one in sight. I gazed across the valley and wouldn't have known if there was a German within a hundred miles.

"They're having breakfast," Dick said. "They'll be around for us later."

"I know, but we told the guy we'd be out before daylight."

"Goddamit, go ahead if you want to. I'll get going as soon as I can." He heaved himself up, took a few cautious steps, and started walking south. We went past the farm buildings, below the rugged upper slopes and along a lane through dozens of small farms. Still we didn't see a soul. House windows were shuttered or boarded up, skinny goats poked around for a few blades of grass in muddy fields, a donkey with his ribs showing stared at us out of sad eyes. The barnyards smelled of manure and human excrement. As we passed the shuttered houses, I felt unseen eyes studying us.

At about noon the roar of a heavy vehicle resounded across the valley. Dick commanded, "Freeze! Don't move a thing; they may have field glasses." We stood motionless, peering across the valley toward the road. "I see him," Dick said. "It's a German armored car. Stay absolutely still until it's out of sight."

The car ground up a long hill, came down the road, and disappeared into the edge of a town. I was sure it was Roccacaramanico, straight ahead of us, straddling a green shoulder of the Morrone.

"I don't like that one damn bit," I said. "But, by God, if we don't get some food there, it's another 12 or 14 miles to Campo di Giove with nothing to eat."

"I understood what you said," Ingegnere said, "Let me go in with the boy. We're less conspicuous, and we don't have the language problem. I'll try to find a place to stay and something to eat."

"That would be excellent," I encouraged him. Dick didn't take very long to agree with the proposal. We watched them disappear along a lane between the farms, then settled down to wait.

About an hour later, I began to worry. "Either they've gotten picked up," I said, "or they found a place to stay."

"Oh hell," Dick said, "they're probably eating their heads off, but either way, it doesn't help us. I think I'll go in and see if I can get some food." I watched him limping down the lane and shook my head.

Charlie and I sat waiting under a hedge. I tried some conversation, but he just didn't want to talk, so I fell silent. Another hour passed. "I don't know what's happened," I said, "but I think we ought to go in after them." Charlie concurred, saying he thought we should have gone in long before.

Just as we started out, Dick appeared, walking slowly. "I spoke to one woman, but it was useless," he reported. "She told me she didn't dare give me any food." I had stalled all I could. "Guess it's my turn. Maybe I can do a little better with the language."

"I haven't the slightest doubt of that," Dick growled. "But I wish I were just as certain you wouldn't eat all the food before you bring it back here."

I produced the frozen smile I reserved for that kind of remark.

With great reluctance, I left my pack behind, because Dick said I looked more Italian without it. I strode out rapidly, past farmyards and pastures, glad to be moving at my own pace for once. In a small gully I came upon a woman washing clothes in a stream. I told her I was an American and wanted to go into the town if there weren't any Germans there. She said they had arrived just a short while ago in *"un carro armato,"* but she thought they'd gone by now.

I thanked her, though I wasn't sure what for. These people never really knew whether or not the Germans had moved out; I could be walking right into the armored car.

Farther along, I came into a narrow cobblestone street where there were no sidewalks and the stone buildings seemed to lean in over my head and close out the sky. Nervously, I glanced behind me, thinking I'd heard footsteps. False alarm. But if this was a blind alley, I was walking into a trap. With every second, I dreaded it more.

Around a curve in the street, an old woman was squeezed back against a doorway, strands of gray hair sticking out from under her shawl. She stared up at me, her toothless mouth agape. Abruptly, she pulled up her black skirts and sprinted down the street and around a corner.

"My God, I'm popular," I said out loud. Up and down empty streets I continued to hunt, until I found one that opened into a little *piazza*, about the size of a tennis court. Here a half-dozen women dressed in dark clothes were gathered around a stone drinking fountain and trough. One glanced over her shoulder at me, then started rattling along in Abruzzese, while two of them darted away, one with a severe limp. The other three waited, but also looked ready to bolt.

"Ladies, Ladies, please wait a moment."

One of them reached into the folds of her dress and produced a chunk of bread. "Leave! Leave right away!" she implored. "The Germans were here a few minutes ago, and I know they're coming back." She was nearly hysterical.

I wanted to run as badly as she did, but I hesitated, holding out my hand. Then the other two women gave me more chunks of bread with a frantic, *"Via! Via!"* (Go! Go!) Thanking them, I started back. Suddenly, the toothless old lady whom I'd met coming into town reappeared and handed me a freshly baked loaf, still hot. Its fragrant aroma forced me to fight an impulse to wolf it down on the spot. Stuffing the bread inside my jacket and feeling a little like weeping, I began to retrace my route. The inclination to run was almost overpowering.

I was nearly out of the village when I heard uneven footsteps behind me. I whirled around to see the woman with the limp hobbling up and holding out a big hunk of prosciutto. I started to speak, but she shushed me and waved me out of the town. Her present tucked inside my jacket along with the bread, I strode out as fast as I could. This time I really choked up — she looked so thin and poor. How could these people do this when they had so little themselves? I had never heard of anything like this back home — except perhaps the Bible story about the widow who gave the farthing that was all she possessed.

Twenty minutes later, I nearly jumped out of my skin when Dick called out to me from behind a wall. "I see from your expression and your eight-months-pregnant look that you were successful. I only hope the food isn't vibrating like that cheese those shepherds gave us."

Dick permitted us the first semblance of a meal in two days. Between mouthfuls, I related what had happened in town. The account left Dick shaking his head. "This time you certainly proved your theory about these people," he conceded.

Half an hour later Ingegnere and Lorenzo returned. They'd had something to eat in town, but had a bad fright when the Germans suddenly returned. Fortunately, the people were able to show our friends a back way, and they had missed the Germans by a scant few minutes. Motorized and foot patrols were now all over the area, so we got moving in a hurry.

We climbed the ridge above Roccacaramanico and, well beyond the town, descended into the valley. From the map it appeared we would have to cross the road only once. Since there were thick woods all along the far side, we agreed to cross right away. With another six or seven hours to Campo di Giove, I knew we'd be spending the night in those woods.

Daylight was fading as we neared the road. The going was relatively easy, and we moved quickly along between patches of cover. This was my first road crossing, and I studied the copses and woods up and down the valley for spots that might hide a patrol. Then I swallowed hard, took several deep breaths, and placed each foot softly so I would hear even the sound of twigs cracking.

A patch of gravel surface was visible just ahead, as we crouched behind some bushes. "I'll go first," Ingegnere whispered. "If you see me in trouble, get away quickly. And if they catch you, you know nothing about me."

"Capisco molto bene," Dick said wryly.

The old boy smiled, and he and Lorenzo moved rapidly over the road and disappeared into the heavy woods. Charlie followed after a one-minute interval, sauntering out and across the road.

In the distance, I heard the roar of an armored car. Dick stepped out, and I watched the broad back of his tweed jacket and his rolling gait, as he crossed at a half-run and was gone in seconds.

I didn't wait the full minute. I couldn't, what with imagining that armored car coming around the corner just as I would be reaching the middle of the road. I sped across at a dead run and arrived at the woods all out of breath.

"Benone! Andiamo, subito!" said Ingegnere and led the way off into the woods.

Chapter 20

The Maiella

Traveling south parallel to the road, we entered a rocky valley that ran along the Maiella down to the San Leonardo Pass, where a late afternoon sun splashed the leaves with brilliant reds and golds. Here and there throughout the woods we came upon the stone beehive shelters for the shepherds.

As I began edging to the east, farther away from the road, Dick eyed me. "Dammit, Joe, quit sneaking up toward the mountain. You know I can't walk up there."

"OK, sure," I agreed and stopped angling away so sharply. Charlie, meanwhile, was insisting that we walk near the road, and carrying on about our being windy to such a point that I got really angry. Out there, he had a far greater chance of being spotted and of exposing us too. To cap it all, he called over, "You chaps are pretty silly, stumbling around in those woods. I'm going out on that road — it's perfectly safe, you can hear those Jerry lorries for miles."

"God help him," I muttered. "He thinks *we're* silly." I wanted to scream at him, but restrained myself and waited for Dick's reaction. He just stopped and stared at Charlie. "You do what you want," he said sounding somewhat annoyed. "I'm not as nervous as old Joe, here, but they do guard bridges, you know. You're just asking for trouble." This time I didn't mind being the butt — Dick and I were on the same wavelength.

Charlie merely shrugged and started off toward the road. "He's one big, juicy piece of bait out there," I pointed out, "and we oughta get out of here in a hurry."

"I know how you feel, Joe," he answered. "But I haven't any choice. I *have* to stick to level ground."

By now, almost completely unraveled, I wanted to shout back, "You just told me that." Every nerve in my body was sending out red signals, like that instinct I had the night the Germans took Chieti. Despite what Dick had said, I turned farther east, but managed to keep him in sight. Ingegnere and Lorenzo walked midway between us. The old man looked worried — the sole of one of his shoes was coming loose. I slowed down to keep pace with the two Italians.

From time to time I watched for Charlie out on the road, occasionally catching a glimpse of him. But he was already a long way off, and the daylight was almost spent. Before long I lost sight of him completely.

It was dark when Dick and I and our two remaining companions reached a clearing with several crumbling stone shelters. We picked one that seemed to be in the best shape, a structure roughly six feet high and six in diameter, with a small opening for a door. The ground inside was covered with dry leaves. The place was big enough for just two of us; the other pair would have to stand guard outside.

While settling in at our new site, I detected a trace of wood smoke in the air, then something caught my eye — the light from a small fire flickering through the trees ahead. "That's got to be shepherds," Dick said. "A German patrol would never light that out here. But I'm worried about Charlie. Let's go have a look for him and then investigate that fire."

Ingegnere and Lorenzo wanted no part of either proposal and said they'd wait for us at the shelter. I was willing to risk going to the fire — at least we could sneak up quietly and hear what language the people were talking. But the thought of Charlie out there had become a nightmare. I had an unbearable premonition of disaster for all of us, and was convinced that a bridge guard or patrol had already picked him up. They'd know he hadn't been alone and would sweat him out, using a hammerlock for quick results. (A guy had got one on me in a fight once and it felt as if he were tearing my arm out of the socket.) Surely Charlie wouldn't be able to hold out, and the patrol would hunt till they found us. Going out there had been so idiotic that I now began to wonder if he'd been a plant. But that didn't make sense. Why would he have waited so long to turn us in? I tried to drive all these notions from my mind.

Walking stealthily through the woods, I worried what would happen to Dick if we had to make a run for it. Lorenzo would take off like a deer. For a short distance, I wouldn't be far behind. Ingegnere would be clever and hide. But Dick . . . .

It was pitch dark now, so I didn't object too much when we went out toward the road to look for Charlie. I searched the woods to the south and east, but felt foolish doing so, because Charlie certainly hadn't gone that way. And I had to admit to myself that this was just a stall on my part to avoid going near the road.

After several minutes I heard Dick's uneven footsteps off to my right. "I looked up and down that road," he declared. "Not a sign of anything. You can hear better out there, and once I heard a vehicle in the distance."

"Dick, I don't like the looks of the situation. You remember I've got Charlie's battledress jacket in my knapsack? That's much too valuable for him to leave behind voluntarily."

"At this point," Dick broke in, "this search is entirely too dangerous," so we continued on ahead towards the firelight. As we approached, I heard with relief the rhythmic cadence of mountain Abruzzese. Two bearded shepherds were sitting on a log by the fire. A third, a huge man, stood with arms akimbo, a sheepskin poncho flung over his broad shoulders, casting a grotesque shadow on the trees, while the red light from the flames flickered on the faces of the other two men.

"*Buona sera,*" said the big one without looking around, his voice coarse but not unfriendly. One of the men on the log stared at us and remarked, "*Prigionieri inglesi.*

"Good evening," I said. "We're escaped American prisoners, not English," then added that we were going down toward the pass — to let them know we wouldn't be hanging around. At that, I asked for something to eat.

The man in the sheepskin murmured, "*Sempre la stessa vecchia storia*" (Always the same old story). He continued, wagging his head, "We never have much, hunger is an old companion of ours, but you can share some of what we have. Come back later, and we'll give you a little mutton and lasagna." Learning that there were four of us, he exclaimed, "*Santa Madonn'!*" and gazed into the coals.

Later that evening, Ingegnere and Lorenzo went back with us, and we all sat down beside the fire. After a few minutes Dick and I held out our canteen cups, but the man stirring the pot appeared not to notice. It had been six hours since we'd had the food at Roccacaramanico, and the smell of the cooking mutton was tantalizing. We waited. And waited. To distract myself, I asked the shepherds about the Germans in the valley, but they evaded the question. Unable to stand it any longer, I asked as tactfully as possible when we might eat. Dick followed what I'd said and spoke out in English, "For Christ's sake, Joe, cut out that Old-World courtesy again and get us some grub."

The oldest-looking shepherd burst out laughing. "I live in States two years. I understan' leetle English — you boys hungry?"

Dick and I forced a laugh, and the man at the cooking pot finally ladled some stew into my canteen cup, announcing, "*Quello è per tutti voi altri.*" The one cup was to be shared among four.

Dick understood as well as I did. "I guess they meant what they said about being hard up themselves," I said, suddenly a little suspicious. "Let's leave well enough alone and not press it any further."

Dividing the stew four ways yielded barely a mouthful each. Even so, it helped considerably. Dick prodded me to try for some more chow, but I advised against it. Furthermore, there were too damn many Germans in this valley to hang around the fire any longer.

Just then, a young boy who had been sitting a few yards away in the darkness blurted out, "I must tell you the Germans come around every morning to get goat's milk from us." Dick said he didn't believe it, but that was just to keep me from panicking. Ingegnere spoke to one of the older men, who remarked casually, "Oh, the boy is only joking."

"Some joke!" Ingegnere muttered.

Stumbling back to the shelter in the dark, I warmed up a little. But the air was cold, and I knew we'd have another frost. We started a fire in one of the stone beehives, shielding the doorway with leaves and branches to keep the light from showing. This made the smoke so bad we couldn't sleep, so we let the fire burn down.

After shivering and tossing for a couple of hours, I heard footsteps outside. Dick got up, carefully stamped out the few remaining coals, then took my arm and whispered, "Now, take it easy, Joe, it may not be anything." Not anything, I thought? Only the patrol that picked up Charlie, or just some German friends of those shepherds. All at once, I had to get out fast — the shelter was a trap! The others agreed. We crept out, making only the faintest rustling. The blood pounded in my head as I strained to listen.

The footsteps moved furtively past on the east side — one, maybe two pairs, measured, even, each foot put down softly, now circling back toward the road. They went off, about 50 yards, then came nearer on the other side. Two men for sure! Crouching over for a sprinter's start, I was prepared to take off, when I heard them over toward the road.

Again they returned, nearer, less than 50 feet away. If I broke too soon, I'd blow it for the others — had to time it to the last second. With my back breaking from the cramped position, I eased up slowly and pressed myself against a tree, taking shallow, silent breaths. Another pair — three now. They stopped. I tried even harder to hear; were they whispering? They turned and began moving to the north, noisier, firmer steps, heading away toward Caramanico. Gradually, the sounds disappeared, until all I could hear was a ringing in my ears.

Still, I insisted that no one move for half an hour. Finally, Dick whispered, "If that was part of a patrol, it wouldn't be logical for them to come back. Let's get out of this cold, but this time we'll post a guard."

13 October

It was after 1:00. For the rest of the night two of us stood watch, tending a tiny fire while the other two tried to sleep. I stood outside, swinging my arms, still straining to listen in the 20° chill. All I could hear were the two Italians rolling back and forth on the leaves inside the shelter. No one did much sleeping that night.

At 7:00 the next morning we went over and asked the shepherds for directions to Campo di Giove. One nodded and said, "Wait!" In a moment, he produced a hunk of bread. He tore it in four pieces and handed one to each of us. No one could convince me now that these shepherds had tipped off the Germans.

The shepherd sat down on the log and pointed down the valley. "We are now at the beginning of the San Leonardo Pass, which begins a gradual ascent up to Campo di Giove. Follow the direction of the road until you see the town off to your right; it is the only one in the cul-de-sac at the foot of the valley." And he added the Italian version of "You can't miss it."

The Guado di Coccia, which was the pass out of the valley, beyond Campo di Giove, was a series of rock slides and cliffs for which even the shepherds had a healthly respect. In the translation, however, I toned that part down substantially so as not to upset Dick. He gave me a quizzical look, then went over to a windfall and broke off a stick to use as a cane.

When we set out, Dick and I had a discussion about routes. I knew the safest way was up on the shoulder of the Maiella, but that it would be far too difficult for him. We at last agreed that he would walk in the valley pastures, while Ingegnere, Lorenzo, and I would take the upper route.

As we climbed, I looked down and was just able to pick him out when he moved — his dark brown clothes were a sort of camouflage. Whenever I did spot him, he was limping and using his "cane" — a sorry picture of a man in a lot of pain, every step a battle. And I guessed he was aware that his chances were diminishing as his injury grew more serious. Desperately sorry for leaving him exposed down there, I recalled again what had originally got him into this mess: it was the fact that he had stuck to his gun positions to help his wounded men, and had remained so long that the battery had been bombed out of existence by the U.S. Navy and Army Air Forces.

Ingegnere saw me looking down at him and read my thoughts. "I'm worried too," he said, "about our friend Riccardo. It's not good to be so close to that road, especially after what happened last night."

"Do you really think they got Charlie?"

He nodded. "This morning when we saw the shepherds, I noticed something in their manner. That piece of bread was to throw you off."

"I can't believe that," I answered.

We stopped to catch our breath, and he put his hand on my shoulder. "Giuseppe, you like my people, and I like you for that, but I've known these shepherds longer than you have."

We walked on in silence and reached a dense forest of beech, chestnut, and wild holly. The cover was good, but long thorns tore our ragged clothes as we labored up the steep slope. The leaves along the way had turned to shades of olive, russet, and burnt umber. Far above us, I could see deep ravines filled with snow. Once, I even caught a glimpse of the snowcapped peak of Monte Amaro, against a cobalt-blue sky. At 9,500 feet, Monte Amaro, meaning Bitter Mountain, was the highest peak of the Maiella. A thousand feet below us stretched the rocky San Leonardo Pass.

By pre-arrangement, I went down to meet Dick, while Ingegnere and Lorenzo stayed up on the shoulder. Delighted to see him, I completely forgot my apprehension at being right near the road. We gazed at the length of the lofty rock massif of the Maiella but couldn't identify the pass where we would have to cross. As I sat mesmerized by the spectacle, I muttered in Italian, partly to myself, "It will be brutal climbing over that mountain."

Dick gave me that steely look of his. *"La guerra è una brutta cosa"* (War is a brutal thing).

Remembering D'Acciaio's observation — if the Allies have many men like Riccardo, the Germans would be in for a tough time — I realized that Dick's remark about war's brutality had applied to himself. While I didn't want to admit it even in my own mind, the odds against Dick were getting longer.

Since the terrain ahead seemed less steep, Dick decided to come up the mountain with me, while Ingegnere and Lorenzo remained lower. Walking the steep shoulder was difficult, so we proceeded slowly, finally coming out in mid-afternoon into the huge open pastures above Campo di Giove. From our vantage point of some 4,000 feet this ancient Roman town, whose name translates to "Field of Jupiter," appeared perched on a hill rising from the valley floor. Its clustered stone buildings were green and brown with moss and lichens, and on the north side of the town there rose the spire and belfry of a medieval church.

Up the valley the road disappeared into the San Leonardo Pass toward Caramanico, with its German patrols. To the south, I could just make out railroad tracks and a station, sure to be guarded by German troops. Directly behind the station, the 7,000- to 8,000-foot peaks of the mountain wall blocked the end of the valley. The pass out of this natural trap was still not visible from our position.

On our way down the mountain we met some shepherds who were chatty and friendly, assuring us that the people in Campo di Giove had an organization for helping prisoners. From the way the shepherds talked, I didn't think it would be a Communist group, and I was relieved to learn that the edginess of the villagers in the upper valley hadn't come down this far.

We sat on the bank of a small pool, where the shepherds had watered their sheep. Ingegnere and Lorenzo climbed up to join us and fill their bottles. We pulled off our shoes and socks. My feet were encrusted with mud that had seeped through cracks in the soles of my shoes. What a heavenly feeling to

The Maiella (9,170 feet) with the Guado di Coccia on the right, and Campo di Giove in the foreground, as it has been rebuilt since the war.

wash my feet and wiggle my toes! "Dick," I asked, "how does it feel to wash your feet?"

"A damn sight better than some tail I've had in my distant past."

At 4:00, Dick and I had just finished a chunk of bread with a bit of jam, when I spotted a tall figure in a brown felt hat and a long black cape striding up the mountain. The gait and manner were decidedly un-Italian. When he approached, I recognized Capt. Colin Campbell, formerly of the Cameron Highlanders, whom I had known at Chieti. I remembered him as a very stubborn, opinionated officer with a fantastic but somewhat insane war record. His appearance on the scene alarmed me, as he was well known for his hair-raising schemes.

Campbell expressed his pleasure at running into us again, and eagerly accepted our offer of something to eat. I thought it a good investment. "Did you hear about the plane crash up on the Maiella?" he asked.

"No," Dick replied. "Whose was it?"

"One of ours. He went down during that fog yesterday. British Intelligence must have gone crackers, because he was cruising at 5,000 feet, when he shouldn't have been under ten. I went up to the crash site with two Italians and some mules. The aircraft had burned and only one crew member survived. We salvaged what we could of the plane's wreckage, collected the ID tags, and buried the bodies.

"We brought the injured chap down on a mule. Bad show — he'd gone through the instrument panel and had a compound fracture of the leg."

His graphic description of the poor guy's injuries made me shudder. "Who's taking care of him?" I asked, thinking of how that guy would be kicked around in those cattle cars if he got picked up and sent to Germany.

"There's a doctor in town who operated on him. Very clever fellow, you know. Did a first rate job with precious little equipment and no anesthetic."

Dick looked at his feet, slowly shaking his head. "By the way," he asked Campbell, "did you escape from Chieti?"

"No. Bad luck, our tunnel wasn't finished. We got out from Camp 78 at Fonte d'Amore."

"When?" Dick asked.

Campbell finished his bread and relaxed back against the rock. "About a week ago. Do you remember a young officer named Ryan?"

"Yes, I do," I said.

"Well, he and an OR and I took some food and water and climbed up and hid between the ceiling and rafters of our building. The idea was to stay there till Jerry left and then come out, but we wound up staying there nine days. The Germans caught onto our stunt and blew up all the other buildings around us, and in some they shot up through the ceilings with those machine-pistols. We watched through cracks and once or twice I rather thought we'd had it.

"They still hadn't found us when all the prisoners had left. When we started to come down, though, we had a bit of a jolt: 3,000 German troops happened to be arriving; we had to stretch our food and water for another two days. Our circumstances were a trifle tight, and when we left our hiding place we weren't in such good shape. But there were only a few guards hanging around, so we had a very easy escape."

Dick looked at me and said with an affected English accent, "That water ration wouldn't have done for *you*, would it old boy?"

"Hardly," I said, dourly.

Campbell went on, "We've been here five days, and the chaps in town have fed us well and given us these civilian clothes."

Dick asked Campbell where he'd been staying and learned that he and the other two men were living in the valley in a tiny cottage, which he pointed out to us. It was about two miles from Campo di Giove and located right on the edge of the road.

Campbell invited us and the two Italians to come by his house later that afternoon, so he could take us into town and show us where to get food. Ingegnere said, "It will be better if the boy and I go in separately as we did at Roccacaramanico. We make less of a crowd and don't attract so much attention. You'll be better off, and it's far less dangerous for us."

"Va bene, arrivederci," Campbell said getting up. He seemed relieved not to have to bring four along.

Our Cameron Highlander marched down the mountain, looking more like a Scottish laird on the moors than an Italian *paesano*. When he was out of earshot, I said to Dick, "What do you think of that escape from Fonte d'Amore?"

"The guy has the nerve of the devil, but in my book a slightly screwy mentality, about in keeping with living on a road where German trucks drive by."

"I'm glad *you* said it," I burst out. Dick gave me a tiny frown. Though sorry I'd let it slip out, I couldn't help adding, "It also makes me nervous about going into town with him."

"I'm afraid you'll have to be nervous for both of us. I don't think I could get in town and back. I've got to give this leg some rest if I'm going to get over that pass tomorrow." I was upset, but not surprised.

The thought of going into the town without him, though, set me on edge. The odds were against you, going into towns, and I hated to push my luck. But I kept my feelings to myself and agreed to go in and bring back some food.

At dusk Dick struggled along with me down to Campbell's house, where we called quietly outside the door. No answer. I knocked loudly. The place was deserted. Dick reminded me Campbell had said "afternoon." Going into town in broad daylight was just like Campbell and his reckless attitude. This was too much, and I burst out, "For God's sake, this whole damn situation is ass-backwards. This town is supposed to be so well organized to take care of prisoners. Yet we know there's always some Fascist spy around, and the Germans are up the valley only an hour from here. Besides, there's a railroad and a station a couple of miles south of us, and it's sure to be guarded."

Dick answered me in a somber tone: "Joe, quite possibly all you say is true, but perhaps there are some risks we just have to accept."

A fat lot of good that advice did me! Now, as it grew darker and it came time for me to set out, I grew tense and fearful. I left Dick sitting outside Campbell's house, roasting a couple of antique potatoes in the coals of a small fire. I'd learned to read his feelings pretty well over the past three weeks, and this time it was obvious that he was in severe pain. For a moment, I wondered if I'd ever see him again.

Striding briskly along the road to Campo di Giove, I kept my eyes, ears, even nose keenly attentive. The sunset over the Sulmona Basin turned from deep red to purple, and it was completely dark when I passed the road coming down from Caramanico. It reminded me of Charlie Rydesdale. The last time we had seen him had been on that road, and, ever since, his fate had lain between Dick and me like an unmentioned ghost. We were both sure he'd been picked up, but the subject was taboo. By now I didn't give a damn how much of a nervous wreck anyone thought I was — his disappearance had convinced me we had to be constantly and totally on the alert. And even with all the precautions in the world, the odds were still heavily against us.

In half an hour I found myself ascending a cobblestone street into town. I jumped when a small black figure slid out of a doorway. Strong, wiry fingers gripped my arm and a woman's hoarse voice inquired, *"Prigioniero Americano?"*

"Si."

"Vieni! The doctor will see you," and she added the word I most wanted to hear, *"Mangia!"*

She scurried off and I followed. A door opened, showing a faint glimmer of light around a blackout curtain, and the old lady whispered, "The doctor, here he is!"

The door closed behind me, and I found myself facing a bespectacled man of about 30, with light brown hair, a broad face with high cheek bones. He grabbed my hand. "Good evening, I'm glad you're here. Your friend told me you would be coming, so as it grew later I became a little worried. We'll help you, but first you must have something to eat." He spoke refined Italian.

In the dim candlelight, I noticed Campbell and two other Britishers sitting at a long table. Slices of bread and a carafe of red wine were set on a clean white tablecloth. Boxes were piled against the walls all around the room. The doctor waved to an empty seat across from Campbell. *"Accomodatevi,"* he said, *"E mangiate."*

"What happened to you? We waited for you," Campbell said.

"I thought it better to come after dark."

"What on earth for?"

The doctor came over and stood by my chair. "But what happened to your American friend?" he wanted to know. "Wasn't he supposed to come too?"

"He's very lame, so he stayed in the woods to rest his leg."

"I wish he had come, I might have helped him," the doctor responded. His offer was something to think about. I noticed Campbell staring at me, looking suspicious and frustrated, and I realized we had rattled all this off pretty fast in Italian, and he hadn't understood.

A young man brought me a bowl of pasta. Campbell and his friends were eating unhurriedly, as if they were back in Scotland in their regimental mess. The doctor pulled over a chair and sat next to me, prodding, *"Mangiate, mangiate!"* I caught the note of urgency in his voice.

While I ate as fast as I could, he went on: "I'm the *sindaco* (mayor) of Campo di Giove, and also a medical doctor."

"May I have your name?" I asked.

Hesitating at first, he said, "Of course you mustn't mention it to anyone, especially if you get caught again." I promised. "I am Enzo Sciuba, the head of this organization that's helping the prisoners. However, that's only the beginning. . . ." His eyes wavered over to Campbell, who was busy eating. "The men we have will also be organized as *partigiani*, and we'll need help."

I said quickly that I knew precisely what he was talking about and that I'd previously come across another situation like it. He nodded and went on, "When you get to the British, or preferably the Americans, I ask you to tell them we are here. By then we'll have an effective group, but we'll need —"

I interrupted, "Guns, ammunition, radios, clothing, food."

"I see you know." He smiled wanly.

When I was halfway through the pasta, a man burst into the far end of the room, jabbering feverishly. The doctor went over quickly, saying, *"Calma, calma!"* But his attempt at reassurance had little effect. The man rattled on at machine-gun speed.

Curious, I put down my fork and listened. Campbell regarded the man casually for a moment and went on eating. The doctor turned quickly toward us — I had made out, amid this stranger's babbling, two words: *Tedeschi* and *rastrellamento*. I sprang from my chair. Campbell seemed either not to understand or not to care. *"Dottore,"* I stammered, "we must leave right away."

"Yes. The information's reliable. There's not much time."

Leaning across the table, I said to Campbell, "Did you get that?"

"Sit down and finish your meal!"

The guy had me so buffaloed, I actually sat down on the edge of my chair and picked up my fork. Then it hit me: What the hell am I doing? Except for Sciuba, all the Italians were running around in a panic. Leaping to my feet, I shouted at Campbell, "You can stay here and get rounded up, but I'm getting the hell out of here."

"Good Lord! You're as bad as the Eyeties," he replied impatiently.

I thanked the doctor and ran for the door, barely a minute after the panicky man had come in. A small boy led me out a back way into a narrow alley, saying, *"Andiamo, rapidissimo!"*

He pulled me by the hand and started running. We careened down some steps behind the house, raced along dark alleys and around corners. He half-turned and alerted me with, *"Scala!"* (Steps!) and bounded up a flight of stairs, across a square, into a narrow street. In a quarter of a mile, this lane led to the road out of town where the boy slowed to a fast walk. Footsteps pounded in the distance behind us, and I assumed Campbell had had a change of heart.

The boy said, "There was a patrol on the other side of the town, but we were too fast for them. Do you know your way from here?"

"Yes, very well."

"Good, you'll probably see the main part of the German troops on your left. Stay that side of them," he said, pointing south.

I thanked him, and he started back to town.

At the junction with the road to Caramanico, I heard the noise of truck engines to the north and turned off into a pasture to the south, walking fast, watching the trucks. Occasionally I saw lights and heard voices. The column of trucks, coming directly south, appeared to be in position to make a wide sweep around the town. Half a mile beyond them, I swung back toward the road and, upon reaching it, stopped, looked in both directions, and listened intently.

When footsteps again sounded behind me, I spun around to make out three dark shapes following, heel plates in their boots clicking in cadence on the hard road. Campbell and his friends had caught up. I fell back in step with them, matching their British stride. No one mentioned our hurried departure.

As we approached Campbell's cottage, I sneaked a look behind me. The line of trucks was now well to the south of our road and seemed to be circling the town. Lights were still flashing and engines roared in low gear. Not one of the Britishers turned his head.

When we arrived at Campbell's house, we found Dick sitting by the remains of his little fire. He got up slowly.

"What happened to you, old chap? We had a good feed in there," Campbell said. I wanted to kick him.

"I told you, I'm lame. I couldn't come in," Dick replied with some irritation.

"Well, then, we'll give you a turn at guard duty. That'll cheer you up." I could feel Dick's anger.

Our "Senior British Officer" began issuing orders for the guard, according to his army's regulations, which included a lot of jargon neither Dick nor I understood. Standing right next to Dick, I heard him mutter, "Fuck that crap!" And with a shake of his head, he whispered, "That's enough for me. This assumption of command reminds me too much of the Chieti fiasco."

"I've had it with this joker," I agreed. "Let's get the hell out of here." After offering our excuses, we headed off in an easterly direction, away from both cottage and town, toward the slope of the Maiella.

"I've had a hell of a wait for my supper listening to that guy," Dick said. "How about some of that grub?"

I'd almost welcomed the hassle with Campbell — it had put off the agonizing moment. With a deep breath, I broke the news, "Let me tell you what happened."

There was a fearful silence, during which I wanted to run away and hide. Finally he said, "Well, haven't you got *anything?*"

"No, we ran into a *rastrellamento* back there, they sent a patrol into town and I —"

"You didn't get anything to eat?" he asked, incredulously.

"Yes, I did at first, but a guy barged in all of a sudden and said the Germans were coming —"

"And you had to run? Couldn't you have grabbed something as you went out?"

"Of course, I should have, and I'm goddam sorry. Do you think I go around doing this for fun?" I shot back, in anguish.

"Don't be ridiculous. What I do object to is the fact you were probably being so polite you didn't have time to —"

I cut him off. "Now look, Dick, I've already told you I was sorry, and I'll also say that if I hadn't panicked, I might have grabbed something. But with a patrol in town, I could've been cornered in that house, so I tore out the door as fast as I could. Now take something for yourself from the reserve, and let's try to forget it." He took a fair sized chunk of bread, small consolation compared to the hot food I'd had.

Midnight had come when we tramped into some woods on the foothills below the Guado di Coccia and lay down. With sleep impossible on such rocky and uneven ground, I tossed and turned, worrying about having to cross the pass in an exhausted state, about Dick's bad leg, about *rastrellamenti*, about a thousand other things.

At one in the morning it started to drizzle and the temperature dropped sharply. The moisture gathered in big drops on the sparse leaves overhead and spattered on my face and hands. Soon my jacket was soaked through. I got up and moved about, trying to get warm. Dick was awake too, so we sat up, propped against a tree and chatted idly.

"Have your parents always lived in New York?" I asked.

"They've mainly lived there since they were married. My father left Germany before World War I and met my mother not long after he got to the States. It seems things weren't too good in Germany even back then."

We remained silent a few minutes. I asked, "Is Sue living in New York too?"

"Yes, in her mother's apartment with our daughter Cynthia, whom I've never seen."

I was sorry I had asked, so I changed the subject. "Do you think we'll ever see Ingegnere and the boy again?" The question must have sounded stilted.

"We may never find out any more about them than about Charlie. Since they're not back yet, I'm not too optimistic. And I'm sorry about the old boy. He was very decent to us, and his maps were a big help."

"Now we'll have to fall back on the Rossbach cartography," I said forcing a laugh.

14 October

After a while we collapsed on the ground for the second time, and I drifted off into a fitful sleep. I woke up with a start at the sound of small arms fire. It was 3:00 by my watch. Bright lights and flares shot into the sky around the perimeter of Campo di Giove. Trucks rumbled in low gear, sounding as if they were moving in on the town.

The shooting went on sporadically for the rest of the night, and the rain continued to soak through our clothes. We turned back and forth on the rocky ground, teeth chattering, until the gray light of dawn appeared through the half-bare trees on the slope above us. I had heard Dick rustling around for a while, when he said, "Come on, Frelinghuysen, kick the blonde out of bed and get your ass over here and help me make a fire. I've got a few shreds of tea, and I'll allow us each a slice of bread from the reserve."

How on earth does he do it? I marveled. Except for the blonde, I did as he said and went and gathered some damp sticks. Dick was struggling to light them, when he began to stare down the hill. "Damned if that isn't Ingegnere!" he explained.

"*Grazie a Dio!*" I said when he arrived. "We're delighted to see you, but where's Lorenzo?"

"He went into Campo di Giove to stay with some cousins, but I'm afraid it was a bad mistake. The doctor sent word to me at the time you left, so I hid in a house outside the town."

By this time it had stopped raining, and Ingegnere spread out his jacket and sat down, his face ashen, his eyes half-shut. Nevertheless, he still seemed to want to talk. He was told by some shepherds that some time during the night the Germans had sealed off the town; despite the doctor's timely warning, a number of prisoners were recaptured. About 150 Italians were carted off for slave labor on the Maiella fortifications, which would stretch for 100 kilometers. "They would have liked to get me, with my experience," Ingegnere said, then sighed. Using his map case for a pillow, he rolled over and went to sleep.

At 7:30, the Germans were still shooting when I saw a tall figure marching along the road below us. In the still morning air, I could hear the click and scrape of his combat boots on the hard gravel. Captain Campbell was wearing his jaunty balmoral at a rakish angle, and his brownish kilt, made from a Red Cross blanket, swung smartly as he walked.

He disappeared below the brow of the hill for a moment, then reappeared. "Good morning," he said. "No need for you chaps to have got in a flap last night; they came nowhere near us."

Dick returned his good morning, but I couldn't bring myself to. I just looked at him. "Don't you think," I said finally, "that it might be better not to advertise our position to the Germans?"

Campbell ignored my churlishness and asked blandly, "You chaps had your tea?"

"We've been trying," Dick said, "but we can't get a fire started."

"Nothing to it." Campbell smiled. "Have it going in a minute."

He took out a metal stand made from Red Cross cans, poured some water from his canteen into a cup and set it on the stand. Then he pulled a thermal grenade from his pocket. "Does a good job, you know, but one must be careful, not too many of them around. This one was from the plane that crashed."

He unscrewed the incendiary fuse and poured some of the filler on the ground. When he pulled out a match, Dick and I took off like two champion sprinters. From a safe distance I peeked around a tree. The filler flared violently for a minute, and dense white smoke rose in a cloud. When it had died down, we crept back, cautiously. Campbell, holding a steaming cup of water, overlooked our temporary absence and said cheerfully, "Have some, lads? I've a bit extra."

"We'll take a little water, if we may," Dick said. "But we have our own tea, such as it is."

Sipping the warm, light-brown liquid, I questioned Campbell about his plans. He said he was waiting for an Italian guide to take him and his friends to the British lines.

"How long are you going to wait for him?" I asked.

"Until he gets here, of course," Campbell answered sharply, "and since you lads are so worried, we'll stand guard all night." I held my tongue. Just then Ryan appeared and began talking earnestly to Campbell.

"For God's sake," I whispered to Dick, "we're trapped here! There's the railroad to the south, shooting to the north and west, and the Maiella right behind us." Inadvertently I glanced down at his right knee. He gave his head that quick little shake and asked, "How badly do you want to get out of this place?"

This meant he was trying to find out if I was in one of my normal flaps, or if I considered this a real emergency. "Dick," I stated emphatically, "I want to get out in the worst possible way."

Ingegnere, who'd been listening attentively, chimed in with, *"D'accordo!"*

"OK, let's go!" Dick added crisply. It was 9:00.

We extended our goodbyes to Campbell and Ryan, wished them luck, and started up the mountain. I turned back once and gave a little wave. Campbell, sitting with his mouth half-open, stared after us but waved back.

Dick had given Ingegnere some wire that had arrived on Red Cross boxes back in Chieti. Our Italian friend had wound it around the sole of each of his shoes, but I could see white ends of thread sticking out of the uppers. I climbed very slowly. At the upper edge of the woods a sand-colored slide of loose, shale-like rock stretched up and disappeared in the distance toward the saddle of the pass. After estimating that it was close to 40°, I sat down and waited for the others to catch up. Gazing back, I was momentarily distracted by the beauty of the tawny orange, olive green, and light brown of the forest along the Maiella and north up the Valle dell'Orta.

My reverie was abruptly shattered by staccato rifle fire from the road just below us. This was followed by the ripping sound of a machine-pistol. "I hope that wasn't Campbell walking back to town," Dick called out.

"He's got more nerve than sense, and all of a sudden my desire to get out of here has tripled," I yelled back.

"No argument from me on that point," Dick said. "You tackle the slide and see what it's like."

When I took a run at the shale, my feet sank in and I slid backwards almost as much as I'd climbed. Again I dug in and this time kept going. Dick put his good leg forward and dragged the other one even. He repeated this procedure over and over; his cane was useless. Ingegnere struggled up, but tripped on the loose soles of his shoes and fell on his hands and knees.

My climb was easy compared to theirs; I found a rhythm for swinging up in the loose scree and only occasionally slipped back. For the next three hours, Dick and Ingegnere panted and sweated their way up, the old Italian having a rough time of it, Rossbach in constant pain. Frequently, I stopped to listen and let them catch up. The firing behind us kept on irregularly, but it grew steadily fainter to the point where my spirits actually rose a little, though we wondered what had happened to Campbell and his friends.

Around noon I reached a rocky crevasse at the top of the slide, with my clothes soaked through for the second time in eight hours. For a moment or two I felt hot, but quickly began to get chilled. Whenever I waited for the others, Dick shouted, "Keep going! I don't *dare* stop."

Picking my way up steep outcrops, avoiding loose stones, I found this ascent precarious and yet far less difficult than the cliff on the Morrone. From this altitude the firing and the roar of trucks were barely audible.

Near the top of the crevasse an icy wind pitched down, nearly strong enough to blow us off the mountain. Grabbing a small pine and hauling myself over the top, I was suddenly staring into a gigantic saddle between two peaks of the Maiella. Just beyond an outcrop of bare rock, a bright green meadow of mountain grass curved up each shoulder of this saddle. Within minutes the others joined me, and together we stared up at the unearthly panorama.

Somewhere I had heard that the Germans guarded this pass, so I walked out knee-deep in the grass, my heart pounding, my senses at a high pitch. But whirling clouds and fog began to sweep around us, and soon I felt as remote as I had on the Morrone.

I had also heard a story that wolves roamed near this pass, but dealing with wolves seemed mere child's play compared to confronting a German patrol. On the far side of the meadow we encountered a shepherd boy, watering his sheep at a spring. "*Buongiorno*," I said. "Have you seen any Germans up here in the pass?"

He shook his head, grinning. "No, they don't come up here. It is too hard for them to climb." We drank our fill of ice-cold water, replenished our canteens, and ate a slice of bread. As we said goodbye to the shepherd, he warned, "Keep on the lookout on the way down." A chill ran through me, but not from the cold air.

With much regret we left the green loneliness of the meadow, and started down the eastern slope, through thickets of prickly wild holly and more scrub oak. A few hundred yards down, Dick spotted four men ahead in brown, shaggy clothes, walking hesitantly and peering ahead through the woods. They had not seen us, so we crept up on them.

When I was convinced they were speaking English, I walked down to meet them: a British commando sergeant and three American soldiers. The sergeant said, "Jerry's raided Palena, and they captured a whole bunch of POW's and rounded up most of the Italian lads in the town to work on fortifications." And he added, "They caught us too outside the town, but we got away."

"How'd you manage that?" I asked.

"I got one of the Jerries aside and offered him my wristwatch if he would let us go. He took the watch, but then got in a row with the other two Germans. We just ran. They fired a couple of times, though I don't think they were actually trying to hit us." I said goodbye to the foursome hurriedly, and they started back up the mountain.

I turned to Dick. "My God," I said, "we're in a box — we can't cross those peaks up there and Jerry's got at least a company on each side of the pass. We've wasted the whole day coming over here. Frankly, I think we ought to go back."

"You do what you want, but there's no question about what I do," His voice was hard. "I couldn't possibly go back over that pass." Christ, I thought, I can't seem to help it, I've put my foot in it again.

Except for the scattered oaks, the cover was still thin as we started down toward Palena. A short way below us, 30 to 40 men, dressed in city clothes, were milling around and chattering in excited voices. A few of them saw us and ran away, but I got close enough to ask one man what the situation was. With frightened eyes, he cried, "Prisoners are a danger to us. Get away from us fast."

"But first tell me where the Germans are?"

"Patrols are all over the mountain, rounding us up for slave labor. Several Italians have been shot for helping prisoners." He glared at me and backed away. I told Dick there was no point in going toward Palena, because patrols were probably between us and the town. We moved a good distance to our right, away from Palena, and lay down in a thick clump of bushes.

Around 3:00 automatic weapons fire broke out directly below us. Flattening myself on the ground, I listened for ricocheting bullets, trying to figure out if the Germans had blocked off the entire slope below us. Dick and I crawled over and got Ingegnere to take out his map. Our route would take us down into a deep gorge with the *Strada Nazionale* at the bottom, running parallel to the Aventino River for the full length of the Maiella. We would have to cross the highway and river that night, despite the Germans who were raiding the area.

When he had put his map away, Ingegnere said solemnly, "We've traveled a long way together, and now I must ask your advice. Look at my shoes!" He demonstrated how the loose sole of each shoe flapped at every step; if he didn't flap it back up each time, he would trip and land on his bare foot. He said he knew a house near Campo di Giove where he thought he could get some fairly good shoes.

Dick said that since he was quite able to walk with good shoes he might be better off to go back and get some. Ingegnere looked at us sadly. The woods had been quiet for some time, so we stood up and shook hands with the old boy and thanked him for his help. I watched him climb slowly up through the woods, a pathetic little figure, stumbling and trying to keep his balance with those wretched shoes.

Chapter 21

The Agreement

3:30 p.m., 14 October

"Joe, I want a council of war!" Dick demanded suddenly.

"OK," I answered, wondering what was coming this time.

We sat down in a thick patch of woods. "Look," he began, "this is the fourth day of this trip, and we're barely across the second of these big mountains. I've no idea how many more there are to cross, but in these four days, we're down from five people to two. And one of them can hardly walk." After a brief pause, he added slowly, "You remember the message Giuseppe D'Acciaio, the Communist Chief, wanted you to give the British?"

Although something in his voice made me very uneasy, I said quickly, "Of course. 'Tell them to drop us guns and ammo, radios, clothing, and food.' "

"With those supplies," Dick went on, "the partisans could raise hell in the rear of a retreating German army, and it could have great military importance. The British can't make any headway against the enemy defense because the Germans hold the high ground; every time the British try to advance, they shoot down their throats, which they couldn't do as easily if the partisans were blowing up their ammo dumps."

"I'm aware of all that, so what's your point?" I inquired, merely as a stall — I had already guessed what he was driving at.

"Just this," he answered, "one of us has to get through with that message to British G-2, regardless of what happens to the other."

"I don't like this conversation," I protested. "The whole idea's crazy." I felt as though I was being deserted.

"It isn't crazy just because you don't like it," Dick retorted. "We're still soldiers, with the responsibility to act like them. So here it is: You have got to agree here and now that if I get captured or am unable to go on for any reason, or if you have to make a running break, you'll keep going on your own to give the British the information."

The suggestion of our separating sickened me. Eventually, I found my voice again. "I suppose your plan has some military rationale, but I hate it. Let's just hope it never becomes necessary." Rather emotionally, I went on: "Now we've got to get going so we can look over that gorge in daylight and see where to cross."

Dick stretched out his leg, rubbed it, and stood up slowly. Pretending not to notice, I led the way diagonally down the slope, moving even farther away from Palena. Somehow I had to get Dick across that highway and the river, to a place where he could rest his injured knee for a few days. Setting as fast a pace as I felt he could handle, I eased off whenever he began to drop back. All this time, sporadic shooting continued below us, interspersed with heavy explosions that sounded like blasting.

In half an hour we emerged from the woods onto a steep shoulder, facing east toward Palena. I didn't like being so close to the town, but we had less than an hour till dusk. Dick pointed to our left. Three figures in gray capes were sneaking along the declivity just below us. "These guys can't be German," he said. "They act scared to death of us."

As we caught up to the three Italian officers at the edge of a cliff, I called out, "We're Americans from the camp at Fonte d'Amore, and we'd like to talk to you."

"You frightened us dreadfully," an older man said with a cultured British accent. "We thought you were part of a German patrol. They nearly nabbed us in the pass."

That shook me. I said, "I wonder how *we* escaped that patrol?"

The old Italian said, "You were lucky there, but how've you been doing for food? You don't look too fit."

Dick smiled ruefully. "I guess we're about as hungry as we've ever been in our lives."

To my utter surprise, the Italians pulled out bread, jam, and slices of salami. I moved over to the youngest of the group, who didn't seem to know a word of English, and told him about the raid in Campo di Giove, and that the food had come just about in time to save my friend's life.

"We can get it more easily," he said. Then he hesitated. "But we were nearly caught in Campo di Giove, and lost our water bottles. Could you spare some water?" I interpreted for Dick, who said, laughing, "Can we spare it?" As we handed them our canteens, he produced, *"Con molto piacere."*

The young man assured me our route would be easier from here on; we had negotiated the most difficult of the mountains. He pointed into the valley. "Get down there before dark. The shepherds said there's a narrow trail just below here. Follow it to your right for about 800 meters. From there, pick your place to cross the highway. At dark, go down to the edge of the road and hide in the bushes. Watch for trucks or anyone on the road. When you're sure no one's coming, cross the road and lower yourself into the river. You can get over most of it on the rocks. Then head for those peaks on the skyline. They're the Monti Pizzi, where there's dense cover and you can hide. Now we have to leave, so goodbye and good luck!" The trio disappeared in the dusk.

"OK, Old-World courtesy, you win that one. After the food, I feel almost human again, and our reserve is in better shape too. Before this donation, all we had left was Giancarlo's Pecorino cheese."

I told him about the route. "I got it," Dick said, "I'm going first, so be damn sure you keep up with me — not like Roccacasale," and he started down. In the growing darkness, I could barely discern his black bulk as he scrambled down the trail. At one point, he went on all fours, at another, he turned around, facing the cliff, and let himself down a steep rock slide.

After a switchback which took us toward Palena, Dick went quickly along a ledge over a sheer drop where I heard the sound of rapids. Now there was a chill in the air. Truck lights gleamed off to our left and swung back and forth as the vehicle took the curves coming out of the town. I caught up with Dick. He ordered, "Get down, and don't move. They're not even using blackout lights."

I spread out flat on the rocky path, holding on with my fingers to keep from sliding. Shifting gears were increasingly audible as the truck rounded the nearest curve. Its headlights swung up across the mountain, etching rocks and bushes in black. "Don't even breathe," Dick whispered.

Just below us, the truck slowed. I thought it was stopping, but the driver shifted down and drove on past. "From the first moment I saw his headlights until he was opposite us took just three minutes. That's what we'll have to get into the river from the time we start to cross," Dick said.

It was completely dark when we reached the bank above the highway and crouched in a thicket of briars. Not much later a truck convoy appeared, coming out of Palena with all headlights on. The nearest hairpin turns were about half a mile away to our left and a quarter of a mile to our right. Beyond these points, nothing was visible. From here, I could make out the black line of the river just beyond the road, and on the far side an old brick power station, which was apt to be guarded.

"I'll go first," Dick whispered. "You follow at 100 yards, that's about 25 seconds, but stay away from the building. Meet me in the first field on the far side."

I tried to answer, but all I got out was a nervous cough. Dick had picked up a long stick. He parted the bushes with it and moved fast out onto the road. I also had a stick to test river depth. I counted endless seconds: 1,001. . . . Headlights glimmered on the curve to my left . . . 1,025 — I jumped out, landed on the run, crossed the road, and crashed into a guard rail on a retaining wall 15 feet above the river. I swung a leg over it, got tangled up, backed off and ran to the left, heading for Palena. Lights drew nearer, truck motors ground in low gear.

Beyond the rail it still looked about ten feet down to the river. I ran farther, jumped over and landed on some rocks, then jumped to another rock, and finally plunged into the current. My feet hit a gravel bottom. Half-swimming, half-wading, I churned with my arms to a place where the water got shallower, and suddenly I was at the opposite bank. There I lay motionless, still half in the river, while truck lights swung back and forth around the curves, going by us without stopping.

Twenty feet beyond the stream, I scaled a stone wall, sank down behind it, and gasped aloud. "My God, we got away with it!"

Since Dick had been well ahead of me, I started up the slope, halfway to my knees in the soft, damp furrows of a plowed field. I kept going, peering into the darkness around me. A quarter of a mile on I heard behind me, repeated four times, the unmistakable whistle of a Carolina quail. I remembered Dick's old way of signaling, whistled in reply, and trudged back down the hill. Dick was sitting on a furrow, chuckling. "If you were a quail, you'd never get a girlfriend with that."

"The hell you say. How'd you get across?"

"I went around the guard rail and found a place where I could slide down some rocks. It was easy, except my pack got soaked, including the bread."

"Wet bread won't keep, no matter what you say. It's been a rough day, we have to eat it," I insisted. He divided the bread between us, dried off the Pecorino and returned it to his knapsack. "Let's hit the trail, I'm freezing."

With a waning moon outlining the black furrows curving across the hill ahead, we gulped handfuls of sloppy bread and plodded on in the soft earth. It was like trying to walk in a quagmire, and in a few hundred yards I was puffing as if I had run a mile.

Dick stopped abruptly, put his head back and bellowed, "Goddam this fucking knee!" He took a deep breath and split the still night with every curse he could think of, while I sneaked a look back along the river. His outburst ended, he stood there, panting. When I reached over and took hold of his pack, he didn't resist, just slipped his arms out of the straps and let me have it.

"Thank you, that'll help," he said so softly I could hardly hear him. He continued, "But now I want you to listen to me. This doesn't make sense. You could walk the distance to the British lines in a matter of days, and this holding you up is bugging the hell out of me. With your Italian, you're better equipped to get through, and if I get caught I'm better equipped to deal with the Germans. You gave me a weasel answer this afternoon. Now I want a definite agreement."

I hesitated, unable to say why I was refusing to agree to leave him. Was it out of loyalty to him, or simply because I was incapable of going on alone? Truthfully, I didn't know which it was myself.

"Joe, is it agreed?" he persisted. "Otherwise I'll demand that you go on without me right now."

"OK, OK," I said weakly. "But it sure goes against the grain."

"All right, then, it's agreed. And don't you forget it."

We labored up slowly in the deep furrows and were out of them in 20 minutes. The next field was good going, a hard pasture that glistened with frost in the moonlight. On up the hill we toiled for two hours, until the black bulk of a farmhouse appeared. This was 1:30 in the morning on a chilly 15 October.

We were a short way from the house when a dark figure slipped out of the shadows. "Who are you?" a man's voice asked in Italian.

"*Prigionieri Americani*," I said. "Can you give us something to eat and a place to sleep?"

His answer poured out in a flood: Palena had been raided. They had killed and wounded many, blown up houses, and taken hundreds of men for slaves to build fortifications. The house was already full of refugees. He stopped and sighed, then said, "But it's a cold night, come in anyway."

We squeezed into a room jammed with people on benches, on rickety chairs, huddled together all over the dirt floor. The air was damp and suffocating with the odors of sour breath and dried sweat. Old and young women sat moaning, many with crying or sleeping children on their laps. Old men stood leaning against the walls, heads bent and shoulders sagging. Yet they cleared a little place so we could sit on the floor near the fire. An elderly lady hesitantly offered us two potatoes, another a small piece of cheese. It was beyond belief that these wretched people, who were totally impoverished, were willing to share what little they had with strangers and foreigners.

I ate my small portion quickly and curled up in a heap on the floor. For four hours I slept, until the stirring of the people woke me at six. We made our way out of the house into a raw, bitter morning and started up the long grade. Dick had had nothing but scraps in four days. There were dark circles under his eyes and he leaned heavily on his stick at each step. After the 16 hours spent crossing the Maiella and the Aventino, I felt pretty much the way Dick looked. Farther up toward the Monti Pizzi we searched for a place to rest in the thick woods that the Italian officer had described to me.

At the top of the ridge a warm sun broke through. Now farther south and at a lower altitude than on the Maiella, we savored the mild autumn air, and, when we reached the forest, sunlight gleamed yellow and red on the damp oak and aspen foliage. The ground was a thick carpet of leaves, and we chose a soft place in a small clearing where we stretched out for a much-needed rest.

Dick still hadn't stirred when I awoke a few hours later, the sun now in the southwest. Seizing the opportunity, I began a major repair job on my shoelaces, which, from constant retying, had become a series of hard knots solidified with black dirt. In about half an hour, Dick opened an eye and looked over at me. Without thinking, I said, "I don't dare take these things off, because if we ever have to make a run for it —"

"You mean, if *you* ever have to make a run for it."

I put my head down, cursing myself for unwittingly raising that obnoxious subject again. To change the subject, I burst out impulsively, "Where do you think we should try for something to eat?"

Dick sat up. "There's a house a little way down I'd like to try. The ground's level, and I've had a good rest. Finish your shoes while I go look into things. Besides, this way I'll know you're not going to eat all his food while you're there."

Though I'd grown accustomed to that old ribbing, I felt my face flush. "God! Did I have that coming."

He walked away at a leisurely pace, and I was actually glad to be alone for a while. I thought about the agreement he had forced on me. One part of me said, "Maybe his knee will get better, if we can rest somewhere until it heals." But deep within, an insistent voice kept saying: "You know he can't make it, no matter what you do."

I recalled how he had coerced me into making the two escapes with him — not only had he masterminded them, but he had provided the initiative and the guts for both of us. Could I possibly go on alone if I had to? I shrank from the very idea.

As a distraction, I tried to envision Emily and the children but ran into a mental block, simply unable to recapture what she looked like anymore. And by the time I would see the children again, I wouldn't recognize them. Surely they wouldn't know me either. Besides, I didn't even know where they were — maybe she had sold the house by now, and why the bloody hell had she moved out in the first place? What had started out as an exercise in distraction had culminated in anger and frustration.

Dick came walking up through the woods, and I glanced at my watch — he'd been gone an hour. "Glad to see you back," I said. "You're just in time."

"For what, a four-course dinner?"

"No," I smiled. "To keep me from going down the drain. Every time I think about Emily and the kids, I just get bitter and angry."

"This may seem rough on you, but did it ever occur to you it might be a good idea not to think about them at all?" He was right, of course.

Dick had found two shepherds who would help us; one had invited us for supper, the other for breakfast. That had to be some kind of a jackpot, I thought. The first shepherd we visited was a small, thin man, proud owner of a little one-room hut lit by a single candle and warmed by an open fire. Two donkeys and four goats stood at a manger, while over in a corner a small boy slept. Scrawny white and brown chickens pecked and clucked around the floor. The stench of animals and manure was acrid.

Our host, Pietro, put a big pot of milk on the fire, threw in a few pieces of lasagna and pork fat, and then told us about the continuing raids on Palena and the neighboring towns and farms. More Italians had been wounded and more men captured to work on the German fortifications. Notices had been posted in all the towns, warning that any Italian caught helping a prisoner would be shot on sight. The Germans were still dynamiting and burning houses — Pietro used the expression *"mettete a ferro e fuoco,"* which I translated as "scorched earth." The Italians felt this would be German policy from now on — they were in for a reign of terror.

We waited and waited, until finally the lasagna-in-milk was ready. The shepherd gave us each a small bowl of it, along with a piece of bread, but took nothing for himself, claiming that he had already had supper. Now we knew the whole pot was for us.

"Don't tell me I can't pick the right shepherd," Dick crowed. "Now we'll see if your stomach has shrunk from starving. As far as I'm concerned, I consider that old theory a lot of crap."

Pietro watched us finish off the pot, and said, "I know hunger well; it's a brutal thing."

"This time, too, I won't object to your Old-World courtesy, Giuseppe," Dick said. Pietro acknowledged my *"mille grazie,"* and waved at some piles of straw on the floor. Two weary Americans lay down and fell quickly asleep — almost, but not quite, as comfortable as if they had been at home.

Awakened around 11:00 by the sound of footsteps outside, and a grunting noise, I looked over Dick's shoulder. Pietro was coming in, driving the biggest sow I had ever seen. She waddled over, sniffed at Dick, went "ngruh, ngruh," and lay down next to him, a maneuver that first took a certain amount of turning around in front of the fire.

"It is terribly cold outside, and she is due to farrow pretty soon, so she must be kept warm," Pietro informed us.

After we shifted around to make sure that Pietro was happy and the sow comfortable, Dick leaned against her back. "She's very warm, almost as good as the fire," he declared and fell back to sleep again immediately.

16 October

We had planned to leave before dawn, but even though Pietro must have stepped over us half a dozen times to feed the goats and donkeys, Dick, the sow, and I slept soundly till 7:00.

In spite of the broad daylight, Dick seemed calm and casual, and said he'd been more comfortable sleeping with the sow than on any night since Santa Croce, and now it was about time to go to the other shepherd for breakfast. We said goodbye to Pietro and went out into a cold morning.

I scanned the vast hillside, with its dozens of small houses and little roads that led down to the *Strada Nazionale*, but could see no cover at all. A German with a good pair of Zeiss glasses would be able to spot us a mile away. The beginning of the woods wasn't far from Pietro's house, if you walked straight up the hill, but Dick said the "breakfast shepherd" lived off at a right angle to our route. He started walking straight across the bare fields.

"Hey!" I shouted after him, "you can't go out there in the open like that!"

"The hell I can't," he yelled back and kept on going.

"For Christ's sake, you'll get us both caught. Stop! Wait! I want to talk to you about it."

He never even turned his head. In disbelief I stood and watched his dark brown figure grow smaller and smaller, until it vanished in the distance.

"Mannaggia!" I heard someone behind me say and I jerked around. It was Pietro. "What a hell of a racket. You'll bring the Germans for sure with all that yelling. Why does your friend walk out in the open like that? It's very stupid. You should go straight toward Monti Pizzi to join your friends the British."

I couldn't have agreed more and walked quickly away on the line of our route. Though I could no longer see Dick, I knew that each step I took drew us farther apart. Cautiously, I picked my way up and hid behind some farm buildings above Pietro's place, always keeping them between me and the open valley. When the owner saw me and asked what I wanted, I said I was waiting for my friend. He told me to get going — that it was too dangerous — I might attract a patrol.

Frustrated, I went to another farm and skulked behind the barns for half an hour. Then I saw Dick strolling leisurely across the pasture. Relieved at seeing him, yet alarmed at our being so exposed, I waited till he was opposite me and sidled over, dreading the meeting and wracking my brain over what to say.

"That shepherd told me there's a very remote valley beyond these mountains," he said, just as if we hadn't squabbled. "Maybe we can find a place to stay where the people won't be so jumpy."

We wound our way through a magnificent oak and beech forest, where a warm sun shone through the flaming autumn leaves, lifting our spirits. By early afternoon we had crossed the three 5,000-foot ridges that separate the Aventino from the Parello Valley, and for the first time there rolled from a great distance the thunder of artillery fire. It was very different from aerial bombardment, far deeper and heavier.

"By God, I haven't heard that in a long time," Dick said, and he pulled out his smudged and wrinkled tracing. He squinted up at the sun and oriented the little map. "It's coming from Larino, on our left — that's got to be British artillery, but what's that shelling off to our right?"

"Maybe from Benevento or Caserta, more likely in the American sector," I commented. It sounded to me like heavy artillery, and I placed it at about 50 or 60 miles away.

"Well, Giuseppe, that's about as far as we'll have to go." He laughed and slapped me on the shoulder. But all I could think of was the German army operating between us and those heavy guns.

We came down a steep pasture above a deep wooded gorge, the Pizzi Mountains behind us, and on the far horizon the southern end of the Maiella disappeared in the haze. Below, to our left, nestled a cluster of stone houses. Dick thought this must be that remote valley the shepherd had mentioned, a place where we could hide out for a few days.

What we would look like to the people here bothered me. We hadn't shaved for a week; grime had collected around my wrists and neck so that the cuffs and collar were a shiny black. As for Dick, his face looked like a coal miner's, and the filth on his shirt had irritated the skin until he had painful swellings that seemed to be incipient boils. We'd had only one day's rest in the five and a half it had taken us to cross the two main ranges of the Apennines; it had now been some 20 hours since I had had anything to eat, and I'd been walking for the last seven. As the day had worn on, I'd had trouble concentrating on what I was doing and felt as though I were walking in a dream.

Halfway down the pasture we came to a long stone wall, beyond which a wiry, slightly stooped man was working the ground with a hoe. With his craggy face and a long black mustache, he appeared to be in his mid-fifties. A sweat-stained hat was perched on the back of his head as he looked over at us, his friendly grin lacking a few teeth.

"Hello, boys, where are you going? Are you hungry?" he called to us in English, his eyes twinkling. I was surprised at how well he spoke.

"We're Americans," Dick said. "We're going south to meet the British army, but we've come all the way from Popoli, and we need a place to rest for a few days. We're very, very hungry."

"You stay around here," the man advised. "Germans don't come here. Now, I'll tell you what. You go down to this stream and follow a path to your left till you come to that group of houses. Knock at the last one on the north side. A lady there will give you food, but don't you tell her you saw anyone up here; you just came in by chance. You understand?"

"That's fine," Dick said, "but will we see you again?"

Immediately, the man's manner changed. He frowned and said crossly, "You go along now. Do as I say!"

When Dick hesitated and seemed about to say something more, I pulled his sleeve and insisted quietly, "Come on, don't push your luck." Slightly annoyed, Dick shook his arm free and began hobbling down the hill. "You're such a bloody mouse, we'll never find out anything."

"Damn it, Dick, you've got to get it through your head that when these people make up their minds, you're not going to change them, so stop arguing with them. That guy obviously had some reason for all that. What worries me is these farms must've had floods of prisoners and refugees through here, and their food can't last forever."

"Well, perhaps you're right, that could be a problem."

Near the bank of a stream we turned left along a path imprinted by the hoofs of cattle, where the ground rose gradually past a thick copse of aspen. Soon we came into a courtyard between two groups of stone buildings. A small black-clad woman of about 50 was standing by the door of the last house on the left. As we approached her, she beckoned and pointed to the door.

Instantly, I was nervous. Things seemed a little too easy; it could be a trap. Dick pushed the door inward and entered the house. The lady motioned me along too, making a shushing sound the Abruzzesi use when they want you to do something and think you don't understand. I slipped in, and she followed quickly.

The room smelled of food cooking in garlic and olive oil, and my stomach did a few cartwheels. Heavy ceiling beams were hung with dried peppers and gourd-shaped cheeses tied with cord. In a niche carved out of the wall at our left stood an enormous copper urn with a ladle. On our right an iron cauldron simmered over a bed of red coals in a fireplace that appeared about five feet high by eight feet long.

Our new friend was a thin little woman with a strong, lined face, her black hair pulled back into a bun. She stood across the room and pointed toward two chairs and a big wooden table.

"*Buongiorno*, Signora. Thank you for letting us come in. We heard you might be so kind as to let us have something to eat," I said, hoping I hadn't given the old man's show away. She gave me a quick look and said a bit impatiently, "Yes, yes, sit down and make yourselves comfortable."

"*Grazie*," I stammered, and collapsed into a chair. For a few moments, I thought I could go to sleep, just inhaling the tantalizing aroma. But this was no dream. I sat up and watched her fuss over the cauldron, expecting one of those interminable delays, while I listened to my stomach's sound effects.

It couldn't have been three minutes later when she came over with a brown pottery casserole full of *polenta* (corn meal) and what looked like two slices of sausage lying in the olive oil on top. Next she brought over utensils, plates, and two glasses of wine. As we began to eat, she hovered over us, occasionally reminding us *"Mangia!"* while pointing to the casserole so we'd take more. The *polenta* was deliciously flavored with garlic and hot pepper blended in oil; I gobbled shamelessly, trying to tell her, between mouthfuls, where we came from in the States, and what had happened on our trip from Fonte d'Amore.

She seemed to understand my Italian, and from her brief answers I gathered she had heard that kind of story before. When we had finished the *polenta* and sausage — I could have gone for another serving, but I knew that by her standards we had been very generously treated — I nudged Dick, and said we should leave. Though he acted surprised, he didn't object.

It was nearly 3:00 when we walked out of the courtyard, a cordial invitation to come back for supper at 9:00 ringing happily in our ears. Descending several flights of crumbling stone steps, we followed a trail down to the river, where crystal-clear water flashed over rocks in the warm sunlight. We picked our way across on big boulders and climbed the rise on the far side, winding up through dark green clumps of mountain laurel and holly. Up on the hillside, we discovered a pleasant glade, where in the quiet warmth, Dick lay down and went to sleep.

My clothes were sticky, and when I tried to rest, I itched all over. Then the stream came to mind, and in a few minutes I was on its bank, stripping. I pulled out a sliver of soap from my knapsack and slipped into a pool. Even though the water was very cold, it felt so delicious — and the sun was so hot — I didn't mind.

My head and shoulders were covered with soap, when all at once I was startled by the sound of someone laughing. I ducked under to splash the soap out of my eyes, and surfaced to see a grinning middle-aged Italian standing on the bank. He addressed me in very good English, explaining that he had spent 18 years in the States and had become an American citizen. He'd come back to Abruzzo with a nest egg and had bought a farm in the Parello Valley. This was Giuseppe di Piolo, known by the nickname "Bepacc'." While I stood there drying off, he offered me shelter in a hut on the mountain. For this I thanked him but pointed out that I already had a place to stay, and that I'd take a "rain check." He laughed at the slang expression and left me to finish dressing.

At a little before 9:00 we climbed back to the group of houses where we'd had lunch. Dick had had a bath too, and we both felt rested and considerably cleaner, though hungrier than ever. As we entered the courtyard there was a scurry of people running off in the dark. One short, husky man, silhouetted in firelight from an open door, called back in, "It's nothing, these are the two we've been expecting."

Wondering how he could be that sure, I said, "That's right, we were here this afternoon. The lady gave us *polenta* and sausage."

His handshake was firm, and he spoke with assurance. "I am Berardino. That was my mother. She told us you'd be returning."

Inside we stood blinking in the firelight. The black cauldron over the fire bubbled and steamed, filling the air with an aroma of *minestra* and garlic. The *signora* and two younger women, also dressed in black, were clustered around a table in the back, and the man we'd met on the hillside was seated by the fire

— he was unmistakable: the sharp nose, the lean, rugged face, though now he had the air of a man with something up his sleeve. He greeted us in English. "Hello, boys, I'm Antonio. You're just in time. But remember, you never saw me before." He gestured behind him. "This is my wife, Rosa, and this is my daughter-in-law, Letizia, and her sister, Filomena."

Three other Italian men sat in a corner but weren't introduced. A tall RAF officer, wearing major's insignia, came over from the fireplace. When we shook hands, I noticed he was a chaplain. He didn't give his name and was known only as *"Il Capellano."*

Rosa stirred the cauldron, while Letizia, eight or nine months pregnant, rolled out the lasagna and cut it on the wooden table. She was about eighteen and strikingly goodlooking, with ivory skin and hair pulled back like Rosa's. It appeared black, but in the candlelight it had a glint of mahogany. Filomena was taller and a little older, with wide-set dark eyes.

When supper was ready, Antonio stood up and invited us, "Come on, boys, let's eat." We seated ourselves at the table, and the lasagna with bread and wine was brought by the women, who didn't sit down but stood behind us, chattering.

As I watched the amount of food being consumed, I wondered about Antonio's generosity. I had counted 14 people, including a British sergeant traveling with the chaplain. Antonio couldn't keep handing out food this way, and I hoped he wasn't under the delusion that "the British Army would arrive any day now." The thought of what the Germans might do to these people if they were caught harboring prisoners sickened me.

After supper we sat in a semicircle around the fire and, as usual, grouped ourselves according to the languages we could handle: Dick with Antonio and the chaplain, I with Berardino, who spoke no English. In his early thirties, Berardino was slightly bald, with a broad, determined face and square shoulders that gave the impression of great strength. As he spoke, he gestured expressively to make a point and seemed to be a man who definitely knew his own mind.

When I asked him if they had had many prisoners coming through, he raised his hands and said, "Eh! Eh! A flood of them. This is the natural route south from Guado di Coccia, where you all cross. There is no other way."

He told me we were lucky to have traveled so far to the west, through the cover of the Monti Pizzi Forest. Many others had been coming farther east, over the pastures. The Germans, hiding in the woods, had picked the prisoners up in their field glasses. Then they had turned loose trained dogs that swept down on the fugitives like wolves. "A few prisoners have been killed and many captured," he added. "That place up there is well named; it's called 'Dark Valley.' "

He stopped and looked blankly at the floor. Breaking the somber silence, I asked, "Berardino, have there been any patrols up here?" His head shot up. "At some time," he snapped, "it will be dangerous. We will know when." Upset, he got up and went over to the others. I sat there for a moment, regretting the question — I resolved to be more careful.

Antonio walked over. "Well, Riccardo, your story is much like the others. Now, some words of advice. While you are in this valley, keep moving around. So far, we haven't had any Fascist spies, but you never know; don't go to the same house too often, and if the Germans start to raid, move quickly to another area. When you do leave, try to find a guide. The Germans are already building fortifications this side of the Sangro River, and you might stumble into them in the dark."

I remained silent a while, trying to take all that in — more hard-nosed advice than we had heard from anyone. Again and again, I went over it in my mind, drilling it into my memory.

It was nearly 11:00 when Dick asked Antonio if we could pass the night in his barn. He nodded, but with a peculiar smile, and taking a lamp, led us across the courtyard to a one-story stone building. There we were shown into a bedroom, which had a bureau with a lighted candle in front of a big mirror. On the other side of the room was a big double bed with spotless white sheets and a pink blanket. I stood open-mouthed as I took in the rest of the room: heavy Italian furniture, a dressing table with a lace coverlet, pictures of a happy, smiling Berardino and Letizia at their wedding.

Antonio, meanwhile, watched us with a broad grin. "Thought you boys would like a comfortable bed for a change. Now, get a good sleep and *buona notte.*"

In vain, we pleaded with Antonio to let us sleep in the barn or in the hayloft. We soon ceased protesting, however, lest he think we didn't appreciate his hospitality. Though I did my best to thank him, he just waved me off and departed, leaving me overwhelmed. About to flop into the bed, I looked down at my boots, then at Dick's. They were even more filthy than usual from the muddy trail on the way up. "What the hell am I going to do about these shoes?" I moaned. "This afternoon it took me half an hour to get them off and an hour to put them back on."

Dick was in the middle of a huge yawn. "As I recall it, some damn escape expert, name of Frelinghuysen, I think, said never take off your shoes in case you have to run for it. So wrap your bloody feet in your jacket, the sheets'll get washed anyway."

The dilemma solved, at least partially, I wrapped my jacket around my feet and tied the arms as tightly as I could; Dick did the same. Then I crawled between the sheets, hoping my damp, grimy shoes wouldn't come out of their wrapping during the night.

Chapter 22

Antonio's Masseria

The next morning I left Dick in the woods with the two Englishmen and went off alone to make a recon of the Parello Valley. The area seemed more remote than any we had been in before, so I wasn't as nervous as usual about leaving him.

Thick woods ran up to about 5,000 feet, where the rocky cliffs of three mountain peaks began, providing innumerable places to hide and making it unlikely that patrols would come up there often. Antonio's house was more than an hour's walk from any road, so when I rejoined Dick that afternoon, I told him I was willing to stay put until his leg got better, and until we knew where the Allies were.

Our conversation was suddenly drowned out by the roar of high-performance engines — a flight of Spitfires zoomed over very low. In disbelief, we both jumped up. RAF fighters this far up? They peeled off and swung around a town called Montenerodomo, or Montenero, a few miles east of Antonio's farm. With all that British personnel and equipment up there, it was like a piece of England just above the the trees, so near and yet so unreachable. "Dick," I said, "there's an RAF guy in each of those who'll eat tonight in a British mess, have a hot shower, and sleep in a nice warm bed."

With a sideways glance he answered, "No doubt he will, if the poor bastard doesn't get shot down first."

The chaplain and his sergeant friend left early for Antonio's farm, but Dick and I waited till dark. We were creeping warily up the hill, when I made out three figures in the shadows and a man talking in German. I started to run, but Dick just stepped behind a tree. Still uneasy, I watched him — he had a hand behind one ear. "They're OK," he said. "Civilians of some kind, and they are worrying about patrols."

Montenerodomo, as it has been rebuilt since the war.

I exhaled in relief. As we caught up with them, the man turned back and said loudly in slightly accented English, "Don't be alarmed. I'm Dr. Eisenstein. This is my wife, Giulia, and her sister, Rachel."

"You scared us, Doctor." I moved up and shook hands.

"I guessed you were the two Americans Berardino told me about. German is our native tongue, but we must remember to speak Italian — sorry we startled you."

We all walked to Antonio's and went in. I saw that the doctor was a small, slight man with a high forehead and sparse, sandy hair. Giulia was a thin-faced, red-haired girl. Her sister was taller, with dark hair and frightened eyes. The doctor explained that they all spoke perfect Italian, and until recently had felt safer in the cities, but when the raids started they had fled into the mountains. He shocked us when he added that the SS had moved into Palena. Dick gave a quick shake of his head — the implications were so bad no one wanted to discuss them. It put a damper on the evening, especially since Eisenstein and the two sisters were Jewish refugees.

When I questioned the wisdom of spending any more nights at the farm, Berardino nodded and offered to come up in the woods and help us build a hut, a *capanna*, as he called it. That night we left early and slept out on the mountain.

18-20 October

In the morning Berardino came up to us with some food. "I hope this will take care of you for today," he began, "because we've had a whole bunch of refugees at the house. They're mostly strangers, and we don't trust them, so it's better if you stay up here for the present. In the meantime, I'll help you build a *capanna*." I told him that we were content to stay in the woods, as long as it didn't get any colder, but Dick grumbled a bit, because those spots on his neck and shoulders were getting worse and he was in a lot of pain.

Each day, Berardino brought food and stayed to work on the hut, with whatever assistance I could give him. My attempts with the axe were clumsy, but he swung it with utter precision. Once, after watching me, he said, "It's better for me to do it, before you chop your foot off."

Dick was more adept at chopping, but the activity irritated his infections, so we were both relegated to gathering branches. Soon Berardino went back for his farm chores, so it wasn't until the third day that the *capanna* was nearing completion. By this time Dick's infections had turned into angry red boils, two of which appeared to be abscessed and were extremely painful. Berardino ordered him to rest, while he and I finished the job.

Berardino looked at the sky. "You'll be all right, at least for tonight, since it won't rain. Now, Riccardo, the situation is much quieter at the house, so you must come down and have the doctor look at those boils, or you'll be in trouble. Come for supper and maybe he can fix your knee at the same time."

After he had left, I said to Dick, "When he mentioned that rain, he reminded me of your remark the morning we crossed the Morrone, 'Maybe the Lord will grant us ten days of perfect weather.'"

"I remember it well, but what about Campo di Giove?" Dick reminded me.

"That was at night, don't you see? It's October 20th; we've had ten perfect days and been damn lucky."

"We have that, but I didn't expect you to call it luck," he said with a smile.

On the way to Antonio's we met Filomena coming up from the river, the huge copper urn that supplied water for the whole family balanced on her head. With her neck and back ramrod straight, she walked with a sliding gait that kept the container level. Upon looking closely, I could see beneath it a little black bag of some kind that fitted to her head and yet gave a flat surface to steady the urn. At a wild guess, that urn had to hold about ten gallons, and that was 86 pounds for the water, plus the weight of the copper. I couldn't imagine how she got it up there.

She said not a word on her way by, her eyes straight ahead as she crossed into the courtyard. Thinking I might help her, I went along, but Dick called, "For God's sake, Joe, leave her alone. You'll screw it up for sure." I was about to argue, when Berardino came out the door. Filomena stopped and put a hand up to the urn to steady it, as Berardino grabbed it, swung it off her head, and carried it into the house.

Just before supper the Eisensteins showed up, and we all sat down together. The chaplain and the sergeant joined us, along with four Italians who, for some reason, remained unintroduced. Antonio seemed to ignore these strangers during supper, so I assumed they were refugees. On this occasion, the portions were noticeably smaller, and with no second helpings the meal was over quickly.

After supper, Antonio and Berardino disappeared. Riccardo, as he was called most of the time, and I sat by the fire with Giulia, Rachel, and the doctor, who asked us how we'd managed for food so far.

"It has been rather extraordinary, in American terms," Dick said, "how we've been helped by people who were short of food themselves. It's inexplicable to us."

"Ah, yes, that's because you Americans are used to affluence. But these people live with deprivation and suffering. They understand what real hunger means. How many Americans know hunger?"

"Perhaps a few of us are beginning to know," I said.

"Perhaps," replied the doctor. "And it will be a good thing never to forget it when you get back."

Dick smiled. "I like your optimism about us. By the way, what are your plans?"

"Like yours, to get through as quickly and safely as possible. Where do you think your Allies are now?"

"We've been held up by my bad leg," Dick explained, "but we heard some artillery fire toward Larino and on the other side toward Benevento."

The doctor shook his head. "They're not up that far. In any case, there's no use going west toward your own troops. You'd have to cross the Monte Meta at 7,400 feet. The passes are already blocked with snow — you'd never make it."

He told us that he and the two girls had come from Casoli, northeast of where we were, through Gessopalena and Torricella, both farther east. The people in those areas nearer the coast had seen British commandos who had rounded up prisoners and taken them back to Bari in motor-torpedo boats and submarines.

"Maybe that crazy colonel back at Chieti had a good idea after all," Dick ventured.

"Perhaps," I said, "but he sure botched it up by making us delay our escape too long." Dick gave me a severe look, one that clearly meant, "Drop the subject."

"Riccardo," the doctor said, "may I ask, are you Jewish too?"

"Yes, I am, though Rossbach isn't normally a Jewish name."

"Well, at any rate, have you had any additional trouble because of it?"

"Not on that count, I've been lucky so far."

"So have we, but some of our relatives haven't — they were picked up by the SS." Silent for a moment, he continued. "You see, once we're out of this house, you and we must stay apart. I believe we could pass as Italians, but you probably couldn't. And if you were caught in those civilian clothes, you might never convince them you were prisoners, and it could go very hard with you. Then we could have trouble too. Now let me have a look at those boils, *foruncoli*, as Berardino calls them, and then we'll see about that knee."

Dr. Eisenstein dressed the sores and advised Dick to try to keep his clothes from rubbing on them and infecting them more. Then he had Dick roll up his trouser leg. After articulating the knee, the doctor, with firm hands, tested movement of the tibia as Dick winced. Then he checked the ligaments with digital pressure. Full extension caused no pain, but when he tried flexion beyond 90°, Dick yelped. Immediately, he told Dick to stand so he could probe behind the knee until he hit the sensitive spot. "Was your original injury a torn meniscus cartilage?" the doctor inquired.

"Yes, in 1938."

"Without X-rays I can't be sure, but I think you've reinjured it. All I can do is strap it up, which should keep you from doing further harm and also give you some confidence." After the doctor wrapped the knee, then unwrapped it,

he taught Dick to do it. "Now keep that on there every time you move about."
Dick thanked him, and we left shortly to spend the night in our *capanna*.

21 October

All day we stayed around the hut. While Dick rested, the problem of his
knee weighed heavily on my mind. Since we had arrived in the Parello Valley,
the injured limb had been improving much too slowly for my satisfaction.

That evening, we reached Antonio's just after dark and found the big room
so packed with people that we had to wait at the door. Men, women, and
children, all dressed in city clothes, were squeezed together with their
hampers and suitcases. Berardino wriggled through the crowd. "There was a
raid in a town next to Montenero, and these people are refugees. They're very
frightened, but I think some will go back later tonight or tomorrow. We'll have
them settled very soon."

He and his father worked their way among the newcomers, talking, asking
questions, calming them down. Some of the exchanges I could understand:
"Our house is too crowded, we can't feed you, we have prisoners around,
making it very dangerous for you." (That's a new twist, I thought; we help
Berardino get rid of some of these.)

Next I heard Antonio suggesting to his new visitors that they try another
house. In half an hour, the room had emptied out, except for ten refugees, the
chaplain, his sergeant, and ourselves. Rosa set a small table in a corner and
then waved at us. The family had already eaten, but she still had "*una piccola
cosa*" for her "*caro cappellano,*" the sergeant, and us two Americans.
Hastily, she served a little pasta and whisked the plates away at the first
chance.

Dick and I were sitting in the corner, getting ready to leave, when the front
door opened. In walked a U.S. Army Air Forces pilot named Magruder and, of
all people, Stony Brooks, the guy I'd had the donnybrook with back at Chieti.
I came halfway out of my chair, but Dick pulled at my jacket. "Sit down, for
Christ's sake, will you? What in hell do you think you're going to do?"

"Leave me alone, dammit! I'm not going to start anything. At least not
yet." I stared across at the man. Both he and Magruder were dressed
completely in jet black. They looked like two huge crows. All the old gut
feelings came back now in a flash. I wanted to kill him — what the hell did he
have to come in here for? Damned if I'd let that Brooks character screw things
up for us with Antonio — even if I had to kill the bastard. I decided to take the
initiative.

First I tensed my arm and shoulder muscles, then relaxed them and walked
across the room and put out my hand, looking him squarely in the eye. His face
was expressionless as he took my hand limply and quickly dropped it. "Where
have you guys come from?" I asked as evenly as I could.

Magruder answered, "Oh, we came from Palena today. There are six of us. The others are at a house down in the valley. How do you like our clothes? We got some peasants to dye them black."

"They're OK. But maybe they'd be better if some of that color came out — they're a little *too* black."

Magruder laughed. "It already has. Look at this." Pulling his collar down, he displayed a neck and shoulder that looked like charcoal.

Dick pushed in front of me, nudging me as he went by. I eased back into the crowd and stood in a corner watching Rossbach talk to them. Within minutes, he had them both talking and laughing. At my expense, I was certain.

Someone tugged at my elbow. "Giuseppe, what's going on between you and that man?" Berardino wanted to know. "You looked as if you were going to hit him."

"It's a long story, Berardino," I replied. "You can check with Riccardo too if you want, but I tell you not to trust those two, especially the one called Stony."

"All right, I'll discuss it with Riccardo, but that's not really what I came to talk to you about. My mother, who has delivered many children, predicts that Letizia will give birth either tonight or tomorrow night."

"That's wonderful, Berardino, although I know it will be a very tense time for you. I've gone through it twice, you know."

"Thank you. But she will be in good hands. Right now I am concerned about so many prisoners around."

"Would you feel better if I made them stand guard? At least that way, we'd have some warning."

"That would be good." He relaxed and smiled. "The air is still very cold. On such nights, I've been able to hear the Germans as much as a kilometer away."

"You just let me organize things," I reassured him, wishing I was that sure I could pull it off.

Having noticed me huddled with Berardino, Dick walked over casually. *"Che cosa c'é, Giuseppe?"* he said with remarkably good pronunciation.

"Just this — apparently Letizia is about to deliver and this place is overrun with enough people to have attracted attention. Therefore, I propose we organize these guys and stand guard outside where we can hear if anyone's coming."

"All right," he said, "but it may take a bit of doing. Let's get the chaplain lined up first; after all, he is a major. Then you take it from there; you're the senior American."

The chaplain quickly agreed with the idea of a guard, but he pointed out that he wouldn't be able to participate, since chaplains were not to perform any military duties. Dick spoke to the sergeant, who also endorsed the idea, while

I went over to Magruder and Brooks with a kind of doomsday feeling. "Have you heard about the notices in the towns that the Italians will be shot for helping prisoners?" I said.

"Of course," Magruder said, "everybody knows that, but it's a lot of bullshit calculated to scare them."

"The Italians in Palena who were shot don't think it's a lot of bullshit, nor do the rest of us here," I rebuked him. "This family is too vulnerable, so I'm proposing that we stand guard outside at night in regular two-hour tours."

"That's a lot of crap, if I ever heard it," Stony growled. The look on his face reminded me of that night in Chieti.

"We're still in the military service," I reminded him, "and I'm willing to make an issue of it, now and in the future."

"Oh, for Christ's sake, Joe," Magruder said, "don't be so goddamn stuffy. We'll do it, we'll do it." He winked, made a quick gesture with his hand for me to get lost, and pulled Stony away.

The rest of that night we all stood guard in turns, and in our thin clothes suffered from the bitter cold. As each guard came off duty, he practically crawled into the fireplace in an attempt to warm up.

22 October

Throughout the next long, frigid night, we also stood guard. Letizia hadn't appeared at suppertime, and by now Rosa and Filomena were scurrying around chattering excitedly. Berardino came in with a load of wood and stacked it in the corner, then stoked the fire and put on a big kettle of water. I smiled — it was such an old cliché in the movies that when a woman was about to deliver the husband was advised to "go boil lots of water!" I had always thought this was a ruse to keep the nervous father-to-be busy, but now I concluded that they really did need sterile water to wash things up.

When the kettle was bubbling, I asked Berardino how things were going. "Eh! Eh! Eh!" he said with a sparkle in his eyes, "big things will happen tonight, Giuseppe," and he ran upstairs.

Dr. Eisenstein was sitting alone, so I went over and said cheerily, "Aren't you involved in all this, Doctor?"

"Not at all. Of course, I wanted to help. These people have been very kind. I'm a general practioner so I asked Rosa about it, but she told me, 'Our women don't expose themselves to strange men. I've delivered enough babies, and since the *levatrice* (midwife) cannot come this far, I shall do very well with the assistance of my daughters.' Frankly, I was a little hurt, but the customs of these people are very old, and in most cases, very well founded on practical experience. This procedure is all right as long as they understand about the antisepsis."

At 10:00 Filomena and the other sister put some bread, pasta, and wine on the table and quickly disappeared. After we served ourselves, we put some aside for the guys on guard duty. Later on I moved over to the fire and sat with Berardino, trying to take his mind off his worries. But it was useless — every moan from upstairs would bring him bolt upright in his chair. Occasionally, he would even put his hands over his ears.

While I was trying to comfort Berardino, I felt a hand on my shoulder. Antonio drew me over to the table and said in my ear, "The baby will arrive tonight. And don't worry about my son, he will survive. Remember how you felt when your first child was born?" He looked wise and winked at me.

Two hours later Dick and I were on duty outside when Antonio stuck his head out the door. "Come in, come in. It's perfectly safe now. It's all over." Not sure whether "safe" meant the absence of Germans or the arrival of the baby, we complied.

A dusty, cobweb-covered bottle of a tawny wine, along with some glasses, stood on the big table next to a plate of bread and prosciutto. The old man poured us each a drink and one for himself. Tears were rolling down his cheeks, and he said, "I am the grandfather of a beautiful boy, who will be named Antonio after me."

We clapped, stamped our feet, and congratulated him in both English and Italian. Then I insisted that there be at least one of us always outside on guard while the rest joined Antonio in the bread and prosciutto and a few rounds of toasts with his finest old wine. At 4:30 Berardino came down, setting off another round of congratulations and toasts. As morning approached, all the older people fell asleep with their heads on the table. The happy old man poured more wine and began reminiscing about his years in the States.

The first rays of dawn were appearing in the Abruzzi skies when Antonio proposed one final toast to young Antonio, II, who had already been affectionately nicknamed "Tonino." Then the proud grandfather and Berardino went off, arms around each other, rejoicing over the evening's blessed event. It was 23 October 1943.

Late that morning Magruder and Brooks left, headed for the lower Parello Valley. A while later we bade farewell and Godspeed to the RAF chaplain and the British sergeant, on their way to meet the group of pilots with whom they'd be traveling.

When they had gone, Antonio confided, "I'm worried about that fine *capellano* in the company of those reckless boys. They've found a young man, a cripple, to guide them. But I don't trust him. He talks all the time with the Germans, and claims they won't bother him because of his handicap." Shaking his head, he then added, *"Mio povero cappellano."* I was concerned about the chaplain too, but I was inwardly heaving sighs of relief that "those reckless boys" were at last out of our hair.

We left for the mountain immediately afterwards, taking along some bread Rosa had given us, tucked away with the precious Pecorino. Most of the day was taken up in fixing the roof of our hut. While we worked, the sheep up in the high pastures were bleating frantically. Despite this, that afternoon we located a group of shepherds and asked them if they might spare us a piece of meat. I wondered if it was a mistake, because they seemed nervous and gave the distinct impression they wanted to be rid of us. When two of them spoke in hushed tones, I heard something that sounded like, "Germans have taken too many." I listened carefully, but they were watching me and said nothing more. One man handed Dick some sheep's entrails wrapped in a piece of newspaper and said, *"Via, Via! é troppo pericoloso!"*

We hurried away. Dick said he'd got the part about it being too dangerous, and that he had an idea the Germans had been raiding their flocks. That was, undoubtedly, why the sheep had been making such a racket all day. Old Giuseppe's warning about shepherds now came back to me, and I said to Dick, "You didn't need me as interpreter that time. Those shepherds are bait for the Germans. The guy was honest when he said it was too dangerous."

The newspaper contained a big chunk of sheep's lung and a small piece of liver. We boiled pieces of the lung in a canteen cup. It came out stringy and as porous as a sponge, and I could hardly choke it down because it had blisters that popped and squirted in my mouth. Dick needled me, saying they were probably tuberculosis sores, which wouldn't hurt us because it had been boiled. I threw the rest out. Although the liver tasted good, half an hour after eating it we were both stricken with violent diarrhea.

26 October

Three days later, completely recovered, I left Dick at the *capanna* in order to explore Monte Lucino, the easternmost of the three mountain peaks.

In about half an hour I discovered a clearing on the eastern side of the mountain, just above a stone hut. As I was scrutinizing it, I heard, faintly, a conversation in good Italian. A man wearing an Italian army uniform with captain's insignia came out the door and up towards me, smiling and extending his hand. "You must be the American prisoner I've heard about," he said in Italian. "Don't be alarmed, we're your friends."

Shaking his hand, I gave my surname as I'd heard the Italians pronounce it. He was tall for an Italian, with a ruddy complexion, graying hair, a lined face, and a straight Roman nose. He introduced himself as Raffaele Valenzani, and told me he had lived in Rome before enlisting in the artillery.

Another man, also in Italian uniform, emerged from the hut. Raffaele was tall, but this man was towering, perhaps six-three and 200 pounds. In his late twenties, he had dark hair and hawk-like features. He wore an Italian uniform with captain's insignia. Raffaele introduced him as Ezio Bartolini. He nodded, shook hands, said, *"Buongiorno,"* and went back in the hut.

Raffaele laughed. "He's a hard one, that. Before we teamed up to come south, he commanded a company of *Alpini*. They're all big, husky, very reserved men, and I believe this one is reliable."

Raffaele explained that for a long time they had been disenchanted with the Mussolini regime and had strong Allied sympathies. But loyalty had compelled them to stick to their units until the Badoglio Armistice. After that, they felt they had an option with honor, and seized it as fast as possible, even though it put them in mortal danger if picked up by the Germans. Raffaele had little use for the military service in any form and now was desperate to get through the lines, a goal that would require a trustworthy guide. He knew about the crippled youth and didn't trust him either.

I told him we would like to go with them if they found a guide and assured him we could obtain safe conduct for them, if we ran into British troops first. He was keenly aware of British hostility to the Italians, so my suggestion appealed to him. We said goodbye, and he added that he hoped to meet my friend Riccardo very soon.

On 1 November Dick and I met a shepherd who seemed to be more friendly than the last ones we had encountered. He told us that an Italian colonel, living in a small house up near Monte San Domenico, had a radio and kept up with the latest war news. When we were alone, Dick said, "That colonel sounds like a good bet to get some idea of where our troops are." I did not like the idea of paying a call on the colonel, but we had a date to go down to Antonio the next night, and I intended to quiz him on what he knew about this man with the radio.

2 November

Antonio was no dissembler, and he had a way of putting his head back when he disapproved of something. "I think there is such a colonel up near Monte San Domenico," he said. "Berardino has heard about him." Then father and son spoke animatedly in their local dialect.

Finally, Berardino turned to me. "The shepherds say there is such a man," he began, "and that he lives on a shoulder of the San Domenico, called *Colle Buono* (Good Hill) for a saintly hermit who once dwelled up there. In fact, there's a shrine to him nearby."

What has the shrine to do with our seeing the colonel? I wondered; it seemed as if Berardino wanted to get us off the subject.

"Ask him if he thinks the man is authentic," Dick said.

"I believe so," Berardino answered, "and they say he has a radio. What I don't understand is why he lives so near a road which the Germans use regularly. It's almost as if he had some agreement with them."

Antonio cut in in English, "You boys thinking of going up there to see him?"

"We were," Dick said.

"I warn you," Antonio said, "it's very dangerous. You must be extremely careful if you go up there."

Letizia crept into the room carrying little Tonino, sat down by the fire, and began to nurse him. Berardino moved over next to her and whispered something. She smiled and invited me: "Come over and talk to us."

Still gazing at his son, Berardino said, "Giuseppe, do you have a religious affiliation?"

"Yes, I'm an Anglican. It's the American branch of the Church of England."

Letizia looked severely at me and said to her husband, "Does that mean he isn't a Catholic?"

"No, he isn't."

"Then he's a pagan?" Letizia said with a frown.

Berardino took a deep breath and gave an explanation of the separation of the Church of England from Rome. Letizia stopped him and asked questions once or twice, but I was amazed at the accuracy of his explanation.

When he finished, she said, "Is Riccardo Anglican too?"

"No, he's Jewish," I said.

At this, her eyes widened and her eyebrows raised. "He mustn't get caught again," she said. "Did they treat him badly before?"

"No, so far he's been very lucky. He did have some trouble with the Fascists, but that was for other reasons. He managed to avoid the SS."

"As you know, they've been in Palena," Berardino reminded me. "You must take every precaution. It could be terrible for Riccardo if he was shipped to Germany."

The room seemed dark around me. I couldn't talk any more, for the thought of the agreement Dick and I had made the afternoon on the Maiella had fallen over me like a shroud.

We slept on the floor in an empty room across the courtyard and left early in the morning in a damp, heavy fog. Dick thought it was very important to see the colonel, and I admitted it was critical to know where the Allies were before we set out. I had been so long in this valley, where I had such good friends and felt relatively secure, that even I thought maybe Antonio and Berardino had overstated the danger.

We stopped at our *capanna* and cooked some potatoes for breakfast. Meanwhile, the thick fog on the mountain began to lift.

Chapter 23

Night Return

Dick heaved himself up wearily and poured water from his canteen onto the fire. His face was gray, dark patches underlined his eyes, and his cheeks bristled with several days' growth of beard. He still wore the old jacket Giancarlo had given him, which had stayed intact only because the sleeves and side seams had been repaired with heavy thread. Though I had escaped serious injury and illness thus far, the black grime on the collar and cuffs of my brown shirt had now started deep, burning infections that resembled the boils Dick had. But worse than these was the hunger that gnawed interminably at my gut and kept me constantly short-tempered and on edge.

Dick broke the silence. "I've got to get cleaned up before we see the colonel. Let's go down to the stream."

"For God's sake, what the hell do you want to do that for? It's too damn open down there."

"Giuseppe, I've learned to estimate your blood pressure pretty well. You want to get out of here as badly as from Campo di Giove?"

His euphemism for my perpetual case of nerves made me squirm a little. "Of course," I snapped, "but not without some troop location and information about the route. Maybe this guy can tell us." But I began to wonder — had I grown complacent? This trip up the mountain was truly dangerous: I remembered that Antonio had insisted it was, and also how right he had been about certain other things. My appetite for this call on the colonel was diminishing fast.

I waited nervously, while Dick washed in the icy stream. The fog and clouds overhead were breaking up, driven by a strong northeast wind. The sky brightened and for a moment the rocky foothills of the Maiella and the main road to Gamberale, three miles away, stood out sharply. "For Christ's sake, let's get out of here," I burst out when I could take the tension no longer. "They can see us from the road!"

10:30 a.m.

The last part of the ascent was about 40°. Here Dick dropped to his hands and knees, crawling at last up and over the top, where he caught his breath and limped out onto a wide, level clearing. At its center stood a stone hut with a mossy green roof. On the far side of the field three dark-faced shepherds in sheepskin capes huddled around their flock. They stared across at us, unsmiling.

Dick gave the hut a once-over, while I scanned the woods and listened for the sound of footsteps, of cracking twigs; but there was only the wind gently rustling the leaves. Without turning, he asked, "Hear anything?"

"No."

Dick pointed toward the hut. "That's got to be the colonel's place."

"Maybe, but keep moving," I warned, "we're too damn exposed out here."

We had started walking toward the little stone dwelling when one of the shepherds called out, "Where are you going?"

"We're looking for a colonel who's been living up here," I answered. The man shrugged his shoulders and looked away. A cold rain had begun to fall.

When I knocked on the double doors of the hut, one of them swung inward a few inches. A tiny old lady in a black dress, a gray wool scarf over her head, peered out at us and, after hesitating a moment, whispered, *"Avanti."* As we entered, a little girl scurried to the back. The interior was furnished with a bench, two cots made from unpeeled branches, and a rusty potbellied stove. The old lady brought out a wicker basket and offered us some bread. "Thank you," I said, "we would like some very much. By the way, where's the colonel?"

"He's gone to Gamberale, but he'll be back soon," she said quickly in pure Italian, all the while never taking her eye off the door. Having wolfed down the bread, we eyed the basket for more. The lady spoke in Abruzzese to the little girl, who crept nearer and stared at us out of round dark eyes. From the stream of dialect, I picked out *"Tedeschi,"* repeated several times. In the past, people had often tried to get rid of us by saying, "The Germans are coming," but there was something different this time. She evidently knew Italian, yet she had chosen to talk in dialect with us around.

I cracked open the door and caught sight of a man in a greenish-gray uniform sneaking through the edge of the woods. "That guy may be another prisoner," I gasped, "but let's get the hell out of here anyway." We barged out the door, clutching our packs. I ran around the hut, and Dick hobbled back toward the steep incline we'd come up.

Two German soldiers burst from the woods at a dead run. A third came at me from behind the hut. Another screamed in German, "Halt! Halt! Or I shoot!" Two of them fanned out on either side of Dick until we were surrounded.

I stopped and stood there — trembling. Three men closed in slowly, rifles leveled at us. One — in corporal's stripes — shouted, "Hands up! Hands up! Or we shoot. Now walk together, but no tricks."

I raised my hands and moved over toward Dick, who was nearer the bank. "Who are you? Identify yourselves!" the corporal yelled.

"Captain Rossbach, United States Army."

"Captain Frelinghuysen, United States Army."

We stood there, rigid, as the man shouted commands at the other two Germans. I thought of the British commando sergeant we'd met on the Maiella. He'd been caught near Palena and had bribed a German to let him go. Could these Germans also be bribed? Not likely, I thought, in view of their Nazi-like manner. Dick stared stubbornly at the noncom and said in German, "Now, listen! I was captured at Tobruk, and I've been in so long I'm finished. Finished! I can't even fight again, so it's no use taking me prisoner. You should let us go, but if you won't you'll have to shoot me, because I'm crippled. I cannot and will not go with you."

Dick snatched the barrel of the corporal's rifle and pulled it against his chest, shouting, *"Schiess mich im Herz"* (Shoot me in the heart). Taken by surprise, the man hesitated, then quickly recovered and wrestled to free his rifle. Dick's feet slipped and he went down on the wet grass, still fighting to hang on to the weapon.

Suddenly, I knew what Dick was doing. I glanced beyond him for a split second at the steep bank we'd come up — 40 yards over wet grass. But I was in shock. I couldn't move.

The corporal swung his body, gave a heave, and tore the rifle from Dick's grasp. "I have no orders to shoot you, unless you try to escape. We have mules with our patrol, so if you can't walk, a mule will carry you."

All this time, the private was covering me with his rifle. "You should let us go," I managed in German. "I have something for you if you let us go." I held out my gold seal ring and wristwatch. The man frowned and shouted, *"Nein! Nein!"* and knocked my hand away with his rifle barrel. Dick looked at me in disgust, and I dreaded what he might do next. For I knew that at the first chance he would order me to make a run for it.

The corporal rattled off a string of orders to the other two men, then took off toward Gamberale, carrying his rifle across his chest. The private still had me covered, while the lance-corporal, now in charge, growled, *"Komm, komm, in die Hütte!"*

Dick explained, "The corporal's gone for his lieutenant and the rest of the patrol. That gets rid of the toughest of the three. In the meantime, we're to go in the hut and wait."

With a smile, Dick turned to the noncom and said in faultless German, "I agree. It's foolish to stay out here. Let's all go inside." It was just 11:00.

Now Rossbach's order was coming, I could feel it. Taking one last look before we went in, I rechecked my distance from the steep bank: 40 yards, and the same to the hut. Still quivering, I followed Dick into the square stone building, through the double wooden doors that opened inward.

The old lady and the girl had disappeared. Once inside, Dick pulled off his knapsack, sat down on a cot, and said affably, "While we're waiting, let us eat. We have some excellent local cheese." He continued smiling at the two Germans as if he hadn't a care in the world, then opened the knapsack and pulled out the Pecorino and a half-loaf of bread.

Still clutching their rifles, the two soldiers looked on in astonishment as Dick took out our old table knife, sliced the bread and cheese, and began making sandwiches. Closely eyeing the whole operation, the private took the clip out of his rifle and dried it on a rag. With a bow, Dick passed around four sandwiches and started to munch his with great gusto. When the two Germans stood their rifles against the wall and bit greedily into their thick slices of bread and cheese, I pretended not to see. Between mouthfuls, Dick commented on how hungry the mountain air could make a man.

"We haven't eaten since last night," the private complained.

In practically no time at all the Germans' sandwiches were half gone. Dick was talking in German a mile a minute, but in the midst of it he murmured to me, barely audibly, "Now, you go!"

"Not without *you*!" I pleaded. Was I stalling because I hated leaving Dick, or because I knew his order was a death sentence?

"You made an agreement," he said coldly, "and you *stick* to it!"

His back was to the Germans, who'd almost finished their sandwiches. He flicked an index finger toward the doors. Though I still dreaded the idea, something inside me suddenly took over, and I whirled around, wrenched the double doors inward, and jumped out, yanking them shut behind me. As they slammed, Dick's body crashed against them from the inside, and they banged and shook with the violence of the struggle.

As I started to sprint across the rain-soaked turf, my boots slipped, and I felt as in a dream that I was standing still. But I picked up speed and tore over the wet ground, casting an eye over my shoulder — the doors were still shut. Racing for the steep bank, I dove over the edge just as rifle fire cracked behind me. Bullets whined past as I pitched headfirst down the bank, skidded on my stomach, and rolled into a somersault. At the bottom of the gully, I spun to my feet and ran wildly, jumping and careening as I slid on the wet leaves.

Shots ricocheted and whistled off through the trees, but by then I was a poor target. Soon completely out of range, I kept the pace, protected by a shoulder of the San Domenico. Gasping for breath, I nearly choked on the bread and cheese, and coughed till I could spit it out, thinking what a stupid waste of good food.

I crossed into the next gully at top speed, well hidden in the hardwood forest. Though no longer afraid of being shot, I ran on steadily for a half-hour more in a drenching rain.

I remembered Berardino telling me the Germans sometimes used dogs, so I had to get as far from the hut as possible. I'd used the downgrade to keep up speed, but now I turned right, up toward Monte Rocca, where the Germans seldom patrolled. I pulled in great draughts of air, slowed to a jog, and began the long climb toward the thick cover of pine and beech on the upper slope.

1:00 p.m.

High above, the glistening cliffs of Monte Rocca butted into whirling clouds that spilled driving sheets of rain. I was soaked through. One of the boils on my left arm had abscessed and was causing a throbbing pain. These things were on both my arms and legs now, especially where the clothes had rubbed in the filth. If I got enough of them, they'd put me out of action. Adding to my misery was the knifing thought of having left Dick Rossbach behind. Though he'd foreseen this very possibility, it really didn't have to happen. Had I only let him know this morning that I wanted desperately to get out of this valley, we would now be on our way. While what I'd done did have some military rationale to it, deserting such a friend went hard against the grain.

I slogged on uphill, every step a test of strength, from time to time pausing and holding my breath to listen for dogs. But there was only the sound of the rain and the wind in the trees. A German patrol would probably use bloodhounds to pick up the trail, I reasoned, and I'd be able to hear them baying. I wasn't afraid of the hounds, but I tried not to think that toward the end they would surely turn loose a pack of snarling German Shepherds. So I plugged on, stumbling over slippery rocks, then wading in frigid streams and crossing rocky ledges and outcrops to avoid leaving any scent.

3:00 p.m.

After two hours in the rain and icy brooks my feet and legs grew numb, so I left the brooks and rocks of the upper slopes and brushed through the dripping branches of the mountain pines, heading east at a slow trot. Each time I thought of Dick, I went through a compulsive fantasy of what those Germans might have done to him. I imagined him being beaten with rifles and kicked to a bloody death. Those two wouldn't know he was Jewish, but if he was taken to

SS headquarters in Palena. . . . The thought was too much, I had to avoid it. I was scared and alone, and uncertain of my direction. Though I'd believed that I'd been going straight away from the scene of our capture, when I looked down into the valley to my right I discovered to my horror that I'd been making a great circle. There below me was the colonel's hut. Again I turned and fled.

By 4:00 I'd been on the run five hours and felt fairly sure the Germans had lost my trail. The wind and rain had let up, and I kneeled down at a stream to gulp the chilled water, wondering whether I could last through the night. If only I could find Raffaele, he might know something about the German patrol and where I could hide out until morning.

I moved on eastward, toward his hut on Monte Lucino. Finally I came down out of the pines into the hardwood forest, reaching the stone shelter at twilight. A man in dark civilian clothes stood near the structure. He saw me and scurried inside.

5:00 p.m.

There was a brief, panicky exchange; several men and boys burst from the door and darted into the woods. They must have assumed the Germans were right on my tail. What a relief it was when Raffaele strode around the building, wearing his heavy army sweater and blue-gray trousers. He stretched out his hand and spoke in his pure Italian: "Hello, Joe, I'm glad to see you. I was afraid I might not ever see you again after what I heard this morning." Abruptly he added, "Santa Maria! Your hand's like ice."

"Have you heard what happened, Raffaele?" I said, hearing my own voice break. "I think they've lost my trail, but still you're taking an awful chance with me here."

"Just relax and come along," he reassured me. "There's a place where we can talk." He strode briskly through the trees, and I followed him for half a mile. He stopped, looked around, and approached a huge rock, which evidently served him as some sort of marker. A few feet away he lifted a matted, rectangular covering of leaves and branches to reveal a wide, gravelike trench. "Quick, get inside!" he ordered.

I crawled in and held up the roof until Raffaele slid in beside me. "Now, if we talk softly," he cautioned, "we'll be safe for a time. Earlier today the shepherds, who see and know everything, saw a German lieutenant with several soldiers and an American prisoner on the way to Palena."

"Thank God, at least Rossbach's alive!" I murmured.

Raffaele nodded and went on: "The people in this area are full of wild stories about you. An *Alpenjäger* patrol of 17 men has been searching the mountain for you all day. They even inquired in neighboring towns, so you certainly are a hot item. Now, tell me what happened and perhaps we can decide what you should do."

My teeth chattered with cold as I related the events of the morning and described where I'd been and what I'd been through. Raffaele fell silent, his brow wrinkling. In a moment, he spoke again, "As you could see, my people are in a panic, so I can't take you in here. But we must get you *some* place for tonight, when the danger will be greatest. It'll diminish tomorrow and more so each day. Where have you been going to eat?"

"To Antonio's."

"Try it there then. But if they won't let you in, come back here. I'll *make* my people take you in, at least for tonight."

"OK, I'll try Antonio's, but I must leave this valley as soon as possible. Have you anything new about a guide?"

"No one we can trust up to this morning, but two men from my people here are going to investigate the area near the Sangro River tomorrow, and on the following night they'll be able to show you where best to cross. However, I don't think it's wise to leave yet; even though the shelling and bombing seem very close, they're considerably farther away than we think."

In the early dusk, when we climbed out of the shelter, I started to run off. Raffaele called, "Wait. Your hand!" He sounded offended. I stopped in my tracks and looked back at him, ashamed at forgetting this custom between friends.

He took my hand firmly in both of his. "Be careful and good luck," he said. "Come back in two days and I'll try to arrange for a guide who will take us all the way."

I attempted to thank him but Raffaele just smiled and waved his finger back and forth. Off into the damp stillness of the woods I walked, more exhausted and confused than I realized. It had been about seven hours since I'd parted from Dick, and for most of that time I'd been running. Concentrating was difficult, yet I knew if I could find the glade where we'd slept so often, I'd be able to get to Antonio's. Even though these woods were very familiar to me, through stumbling and falling in the growing darkness I eventually lost my bearings and any sense of how long I'd been on the move. In the misty gloom, all the trees and foliage looked the same and time stood still.

Wandering along a steep hillside, obsessed with the thought of just lying down, I suddenly realized I was right above the Parello. My mind began to clear as I bounded down to the river and groped my way across. Above the bank on the far side I recognized the familiar path to the farm. Veering right, I followed it up the long grade, and shortly the silhouettes of Antonio's farmhouse buildings loomed up.

Cautiously I tiptoed into the courtyard. My heart jumped in my throat when a child ran into me in the darkness, let out a scream of fright, and ran off to one of the houses. In a moment a ray of light from a doorway fell on me. God, what a relief to hear Berardino's voice call out evenly, *"Chi siete?"* (Who is it?)

"It's Giuseppe. There's been a disaster! Riccardo and I were captured this morning!" I said, my words tumbling out in a torrent. "I escaped and they chased me, but I think they lost my trail some time ago. Of course you know how risky it is for you if I'm here."

For a moment, Berardino didn't respond. Then he asked incredulously, "And Riccardo isn't with you?"

"No," I whispered, my voice breaking. After another brief silence, he suddenly spat out. "The devil take those accursed Germans, Giuseppe." He put his hand on my arm. "I'll never turn a man away at night in your condition. Come in!"

8:00 p.m.

I followed him, with a brief release from tension at the momentary safety. But I hated the thought of having to break the news to everyone that I had run out on their "Riccardo." The door opened on the familiar smell of burning wood from the huge fireplace. Flickering red and yellow light gleamed on the great copper urn in the alcove, as I slowly looked around at the dark-clad figures, the hardy mountain folk who'd become my friends. Their eyes all turned to stare at the bedraggled man in their doorway.

Rosa raised her apron to her face and cried, "God have mercy! Santa Maria have mercy! What's happened to you? Where is Riccardo?" Letizia looked at me, her young face pale. Her sister began to cry, while Antonio jumped out of his chair and grabbed my arms. "My God, boy, what happened?"

Recovering her voice, Letizia said reprovingly, "Giuseppe, where have you left Riccardo?"

"Be quiet, all of you!" Antonio scolded. "Let's hear what he has to say."

Clutching a blanket around my shoulders, I sat in front of the fire between Antonio and Berardino, agonizing through an account of the day's occurrences and of what I suspected the enemy had by now done to my friend. Again and again, I emphasized to the family that despite the agreement Riccardo had imposed on me, I felt horrible about leaving him.

Letizia turned her back and began to work at the table while I was talking, and Rosa periodically moaned, *"Povero Riccardo!"* while she stirred the pasta in the cauldron. Soon, echoing voices came from the two sisters, *Povero Riccardo!"* until, finally, the sounds became a rhythmic chant, to which their heads swayed in unison.

My story told, I sat in silence, listening to this ancient mountain ritual of lamentation, each moan a stab to my conscience, adding to my misery. The abscess on my arm had begun to throb again, and the smell of cooking brought on waves of ravenous hunger. Still cold, I sat shivering between father and son and edged closer to the fire.

Chapter 24

Bart Pyle

<u>11:00 p.m., 3 November</u>

An hour later Rosa took me by the arm. "Come, I've fixed a nice warm bed for you upstairs."

"Oh, Rosa, thank you, but it's much too dangerous for all of you if I'm up there, and it's no good for me either. I'll sleep in the kitchen where there's a back door."

"No, no, no, Giuseppe. You'll be safe and comfortable up there."

"But I can't even take these muddy shoes off!" I pointed to the congealed knots in the makeshift laces. As if to say it didn't matter, she shook her head and tugged me along. With Dick no longer around, I seemed to have lost the will to make a decision and stick to it. Looking hopelessly at Antonio, I pleaded, "You tell her."

"Go on, you do what she says, Giuseppe. But you must be sure to leave early in the morning."

"I know, I know — I'm trying to get a guide. Then I must leave at the first possible moment."

He grimaced and stressed firmly, "Yes, as soon as possible is right. It gets worse every day." He turned back to the fire as I followed Rosa up the steps. She removed from the bed a brazier full of redhot coals and commanded, "Get in!" Again, I pointed at my shoes. Getting impatient, she gave me a little push. Reluctantly, I wrapped my feet in my jacket and crawled in. The bed was deliciously hot, and I slept dreamlessly until 4:30, when I woke, instantly alert, but the house was quiet.

<u>4 November</u>

Rosa was the only one up when I went downstairs. She fussed at the fire for a few minutes and gave me a cup of a mysterious hot brown liquid. It was roasted barley "coffee" with hot milk, I learned; she said it would cure my dysentery. As rapidly as I could, I ate the bread and drank the coffee. As I finished the last morsel, she handed me a batch of potatoes and two eggs she had cooked in the ashes. I was keenly aware of how precious the eggs were to this household, because heretofore only Letizia had been allowed them. Yet when I tried to thank her, Rosa merely waved her finger at me. "Have a good trip and good luck," she said, with tears in her eyes, then kissed me on both cheeks. It was Wednesday, the fourth day of November.

At 5:00 I departed while it was still dark, crossed the river, and climbed the hill on the other side. There I started a small fire and warmed the eggs in the ashes and roasted two small potatoes in the smoldering coals. The eggs were a rare treat indeed, but even along with the potatoes they made not the slightest dent in my hunger. After running and walking for some 11 hours the previous day, I still felt physically spent and desperately famished.

My improvised camp faced north, and I sat looking out at the snow-covered Maiella, wreathed in feathery clouds. As I stared, there came to mind an old Abruzzese proverb: "Never let the snow catch you in these mountains." Struggling to figure out a course of action, I found it impossible to sustain any train of thought. I had functioned well enough in a team or in a twosome. Now the prospect of crossing the Sangro alone, then walking 45 miles through unknown country and somehow sneaking through the German lines, paralyzed me mentally and physically.

The pain of separation from Dick, whom I had depended on, ran very deep. I had only a third-hand report that he had survived, and, at best, he had paid a bitter price to cover for me while I escaped. Now it was imperative that I reach the British and deliver the partisans' message. Then, at least, Dick would not have paid the price for nothing.

Rosa's remedy for my dysentery and the sympathy that came with it had helped, for by afternoon I felt better and started down to see Raffaele a day sooner than expected. He must have heard me coming, for as I approached he stepped out and shook my hand. "Those two guides have gone," he said with a shrug. "They left without a word."

"What do you mean? Didn't you have an agreement with them?"

With a wan smile, he put his hand on my shoulder. "Just forget about it. If these people don't want to do something, no one can force them to — they're too stubborn. Anyway, it's better to wait until the British get nearer. Now, have you heard of a British infantry sergeant named 'Bart,' like *Bartolomeo*? I told him about you and he wants to meet you."

"No, I haven't, but I would like to meet him."

"*Va bene*, he's staying in a mud hut up on the mountain." Though still upset about the guides, I agreed to go up and talk to this "Bart." Raffaele gave me precise directions.

Upon my arrival, I was greeted by a broad-shouldered, ruddy-faced British soldier. Perhaps 24 or 25, he was wearing battledress trousers and a dark gray civilian jacket with torn pockets and sleeves; thick brown hair protruded from under an ancient tweed cap. There was another prisoner with him.

"Might you be the Yank Raffaele's been talking about?" he asked in an unmistakable north of England accent.

"Yes, my name's Frelinghuysen."

"Mine's Bart Pyle," he said, extending a square, powerful hand with fingers so thick I could hardly grasp them. "Joe, isn't it? I heard you wanted to move out of this valley as much as we do."

The man seemed to be a solid British soldier — good guy to team up with, but probably as reckless as the rest of them. Expecting an argument, I said mechanically, "Not without a competent guide and some idea where the Eighth Army is."

Bart nodded as if in agreement and introduced me to his friend, an Irishman named Dan, who had been in the British army. "I've met a man who agreed to guide us out," Bart said. "I get along pretty well with these Eyetie chaps, but don't always understand them too well. Will you come along and check him out?"

In spite of myself, I said huffily, "First of all, I prefer not to call them Eyeties. Where is this guide?"

Detecting my irritation, he said in a conciliatory tone, "He'll meet us late tonight where me and Dan's been living. The farmer there's killing a pig today. Said if we come down he'll give us some fresh pork. Like to come along?"

Such a generous offer quickly shamed me out of my stuffiness. "That's one invitation I'll take you up on," I said smiling. "When do we start?"

"Right now, if ye're ready?"

It took an hour to get to his friend's house, farther down the Parello than I had been before. The valley opened out into pastures and farmland, cut by the gorge of the river, which eventually cascaded into the Sangro between Quadri and Villa Santa Maria. The country was not as rugged as where I had been living and lacked good cover.

The farmer had a great batch of fresh pork frying in an immense skillet with olive oil, garlic, and hot peppers. I came close to grabbing some of the meat right out of the pan. While we waited, Bart informed me that our guide's name was Paolo, and that he came from Quadri, in the lower Sangro River Valley — he would know the river well. Bart also told me that Paolo was inclined to talk too much and to drink too much wine. The *vino* part didn't bother Bart; he figured we could walk it out of him. Paolo was to meet us outside the house at 7:00, in about three hours.

After what seemed a lifetime, the farmer announced that the pork was cooked. It was still pink inside, but we were all so hungry we would have eaten it raw. Our host gave us two platefuls each, with some bread, which we polished off in short order. It was the first meat I had had since the sheep's lung, but this time I had no unpleasant reaction.

For the next half-hour or so we sat around the table talking with the farmer and his family. Bart seemed to communicate with them quite well, in a mixture of gestures and a few mispronounced words of Italian. Occasionally, the farmer would understand him and respond before I could. Bart was clearly popular with this family, but I wasn't too sure about Dan's standing with them. As we chatted he sat across the table from me, next to one of the daughters. Every now and then his hand would disappear under the table; the girl would jump, squeal, and burst into peals of laughter. Her face and neck would turn scarlet. Each time, her father looked angrier. I wondered if at any moment now Dan would find himself propelled out the door by the seat of his pants.

It was nearly dark when we heard people talking excitedly outside the house. A man and two women burst into the room. The man gasped, "Two houses, only 400 meters away, have been raided by the Germans!" One of the women slumped down in a chair next to me, put her head in her hands, and burst into tears. "One was my house," she wailed. "They threw everyone out except five of our girls, and they've kept them for the night!" She broke into uncontrollable sobs.

The farmer jumped to his feet, staring at me with sheer terror in his eyes. I felt desperate that I couldn't help them in any way. I translated to Bart what had happened. "The bloody bastards," he said. "Let's get out. Paolo'll be here soon anyway." Not waiting to be asked, we made a beeline for the door.

"Where the hell you blokes going?" Dan demanded.

"Out fast," I ordered. "Jerries in the next house!" Dan didn't budge.

Bart and I waited outside listening. In a couple of minutes Dan wandered out. "You laddies sure get the wind up fast," he said.

"Look, Dan," I said, "you keep on with this horseshit and you'll get your ass back in the bag real quick. I'd be there myself now, if I didn't have the sense to move fast." Dan let out a long sarcastic whistle. I thought the sooner we get rid of this guy the better.

The Italians have a method of walking in the countryside in the dark of night: They take a burning stick and swing it back and forth just above the ground. The flame soon dies out, but the ember that's left glows enough to illuminate the path. Such a stick now came swinging up the trail toward us. *"Chi siete?"* Bart called out.

"Eh, eh, Bartolomeo, son' Paolo," a loud, thick voice answered.

Paolo approached, waving the firebrand and swaying so badly I couldn't understand why he didn't topple over. Our would-be guide smelled of sour wine, garlic, and acid indigestion.

"I've come a long way to tell you it's no good to go tonight." Paolo hollered in a voice like a hog caller's. "The river's too high, too many Germans —" "Paolo, be quiet," I interrupted. "There are Germans in the next house!"

Lowering his voice perhaps a decibel or two, he kept on ranting, his speech slurred and nearly incomprehensible, as he cited every reason he could think of against going. His litany of excuses told their own story; the man was both too afraid and too drunk to guide us anywhere.

Suddenly, about 50 feet away, a shot was fired. All three of us turned and ran, leaving Paolo standing there. Racing up the valley along a field, I heard whistling back to our right — it sounded like a signal. Somebody was on our tail. Getting our second wind, we kept going. Twice more I heard whistles, each time a little farther back. We had gained a little.

Holding the pace till I was pretty sure our pursuers had given up, I slowed to a walk. Bart and Dan were panting and heaving, and whatever they had thought back at the house about my being "windy" was not mentioned. Bart led us to a big stone barn far up the valley, where a man named *Gio'an'* (Giovanni) kept his cattle. We reached the place after midnight, pried our way in, and built a small fire on the dirt surface of the floor. Each man took his shift tending the smoky flames, while the other two did their best to get some rest.

Getting to sleep was difficult to me. My arm had begun to throb viciously. The shiny filth on my clothes rubbed the boils continually, and for each one that was abscessed two or three more were on the way. In the flickering firelight I examined the skin above each one for red streaks that would indicate blood poisoning and was satisfied that conditions had not reached that stage.

For several days we stayed up in the mountains, coming down only to get food. Dan had been for some time growing more and more uneasy, until finally on the morning of 6 November he erupted and left in a huff. We never saw him again.

By this time, my civilian clothes were so tattered I had to wear them under my army pants and sweater, where they still afforded scant protection from the cold. Apart from my personal troubles, a very different problem had arisen from the situation among the local farmers, which was worsening by the day, with more and more refugees streaming up into the woods. At sundown I informed Bart that I had made a firm decision never to go to the same house two nights in a row. He simply shrugged and made his way down to Gio'an's, while I remained in a *capanna* he and I had built.

On the evening of 8 November Bart arrived up at the *capanna* with an invitation for me to join him for supper at Gio'an's. I accepted with alacrity, though I had mixed feelings about the position I was in. While Bart had made several of these arrangements for me, I had never reciprocated by asking him to Antonio's. The place had been far too crowded all along, and Antonio and his family had done much more for me than anyone else. It simply wasn't fair for me to go back. I was determined not to, unless I was in real trouble.

On the way to Gio'an's, we stopped at Raffaele's to see if he had located a guide and found him surprisingly evasive. Bart became very suspicious, and even I, who had had up to now complete faith in Raffaele, was left wondering.

We met Gio'an' and his wife Maria in another barn, where they were living. He was thin and dark; his wife, a slender, gaunt-faced woman, had a yellowish-brown tint to her skin. She was nursing their infant daughter, while a six-year-old son whined and cried on her shoulder.

When we had squatted down on wooden boxes around an open fire on the barn's dirt floor, Maria put down the baby, who began to howl, and brought over some pasta in a crockery bowl. She served me a small portion on a cracked plate and handed me a rusty fork, then served the others equally small portions. As soon as she had finished her helping, she lowered her blouse and began to nurse the six-year-old. I was shocked at a child that age being nursed.

Gio'an' looked at me sharply and said, "Indeed, if my wife didn't nurse our older son, his health would really deteriorate. We just don't have the meat and eggs a growing boy needs." That people in such destitution would even consider feeding strangers continued to astound me.

That night Bart and I slept in their hayloft, but in the morning we returned to our hut. He had borrowed Gio'an's axe so we could expand our little shelter into a better hideout. At first, he swung the blade very energetically, but after about an hour he sat down, sweating profusely. While both my arms were aching from the boils, and at times I felt dizzy, my conscience impelled me to offer, "OK, it's my turn now."

Bart wasn't the woodsman Berardino was, but even so he was an expert compared to me, especially in my present condition. Still, I lined up the branch the way Bart had and swung the axe. My sleeve scraped the open head of a boil, and a stabbing pain ran up my right arm. The blade barely cut the bark. I tried again, attempting to ignore the pain. At last I cut through the branch. It looked shredded, as if some animal had chewed it off.

When I started on the next branch, Bart got up. "I can't even watch ye," he said, grimacing. "Ye'll hurt yourself bad with them filthy boils." He seized the axe from my hand. Feeling sick and useless, I collapsed on a rock and watched him finish the task.

The next evening I was lightheaded from the lack of food. I had had only one meal in two days; with the infection, I had to get something to eat as soon as possible. I went down toward Antonio's and crossed the Parello where it passed through his fields. From all my weeks in the mountains, my intuition had been honed to a razor sharpness, and at this moment I sensed something was wrong.

Climbing the rise above the river, I saw some figures running into the woods. Though they looked like Italians, there was something different about them. At a house near the trail, people were whispering in small groups. When they saw me, some women cried and ran away. *"Aspett', son' Americano,"* I called out.

One young woman stopped and warned me: "The Germans have just raided a house not more than 200 meters down the trail. You better beat it, full speed, the other way."

"Are there any Germans at Antonio's?" I asked her.

"No, they came up from below his house."

Thanking her, I sneaked up the hill toward the courtyard. When I got to the door of the house, I stepped quickly into the big kitchen without being noticed. The room was jammed with people: 15 or 20 refugees milling around, sitting and lying on the floor, squeezed between bundles and packages. Across the room, Rosa, a black shawl wrapped around her head, was packing things into wicker hampers. After picking my way through the people, I tried to speak to her, but she kept moaning to herself. Then I found Berardino.

Despite the situation, he and Antonio were calm, as I had always seen them. Berardino insisted I stay, that they would get things organized. These were new people who had just been bombed out of Montenero. The Eisensteins had left some time ago, and the refugees were all strangers to me. Among them was a very attractive young girl, but she said to me, "You have no business to be here, you're a danger to all of us."

Choking back an angry reply, I asked politely, "Where are you from?"

"Chieti."

"Why, I spent eight months there," I told her, with my friendliest smile. Still indignant, she turned her back on me, walked out, and I forgot about her.

Not ten minutes later, this same *signorina* ran back into the room and shrieked, "The Germans are coming!"

Women cried out, men echoed her alarm, *"Via! Via! Vengono i tedeschi!"* The refugees pushed and elbowed their way toward the door. A few got out, but it quickly became a mass of bodies, shouting, struggling, all heading toward the narrow exit.

I squeezed against the wall, wondering how I could get into the room behind the kitchen that led to the back door, while a man wormed his way toward the girl. He took hold of her arms roughly and demanded, "What did you do? Another of your tricks? Is this true or not?"

The girl shook her head and began to whimper, *"Era uno scherzo, uno scherzo!"* (It was a joke, a joke!)

The man muttered, *"Maledetta!"* disgustedly, then faced the room and announced, "Pay no attention to this girl. That's her idea of a joke."

Gradually, the women stopped crying, the people at the door extricated themselves, and in a while the group calmed down. Afterwards Antonio and Berardino moved among them, helping them to get into better positions, rearranging their belongings, until the room took on some semblance of order. I moved over and waited near the door.

About 15 minutes later, a man rushed through the door and cried, "They're *really* coming this time! They're on the path below, headed this way!"

Clinging to my knapsack, I whipped out the door and around the side of the house. Running at top speed, I reached the hill above it and ducked behind some haystacks. After a brief pause there, I ran across the upper field, expecting to hear any second the crack of a rifle, slipped through the hedge on the far side and listened: not a sound. I'd moved so fast I was confident the Germans hadn't spotted me.

Minutes later I rejoiced at the sound of Berardino's calm, reassuring voice: "It was nothing, Giuseppe, you can come back right away." Still worked up, I ran down to him and grabbed his hand. *"Calma, calma, Giuseppe,"* he advised, "it's better not to run if someone is watching. I don't think they're up this far, but that was a very bad raid earlier."

"What happened?"

"They came at dusk and surrounded two houses. A few got out, but they caught about a dozen men — no one is sure, because they may be hiding somewhere. But then they also took some of the women." Here he stopped and let loose a torrent of curses. In the early gloom I could feel him struggling for his composure and looked away.

"If it's as bad as you say," I suggested, "maybe I better not come in."

"No, no, no, Giuseppe, it's all right now — they've gone. But this is why the others all believed the girl's lie. Her false alarm ran through the neighborhood and came in a circle back to our house."

Once again, I felt an attack of cramps coming on. When I told Berardino I'd be back in a few minutes, he returned to the house. The dysentery, while not as severe as the day Dick and I ate the sheep's lung, still left me weak and sore inside. I knew I shouldn't go back, but my willpower had gone.

When I sneaked into the house, Rosa caught sight of me and took me over to a corner, out of view of most of the refugees, and fed me some bread and pasta. Later on, as I moved about, I found myself face to face with the girl. "Please forgive me," she begged. "I didn't realize it would cause so much trouble. Do come over here and talk to me and cheer me up." She tried to take my arm, but I quickly withdrew it and backed away in disgust.

Eventually, when the refugees had fallen asleep in uneven rows on the floor, Rosa stepped carefully over their inert forms and led me to a pot of boiling water where she motioned to me to take off my sweater and jacket. Complying, I pulled my shirt down off my right shoulder, exposing an abscess. When she dipped a poultice into the steaming water and pressed it tightly over the yellow head on the boil, I almost let out a shriek. Somehow I suppressed it, grinding my teeth while the pain shot down my arm like a streak of fire. I wanted to yank my arm away from Rosa, but she had her purpose and showed no more feeling than if she had been putting the scalding poultice on a stone. When it cooled, and I relaxed a trifle, she slapped on another. I sat on the edge of my chair, and after a while the excruciating pain leveled off into one long, pounding ache up and down my arm. It seemed like hours until she finally looked at the boil and said, *"Esce"* (It's coming out). She let it drain thoroughly, then threw the poisonous debris in the fire and washed her hands right in the boiling water until they were purple red. "Your poor hands," I said sympathetically, but she just shrugged her shoulders.

Berardino came over and settled himself on a bench next to me. He sighed and began to talk in that philosophical way of his, as he had when he had patiently explained to his wife about the church of England. He launched into a description of how his beloved *Patria Italia* would have troubles after the war, and observed that he thought America would undoubtedly have them too, because her citizens were much too profligate and wasteful with their natural resources. "You people don't understand," he said, "so you eat such food as eggs and milk, which we wouldn't think of using, except for babies and pregnant women. That's food of the third stage; the cow or chicken uses even more food and energy to make the milk or eggs. In Italy, we can't afford those luxuries; they're too expensive and wasteful. Our food must consist mostly of the crops that come directly from the ground. Some day, you in America will no longer be able to eat meat."

At Berardino's words, I had a fierce surge of guilt. Since Dick's recapture, I had lost my spirit, my drive to keep going, and I'd stayed here far too long. Despite Antonio's earlier hints, I had kept coming back and taking food that should have been left for their family. This time I vowed to myself I would not return again.

Antonio, picking up a candle, beckoned to us from across the room. Berardino and I started after him as he disappeared through a door in the back of the kitchen, where Rosa caught me in her arms. Her face wet with tears, she kissed me on both cheeks, saying, "Goodbye, my prayers go with you."

I followed Berardino out into an old storeroom. It had a door leading out the back and a wooden bin half full of potato culls. Berardino piled the culls up at one end and pointed to the bin. Without a question, I crawled into the bin and nestled down as far as I could. He and Antonio piled potatoes on top of me until just one hand stuck out and a hole was left for me to breathe. They each shook my hand and told me to pull it down under the potatoes. Satisfied with the appearance of the bin, Berardino commented, "It looks all right now. Goodnight, Giuseppe."

"Goodbye, Giuseppe," Antonio added, took his candle, and went out. I remembered my vow.

After squirming around for a few minutes in the earthy-smelling culls to get as comfortable as possible, I dozed off, not to awaken until 4:00, when everyone was still asleep. It was 10 November.

The morning was icy but windless, and as I went out all was still. The half-moon had set and the early November stars were brilliant. By way of the boulders among the rapids, I crossed the Parello and went back up to the *capanna*, where I built a tiny fire. When it had burned down, I roasted a small potato in the ashes. My right arm, the one Rosa had treated, felt weak, but it had stopped throbbing. Exhausted, I tried to take a nap, but in the freezing cold found it impossible and could only turn back and forth on the rocky floor. My body seemed to have lost the capacity to withstand cold the way it used to when Dick and I first broke out of Fonte d'Amore.

Unable to get comfortable, I sat up and pulled the potato out of the ashes. And though it was cooked enough, when I took a bite my stomach revolted and I could hardly choke the damn thing down. Since our break from the prison camp, I'd been living almost exclusively on starchy food, a lot of it potatoes, and I was reminded of a refugee I had seen who had turned yellow from a strict potato diet and looked as if he'd had jaundice.

At 9:00, sitting outside the *capanna* trying to catch a few rays of the sun, I heard someone making his way up through the woods. Always ready to take off, I grabbed my knapsack, scrambled up and hid in the rocks. But a familiar English voice rang out, "'Allo' Joe, where be ye?"

Relieved, I peeked over a rock. "Oh, Bart, thank God it's you!"

He looked up at me and laughed. "And what'll ye be doing up there?"

"After that calamity with Dick, I'm damned if I'll ever again get caught in a trap. By the way, have you had anything to eat?"

"I was lucky; had a bite at Domenico's. He's the very old chap I was telling you about; told me to come back tonight and bring my mate."

"That's great, if we don't pull out before then."

Bart's voice rose, "You mean it's laid on for tonight?"

"Well at the very latest, one of the next two or three nights."

We talked for a while, and when I brought up the incident with the girl from Chieti, he shook his head. "Girls and war don't mix for my money. Better stay away from them on any account. Mate I had some time ago shacked up wi' one at Pizzo'. Caught a bloody dose, he did. Had to turn himself in to Jerry to get treated. Had no choice. 'Twas a cryin' shame that."

"Bad show," I mumbled, not knowing what else to say. "Was the girl an Italian?"

"So he said."

"She probably caught it from the Germans; you remember what they did that night down in the valley?"

"How could I forget it? Those blasted Huns."

Then Bart listened patiently while I waxed nostalgic about my wife, our two children, the house I'd left back in New Jersey, and the kind of life we had led before the war.

"Lovely story, that," he reflected. "Dirty shame to have to leave your family. For me, there's the guv'nor. He's worked most of his life in the coal mines, but he's on the Home Guard now. You know, I started in the mines, too, when I was a young lad, and worked there for four years. It's a bloody rum go, that job. Then my mum's been working in hospital. Our place is just north of Newcastle — raids been terrible there, they say."

He broke off to listen to the distinctive whine of German planes and the rattle of machine-guns that echoed up the valley. In a few seconds, this din was joined by the thud of bombs which seemed to come from the southeast, somewhere in the Sangro Valley.

The afternoon passed quietly, and at twilight we went off through the woods to stop at Raffaele's on our way to Domenico's. Raffaele appeared fit and as confident as ever. Clearly he was getting along better than we were, because he still retained his florid complexion, looking as though he had just dined in a Roman restaurant. As we shook hands, he said, "I'm sorry to have to tell you, but I don't have a guide as yet."

"I could've told you that," Bart muttered behind me.

"Cool it, Bart, you'll mess up the deal." Switching into Italian, I spoke to Raffaele. "Just what's the problem with those guides?"

"The obvious one is the heavy rain in the western Apennines, and the Sangro is at flood stage. Even an expert swimmer couldn't make it in that icy water, and it's far too deep to ford on mules. The less obvious reason is that very few men want to take the risk of getting shot."

"And the bridges?" I said.

"According to the shepherds, every one guarded. And they ought to know — they use them at the cost of a lot of sheep."

This time Bart growled at me, "Let's get moving, we're getting nowhere this way."

Raffaele glanced at Bart, then said to me, "Come back in two days. I might have someone then. By the way, what's bothering your friend?"

"He just doesn't like this waiting," I said with a smile he did not return.

After we left, I got to thinking that in spite of my fussing about Bart's impatience, he was the one who was finding us the places to eat. He interrupted my thoughts with the startling news that Domenico was totally blind. I had a sudden feeling of prescience — was this the blind ballad singer of the old Italian poem that I had learned back in Chieti?

Domenico's house was beyond the Parello, on the saddle at the head of Dark Valley. In the blackness, we sneaked into the courtyard. A small boy came out and spoke softly to Bart, then went back inside. How he understood the child's Abruzzese was a mystery to me, but he whispered to me that we were to wait.

From the way he put it, I got the impression we were "waiting upon" a personage of considerable importance.

A few minutes passed before the boy reappeared and took us behind the building, past the animals in a stableyard, and up a narrow staircase built on the outside of the old stone house. From the upper landing we entered a large room, bright with lantern and firelight. After the darkness, I stood there dazzled, until I was distracted by shaking hands with people who met us at the door. Then I saw him. Seated by the hearth, his gnarled hands resting on an oak stick between his knees, was Domenico, a patriarch with a great curling white mustache and beard. His sightless eyes stared out across the room as though they saw both vistas of the past and visions of the future.

In a reverential tone, usually reserved for speaking of nothing less than royalty, Bart said, "I'll introduce you to Domenico in a moment." Then he greeted our host in a booming voice, "Greetings, Domenico, it's good to see you again!"

Reading wisdom in the rough-hewn old face, I was reminded again of the poem I'd memorized at Chieti: *"Sono il cantastorie cieco all' angolo della via"* (I am the blind ballad singer at the corner of the street).

I was shaken from my daydream by the old man's roar — in rather good English: "Hey, Bart, what'sa matter with you? You think I'm deaf as well as blind? Bring your friend over and introduce him to me!" Bart laughed and said, "Domenico, I'd like you to meet Giuseppe. He's American."

Domenico's grip was like iron. "Damn you, Bart, now you tell me I can't speak English. His name is *Joe!*" They both roared with laughter.

The old man's sallies at Bart were goodnatured, and we sat by the fire, soaking up the heat, while he related to me tales of his years in the States, working in the steel mills of Pennsylvania. Our conversation was interrupted when his daughter, Maria, already middle-aged, brought the meal, a lavish repast featuring lamb, pasta, bread, and wine.

This situation, startlingly analogous to the poem, seemed to me an augury, and the old Italian verses kept running through my mind, until Domenico broke into my reverie. "Bart, bring your friend closer," he shouted. "He's wondering in his head, what can I learn from that old blind man that will help us in our misery?"

"Much, I am sure, Domenico," I murmured, feeling awkward.

"Because I am blind, my friend, I have second sight, and because I am old, I have no fear. At 87, what do I care if the Germans kill me? It's near my time anyway. But you're young and you're afraid. I can feel it in the room when someone is afraid. And because of your fear, you can't make up your mind what you should do. So I tell you, you mustn't wait any longer. It's your duty to go now and join your Allies and your countrymen, for two reasons: one, because you have taken an oath as a soldier, as I did many years ago, when already an old man I fought at Caporetto. And the second reason is that you bring danger to these good people."

I looked at the ground. Bart looked embarrassed. Finally I found my voice. "Domenico," I said, "you're right. That's sound and honest advice. We're grateful to you for it and for the best meal we've had since we left home. Now we must leave." As I finished speaking, I stood up to go.

Bart got up too, but the old man grabbed his arm and pulled him down. "A glass of wine before you leave." He called, "Maria, *vino!*"

A hush fell over us as we drank. When we at last shook hands and extended our farewells, Domenico gave us advice and encouragement, "Go carefully and quietly. I feel in my heart you will have good fortune. God bless you!"

With the moon so bright, we slipped along in the shadow of the hedgerows till we reached the woods. After we had settled down back in our *capanna*, I told Bart the story of the Italian poem and of its strange analogy to Domenico.

"Kind of gives you the creeps," he said, after some reflection. "It's like those old prophets in the Bible who foretold the future. Now maybe we'll get going. It's a good job the old man said we'd have good luck on our side."

11 November

We passed a miserable night stoking the fire and trying in vain to sleep in the smoke and the cold. In the morning Bart left early to locate a shepherd he knew to try to get some food. An hour later I was alarmed by the sound of someone coming up through the woods. This was much too soon for Bart to be back, so I was about to run when I recognized him hurrying up the slope. Running up to the hut, he exclaimed, "Christ, my friend's gone and the whole bloody valley's in a flap."

"More than usual?"

"Hell, yes! Jerry's got those signs up all over, which is nothing new, but he's also told the *paesani* he's going to blow every town flat. I heard the Jerry sappers blasting in the Sangro Valley this morning. The sound is altogether different from their guns."

I was getting edgier by the minute, but I managed to change the subject. "You got any ideas where we might eat?"

"Well, I know Gio'an's in a bit of a flap, but we might try his place anyway. He's been pretty good to me all along."

We lost no time going down, and we met Gio'an' and his wife leading their cattle up to hide them in the mountains. She was carrying on her head their old crockery bowl with some hot pasta, which must have just come off the fire. They shared it with us, in spite of their own misfortune. I was too hungry now to feel guilty.

This was the first time I'd seen Gio'an' show any fear. He told us the entire valley was in a panic and confirmed the rumor that the Germans had sworn to level all the houses, and that the people had been ordered to evacuate them.

Fortified a little by the pasta, we climbed back up the mountain. I reminded Bart of what Dick had forecast: that the nearer the British got, the nastier the Germans would get. "I wish I'd known yer friend Rossbach," he said. "Him and me would'a got along fine."

That afternoon a flight of B-26's and Boston A-20's roared over so low they looked as if they would hit the mountains. The thunder of their bombing was equaled only by the earthshaking cannonading of the German antiaircraft guns. An hour later a hundred or more of the bombed-out townspeople came trudging up the mountain, loaded with every kind of bundle and package. The men were grim; the women and children sobbed.

For supper that evening, we shared scraps of bread and an old potato. During the night the wind blew and the temperature dropped so low we again had to alternate sleeping in shifts and stoking the fire.

12 November

To my horror, when I woke up in the morning, I looked out at five inches of snow piled on top of the *capanna*. "For God's sake, Bart, look at this!" I wailed. "The worst thing that could have happened."

"Now they can trail every bloody step we take. I been tellin' ye, we got to get out of here." This was Bart's tired litany. It galled me, even though I knew he was right. With no small effort, he got up and started to light the fire. I didn't have the energy to help.

Seven weeks in the mountains, living in constant fear, weighed down by exhaustion and near starvation, had exacted their toll. The boils had aggravated my problems, and I guessed I was 10 or 12 pounds lighter than at any time in Chieti. Bart, seven years younger than I, with his rugged north of England background, showed little sign of being touched by the ordeal, except for his ragged clothes. He still had his ruddy complexion, and only his frequent impatience revealed his underlying tension.

All day Italian refugees were around and above us in the high rocks, building shelters and driving their cattle up from the valley. By 4:00 there must have been about a thousand of them: the *"Sfollati,"* or scattered people, as they were called. They looked the epitome of human misery, but my instinct told me there would be far worse suffering to come.

The day had been warm, and by evening the snow was gone. I decided we should check with Raffaele about the guide. I saw a shepherd tending a small flock, staring at me. He looked somewhat familiar. We went over to talk to him. He gave us a piece of mutton, for which I thanked him, but something about the man still bothered me. Bart managed to ask him if he knew of a

The way the Maiella looked from the saddle above Dark Valley on the day it snowed in November 1943.

guide, and the man said he might know someone who would take us across the Sangro. That was the last thing I wanted to hear from this shepherd — I had to warn Bart. Yet when I tried to, he swung around and snapped, "Dammit to hell, Joe, here's our chance to get out of this fookin' valley; what in God's name are we waitin' for?"

While Bart was scolding me, I suddenly remembered: This was the shepherd I had seen outside the Italian colonel's hut just before Dick and I were recaptured. Stepping between Bart and the shepherd, I said to the man, "When do you think this guide would be able to go?"

"Perhaps tomorrow. I could find out later."

I decided to play along with him so he would not get suspicious. "Tomorrow would be good," I told him. "We'll meet you here, just about this time. Will you bring the man with you?"

"I'll try."

I said to Bart, "Before we get tied up with this guy, we must go down and check once more with Raffaele."

"All right, but don't lose this bloke. Raffaele didn't get us that guide the other day."

The shepherd gave us some ricotta wrapped in paper as we exchanged goodbyes, but it did not diminish my distrust of him. The wet cheese had soaked through the paper, so we hurried down the hill toward Raffaele's, munching dirty handfuls of it.

But Bart and I forgot that shepherd in a hurry when Ezio Bartolini stormed out of Raffaele's hut to meet us. "Get yourselves ready," he ordered. "The guide is here and we leave in ten minutes." The news went through me like an electric shock. I flopped on the ground and began frantically to repair my shoelaces.

"We're on our way, Eighth Army!" Bart sang and went to work on his.

Chapter 25

The Valley of the Sangro

5:00 p.m., 12 November

When my old U.S. Army combat boots had worn out back in Chieti, I had managed to get a new pair of British boots through the Red Cross. In the weeks since Dick and I had crawled our way out of Fonte d'Amore, I had had them off just three times; the soles were thin and cracks were opening in the sides. Glancing at them, Bart tore up his handkerchief and gave me a strip, which I used to repair the laces in one of my boots. I patched the other with bits of string I had clung to for months. Ingegnere's disaster with his wretched sport shoes taught me that adequate footwear would be critical in this final drive for the British lines.

We had waited considerably longer than ten minutes when Raffaele finally stuck his head out the door and announced, "Come in now, we have some pork stew." On a bench inside the hut sat a short, muscular man in his forties. He was Vincenz' and would be our guide. When I shook his powerful hand, the man nodded but continued to sit in silence, while Bart and I put away helpings of hot stew.

Raffaele detailed the plan he had worked out with Vincenz': Ezio and he would travel up front with our guide; Bart and I would follow at no less than 200 meters, to reduce the chances of their being caught with Allied prisoners. Bart appeared indifferent to the size of the interval, but considering the terrain and the darkness, I thought 200 meters far too much. While I was mulling this over, he caught my eye and motioned toward the door. Outside, he grumbled, "These damn Eyeties, ye can't trust 'em; they could turn us in, ye mark my words!"

"For God's sake, Bart, make some sense. They could've done that any time before this without the risk of getting shot." Still unconvinced, he shook his head, muttering, "Well, we better look sharp."

Bart was angry enough already, but I was paranoid about night ambushes and when I told him I thought he should precede me, he flew off the handle. "What in hell? Ye're the officer, you go first!" I protested that I had been captured precisely because of my lack of knowledge of infantry tactics, while he was a trained infantryman. All at once, he changed his mind and conceded, "I suppose I better go first, or you'll be hangin' back, and we'll lose 'em for fair."

At 7:00 we started out, in the order finally agreed upon, with Vincenz' leading the way south from Monte Lucino toward the lower Parello Valley. I was so wild with excitement that for a short time I actually forgot my fears. This for me was the culmination of months of planning, of living with the concept of escape, of crawling out under the wire, of brutal hiking for weeks, all in the constant company of fear and hunger. Now I was betting everything I had worked for on what was about one chance in ten of getting through.

The air was clear and cold, the night very dark except for glimmers of a moon that barely penetrated the blackness of the forest. Though Vincenz' moved swiftly, we had no trouble keeping up while we were still on a downgrade. We were out of the woods in little more than half an hour. The lower valley, which I thought I knew from my mountain-top observations, turned out to be a complex maze of plowed fields and pastures, laced by stone walls and brooks running in little gorges.

Now a brilliant full moon caught us on the crest of a rise, where we came upon a cluster of houses that were silent and ominous. Raffaele was waiting in the shadows. "We're going in with Vincenz' to try to get some food. You wait here."

"Bastards are going in to get Jerry," Bart growled. I sighed. He started out into the moonlight as if he were going off on his own, but I pulled him back. "For God's sake, knock it off, Bart, Jerry'll spot you out there!" He yanked his arm away.

After about a quarter of an hour, our companions emerged from the house, and Raffaele spoke to me reproachfully, "You've been trailing much too close. From here on it gets very dangerous; you must stay further back."

This time Ezio and Raffaele really picked up the pace and were out of sight almost immediately. I ran up with Bart, and we followed the faint sound of their footsteps till we lost it completely while crossing a brook. Neither of us had the slightest idea which way they had turned. I was in a turmoil. I knew we were near the German fortifications, but other than a vague idea of compass direction, I had no idea where in hell we were. "Bart, for Christ's sake, which way did they go?" I sputtered.

"Dammit, don't ask me. If ye'd been up here where you belong, this wouldn'ta happened. It's your job to get us out of this mess."

Bart then proceeded to rail at me, the Italians, and everyone he could think of. Muddled though I was, I knew I had to do something — and fast. I made a wild guess at where they had headed, whispered, "Let's go," and took off on the run, Bart right beside me.

By now the moon was high overhead and so brilliant it seemed almost like daylight. A minute or two later we hit a plowed field, and I sank into the soft loam halfway to my knees. Bart dropped back, swearing. A hundred yards farther up I came to a small stream and paused there to rinse the mud off. Turning to look for Bart, I caught a movement near a thicket at the edge of the field. Creeping back and crouching to stay in the shadows, I wondered if it might be a trap. Then I heard Raffaele. "Giuseppe, is that you?" He said we had gone right by them.

"This system isn't any good," I told him. "Your last man has got to keep contact with us."

"All right, so be it. But what's the matter with your friend?"

Bart was grumbling about the Italians leaving us, until I became afraid Raffaele would catch on. I searched my mind for a way to explain to him. Unable to find the right words, I had to settle for a translation of, "My friend has a bee in his bonnet." Raffaele let out a guffaw.

"What're you sayin' to him 'bout me?" Bart asked.

"Forget it, Bart, and stop bitching," I demanded. "First thing you know, you're going to screw up our arrangement with these guys."

"Might be a bloody good idea," he retorted loudly.

Out in the next field, one of Bart's laces broke. At first, he made a gallant effort to keep going, carrying one boot. Then he gave up and sat down to make repairs, and Raffaele disappeared over a ridge. Terrified at the idea of losing him again, I ran ahead across a pasture, peering forward and backward, trying to keep an eye on both the Italians and Bart. When Bart caught up to me, we ran on up a steeper grade, our breath coming in noisy gasps. At the top, Raffaele stood waiting.

"His shoelace broke," I explained.

Raffaele ignored my excuse. "This is the most dangerous part," he began. "We're about to pass through the fortifications of the Sangro Valley. Whatever you do, don't lose us here."

"Then don't go so bloody fast," Bart protested. Raffaele tapped my arm and set off.

A little while later we found ourselves crossing the bare, rocky shoulder of Monte Lucino. High up to our right, perched among the crags, were the houses of Pizzoferato, spectral in the moonlight. Massive rock promontories bulged out like heads of giants above and below the town, now a German stronghold. Tensely, I studied the village for signs of movement, as we plunged through more deep furrows, thick clods of earth clinging to our feet.

A group of farmhouses now lay directly ahead of us, a collection of sharply angular shadows. We moved stealthily past them, behind a hedge that ran right next to the buildings. I agonized: Why the devil does Vincenz' have to go so close to them?

The eerie stillness was shattered by the barking of a dog, but this was soon drowned out by a burst of raucous German singing. We crept closer, our footsteps silent in the damp earth. A few feet away a door opened, casting a gleam of yellow light, and a girl's soft Italian voice sighed, *"Auf Wieder-sehen."* The murmured response was low and indistinct. With fear tightening my throat, squeezing like a chain around my heart, I eased by on tiptoes.

Then Vincenz' sped on down into the valley and swung to the right, just below the shadowy buildings of Pizzoferato. Up ahead, Ezio and Raffaele ran hunched over, low to the earth. Bart and I followed the others across a gorge and up a sheep trail on the other side, cowering in the darkness behind every bush. Soon the grade grew steep, and I had to fight the gasping, trying to avoid making any sound.

Off to our left the grinding rumble of a German armored car echoed off the hills. At the top of the ridge we darted over a main highway. Much nearer now, the noise of the armored car changed pitch as the driver shifted gears. As the vehicle passed close behind us, we sprinted down the mountainside.

Raffaele was waiting in a little swale when Bart and I drew up. "Be extremely careful from here on," he whispered. "We're going between the gun emplacements of their main line between Gamberale and Pizzoferato. Don't make a sound."

A quarter of a mile farther on I caught up with our leaders once again when they paused on a shoulder overlooking the 14-mile expanse of the Sangro Valley. Its upper slopes were bathed in bright moonlight, and in the shadows lower down the fires of burning houses blazed in both directions as far as I could see. The deep booming sound of blasting echoed up from the depths, and the air was acrid with the smell of gelignite, its bluish-gray smoke hanging in layers all across the valley. This was the scorched earth the Germans had threatened. It was a scene right out of hell.

Bart seemed too stunned even to utter a word. We continued onto a long exposed ridge where, just below its crest, the black bulk of a gun position loomed on our right. Another appeared off to our left, and for some inexplicable reason Vincenz' decided to stop by it. "Come here, I want to show you something," he said casually.

I was aghast — childish curiosity in *this* situation? The man had to be insane. I heard Bart mutter, "Stupid bastard!" As I tried to pull our guide away, a huge dog tied to a tree began to bark furiously, flinging his great bulk against the taut rope. That, fortunately, yanked Vincenz' back to reality, and he took off like a deer. In sheer terror, I raced down the hill after him, certain that the enraged watchdog would bring out a patrol. Everyone held the exhausting pace until the frenzied barking had died out and we were safely concealed by the darkness of a steep ravine.

Two miles beyond, Raffaele stopped again. "We're at Vincenz's house. Ezio and I are going in, but it's dangerous for this family with you here; so you and Bart will please stay outside."

"Of course," I said, "I'd prefer that anyway."

Bart had understood our exchange. "Makes no sense to stay out here in the bloody cold," he protested.

"We're better off in the open, Bart," I said. "That way we can hear someone coming." Perhaps the running had calmed him down a little, because he was still for the next 20 minutes. Shortly afterwards, some teenage boys and girls joined us, laughing, chattering, and carrying wicker baskets. Introducing themselves as members of Vincenz's family, they told us they had brought some bread and prosciutto. When they continued to talk loudly and the girls occasionally broke into peals of laughter, I told the oldest boy they would bring the Germans down on us and asked him to please quiet the group.

"On the contrary, it doesn't work that way," he said. "The Germans are used to the sound of loud Italian voices. If they think we're tiptoeing around, *then* they suspect we're up to something. Things will be all right as long as you two don't talk above a whisper." Though unconvinced by his rationale, I didn't argue. Bart and I were too hungry. Finally the kids left and we ate the food gratefully, though by now we were shuddering in the frigid night.

Half an hour later some other youngsters came out and invited us into the house. Though we had no idea why we were now welcome to come inside, we quickly accepted to get in out of that merciless cold.

Vincenz's house, a long, low building — dug into the mountain to afford a big storage cellar under the living quarters — sat perched on a steep hill at the edge of a clearing. We followed the young people into an enormous room, almost bare of furniture, that ran the full length of the house. Heavy wooden beams spanned the ceiling, and at the far end of the room glowed a fire of solid coals. In the middle of the floor was a trap door through which two boys were throwing up sacks of grain and potatoes. The sacks were being caught effortlessly — in spite of their weight — and stacked in piles by a young girl, maybe 17 or 18. Another pair of boys then lugged them outside and loaded them on the backs of mules.

I joined Raffaele and Ezio by the fire. "I'm worried about this," Raffaele said. "Vincenz' told me he had to load all this stuff up and hide it in the mountains. He says he's lucky the Germans haven't gotten hold of it yet."

"What does that do to our plans?" I asked.

"Nothing good. These are the same mules that are supposed to take us across the Sangro."

"My God, how long is all this going to take?"

"Vincenz' says an hour, but I don't believe him," Raffaele warned. "These kids work in shifts, and they're moving the bags as fast as they can, but it looked to me as if there was a carload of stuff in that cellar."

Bart wanted to know what was going on. After I told him they'd said we'd have to wait an hour until the job was done, I began to wonder what I'd next say to Bart if the hour came and went and we still hadn't gone. He lay down on the floor near the fire and went to sleep. Having concluded that I couldn't do anything at the moment about the situation, I lay down, too. Soon our whole foursome had fallen asleep.

At about 1:00, I woke up abruptly to find Raffaele's eyes riveted on me. "I'm glad you're awake," he said agitated. "This is getting serious. Every time I've asked one of them how much longer, he says 'Another hour.'"

One of the girls came over with a long-handled metal container and shoved it out over the coals. She shook it continuously, and in a few minutes white, fluffy kernels popped up against the container's screen top. When I showed an interest, she handed me the gadget, saying, "I have to go back to work now."

The four of us took turns popping the corn until we had eaten the whole bag of kernels the girl had left. Half an hour later, Raffaele confronted Vincenz', and this time our guide admitted that he wouldn't be through until nearly three. Disgusted, Bart and I tried to get some more sleep, but I was restless, plagued by dreams of getting caught crossing the Sangro in broad daylight.

Three o'clock had passed when Raffaele broke some disconcerting news to us. While we'd been asleep, Vincenz' had confessed he'd been tipped off by a spy that his place was scheduled for demolition the following afternoon, and that was why he was now trying to move everything out.

When I related this to Bart, he blew up. "What in bloody hell have I been telling ye? These Eyetie boogers're goin' to do us in one way or another. Here we are right in the middle of the Jerry lines, in fact, right in front of their main line of defense, it looked to me; we'll get our arse blown off yet."

I tended to agree and said so, for if Vincenz's informant was mistaken about the timetable, the Germans could be arriving any moment to level this house. Planting information was a well-known German trick to catch people off guard, as I remembered bitterly from Chieti.

Keenly aware that the danger was increasing with every minute, Raffaele discussed the idea of leaving without Vincenz'. But swimming the icy Sangro at near flood stage wasn't much of an option. We finally decided that we should wait till the last chance to get across before daylight; if Vincenz' wasn't ready then, we would go off on our own.

For the next hour, I tried to sleep but the dysentery I'd had for the last several days had returned suddenly, the cramps worse than ever, and I had to run outside. I came back, limp, shivering and sick with worry. We were now, I was convinced, between Scylla and Charybdis. The choices were to stay in the house and get killed or captured (but we couldn't even do that — the Italians would throw us out), or to head out on our own and, ignorant of the route, stumble into a German pillbox or a patrol or risk drowning in the Sangro. In truth, we had scant chance of making it. Yet, if we stayed, there'd be no chance at all.

Ashamed of my procrastination, I shook Bart and said decisively, "Let's get going!" It was 5:00.

"It's fookin' well about time," he said as he picked up his canteen and sweater.

Raffaele, standing next to me, said at the same moment, barely audibly, "Ezio and I are leaving without the guide. Do you want to come with us?"

"As fast as possible!" Bart cried out. "We shoulda left three hours ago." I agreed, and we ran for the door.

Out in the open, the moon was still so bright that we could be spotted for half a mile. Dawn would be breaking soon, and I mentally kicked myself over the time we'd squandered. We had descended the hill on a rough trail about 200 yards when I heard hooves clattering on the rocks behind us — Vincenz' and two of his sons were leading down their string of mules. "Everything is all right," our laconic guide reassured us, sounding almost bored. *"Non vi preoccupate* — don't worry about it. We'll get across the Sangro."

Counting the entire cavalcade, I discovered in the rear two Italian refugees who also wanted to cross. Oh, God, I thought, is the whole damn bunch coming with us? Vincenz' had but three mules, and, try though I might, I couldn't figure out how we'd all get across. Nine people, counting Vincenz' and his two sons, would have to be carried over to the opposite bank.

We traveled southeast, crossing silvery fields where our feet grew wet with the heavy frost on the grass, while I kept my eyes on the dark outlines at the edges of the fields. As we approached the bottom of the valley, I expected any second a sharp challenge to ring out in German, followed by a blast of gunfire.

We had walked about ten minutes when faint streaks of gray began to appear in the sky, and the valley flattened out as we approached a railroad embankment. Raffaele had heard that this area was mined on both sides, and that the Germans had sited machine-guns to cover their minefields. If ever there was a zone for maximum alertness, this was it. Each footstep was placed with care.

The mules labored up the jagged stones of the embankment and clanked over the rails. We followed while I held my breath, realizing what a fine target we were providing, even in the hazy light. Two hundred yards beyond the track, we came to the bank of the Sangro — a river broad and swift, its clear flow flashing in the fading moonlight. The water looked deep and forbidding in the slower-moving swirls, while mist shrouded the far bank. Vincenz' signaled to us, and we gathered around the sweating mules, which were no bigger than ponies.

"Raffaele and Ezio will go with us on the first trip," he stated to the group. "My sons and I will bring the animals back and then take the two prisoners. "You two," he said to the nervous refugees, "will come on the third trip."

"Hell," I said to myself, "that'll take an hour and by then it'll be broad daylight. We may have to swim the damn river yet." I shuddered at the idea.

Vincenz' explained that we would ride two men per mule; that each animal would have to follow exactly in the tracks of the one ahead, lest it miss the ford, plunge into deep water, and drown. If I hadn't been so scared, I might have laughed — for it was also rather obvious what would happen to the riders in the process.

The guide led the procession. The wretched beasts went back on their haunches and slithered down the bank into the river, Raffaele and Ezio's animal stumbling off and floundering for a foothold in the swift current. Both men held their feet up as the little mule braced himself against the powerful force of the water. They vanished in the mist.

It was half an hour before I saw Vincenz' and his boys bringing the mules back, still sliding and stumbling on the rocky bottom.

All this while, the two refugees stood on the bank watching us, their heads slumped, their shoulders drooping. Picking up the rope reins, I mounted the little mule and gripped his narrow withers with my knees. Bart vaulted up behind, grabbing me so hard around the waist I could scarcely breathe. I leaned back, pushing Bart well back too as the mule went over the edge, did a sliding scuffle down the six-foot bank and plunged into water that reached up to my knees. I pulled them higher, rendering our balance even more precarious. The little brute was incredibly strong, but at one point he swayed so much that I thought we were all about to go over.

We followed Vincenz's son, heading almost downstream, so that the force of the rapids would never hit the mule's body broadside and upset it. But Bart and I had to pull our legs up more so they wouldn't create a drag and throw the creature forward. The deepest part was near the far bank, where the water came over its withers. The instant the mule's feet touched the bank, I threw my weight forward and wrapped my arms around its neck, pulling Bart with me, while the mule clawed its way up onto dry land. I leaned over and hugged the creature.

Raffaele and Ezio met us under a huge oak. "Snap it up!" Raffaele commanded, "this is very bad. Get up there under that tree and stay out of the moonlight." I had never heard him talk like that before. Shaken, I ran close to the ground, keeping in the shadows till I got to the tree, while Bart stayed behind, out in the moonlight. "For God's sake, Bart," I called to him, "get up here under cover. Those guys know what they're talking about."

He strode over and I could feel his anger. He grumbled something about "you and those Eyeties," but he came back in the shadows. I should have left it there, but I was right at the edge. "Damn it, Bart, we'd be nowhere without those guys. I didn't like the whole operation back at Vincenz's any better than you did, but Raffaele had no control over what happened." This time Bart said nothing.

It was 6:30 and almost daylight when the others caught up. Vincenz' said abruptly, "Come with me," and took off at an angle to the river. I followed Raffaele at about 50 yards, all the while glancing behind us, once to see our guide's sons with the mules and refugees moving way to our left down in the river valley.

Vincenz' led us upgrade through patches of woods and across gullies till we came out just below the main highway between San Angelo and Quadri. We scooted over the highway in clear morning light, then crossed fields and passed houses where dogs barked furiously. From here we turned uphill toward a grove of the tallest trees I'd seen in Italy. The sons with the mules reappeared on our left, but the two Italian refugees had disappeared.

Vincenz' stopped and conferred with Raffaele, who in turn beckoned to me. His eyes were bloodshot and his normally reddish face was a chalky gray. Our guide reported that the boys had gone off separately to get away from Bart and me. This area was dangerous because they had been captured here a few days earlier. Fortunately, they had escaped the next day. Now, I hardly had time to thank him and say goodbye before he, the boys, and the mules had headed back toward the river. This late, their only chance was to get back fast, but after the risks Vincenz' had taken for us, I felt our farewell had been far too abrupt.

The four of us ran quickly into the forest. There, Raffaele took my arm. "You understand," he said, "that being here with you two is just as dangerous for us as it was for Vincenz'?"

"Of course I understand. Let's separate temporarily and meet back here about an hour from now." He nodded and they started off. As we watched them leave, I said to Bart, "There they go, on their way to get Jerry." He glared at me for a moment, then laughed and slapped me on the back.

About half an hour later automatic weapons fire broke out from the direction of the ford in the river. Bart and I looked apprehensively at each other. "We're thinkin' the same thing," he observed. "Bad show if that was for Vincenz'. Good man, that; he got us over in spite of the delay."

In my estimation Vincenz' was more than a good man. He was a man who had helped two foreigners in adversity at the risk of his life and lives of his two sons; he was a human being who was courageous beyond my comprehension and beyond the power of my words to express.

The two Italians returned on schedule. Ezio was as impassive as ever, but Raffaele's face was twisted with anguish. "I am most unhappy to bring you bad news. We just heard that three Italians and three Allied prisoners were executed in San Angelo del Pesco yesterday. The Germans lined them up against a wall and machine-gunned them. We've got to stay apart and meet later. However, I did talk to a young Italian who said he'd guide us to Castiglione, which is currently in British hands."

"How far is it?" I asked quickly.

"About 30 kilometers, the way we'll have to go. This kid says he can make it in three hours, but I can't believe him."

"Do you think he'll really come back?" I said.

Raffaele made a wry face. "I'll tell you when we get together again."

We shook hands, and they departed. Despite my confidence in Raffaele, this arrangement sounded very flimsy, and though I tried not to show my doubts, Bart was watching me closely. "I know what you think about these lads, all this shaking hands, but they still worry me. Now that we're across the river, they could easily go without us." I kept my own counsel.

Through the rest of the morning we slept in some thick undergrowth. Eventually we ventured out in search of food. Catching sight of us, several people moved off before we could approach them. One small group shouted the now familiar refrain, *"Basta di prigionieri,"* with one man adding, "Go join your British countrymen; all you do is bring us trouble."

Deep in the woods we came upon an old man and his wife sitting around a little fire. He was dressed in torn and patched clothing, and she was wrapped up in a black shawl, so completely that all I could see were her eyes. The man invited us to sit down and offered us some *polenta*, which Bart and I ate with our fingers right from the bowl. In the meantime, the sun had warmed the air to the extent that I was able to shed my sweater. The old lady, pointing to the tears in my jacket, made a sewing motion with her hand. For some reason I decided not to speak too much Italian, so I nodded and smiled and handed her the jacket, which she mended neatly. She then pointed to my pants. With a little maneuver behind a bush, I removed them and handed them to her for mending also. Her kind gesture completed, I thanked her in English. Once again, I could wear my civilian clothes on the outside.

The husband, after saying something to his wife that seemed to be about us, came over to me. Partly in sign language and partly in a few words of English and Italian, he briefed us on Raffaele and Ezio. They had gone on without us. I jumped up. I couldn't believe what I was hearing.

"What's the old booger say 'bout Raffaele and the other one?" Bart demanded.

"That they went on without us," I replied, bracing myself for the storm.

"I knew damn well we shouldn'ta let them out of our sight. See, now that they're across the river, they've gone ahead on their own!"

"Bart, that doesn't make any sense. The only thing they want and need is that safe conduct they can get only through us. The British would never believe their story —"

"Nor do I."

"I just think this old fellow wants us to shove off," I said. "He and his wife have done their bit for us. Why should we hang around here and let them take the risk? I guarantee Raffaele will be back." Thanks to the hot *polenta* and my refurbished clothes, my morale had begun to revive and along with it my faith in Raffaele's last handshake, but I didn't attempt to explain this to Bart. I was afraid he wouldn't believe me.

When we had left the old couple, Bart declared, "We'd be better off going right on by ourselves. We'll live to regret hanging around here."

"OK, you go along if you like, but I made an agreement with Raffaele and I'm going to stick to it." As I spoke those words, I remembered where I had last heard a similar phrase, and I drifted off into a reverie: Dick had insisted that I stick to the agreement we had made. Now I wondered if this pact would be as hard to keep as the other had been.

We had settled down on the forest leaves, and when I came out of my reverie, Bart was gazing at me with a puzzled grin. "Penny for your thoughts," he said. "You *were* off in a brown study."

"I'm worried sick about what might have happened to Dick."

"He must've had a rough time, but from what you've told me about the man maybe he could handle it." I didn't answer, and in a few moments Bart stretched out and dropped off to sleep.

I sat silently in the warm sun, listening to the bombing and blasting off to the west toward San Angelo. Gradually, I became aware of a strange murmur coming up from the lower woods. It was a moaning sound, much like the keening I had heard back at Antonio's when I broke the news of Dick's recapture. But this sound was accompanied by the crackling of brush, and within minutes, a line of *sfollati*, dressed mostly in dark clothes, came toiling up through the woods.

The women were crying, holding children by their hands. The men were grim and silent. They all had heavy bundles strapped on their backs, and some were carrying infants. Many had bloodstained bandages on their faces, arms, or legs. One man, apparently their leader, saw us, looked away, and took his people off in a different direction. As I watched them disappear into the woods, I tried to imagine what it must be to lose your home and all the things you loved.

Before long an old man in a tattered cap came stumbling up the trail alone. In shirtsleeves, his torn trousers held up by sweat-stained suspenders, he made no attempt to avoid us but rather sat down on a rock just a few yards away, staring out over the valley. When I approached him, I noticed tears streaming down his face.

"My house, barns, cattle, all destroyed by those dirty pigs," he said, weeping.

"And your family?" I asked, as reverberations from a bombing raid shook the ground under us.

He didn't respond for a long time, and I wondered if he was angry at my intrusion. But then he poured it all out: "My wife is wounded and with her sister up on the mountain. I foolishly stayed behind and tried to save some things, but I had to run. I'm going off to find her now. My son is on the Russian front. My three daughters ran off two days ago, and I haven't seen them since. But they're young and clever, maybe they've hidden somewhere. Those rotten Germans even blew up the well my grandfather dug and poured dirty oil in it. They mine and blast down every building one by one." He sobbed and shook his fist at the sky. "O God, why don't you punish those barbarians?"

I asked a few more questions, just to keep him talking, and finally he looked at me with a wan smile and said, "I've had a rest and a good talk, now I must go find my wife."

"And your daughters, too, I hope." We shook hands sadly, and he dragged himself off into the woods.

Next I roused Bart, and we headed for our rendezvous with Raffaele and Ezio, who arrived shortly after 3:00. They were strangely silent.

"What's going on? Is something wrong?" I asked.

"We thought there was, very much so. An older man told us you'd left without us."

"What did he look like?"

"Well, he had an old coat with lots of patches —"

I interrupted, " — and gray hair and a long mustache, and his wife had a black scarf around her head that covered her face?"

"How did you know?"

"They told us the same thing about you."

We all laughed. "I should have known. It's their way of letting us know we should beat it," Raffaele said. "I can't blame them, they've had so much trouble because of prisoners and refugees."

I assured Raffaele that I'd never doubted his word and didn't think he and Ezio had doubted mine. For ours was an agreement between friends, I emphasized. Once more, we shook hands and resolved never to let any outsider cross us up again.

Raffaele then told me that although he expected to meet a guide the next day the situation for the local people was steadily worsening, and we could expect more of the same trouble we had just had — people would try to get rid of us, one way or another. The new plan we devised called for us to meet at this same place in the morning, if possible with the guide.

Bart and I found a sheltered spot with good cover and began to look for firewood. Since the ground had been stripped bare of dry sticks by the *sfollati*, we broke branches off the trees. After several tries with the green wood, we got a little fire going and gradually warmed up. At dusk we went out in search of food. Not far away we discovered an enormous *capanna*, built of pine branches. It had a gable roof and must have been 40 feet wide by 80 feet long. Cautiously, I pushed open the door, made of trimmed branches bound with string. Inside, the building was lit by two lanterns and a few candles. The walls had been woven with branches, and three center poles of trimmed trees held up a roof built of layers of pine on long stringers — I couldn't imagine how the builders got them up there.

Refugees were huddled in clusters here and there on the muddy floor, and the air was fetid with the smell of sweating and dirty bodies. When they saw us, several women began to wail. One man calmed her, "Don't worry, they're only prisoners."

Another called out angrily, "Enough of the prisoners!"

Bart looked as uneasy as I felt, and we both wanted to get out of there as fast as we could. But a young couple standing next to me had smiled at us when we came in, so we were encouraged to take a chance: "If you please, could you possibly give us something to eat?"

"We've almost nothing ourselves, but you may have some of this," the man said, showing me a basket of little shiny-brown chips of some kind which had a faint smell of bacon.

"*Mille grazie,*" I said, as we stuffed handfuls of them into our pockets.

Right then, a man crashed through the pinebough door and yelled, "The Germans are coming! They're only a couple of minutes away!"

Even though I was skeptical, we couldn't take a chance. So I shot out the door, Bart half a step behind me, and circled the *capanna* to make sure we were not being followed. When we realized no one was after us, we tried some of those chips — they turned out to be dried pork rind — and it was literally chewing leather. Still, there was some flavor to them, and they did fool my hunger for a time.

The temperature dropped as the night wore on, and a vicious wind sliced through the trees. Bart, sure that the alarm back at the *capanna* had been a fake, suggested we return, but I was against it — they could give that alarm every few minutes and drive us crazy. Through the night we took turns trying to sleep and keeping the fire burning.

The next morning I was numb and stiff from the cold and from lying on the rocky ground. Taking both our canteens, I walked down to the spring to fill them. On the way I saw hordes of Italian families driving their cattle up into the forest, and realized we had very little time left. Breakfast was more pork rind, which I chewed for half an hour — and then had cramps and dysentery for the rest of the morning.

Raffaele and Ezio were waiting for us at the rendezvous, with the guide. Compared to the rugged, capable Vincenz', this teenage stripling's appearance did little for my confidence. He was about five feet tall, and so thin that his black clothes seemed to be hanging on a skeleton. He wore a black felt hat, and the skin on his pinched face was a translucent gray. Adriano, as he was called, coughed a deep, gurgling cough and spat brown phlegm on the leaves.

He shook hands with us and declared, "I've just returned from Castiglione, which is occupied by the Gurkha troops of the British Fourth Indian Division." Bart studied him closely, frowning.

"Did you get what he said?" I asked Bart.

He nodded. "The laddie's right so far."

"How long did it take to get here?" Raffaele asked Adriano.

"For me two and a half hours. For you it would be more like three and a half."

"How many kilometers is it?" I wanted to know.

"About 15 in a straight line, but through the mountains it's 25, more or less."

"Are you sure you can find your way back there?" I said.

Adriano let out a hoot of laughter and crowed, "It's impossible for me to get lost in these mountains."

For his service he wanted 500 *lire* apiece from us, plus a few hundred cigarettes. No one had a cent except me, and all I had was 600 *lire* from selling my excess clothing back at Chieti. Nevertheless, I said very quickly, *"D'accordo!"* I would just have to rely on the British army to put up the rest. While I felt less than honest, at this point I didn't care. With freedom almost in my grasp, it would take a lot more than this to stop me.

Evidently my flimsy promises were enough for Adriano, for he sealed the agreement with a handshake and announced that we'd be pulling out that same night. His aim was to arrive at Castiglione just at daylight, lest in the dark the Fourth Indian Division machine-gunners mistake us for the enemy and start shooting. Bart grinned approvingly. "This one knows what he's talking about."

Bart and I returned to our fire, and got a good blaze going. But waves of hunger came over us, so we chewed on more of the pork rind until we had very little left. For two days, all we had had was the popcorn and this rind. I still had my reserve of the New Zealand chocolate, but I didn't dare eat it — it was my last critical reserve for that 25 kilometers to Castiglione.

An Italian family who had been living in the woods came over to pay us a friendly visit, with nothing to offer beyond a few potatoes. But these we eagerly roasted in the coals. Unhappily, though, we could hardly get them down, for from our prolonged starch diet Bart and I had contracted the "potato sickness." In addition to these problems, the boils on my arms were getting bigger and more painful, and infections had started on both feet.

Raffaele and Ezio came over to wait with us for the guide. As it grew late, the wind rose again, and the temperature dropped to near freezing. Now Raffaele was doubtful. "I'm afraid that guide won't ever show up in such weather."

"I could've told you that this morning," Bart said. "Ye'll not see that lad again." I was about to argue the issue with Bart — for it seemed to me it would have been senseless for Adriano to make the deal with no intention of following through. But I decided to bite my tongue.

At midnight Raffaele asserted, "That man isn't coming tonight; let's meet here again in the morning, and I'll try to locate him." The two Italians went off to a small *capanna* to spend the night with a *sfollati* family.

Bart and I drew as close to the fire as possible, but as the wind increased we froze on one side and were nearly roasted on the other, while the smoke and flying embers stung our eyes. At about one o'clock it began to rain, and with that I decided to quit worrying about the guide — we already had enough problems. The rain soon escalated into a driving, icy downpour that pricked like needles on our hands and faces. Both of us were soaked to the skin, and the fire expired in a wet sizzle. Over the roar of the downpour, Bart yelled, "It's not likely Jerry's out in this. Let's try that big *capanna* before we freeze."

I grabbed his arm. "Come on, let's go!" Through the sodden underbrush we stumbled, falling repeatedly, as we followed the rise of the land. At last, a glimmer of light showed ahead and soon we bumped into the side of the *capanna*. We crawled around to find the door, pushed it open, and went in.

In places where the storm had broken through the branches the roof was streaming water. Some areas of the earthen floor were lakes of mud, and people were lying in contorted positions in order to stay in the driest spots. The place reeked with a sickening stench I didn't recognize. My watch was still running: it was 4:00.

The people were still, as if in a stupor, but when they became aware of us, up went the familiar cry of, *"Basta di prigionieri!"* It came from all over the room, in rhythm, until it was like a dirge.

A man in his sixties stepped over the forms on the ground to get to us. "You can see they don't want you around," he said. "And I can't blame them."

"Nor can I," I said hurriedly. "But we won't last out in that rain, it's near freezing. And certainly the Germans won't be out in it," I added.

"Eh! Eh! Who knows? Well then, you can stay, if you promise to leave before daylight. I'll arrange it for you."

"Definitely. You have my word." (I would have promised him anything.) He went over to a middle-aged blond Italian, evidently a leader in the group. The older man pointed to us and the other nodded.

The roof leaked sporadically, seeming to store pailfuls of water only to dump them maliciously on the people below. The men had built a big fire, but neither of us attempted to get near it; women and children were crowded around the flames. The young man I'd seen before told me that they were the *sfollati* who had been bombed and blasted out of San Angelo, and that the blond man was their mayor.

We moved a little farther toward the middle, where it was perhaps a degree or two warmer. Along one side, wounded and sick people of all ages, with parts of their bodies wrapped in wet, dirty bandages, were stretched in even rows. A small boy with a wounded leg hobbled around on a crutch made from a branch. When I drew nearer the casualties, that sickening smell I had failed to recognize earlier grew stronger, and I realized now that it came from infected wounds.

A young woman with long wet hair and dark circles under her eyes was nursing the smallest baby I'd ever seen. I asked her husband how old the child was. "Two hours," he said. "Our baby girl was born out in the woods in that deluge."

Suddenly the mayor of San Angelo leaped onto a table, raised his hands in the air, shook his fists, and screamed a torrent of curses: against God, Germans, British, and Americans, all of whom, he alleged, had brought these miseries upon his people. As I studied the clenched fists and the splotchy red face and listened to the impassioned maledictions, my feelings ranged from embarrassment, to puzzlement, to wonder.

Bart caught my ear: "His lordship the mayor won't last long at that rate."

"Probably not," I said, though I wasn't so sure. The mayor must have organized the people to build this *capanna* and, poor as the shelter was, it had at least gotten them out of the icy rain. Indeed the construction seemed to me a marvel. It was clear that thus far this man had done everything in his power to help his people. Was this public display of anger still another way of helping them? Was it intended to provide a symbolic catharsis in face of the tragedies that beset them all?

When Bart and I left at 6:30, the rain had stopped, and overhead swirls of nimbus were scudding past on a strong northeast wind. We ate the last of our pork rind, drank some water at a spring, and filled our canteens. When we met Raffaele and Ezio coming up from the lower woods, both looked ill. Raffaele's face, in particular, had a gray tinge, and there were dark smudges under his eyes. He spoke in a rasping voice: "Joe, this place is beyond desperation, and very dangerous. I'll guarantee you, it'll be raided sometime today. We've got to get out of here. Right now. Guide or no guide."

Bart, who had been listening, smacked his fist in his palm and sang out, "Here we come, Eighth Army."

Chapter 26

The Final Agreement

Raffaele strode away toward the southeast, but he had gone only a few hundred yards when Adriano came up, wearing a sheepish smile. The older man spat out a curse and railed, "Santa Madonna! Where the devil have you been?" He scolded Adriano at such a speed I couldn't catch a word. Each time the boy tried to explain, Raffaele lit into him again.

Finally I got angry. "Raffaele, shut up," I demanded, and pulled him away from Adriano. "This guide is the only chance we have, and he's got us in a corner. He can tell us all to go to hell. He might choose to find some rich Italians who'll pay him ten times the price." Raffaele's eyes still blazed, but I smiled and took his arm. *"Calma, calma, mi'amico,"* I said soothingly.

He hesitated, then grinned and replied in English, "OK, Joe."

About two minutes were all it took to reconfirm the deal. We all shook hands with Adriano, then with one another, and Raffaele proclaimed: "Now we'll have one final agreement — this one among the four of us: This day, November 15, 1943, will see us shot, captured, or free men in Allied territory!" Bart let out a cheer, and Adriano led off up the trail.

Oh God, my exhilaration was so great as I swung out with them that I wanted to shout and sing! Raffaele's row with Adriano was forgotten, and in my excitement I felt as if I could walk the entire length of Italy. This called for a tin of the precious New Zealand chocolate that I had been saving for so long. Bart and I split it.

We had made only half a mile when we ran into another refugee camp; instantly my euphoria vanished amid the miasma and decay of the place. People came to meet us, walking, staggering, crawling out of tumbledown *capannas*, their faces yellow with starch sickness. They were attired in pieces of burlap bags, old towels, and rags. One wore something that looked like a cut-up horse blanket. Nearly everyone had some injured part of his body bandaged with muddy strips torn from old clothes. In all their wretchedness, these souls crowded around and implored us in anguish, "Help! Help us, take us with you to the British!"

A young girl hobbled up on a homemade crutch, one of her legs a bandaged stump. Another child had patches over both eyes and had to be led about. Her young companion explained, "She is blind, she lost both eyes." Even out in the open air the place reeked of sick breath and infected wounds. Many of the children pawed my sleeves. "Take us with you." one child cried, "so the British will give us food and medicine." My eyes welled as I stammered phony excuses and tried to offer words of sympathy.

Adriano had halted and was standing on a hummock. "Let me tell you something," he shouted at us in a commanding tone. "Twenty-five of these people are going with us to Castiglione!"

I simply stood there, looking at him with my mouth open, but Raffaele turned on him. "You're insane! This trip is much too long for them. These miserable people couldn't possibly walk those distances through the mountains — look at them! Most of them couldn't make another hundred meters!"

Adriano broke in, "The British have reached Castiglione."

I caught Raffaele's eye and shook my head repeatedly to let him know I agreed that Adriano's idea was sheer madness. But at the same time something stabbed at my conscience, telling me that we should try it. Good Christ, what a decision to have to make! All I could think of was these poor *sfollati*, all sick and some dying, stretched out for miles across a mountainous no-man's land. Any patrol could spot them with field glasses, and even if the patrols missed them they would eventually starve or die of wounds or exposure. Yet all the while these rationales raced through my mind, I knew I was simply copping out. Then, finally, I sought refuge in the excuse that if Dick hadn't been able to make it with merely one bad knee, nearly all the members of this group, far worse than that, would fail.

Suddenly it dawned on me: We hadn't arrived at this camp by accident. These wretched people were the reason Adriano had been behaving so strangely. Raffaele beckoned to me. "Come, I'll lead the way," he announced. "This is too much." He kept repeating, "But to take them along isn't possible, it just isn't possible," and he strode off fast in the direction Adriano had been going. Ezio, Bart, and I followed. We had not gone a quarter of a mile when Adriano caught up with us and cut in front of Raffaele, then continuing to lead as if we had never seen the refugee camp. For some reason, Adriano chose a path that ran along the edge of the woods up toward a mountaintop town called Pescopennataro. It was visible off to our right, nestled up against a huge spear of rock that soared into the heavens. Adriano told us offhandedly that the town was occupied by German demolition teams who were systematically dynamiting one building after another.

At the top of a hill opposite Pescopennataro, he angled to the south and led us out into wide-open fields until we were scarcely a few hundred yards from the nearest houses.

"What in God's name is wrong with this kid?" I asked Raffaele. "I'm getting damn suspicious. Those Germans could see us even without glasses. I'm all for dumping this guy."

Raffaele went on ahead to find out what Adriano was up to. While I couldn't hear what he was saying to the guide, I could see that the boy wasn't paying the slightest attention to him. Bart ran up to me and demanded angrily, "What the bloody hell are we doin' out here?"

Not sure myself, I just told him to cool off and keep going. Tramping along and peering at the gray buildings, I expected at any moment a hail of machine-gun bullets, or at least a patrol or an armored car to come tearing out of town across the open field. Adriano, scanning the woods below us, started to swing back toward the east. What in the world did he have in mind?

But now each step took us further and further away from the German-occupied town. And with each stride I breathed more easily, especially since the drizzle had become a heavy rain, reducing visibility by half. The downpour continued as we crossed close-cropped pastures with stone walls and rocky cairns that reminded me of the Scottish Highlands. Shortly the wind came up again, the rain beat harder, and the temperature began to drop. Nevertheless, the worse it got the better I liked it, for it meant that visibility declined for the Germans.

With a long look at the hillside below us, I searched for any movement, and gradually realized that instead of the route Adriano had selected, the little conniver could just as easily have taken us the whole way under cover of a parallel line of woods, without exposing us to the German troops in the town. His whole plan continued to puzzle and irritate me, and the more I thought about the way he had handled things, the madder I got.

Soon, with the rain pounding down in frigid sheets, Adriano decided to stop at a shepherd's stone shelter. "No sense continuing in this," he said. "We'll wait here until it lets up."

"Bullshit to that!" I shouted. "If you don't keep going, we'll go on without you." I stomped off alone, and the others followed. Two minutes later Adriano ran up and resumed the lead.

When two men appeared off to our left, walking very fast and cutting diagonally toward us, I yelled at Adriano, "Who're those men over there to our left?" He didn't turn around to answer my question, nor did he look toward the two men, but I heard him say, *"Non è niente"* (It's nothing). Still, I kept my eye on them, ready to make a break, until I realized that their clothes were much too dark for German uniforms. I felt a surge of relief, especially when we pulled far ahead, and they disappeared behind a wall of rain. The downpour began to turn to sleet, which beat at us almost horizontally. The others seemed well enough protected. Bart had a fairly good jacket, Raffaele and Ezio had put on their camouflage slickers. But my torn clothes were soaked through, and I was growing colder every moment. The temperature plummeted, and I knew there were limits to the degree of cold I could stand. But freedom was uppermost in my mind, in my heart, in my soul. Though I hardly dared to hope, I could not help but feel euphoric and quickened my gait. The faster we went, the better I felt. I found myself humming "The Battle Hymn of the Republic."

We traversed a wide plain, maintaining a rapid pace until we had to ford a swollen stream of rushing brown water. With the icy flood chilling my legs, I paused and looked back. The two men I had seen a while ago again came into view, this time much closer. Now, something about them appeared familiar — I was sure I had seen them back at the big *capanna*.

All at once it dawned on me what Adriano had been up to. Every one of his maneuvers had been a calculated delay to let those two catch up: the wide circle around Pescopennataro, the slowdown at the stream, the pretext to stop at the beehive shelter. I was ready to throttle him. Those two men had come safely through the woods while we had paraded under the noses of the Germans in the town. When I mentioned this to Raffaele, he said that he and Ezio had recognized the delaying tactics, too. To make up time, they now went on at a rate that might as well have been a run. Soon the two mystery men had dropped from sight.

Descending into a narrow valley, we met two shepherds tending their flock. *"Buongiorno,"* they called, and we returned their greeting. Adriano told us he had to talk to them to learn more about German patrols, but when he stopped I kept right on going. Having had quite enough of his stalling, I didn't give a damn whether he was telling the truth or not. Ten minutes later he caught up and reported, "They saw a British patrol two days ago, and haven't seen the Germans recently. This is no-man's land. We'll be in it till we get to Castiglione."

Raffaele explained that we were in a desolate area some 20 to 30 miles deep. For weeks it had been the scene of fluid, guerrilla-style attacks, until the Germans had withdrawn to dig in on the high ground to the north that formed the natural line of defense. He was a student of the Roman and Saracen campaigns that had ravaged this territory in ancient times and couldn't understand why the British hadn't moved forward in force to fill the gap.

Thus far, a crazy excitement had kept me going, but for the last half-hour, I'd had some mild cramps. Suddenly, they really grabbed my gut. I ran for cover between some rocks — I had no wish to show a big white target to a guy with a telescopic sight. I crouched, scanning the hills in the northwest, and afterwards I felt drained and weak, and had to force myself to run. Raffaele sympathized. "It's no fun. Do you feel better now?" I merely nodded, unable even to speak.

We crossed monotonous, treeless ridges in the most desolate country I'd seen, until I lost all sense of time and place. At another surging stream that had overflowed its banks, Ezio waded across and stood on the far side, staring back at us. Raffaele stopped and pulled out the last of his bread.

Ezio called, "Come on, all of you; hurry up, we must get moving!"

Raffaele shook his head. "No, we must rest." Ezio snorted and leaned against a tree, yawning. Bart nudged me. "Look at the bloke, doesn't even know he's been on a walk."

Adriano had also crossed the stream and was standing on the other bank, trying to light a damp cigarette. Finally, in disgust, he threw it on the ground. I couldn't imagine why a guy who apparently had some kind of a lung problem would smoke on a hike like this.

My whole body felt hollow and I pulled out another tin of New Zealand chocolate, again dividing it with Bart. That left only half a bar for the last-ditch effort to get us to Castiglione. It was 1:00; we'd been on the go two and a half hours. I called over to Adriano, "How far have we come?"

"Mezza strada" (Halfway), he said and turned away.

While I forded the stream, the rain slackened and the sky grew brighter. For the first time, as the fog and rain lifted, I could scrutinize our setting. Behind us, among the rocks, rolling pastures, streams, not a moving thing was visible. On the far horizon misty mountains met the rain clouds to the west. Where we found the energy, I didn't know, but with the increased visibility, each one of us drove himself to put on a burst of speed to follow Adriano's fast-moving figure toward the lightening eastern sky.

Raffaele noticed me eyeing a big white house off to the northeast. "Don't worry, Giuseppe," he assured me. "Even with glasses they can't see us from that distance." I relaxed a little, but lost my brief elation when I spotted a high-tension line. Surely it would be guarded. Nervously, we looked in both directions, but we saw no one and started to climb the first real mountain of the day.

At the steepest grade I drew abreast of Raffaele. His shoulders were slumped and his eyes bloodshot. The trip wouldn't be over for him and Ezio even when they reached the British lines, so they had to hang onto all the equipment they could carry. He started walking more slowly and soon stopped altogether, letting out a sigh. I took hold of his pack. "Here, Raffaele, give me that!"

"No, no, no! I'll do it. Why do you take it?"

"Because you're so damn tired from screwing all those girls last night."

When he started to laugh, I succeeded in unhooking the pack. He released it to me and gave me a slap on the back. "Only an hour more, maybe," he said.

My body, particularly from the waist down, had become a solid ache and I wondered how long I could keep going. At every ridge we crossed, Adriano pointed to the next one and said, "Castiglione is just beyond that one."

This mountain didn't seem very high after the big ones up north, but Adriano claimed it was 4,000 feet. Our trail now wound around great boulders rising up from deep pools of rain water.

One of my major worries all along had been that my shoes might fall apart, because I recalled with near panic what had happened to Ingegnere. Now my fears became realities: The sole of my left shoe had worn through, and my bare foot began to strike the ground at every step; the cracks in the other shoe had completely opened up. My trousers, too, where the old lady had patched them, had ripped open, and in spite of the speed at which we were walking, a numbness began to set in. First my feet — but I almost welcomed that, for at least I wouldn't feel that bare foot so much. Then, however, I lost the feeling in my upper legs. For a last little scrap of energy, I pulled out the final half-bar of chocolate and split it with Bart.

In about half an hour, we reached another ridge, much higher than the previous ones, and I realized it was the one Adriano had been pointing to earlier. Glassy-eyed and drawn with fatigue, he dropped back and explained the route to Ezio, who then took over the lead and began to set the fastest pace yet. Near the summit of the ridge the wind escalated to an icy gale and our clothes froze stiff.

As we came over the crest, the long, deep valley of the Trigno River spread out before us. A couple of thousand feet below, the *Strada Nazionale* twisted westward toward Agnone. A short way east was Castiglione, a cluster of gray buildings perched on a high hill. Bright shafts of sunlight pierced the breaking clouds and glistened on the red tile roofs of the houses. We've made it, I thought. Tears started in my eyes and were whipped away in the wind.

My exhaustion was forgotten as we pelted down the hill like a bunch of kids, running and jumping over rocks and ditches till we came to the national highway. It was at once exciting and frightening to walk along a paved road for the first time in a year. A shepherd driving some sheep passed us, ignoring my greeting, apparently afraid to even look at us.

Here, at the edge of town, Bart and I went first — right down the middle of the street, expecting the challenge of an Indian sentry, not sure if we'd have to duck a bullet or the razor-sharp blade of a Gurkha sword. But there was no challenge, and we saw no one. The deathly silence of those bombed-out towns in North Africa came to mind. Yet somehow I knew this was different. Certainly there was life here somewhere. I had a feeling we were being watched.

When Bart and I walked warily into a small *piazza*, a man called out in

Italian, "Who are you?" Taking a chance that the guy wasn't a German, I answered loudly, "We're British and American, with Italian friends." Then they came out, first one by one, then in droves, and in a few moments they had us surrounded, a group of townspeople, all talking at once.

One man cautioned, "The Germans are expected any moment. The British cleared out of here this morning." I looked down a narrow street, out across the Trigno Valley, and wondered if I could make the distance to cross the river. We had walked 30 kilometers in five hours, mostly through mountains, and the thought of going one step further was more than I could bear.

Raffaele read my thoughts: "It's not possible to go on without drying our clothes and getting some food," he said, swaying. His eyes were bleary and seemed not to focus.

More and more people emerged from the buildings until Bart and I were leading a little procession. Soon they crowded us until we couldn't move. When I explained that I was an American, they began shaking my hand. "I have a cousin in Allentown, maybe you know him." "My married sister lives in Ohio, are you near there?" On and on it went, people laughing, taking my arm, competing for my attention. At last I got a chance to ask, "Is there a hotel in town?"

"Si, si, si!" And they directed us to the only one, a dilapidated building in a row of stone houses, its windows boarded up, its front entrance locked. I pounded on the door and shouted, *"Aprite la porta, siamo Americano ed Inglese!"* Through a crack in the door I could make out a woman's gray head. Then I saw her eye at the crack, peering back at me.

"The hotel is closed!" she shouted back. "How do I know who you are? The accursed Germans ransacked my hotel before, and they'll kill me if they find you prisoners here. Go away! Why should I give my place to Allied prisoners when the British left here this morning? The Germans will be here any minute."

Her refusal was unacceptable to Raffaele and me. We had to have help. Thinking it might get her to open the door, I offered her money I didn't have, but she showed no interest. I took a deep breath and began again, "Two of us are in very bad shape and must have help. The British will return sooner or later, and if I report you to them, you will be in terrible trouble." I felt guilty for threatening, though my companions seemed to find nothing wrong with my tactics.

The door opened and I heard, *"Maledetti prigionieri, porca la miseria!"* The *signora* led us upstairs, grumbling to herself.

We came into a huge kitchen with a fireplace and a few benches. As our reluctant hostess lit a small fire, I asked her if we could get something to eat, but she just put her hands on her hips and grunted. Nevertheless, I smiled at her, thanking her for letting us in, and said I was sorry if I'd been a little rude.

In an attempt to thaw her, I told her about my wife and two children back home. But she just went on working on the fire. Finally she promised to get us some spaghetti and wine in a little while.

Satisfied with the fire, the *signora* let us have a pot to boil some water in. I pulled out an ancient, rusty razor from Chieti, with which I got off an inch of beard and grime, along with a certain amount of skin. Clearly it was the most painful shave I'd ever had. The *padrona* gave Bart and me a couple of blankets, which we wrapped around ourselves as we crowded nearer the fire, trying to dry out our clothes and warm our numb arms and legs.

But when the heat began to penetrate, I started to shake violently, and when the shakes stopped, I lapsed into a kind of trance, somewhere between sleep and a drugged consciousness. Even then I did not dare accept the idea that we had made it — my habit of apprehension was so strong that I expected at any moment to hear shouting in German and footsteps on the stairs.

Eventually, though, I slipped off into a doze. A half-hour later I awoke with a start when a door slammed and heavy boots pounded up the stairs. My heart jumped, then felt as if it had stopped beating. I held my breath, no more able to move than if I were in shock.

The door leading into the kitchen flew open, and in walked a trim British captain in garrison cap and long tan winter overcoat. Four bulky Gurkhas crowded in after him, bearing Sten sub-machine-guns and wearing turbans and the olive-tan battle dress of the Fourth Indian Division. I had heard about them in Chieti — they were the Rajput Hindus from Nepal who had remained loyal to the British for nearly 100 years.

Bewildered, I stared at these imposing warriors, but I could not take in what was happening until I heard the captain asking in English who we were. Even with deliverance almost at hand, I did not dare to believe. I had lived in constant fear for so long that the emotional acceptance of freedom and security was, for the moment, still far beyond me.

Chapter 27

Ave Atque Vale

Painfully intent on making a good impression despite my rags and filth, I stepped up to the British officer and sounded off: "Captain Frelinghuysen, 5th Field Artillery, 1st U.S. Infantry Division."

For a moment, he stared at me, unsure; then he shook hands and nodded unsmilingly. Bart cut in front of me, stood to attention, and stated his rank, name, and former unit. Upon hearing Bart's north country accent, the captain broke into a smile. "Well, I do say, you sound authentic enough. Now, what about these other chaps?"

Bart sidestepped the touchy subject of Raffaele and Ezio. "Yes, sir, Joe Frelinghuysen and me has been mates on this trip these last three weeks, and I can vouch he's the pukka type, sir."

Seeing the officer's skeptical look, I had no choice but to meet head-on his question about our Italian friends: "Captain, these other two men are former Italian Army officers." With that, the British officer's eyes narrowed and he frowned. I plugged on, "I've known them now for a month, and they've been invaluable in assisting us to get guides and food. In fact, neither Pyle nor I would be here were it not for them." Bart shifted a little, but kept silent.

"That's all very well, old boy, but I'm afraid you'll have to do better than that. We're not so keen on them, you know."

"May I have your name, then?"

Still frowning, he replied, "Mannington."

"Captain Mannington, in accordance with my orders, I've escaped and returned to Allied Military Control with the help of these officers. Furthermore, I have useful intelligence to report, so let's get on with it."

"Save the 'gen' and speeches until later; I must get my men settled in, but first tell me more about those two."

Stifling my irritation, I introduced Raffaele, who smiled and said in halting, but understandable, English, "I'm glad to meet you, Captain." Mannington shook hands with Raffaele, but he didn't appear exactly pleased. Next I introduced Ezio and suggested to our group that we sit down by the fire. The captain turned to his men and spoke with them in a language that I assumed was Hindustani. I hoped he was telling them we were OK and not to use us for practice with those curved Kukri blades they were carrying.

Bart saw me staring at the knives. "Chap I knew was in the Fourth Indian," he began, "told me Jerry's got no stomach for those Kukris. My friend was in a scrap alongside some Gurkha types one night when they moved in on a Jerry company. Walked real quiet, they did. Jerry never heard a sound, and those blokes slit the throats of the whole bloody lot — wiped out that company. All the Jerries in that area weren't worth a fookin' ha'p'nny after that."

Raffaele seemed alarmed by his and Ezio's position with the British, having a good idea how they felt about Italians and fearful that I might not be able to handle them. Despite my own doubts, I assured him I could, and in an effort to cheer him up, I told him Bart's story about the Gurkhas' night attack. But it didn't cheer him at all. In fact, it dismayed him, and for a while after that I could see him fingering his throat.

Mannington meanwhile had stopped talking to his men and had been tuning in on me. "I say, where did you learn to speak Italian like that?" he asked, sitting on the edge of his chair, still not smiling, and I realized I hadn't convinced him of my identity.

"In Chieti," I answered. "For nearly a year I was in Italian camps. About a year ago, an officer from your 1st Parachute Regiment tried to escape from the camp at Capua. His escape plan was first-rate; he had the uniform and a forged ID card. The only problem was that he could speak only a few words of Italian. I made up my mind to learn the language, and I worked very hard with two Americans at Chieti who were rather fluent. Now if you're sufficiently convinced, I'd like to give you my report, which may contain some interesting information, or 'gen' as you term it."

He relaxed and let me continue as I reported in full on D'Acciaio's partisans and indicated to him the location of their camp on his map. He recommended strongly that I make it my business to see the top British Intelligence officer when I got back to his division headquarters. Partisan support was outside his authority, he explained, and, furthermore, Giuseppe's group might not even be situated in his sector. When I described to him the gun emplacements on the north side of the Sangro Valley, Mannington showed far more interest and made careful notes. In addition, I raised with him the subject of Adriano. Though I had questioned some of our guide's actions, and certainly his judgment, I had to concede that his motives had been of the best. Thus I gave him the finest written recommendation I could and said to Mannington that I hoped the British would help him, since he had done a splendid job of getting us through.

I scraped up all the money we had among our group for Adriano and also got him some British cigarettes. Then I took his address so I could send him something after the war.

At last, nearly two hours after our arrival at the hotel, the *padrona* brought us the pasta and *vino* she had promised. Later, she showed us to some rooms with wire cots. After washing up in a little basin with cold water, I slept for close to ten hours, while the Gurkhas stood guard. Any big patrol could have overcome them, like the one that chased me after Dick was captured, but after sleeping in the woods unprotected, with nerves on edge, I felt as safe with these Gurkhas as I would have with the entire Eighth Army.

16 November

Early in the morning, a unit of rugged New Zealanders, on their way north to patrol, arrived in a column of light armored vehicles. Mannington told me that one of their jeep drivers would shortly be returning to the rear and would take us along. When the driver was ready, Ezio, Raffaele, Bart, and I all piled in and three hours later found ourselves stopping at Torrebruno for lunch at a battalion HQ of the Fourth Indian Division. There Bart went off happily with another sergeant to eat with the OR's, leaving the three of us to find the officer's mess, where we were not likely to be warmly welcomed. This famous, much-decorated division had fought bitter battles against the Italians in the Libyan Desert, and its officers would not soon forgive Italy, England's ally in World War I, for deserting her to side with Hitler and his Fascist henchmen. My hunch was right. When we walked into the place, the mess officer accosted me with, "You don't expect to bring those bloody sods in here, do you?"

When the routine I'd used with Mannington didn't work, I offered to go to the OR's mess. But after snorting in disgust, he let us come in, muttering something that sounded like, "Cheeky Ameddicans."

That afternoon we rode south in a Land Rover with a British lieutenant. Bart and the two Italians sat in back with the officer's sergeant, swapping yarns. An occasional remark in English from Raffaele got a laugh, but the lieutenant up front with me was anything but amused. "What on earth are you doing," he asked me, "bringing those Eyeties back here?"

When I'd explained all that had happened, he inquired angrily, "How much of that do you expect me to believe?" He pointed to a steel bridge spanning a river that we were about to cross. "I lost 32 men getting that bridge across here, while you were sitting in that camp doing bloody fuck all. When in hell are you people going to get off your tails and give us some help?" He grunted and stared at the river. A dead soldier was lying on the shoulder of the road, his helmet still on. Both hands with palms outward were in front of his face, as if to ward off the gunfire that had killed him. For the rest of the ride the British lieutenant and I stared ahead in stony silence.

That night it was a pleasant surprise to be received at a regimental headquarters by a cheerful captain, who said to Bart, "I'm going to take you over to meet Sergeant Welford. They'll have a keg of bitter this evening, and you'll get a first-rate feed. They're good chaps there." Bart grinned. Then the captain invited Raffaele, Ezio, and me to the officers' mess, where, for the first time, the Italians were accepted. We, too, were treated to a couple of pints of bitter and a good supper. Toward the end of the meal, I told the captain I needed to make a quick trip outside, having in mind some nearby bushes. When he got up to accompany me, I tried to dissuade him: "Don't bother, I'll be all right." Disregarding my opinion, he held my arm in a vise-like grip while I performed.

"Don't you see," he said, "if I left you out here and one of our Gurkha guards were to challenge you, he wouldn't recognize your American accent and you'd never know what hit you — those blades are sharp." His words brought to mind the way Raffaele had fingered his throat.

The next day we reached British Eighth Army Headquarters at Foggia. At breakfast in the officers' mess, I was invited to join the brigadier at his table. Obviously I was coming up in the world since my encounter with Mannington. When I arrived with Raffaele and Ezio, the brigadier's aide took me aside and protested, "I say, you're not bringing those two blokes in here, are you?"

"Most certainly I am, because I wouldn't be here if it hadn't been for their help."

After some more bluster, he spoke in a stage whisper to the brigadier, from whom I got a frosty nod. My introduction of Raffaele and Ezio was greeted with a thunderous silence. Throughout the meal the brigadier continued to ignore my two friends and peppered me with questions, though I was far more interested in eating.

After breakfast, British supply very generously issued me some new boots and a clean shirt. Then off I went to Army Intelligence to see one of the Britishers' top men, the equivalent of our G-2. This guy knew his job and listened intently while I detailed the partisan activity from D'Acciaio's aerie to the Sangro Valley. I came away from the exchange knowing I had placed all the emphasis I could on the potential value of the partisans, but I realized as I left that it would be a long time before the British would reach the Morrone and Giuseppe's *partigiani*.

That afternoon, with great regret, I said goodbye to Bart, having first told him he had been the mainstay of our partnership, and that I was damn lucky to have joined up with him. Before parting, we exchanged addresses. Then I wished him a safe trip back home. Bart was a stalwart — the kind of man I'd seen in the 1st Parachute Regiment, the kind who made these British fighting outfits among the best of the war.

Raffaele and Ezio continued on with me to Bari, where Raffaele said they could arrange for their own transportation from then on. As we were uttering our *"arrivederci's,"* he suddenly gave me a bear hug and turned away quickly. Then the two of them went on to Rome.

As they disappeared into the Bari traffic, I had a profound feeling of loss — especially for Raffaele. While Ezio had been a rock throughout the ordeal, he had also remained somewhat distant. It was Raffaele with whom I had worked closely. He and I had come to depend on each other through all the worst crises. I would miss him acutely. Now I wished I could have gone on with him and somehow grabbed a plane back from the American sector.

In Bari I reported to an American Army Air Forces HQ to obtain a billet for the night, but a new shipment of pilots had just come in, and there wasn't a bed in the place. The lieutenant at the desk told me that over in one of their office buildings there was a latrine, and that I could sleep on the floor there. "And," he added cheerfully, "there's heat too, and once in a while a little water. There won't be too many patronizing the place."

"After what I've been used to, it'll be the Ritz," I laughed, and set out for my new quarters. The floor was pink terrazzo, and so were the walls and the partitions. Even the urinals were pink. The only inelegance was the old steam radiator, a rusty gray affair. Figuring there might be less spray in front of the partitions, I selected a spot there, folded my sweater for a pillow and stretched out just as night was falling. Before I fell asleep, I thought happily: no hunger, no cold, no Germans. Other than an occasional disturbance from someone stepping over me, I slept on the hard, shiny terrazzo for 12 hours straight.

The next day a quartermaster finance officer let me draw against my pay and then directed me to a newly arrived officer's uniform and supply store. There I bought a whole new outfit, replete with insignia. Since it fitted well enough, I paraded smugly up and down the streets of Bari, saluting and being saluted. I walked past bombed-out buildings, thinking of my Italian friends, wondering whether it had been Germans or the U.S. Army Air Forces who had blasted those buildings.

In the course of my stroll, an old nuisance came back. The throbbing of the boils made me dizzy and sick, so I went back to the billeting officer, who relented and assigned me a room in a hotel. There I promptly collapsed on the bed and reflected on the way the Germans had missed me all through the mountains. That night I went to sleep with the same reassuring thoughts I had had in the latrine the night before.

The next morning I left for Tunis in a beat-up DC-3, with two pilots who looked as if they could be in high school. While they negotiated their way through a pea-soup fog, down mountain valleys at about 500 feet, I bounced around on a metal bucket seat. When we came out of the cloud cover over the northern coast of Sicily, at around 5,000 feet, I sighed explosively. Far below us was the sparkling blue Mediterranean, and I gazed at the white line of breakers, trying to guess where Dick had made his landing near Brolo. I thought of him now, somewhere deep in Germany — and kept my face to the window, while we banked and turned southwest of Tunis.

We touched down on a metal strip runway at El Aouïna, just about where I had taken off in the Ju-52 almost a full year earlier. This time, though, there were lines of U.S. and British aircraft around the field.

The airport personnel officer assigned me to a hotel in Tunis for the night and instructed me to report back to him in the morning for a flight to Algiers. The lobby was so full of Air Forces pilots either heading home or arriving for duty, that I couldn't see across the room. Many were singing and reeling, coming in and out of the bar. The whole place smelled of cheap wine and cigarettes. While I was waiting to get near the desk, I happened to overhear a pilot describe a German air raid on Bari. I turned cold when I learned that the hotel where I had slept had been leveled and many lives lost.

Gradually I fought my way to the desk, where a skinny little Air Forces corporal coolly told me he had no rooms available. "What are the chances later on?" I asked.

"None. There are five colonels and three majors ahead of you."

Just then a captain walked up, a dental officer in his early forties. "My name's Welkind," he said cordially, offering his hand. "I have a single room I'll be glad to share with you."

"That's the best news I've had today," I exclaimed. "Don't worry about the bed, I'll sleep on the floor."

"We'll see about that. But first let's get washed up and have some food. You look as if you could use it."

At supper in a makeshift officers' mess, Captain Welkind told me he had arranged for some kind of through flight and would be reaching New York in a few days. So I gave him Emily's and my parents' phone numbers. When we got to the room, he pulled out his kit and dressed a boil on my left wrist. After I showed him a few others, he urged me to get some medical attention as soon as I reached Algiers. Then, as I prepared a place on the floor, he insisted I share the bed with him.

Soon after his plane landed in New York, on Thanksgiving Day, he called Emily from the airport to tell her I was back on the right side of the wire. This was the first word she had had that I had escaped.

I flew to Algiers, where a medical officer at the airport took one look at me and sent me at once to the base infirmary. From there, I ended up in an American hospital and quickly became a prime exhibit of pellagra and furunculosis before a dozen doctors and nurses, while I shivered in nothing but a small towel.

Along with two other officers I was put in a ward, an old hotel room taken over by the 29th Station Hospital. Two of the three beds stood along one wall, and a cracked basin with rusty fixtures hung on the far side beneath a glass shelf littered with swabs, bandages, and adhesive tape.

Dave, the man next to me, who had been a deck officer on a destroyer until he caught an eight-inch chunk of shrapnel in the gut, had a badly infected wound. A drain made out of old enema tubing stuck out of his stomach, dripping a greenish-yellow pus into a big glass bottle between our two beds, barely a foot and half apart. All through the night — every night — Dave groaned and thrashed around in the bed. One night he let out a blood-chilling scream, which trailed off into a string of curses — against God, the hospital, the doctors, and, for some reason, me. As he writhed, the tube came out of the bottle and the pus went all over the floor. Barely able to speak, he asked me to put the tube back in place. The task didn't take me long, but the odor was foul, and it reminded me of those wounded refugees from San Angelo. With fistfuls of wadded-up toilet paper, I mopped the floor and then scrubbed my hands.

Later, I dropped off to nightmares and was soon running, running through the woods, the patrol getting nearer, when the nurse shook my shoulder. "Time to take a pill." I grabbed her arm and lashed out, *"Via! Via! Vengono i tedeschi!"*

She shook me hard and yapped, "Stop that! Stop it! What's the matter with you? Any more, and I'll call the officer of the day."

I sank back on the pillow. "I'm sorry, sorry — just a dream." I swallowed the pill. What the hell did she know about anything? Then in the dim glow from a night light, I saw Dave grinning at me. "They're all like that," he assured me. "Always think someone's gonna rape them. Trouble is 'bout half the time they're right."

"Not this time," I said dryly.

"She's in no danger from me either, mine's been like a wet noodle since I got this thing," Dave chuckled. Though he sounded kind of bitter, it was the first time I'd seen him smile, and I was glad. In a few moments I heard a light snore.

One day, after three weeks in the hospital, I was able to walk around the city, so I set out to see a dispatching officer. "You might be just the guy I'm looking for," he said. "A responsible type who can be a courier to Washington. It means special air travel, you know."

"You got your man!" I said, unable to contain my excitement. "What do I have to do?"

He asked me a lot of questions, filled out a pound of forms, made a couple of phone calls, then, at last, announced: "You're all set." He showed me a red dispatch case equipped with a chain and fastener. "This is of the highest priority short of Top Secret," he said. "It's General Eisenhower's Christmas mail for his family, and this is the only damn way I can figure out to get it to them on time. You'll take a plane out of here in the morning to Marrakech, then to Dakar, where you'll make a connection with a special plane going to Washington — I can't tell you where it's coming from or who or what's on it. You must chain this red packet to your wrist; don't take it off for any reason whatsoever till you deliver it to the main United States Post Office in Washington, D.C." He gave me a special form addressed to Mrs. Eisenhower to give to the postal clerk, and added, "Is all that clear?"

I stood up and saluted. "Yes, sir." He looked surprised, and returned the salute rather sloppily. Obviously, that young man hadn't been in the 1st Division.

On the morning I was to depart, I went to the transient officers' mess, a big room in another hotel, with a long table loaded with cereals, milk, eggs, bacon, sausage, and coffee. I would have liked to have had Bart, Raffaele, and Ezio there to share the feast. I still retained one hell of an appetite, so I filled my plates and crowded them on a tray, as a scowling mess sergeant muttered, "Why don't you leave something for the other guys?"

The breakfast was truly good, and while I was stuffing it down, I saw a small man with the kind of Italian army cap and blue denim fatigue uniform I had seen on the work details at Chieti. The guy turned out to be an Italian POW. He was a busboy for my section, so I waited till he came to take away my dishes, and said quietly, *"Siete Italiano, da dove venite in Italia?"* (Are you Italian? Where do you come from in Italy?) The ritual first questions.

His eyes swept the room before he whispered, *"È meglio non parlare. Sono prigioniero di guerra"* (It is better not to talk. I'm a prisoner of war).

"Si, si, lo so molto bene. Ero prigioniero in Italia anche io stesso" (Yes, yes, I know very well. I was a prisoner in Italy myself).

When two Air Forces second lieutenants wandering by stopped at my table and stared at me, my Italian friend nervously scooped up the plates and slithered off through the packed tables like an eel.

"I don't know what the hell you think you're doin', Captain, gettin' so chummy with those guys. Sons-a-bitches were shootin' at us not so long ago," one complained. The other one said, "Who the hell are you anyway?"

I stood up and declared, "I'm Captain J. S. Frelinghuysen, a returning prisoner of war. But in my branch of the U.S. Army, we use more courtesy in addressing a senior officer."

"Aw, come on, Charlie," the second guy grumbled, "he's probably kinda stir crazy like that guy came through here last week."

But the other was more cynical. "How do you know that story's true — a guy speaks Ite like that. I've half a mind to call the MP's."

"I wish you would," I said. "I'd have quite a lot to say to them, too."

The first man grabbed his friend and pulled him away, and I heard them laughing as they went out the door. I would have liked to throttle them.

The second day out, our DC-3 cleared the 13,000-foot Grand Atlas by a few hundred feet, while my head and stomach went in spirals. We flew on across the Sahara and late that afternoon landed at Dakar, where I got a look at the mystery plane. It was a DC-4 or C-54, which meant two more engines, and I took off in it the following afternoon for Belem, Brazil.

On the plane were ten tough-looking men, dressed in uniforms without insignia. At each stop, we would be cordoned off by MP's. The ten men would emerge, draw their guns, and take positions around the plane. Then the MP's would depart. When we left Belem, I asked one of the men what this was all about.

"How would you like to walk the rest of the way?" he inquired, in a frigid tone. They were all cold as ice, and they handled their guns too well for me to ask any more questions.

Next stop was the U.S. Army Air Forces Base at Borinquen, Puerto Rico, where the plane had to lay over for landing gear parts, and where I promptly checked into the hospital with blood poisoning.

Luckily, the abscess was in my left arm. I say luckily because the red packet was chained to my right. The hospital was steaming hot, in the high nineties, which was to my liking. The nurse had left me bare to the waist. Some time that afternoon, a ravishing, dark-haired USO girl came in to sing a few songs. The only other guy there with me was a fighter pilot, recovering from some bullet wounds. The girl went to his bedside and asked him what he wanted to hear. It was great, the way he spieled off the names of the newest hits. Never having heard of any of them, I felt more out of things than ever.

Next she came over to my bed, and asked me what my selections were. Suddenly, it was all too much for me. I was lying there half naked, and would have to watch this perfectly lovely girl gyrate and roll her eyes at me as she sang. All at once I wanted to run — and might have, if I hadn't been so damn tied down with compresses and gadgets on my left arm. But she was still waiting for my answer, looking a little puzzled. I wracked my brain: if I asked for *"White Cliffs of Dover,"* or *"White Christmas,"* both of which Don Waful had sung at Chieti, I'd come apart. So I asked for *"I've Got Spurs that Jingle, Jangle, Jingle,"* and *"When Johnny Comes Marching Home,"* numbers that seemed harmless enough for my confused emotions. Yet the whole scene, despite the girl's sincere efforts to cheer me, grated on my nerves, and I resented her very presence. In my view, this was hardly a time for singing. Didn't she know *anything* about the anguish over there and the devastation taking place? How could she be so insensitive as to fail to realize that I had no way of relating to what she was doing? Silently I pleaded with her, I implored her to please go away, to let me try to figure out all this in peace.

In the morning, I was visited by a doctor to whom I took an instant dislike — why, I didn't know; perhaps I resented his pudginess, which showed he had no idea of what the word "hunger" meant. We went to an operating room, where he waved me to the table. As I stretched out on it, skinny and still feeling washed out, he prepared his scalpels as if he were about to carve a Sunday roast. My eyes became riveted resentfully on the blubber hanging over his belt — what had put that on would have fed Antonio's family for a month.

Though the doctor's crass attempt at humor ("We'll use 'vocal' anesthetic") did little to endear him to me, I was damned, now, if I was going to let this clod get a peep out of me, no matter how clumsily he carved me up. When he turned the scalpel upside down and ripped it upward through the boil, I made no sound. In the aftermath, I resented passionately this whole world to which I had returned.

Two days later our C-54 took off from Borinquen Airport for Washington. As we climbed high above an aquamarine sea, I was fascinated with the agility of our pilots, and how they dodged the antiaircraft fire of, believe it or not, the U.S. Navy. They did dives, vertical banks, wingovers, while I wondered if this plane was built for that kind of stuff. But the pilots didn't seem to worry. In fact, the captain came aft later on and wisecracked, "Those guys never learned their aircraft identification; they'd fire at anything. It's a damn good job the sons-of-bitches don't know how to shoot, for I'd have had a hell of a time without any cloud cover."

Dusk was setting as I awoke from a doze and heard the guy next to me say, "I can see it, there's a Hot Shoppe!" Not bothering to ask what a "Hot Shoppe" was, I slid over to an empty window seat to peer out into the gathering darkness. Odd, I mused, why isn't Washington blacked out? This concern I quickly forgot, however, at the sight of the white shaft of the Washington Monument, shining in its vertical lighting, thrusting up into the night, a symbol of the freedom I had regained. The plane banked and swung over the brightly lighted portico and marble columns of the Lincoln Memorial; at another turn, when I saw the full length of the Capitol building, I pressed my face close to the glass and said quietly, "This is my own, my native land!" My chest and throat clenched, and I was glad the cabin was dark; for none of these guys could possibly understand.

Following orders, I reported to the base commander, an overage major who had fought in World War I, as I could tell from his ribbons. He was soft-spoken and gentle with me, and, best of all, didn't ask a lot of stupid questions. "You don't look so well," he observed. "I'm sending you to Walter Reed Hospital. You'll be in a ward for tonight, but by tomorrow they'll have a room for you. You'll be needing some tests." He paused a moment then inquired, "Have you been able to draw any pay?"

I smiled. "They fixed me up in Bari, sir. I'm in good shape."

To which he replied, "Financially, at least, if not in other ways. By the way, we had a man fly in here a few weeks ago, who had also gotten through in Italy." The major mentioned the man's name, but I shook my head and told him they'd been loose by the thousands, though I had no idea how many had made it to the Allied lines.

The phone on his desk rang. "Major Hawkins . . . oh, thank you, he'll be right out," the commander said, then turned to me. "I had to get you a taxi. Sorry, our own vehicles are all on assignment. Can you manage?"

"Of course, Major," I laughed, "but I have to stop at the main Post Office on the way." I showed him the red packet and added, "I'm a courier, sir." I didn't tell him what was in it — for all I knew the business of "Christmas mail" might well have been a cover for some Top Secret stuff.

He rose and saluted. Wrestling with the packet, I clumsily returned his gesture.

In the car, the driver looked at me peculiarly — I suppose because I couldn't get my arm through the sleeve of my overcoat, so it hung empty. When I walked into the huge Post Office building, the scene was suddenly unreal, and I felt lightheaded. People swung around — I could sense their eyes following me right up to the window, where I handed over the packet and got a receipt. Then they stared again. Embarrassed and confused, I began to think I must be a freak, but gradually it came to me: In Washington, D.C., I was not yet at home. The essence of my life and being was still 4,000 miles away, still on the run, a hunted creature suspicious of everyone and everything — I had not yet come back to this world, so familiar, yet so strange and so difficult.

My bed that night was in the terminal cancer ward. I was surprised to find that the guy next to me came from a town ten miles from home. As a matter of fact, though we didn't know each other, I knew his family and he knew mine. After we compared notes, our dialogue turned solemn, then grim, and finally rancorous, when he pointed out what a lucky son of a bitch I was to be alive. I wholeheartedly agreed, but that threw him into more of a rage. Because what this poor embittered man actually meant was that I was truly a bastard because I was going to live, and he wasn't. Two hours later, near midnight, his tirade continued to echo in my brain until, finally, I fell asleep. In the morning, I made an attempt to bid him goodbye, but it was a dreadful mistake. There was simply no way he could accept the implication of the word.

Later that same day Emily arrived at the hospital and I met her in the hall outside my room. For several overwhelming, devastating moments we simply clung to each other. Soon I was able to talk the doctor into giving me a four-hour pass. Then I struggled into my uniform, but kept it on for only ten minutes, which was just the time it took me to walk over to the nurses' quarters, where Emily had managed to get a tiny private room.

A few days later, there began a beautiful, though sharply poignant, breathing spell, a few weeks when we treasured every priceless day. But, inexorably, my reassignment came through, and we were subjected to another heartbreaking separation. With the war still raging, I would serve two more years, with a second overseas tour, this time in the Pacific, before I would return home to stay.

Epilogue

During the ten days or so that I was at Walter Reed, I obtained several passes to visit a foreign news section of the War Department. There, microfilm copies of most enemy newspapers published since the outbreak of war were filed. For many hours each day I searched through Axis newspapers for a photograph that Marty Lawler, Len Warren, and I had seen in an Italian daily, while we were prisoners. In the front row, looking dejected, had been an American captain who closely resembled Tom Stafflebach — the same eyeglasses, field cap, and uniform, in addition to a strong facial likeness. But my research proved futile. Through subsequent investigations in the labyrinthine corridors of the Pentagon, I came to learn that Lt. Col. Warren C. Stout and Capts. Gordon Bilat and Tom Stafflebach were recorded as "Presumed Killed in Action," as was the colonel's driver, PFC Harold W. Smith. All are listed on the bronze plaque on the 1st Division War Memorial Monument in Washington among those who lost their lives in World War II.

As soon as I got home, Emily put me in touch with a group of prisoners' wives and families who exchanged news of their absent husbands and sons. Through these sources I was happy to hear that some of my old friends from Chieti had escaped successfully. Connie Kreps, for one, had broken out of Camp 78 at Fonte d'Amore and was now at the big U.S. Army Air Forces Reception Center in Atlantic City for debriefing and reassignment. During a jubilant reunion with him there, I learned from Connie that Claude Weaver and Harold Rideout had hoofed it from Chieti to some railroad tracks on the east coast of Italy and, still in their Italian uniforms, had squeezed on a crowded train south to Taranto, where they met up with units of the British army. From there, Weaver went back to England and ultimately rejoined an RAF Spitfire squadron. (One day in the spring of 1944 I chanced to read, with great sadness,

Shortly after arriving in Montenerodomo in February 1956, JSF is bombarded with all kinds of questions.

that this singularly courageous man had lost his life in a battle in the skies somewhere off the coast of England.)

In time I ascertained, too, that quite a few other Americans who had been in Chieti had managed to escape, but most were ultimately recaptured. Len Warren, for example, jumped from a train near Tagliacozzo in the Simbruini Mountains of Abruzzo and did very well for a number of weeks, only to be caught in a late-night *rastrellamento*. Most Americans from Chieti ended up

Berardino and JSF meet again after 12 years.

in camps throughout Germany and Poland, where they were forced to endure unspeakable hunger, cold, and forced marches in the snow until they were finally liberated by the Russians or the Americans.

Upon my final return home in late 1945 I learned of Dick Rossbach's story from his father. Just after I had left him, Dick had survived a brutal beating at the hands of the Alpenjäger patrol that had recaptured us. Then he spent a year and a half in German prisons, until Poland was overrun by Marshal Zhukov, whose troops again imprisoned him, this time in a Russian concentration camp. After six weeks there Rossbach made his fifth escape, eventually reaching the American embassy in Moscow, where he was personally extended the warmest kind of welcome by Ambassador Averell Harriman. On his return to the States, Capt. Richard M. Rossbach was notified that he had been awarded the Silver Star for his part in the landing at Monte Brolo, Sicily, and a Bronze Star for his action at Monte San Domenico.

After the war, Dick stayed in the Army for a while, stationed in Washington. I saw him once or twice, and though we had a world of things to talk about, we were both tense and having trouble adjusting to civilian life. Besides, I felt we

Berardino and Letizia do a little "catching up" with Emily and JSF before they visit some of Letizia's relatives.

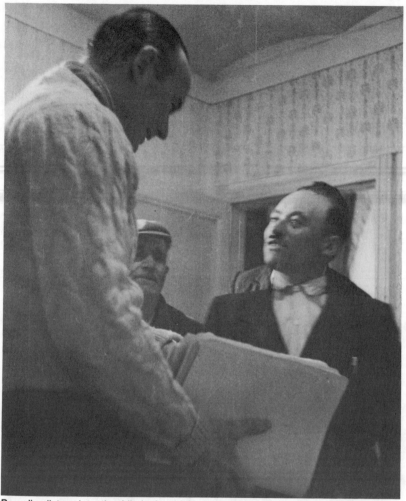

Berardino listens intently while he is told the status of his papers for entry into the United States.

each had a sense of frustration at the time wasted in prison, unable to serve in the ways for which we had trained so hard.

When Dick switched to a job in New York, where I was working, we began to see each other more often. Then a splendid business relationship developed, in which, as before, Dick assumed a leadership role. It worked like this: We met at his office and took care of the business first, which Dick handled with skill and efficiency. Then we went off to lunch, and, in time, the stories began to unfold — his and mine as well.

The bond between us was for life, as are many that are forged in danger and extreme stress. This was special, however, because of how he kept our agreement, even while enduring the excruciating disappointment of being recaptured and the prospect of more time in prison and near starvation.

Even long after the war, there were difficult moments when I unloaded my guilt for leaving him to a beating and perhaps even death. One day Dick had heard enough, and he burst out, "Oh, for God's sake, Joe. You did what we had agreed to, which had its military purpose, whether you liked it or not. Hell, I was the one who felt guilty, holding you up all that time; you could have made it to the British in a few days on your own."

My good friend had let me off the hook, the dragons were slain, and we had our occasional meetings until he began his long and unsuccessful battle with a fatal illness that took him in the summer of 1987. Dick was a man of unqualified courage, valiant in war, brilliant and forceful in peace. You knew where you stood with Dick, which, after all, is the best kind of friend to have.

In the months and years after the war, through bits and pieces from many sources, I was also able to put together this information:

James Cleminson and a number of other British prisoners escaped from Chieti by hiding in a tunnel, sneaking out only after the Germans had left. James and a companion trekked south and in a fortnight actually rejoined their own embattled 1st Parachute Regiment north of Taranto, down in the heel of Italy. James' battalion commander put him right back on full combat duty, which was fine with him, but the British high command back in London wanted him for debriefing. James didn't like the idea, nor did his battalion

Berardino, Letizia, and Emily stop for coffee.

commander, but he did return to London, when threatened with court-martial. After some months in England, he jumped with the 1st Parachute Division at Arnhem. Severely wounded in that valiant though devastating action, which was recorded in Cornelius Ryan's *A Bridge Too Far*, James spent most of the rest of the war in a German military hospital. Years later, James was knighted by Queen Elizabeth II and is now Sir James Cleminson.

No one to my knowledge ever heard of Charlie Rydesdale again, nor of Rosa's beloved chaplain. Nor have I ever heard from the Eisensteins, for whose safety I greatly feared. Always I have recalled them with warmth for their friendship, and have hoped in my heart that somehow they made it through.

As for Bart, I lost touch with him for many years after the war, in no small measure because of my extreme reluctance to resurrect and relive memories that were simply too painful. Though frequently in the narrative he and I appear critical of each other — because, in truth, that was the nature of our relationship for those weeks in the mountains — over the years, his courage and determination came through to me crystal clear; and I acknowledged his decisiveness and leadership in the face of my indecision and procrastination.

Just recently, to my surprise and delight, I got a letter from Bart. It was from Cameron, Ontario, where he and his wife, Mary, moved after the war. They have three daughters and Bart, Jr., who has a son, Bart, III. I also learned that my old friend was given a medical discharge because of a bullet in the knee in the fearful Battle of Halfaya Pass, west of Cairo. Yet during those rugged weeks on the run, he had never once complained. So far our reunion has been only by mail and telephone. One day we hope to have it in person.

While I never again saw Ezio Bartolini, Emily and I did meet Raffaele in Rome in February 1956, and again in 1958, when we visited his vineyards in Frascati. Rather incredibly, his house in that medieval town south of the Eternal City had been occupied, at one point or another during the war, by troops of nine different nations. A student of the military history of his province, Raffaele always maintained that if the U.S. generals had studied the ancient campaigns they would have gone around Frascati instead of attacking it head on, and would thereby have avoided the severe loss of life and almost total destruction of the town. On every subsequent visit to Rome after that, I made it a point to see Raffaele, and we remained close friends until his death in 1970.

On our 1956 trip to Italy, Emily and I drove up from Rome to Abruzzo, past snowbanks ten feet high to a place where the road ended in the cobblestone *piazza* of Montenero. When we stepped out of our ancient rented Fiat, I was engulfed by welcoming, smiling townspeople, grasping my hands and my arms. Cheerful cries of *"Ben arrivato, Giuseppe,"* and *"È molto tempo che non ti abbiamo visto,"* filled the air. People hung on me, everyone talking at once.

Berardino and Letizia's younger son, Lorenzo, and Emily made friends quickly.

After these pleasant and hearty greetings, the crowds parted, creating an aisle, and I beheld my old friend Berardino striding in stately fashion down the hill like a welcoming chief of state. When I'd last seen him it had been under such fierce emotional strain that this was now simply too much for me, and I was speechless for a moment. And so was he. Then his wife, Letizia, came up, and we all exchanged enthusiastic greetings.

Emily and I chatted with the people for a time, until Berardino pulled us into the house of his brother-in-law, Nicola, and bread and wine were brought. After several rounds of toasts, we began to catch up with each other's news across 12 intervening years.

Later on that reminiscent afternoon Berardino led us up through the mountains toward the group of houses where for generations his family had dwelt, and where for weeks I had been fed and cared for. Along the way he stopped and called my attention to an ancient, crumbling stone wall: "Giuseppe, do you see that wall?"

I nodded.

"Just after you left us, they machine-gunned 26 of our people there for helping prisoners."

My eyes filled and I was unable to express any of the things that flew into my mind: Were they any of the people I'd known? Had they been killed because of me? I had not the courage to ask.

Even after Berardino's revelation I remained for some time unaware of the extent of the slaughter and destruction that the Alpenjäger had wrought on the people of Abruzzo. Certainly, the *partigiani* had taken their chances, knowing what the Germans would do to them if they were caught. And the farm families out in the country knew they were taking risks too. But the brutalities inflicted on women, children, and the aged here were on a par with the worst of the war anywhere. Only the remoteness of the mountains made it possible for some to escape. Survivors of the Alpenjäger atrocities to this day set aside the latter part of March as a time for prayer and meditation, a time of recollection and mourning for the Abruzzesi who died in December '43 and early '44.

That winter the *partigiani* had formed the Brigata Maiella, a regular brigade, which joined the British Eighth Army. With no little difficulty, British and Italians, former enemies, managed to join forces and fight side by side north through the Apennines. On 1 May 1945 the Brigata crossed the Po Valley and reached Asiago, its final objective. On 22 June the unit was cited for bravery by Lt. Gen. R. L. McCreery, Commanding General, British Eighth Army.

The Brigata Maiella has been memorialized in a book of that name by Nicola Troilo, son of the unit's commanding officer, Col. Ettore Troilo. The book describes the fate of several of the towns that lie on either side of the Parello Valley. What follows is my abridged translation of the author's accounts of the worst disasters:

Lama and Torricella were 85 percent destroyed: Quadri, 98 percent, and Civitaluparella, 85 percent. Ruins were piled up under the snow, completely blocking streets and changing the town so drastically that it was extremely hard to find any given houses. . . .

Antonio and Rosa DiGiacomantonio.

Remains of murdered civilians, of foreign refugees, of stray dogs . . . of pigs with their throats cut, of donkeys insanely beaten to death with clubs, of cows, horses, and decapitated chickens, lay everywhere — in the streets, in the corners of houses, against walls red with blood, even in the living quarters of the houses. . . . Parts of human bodies, with revolting mockery, had been smeared with excrement and arranged in horrible and grotesque positions.

1st row: Tonino; 2nd row: his parents, Letizia and Berardino, with relatives.

In Torricella, over a hundred civilians were slain, half of whom were women, children, and old people. But in Pietransieri, a small, secluded hamlet in the mountains, the entire population was hunted down and shot like animals.

Forty-one died in the barbaric St. Agatha massacre, entire families murdered. Afterwards, red-hot brands were put on the necks of the victims to make sure they were dead. During the night, houses were set on fire and by morning none of the burned bodies could be identified.

In the Rigata di Torricella massacre, young men were used as targets by German soldiers. Young women were raped and killed — old people dragged from their houses and shot. Two very young children were clubbed to death and a newborn baby's head was crushed with a rock. Two pregnant women, on their way from Palena to Sulmona were insanely beaten until they aborted and were left bleeding in the snow.*

Through great courage and resourcefulness, Antonio and Berardino and their families survived this horror, although once Antonio was captured in a *rastrellamento* and taken to work on the fortifications of the Maiella. Eventually he and a friend escaped through the German minefields, and, in time, Antonio's whole family returned from months of hiding and near-starvation to their *masseria* in the Parello Valley. After the war I stayed in contact with them while I struggled with the rigid red tape to pave the way for their entry into the United States, a goal that Berardino had expressed to me shortly after we met.

During our 1956 visit Emily and I stayed at Antonio's, in the same house to which I had returned the night after Dick was recaptured. In addition to Tonino, we now met the younger children: Rosa, Maria, and Lorenzo. But there was still work to be done on Berardino's project, so after three days we left for appointments in Rome. With snow-covered roads impassible for vehicles, we abandoned our car in Montenero and, accompanied by Berardino, Letizia, Nicola, and a friend to break the trail, we trudged eight miles through a driving blizzard to reach the nearest plowed road.

Late the next afternoon I walked down the marbled and frescoed hall of a Vatican building on the *Via Conciliazione*, down a corridor lined with Italians, standing, sitting, some lying on the floor, as they waited to see someone who might help them to get to the U.S., or perhaps to South America.

I proceeded to an office at the end of the hall, where I met a Monsignor Landi for an appointment arranged by a friend of Raffaele. The *monsignor* was a charming, friendly American priest and an expert on emigration matters. Our conversation was to prove fruitful. I sent my affidavit of support to Berardino, and in 1958 he and Tonino arrived in America. Four years later, after Antonio had passed away in Italy, the rest of the family came over.

In late October 1972 our daughter Susan, who is fluent in Italian, drove up to Abruzzo with me from Rome. One day, wearied of my poking-around, she asked to be dropped off for a rest at a little cafe in San Angelo del Pesco. On

---

* From *Brigata Maiella*, by Nicola Troilo, distributed by NUOVA ITALIA, Florence. Printed by S.E.T.I., Via della Guardiola, n. 23, Rome. Translated by JSF and reprinted with the kind permission of the author.

that sunny afternoon I wandered alone in the valley of the Sangro, searching for Vincenz's house. Though the nights had been cold, this day was pleasantly warm, and the trees were the russet, red, and gold I remembered so well.

As I paused on the bridge over the Sangro, I was keenly disappointed to find the swift, majestic river I had known now nothing but a deep rocky crevasse, dried to a trickle by the diversion of its flow to a hydroelectric project up in the mountains. Recalling that night when we had forded the river, I had a strange feeling of remorse, and wondered if this might have been the place where Vincenz' and his two sons had tried to get back across, and from which Bart and I had heard the foreboding machine-gun fire.

On the southerly shoulder of Monte Lucino I came to a narrow gravel road where two workmen were finishing some repairs. Their faces were brown as leather from the Italian sun, and they looked curiously at the tall, light-skinned foreigner.

In response to my question, the older of the two said, "No, I've never heard of this Vincenz'. Don't you know his surname? But then, almost all the houses in this area were destroyed and many people were killed."

"Yes, I know."

"Eh! Eh! La guerra, che brutta epoca!" he said with a sigh, and the two men started putting their tools in the back of a little three-wheeled truck.

I waved as they drove away, then walked out on a ridge to gaze at the vast expanse before me. The shadows had lengthened, but San Angelo and Pescopennataro high above were edged in gold. The valley was silent and still, and above the tranquillity there was an overwhelming sadness, as if the memory of those who had died here would always linger in the air of this valley.

I thought of Antonio with his tenacity and courage, of Vincenz' and his bold crossing of the Sangro, and I remembered Jan Struther's poignant and beautiful words:

> Lord of all gentleness, Lord of all calm,
> Whose voice is contentment, whose presence is balm,
> Be there at our sleeping, and give us, we pray,
> Your peace in our hearts, Lord, at the end of the day.

Index

Compiled by Lori L. Daniel

Other Works
by
Joseph S. Frelinghuysen

Keep Your Heart Running
(Published by Winchester Press)
Co-authored with Paul J. Kiell, M.D.
First Edition, November 1976

Paperback Title:

The Complete Guide to Physical Fitness
(Published by Stoeger Publishing Co.)
First Edition, January 1978
Second Printing, November 1978